IN THE MIDST OF THE KINGDOM

The Royalist War Effort in the North Midlands 1642-1646

Martyn Bennett

'This is the Century of the Soldier', Fulvio Testi, Poet, 1641

Helion & Company

Helion & Company Limited
Unit 8 Amherst Business Centre
Budbrooke Road
Warwick
CV34 5WE
England
Tel. 01926 499 619
Email: info@helion.co.uk
Website: www.helion.co.uk
Twitter: @helionbooks
blog.helion.co.uk/

Published by Helion & Company 2021
Designed and typeset by Mach 3 Solutions Ltd (www.mach3solutions.co.uk)
Cover designed by Paul Hewitt, Battlefield Design (www.battlefield-design.co.uk)

ISBN 978-1-913118-89-1

British Library Cataloguing-in-Publication Data.
A catalogue record for this book is available from the British Library.

Contents

Abbreviations

BL	British Library
BL Add Mss	Additional Manuscripts
BL Eg Mss	Edgerton Manuscripts
BL Harl Mss	Harleian Manuscripts
BL TT	Thomason Tracts (these will be followed by the individual number of the tract, e.g. E345/2.)
Bod Lib	Bodleian Library, Oxford
CCAM	*The Calendar of the Committee for the Advance of Money, 1642–1656*, ed. M.A. Everett-Green (Liechtenstein: Kraus reprint, 1967)
CCC	*The Calendar of the Committee for Compounding*, ed. M.A. Everett Green (Liechtenstein: Kraus reprint, 1967)
CSPD	*The Calendar of State Papers Domestic Series*, Charles I, Charles II, ed. J. Bruce (Liechtenstein: Kraus reprint, 1967)
DRO	Derbyshire County Record Office
Firth and Rait	*Acts and Ordinances of The Interregnum 1642–1660*, eds C.H. Firth and R.S. Rait (London: HMSO, 1911)
HMC	Historical Manuscripts Commission
JSAHR	Journal for the Society of Army Historical Research
LAO	Lincolnshire Archives Office
LCL	Lichfield Cathedral Library
LJRO	Lichfield Joint Records Office
LRO	Leicestershire County Record Office
NRO	Nottinghamshire County Record Office
North. RO	Northamptonshire County Record Office
Rushworth	J. Rushworth, *Historical Collections* parts three and four (London, 1721–1722)
SHC	*Staffordshire Historical Collections* (New Series I, 1898)
SRO	Staffordshire County Record Office
WSL	William Salt Library, Stafford
WSL SMS	Salt Manuscripts

All dates used in this book are based on the modern calendar, with the year commencing on 1 January. All spelling has been modernised; however, punctuation is unaltered.

Preface

This book is the product of four years of work on a doctoral research programme at Loughborough University of Technology between 1982 and 1986. I was attracted to the area of study a few years earlier whilst an undergraduate, when I realised that there was more to the history of Henry Hastings' war than the few historians who had covered his career had credited him with. Portrayed as one-eyed 'Rob-Carrier', the best that both J.H. Hollings and E.W. Hensman said of him was that he was involved in intercepting dispatches, attacking parliamentarian convoys and that he was a daring partisan. Yet is was abundantly clear that there was more to his role in the First Civil War than that. The way in which I was able to tackle the problem was not through a standard biographical approach; I tended to be wary of such things until I became a biographer myself, but through an exploration of the wider picture. I had contemplated a county study of Leicestershire, which would have fitted into the genre established by Alan Everitt and J.T. Cliffe amongst others and which was at that time being continued, even though their conclusions about county society integrity was by that time being challenged by Anne Hughes and Clive Holmes.[1] However, unbeknown to many of us such studies in any case were going out of style. Despite the fact that Professor Everitt had not followed up on his very tempting pamphlet on Leicestershire and Northamptonshire I jumped at the opportunity for regional examination of the Civil War prompted by Ronald Hutton's pioneering *The Royalist War Effort*.[2] Whilst not following the same methodology as Professor Hutton, I explored the East or North Midlands in the same way that he had explored the West Midlands and Wales; taking the form of a regional study.

Henry Hastings seems to have had little military experience before the war, but in 1642 he was given colonelcies of a horse regiment initially and then both dragoon and foot regiments before the end of the year. In early 1643 he was appointed colonel general of the Midlands counties of Leicestershire, Rutland, Staffordshire, Nottinghamshire Derbyshire and Lincolnshire. In effect he was the senior colonel or serving in the role of a brigadier of the regiments being raised in those counties for the King. Initially his commander was William Cavendish, Earl of Newcastle, who commanded England north and east of the Trent, but as the war progressed the lines of command were to become more complex. Hastings amassed a small army in the region in his remit which was subsequently involved in many of the major campaigns of the war.

Hastings might be the central figure in this book, but this is still not a biography. Rather, it is an analysis of the North Midlands royalists' cause as a whole both militarily and administratively. The devil is in the detail they say, and some of the reasons for the failure of the royalist cause as a whole can be seen clearly in this region. In terms of controlling the royalist armed forces, there was confusion in command structures, sparked by the fact that Hastings was in charge counties which were under the overall command of different commanders. Derbyshire, Nottinghamshire Leicestershire and Rutland were under the Earl of Newcastle's purview until July 1644 when the command collapsed, never to be re-established, but Staffordshire would be under various commanders including princes Rupert and Maurice throughout the war. This division caused problems early on with rival colonels, bridling under Hastings' command and appealing above his head to superior commanders. This problem was only exacerbated by the collapse of the royalist northern command in mid 1644 and inconsistencies in command structures in the west. The colonels and garrison commanders subsequently quarrelled over orders, billeting allocations and tax appropriation; sometimes refusing to accept Hastings' decisions. All of this would weaken the royalist cause, without any need for the local and regional parliamentarian to raise a hand. In military terms, Hastings' army was weakened by the strategic decision to dominate territory through occupation. The 5,000 or so royalist North Midland forces were as a result divided between a large number of garrisons because the opening strategy of the war had been directed at holding down territory in order to exploit resources. Subsequently there was no initiative to change this. Even a small army such as Hastings' could have made an important contribution to a larger field army, but that was rarely to be. As a result, when Hastings' forces were incorporated into marching armies, it was generally piecemeal such as in the campaign in the north in early 1644 or in the march to relieve York later that same year. On a small number of occasions, the siege of Lichfield and the battle of Hopton Heath in 1643 and the battle of Newark in 1644; however Hastings' forces did fight in larger concentrations. Hastings himself did act in a greater role. By the end of 1643 he had been appointed lieutenant general: this was a regional rather than field command but in the following March Hastings, or more properly Lieutenant General Henry, Lord Loughborough served as Prince Rupert's second in command at the prince's greatest victory, the battle of Newark. The two men had worked together the previous year at the siege of Lichfield, but this was the only major battle in which they fought together.

Since the completion of the thesis in 1986, there has been only a small amount of work on this area. The thesis itself generated several articles before and after its completion, but it was never published as a complete work.[3] Some further work was conducted on the issues it raised, but my attention was diverted by the larger debates over the very nature the Civil War.[4] Whilst applying the same research techniques regarding the type of sources used in the thesis my chief concern was to look at the broader issues of the Civil Wars across the four nations or three kingdoms, which took up a pair of books.[5] This was then followed by concentration on Oliver Cromwell, rather than on the royalists in the North Midlands.[6]

It is also true that there has been little engagement with the region by others since I wrote the thesis. There are exceptions. Jeff Richards has produced two books focussing on Leicestershire and Thomas, Lord Grey of Groby, and has been keen to present a more sympathetic case for the young aristocrat.[7] Ian Atherton has also re-examined the history of Lichfield during the Civil War, making extensive use of the sources I used back in the 1980s and has been able to usefully develop the history of the town and its garrison's roles during the war.[8] Brian Stone and Andrew Polkey have both explored Derbyshire and the Trent Valley in very useful studies: Stone had made accessible the accounts of the war in Derbyshire written by the Gell brothers and Sir George Gresley.[9] Exploration of the war has developed in ways which have reflected the social and economic considerations such as those I raised in the 1980s, but now pursued in more depth by authors such as Peter Edwards and Gavin Robinson who have explored the exploitation of materiel and the acquisition of horses for the large number of cavalry regiments.[10] There are new and ongoing exciting studies of garrison management and the powers of garrison governors which will enhance our understanding of the management of resources, towns and fortifications and how they contributed to administration, control, victory and defeat.

Looking back over the past 30 or so years at my conclusions, I am still largely content with them. I was disappointed that the records from other counties which I researched for chapter six of *The Civil Wars of Britain and Ireland 1637–1651* were not more forthcoming in terms of constables' or other relevant accounts. Whilst there are some which stand out in terms of content, such as those from Nottinghamshire, Herefordshire and Hertfordshire, none of them actually contained full details of income, disbursements and records of from whom the taxes were collected, although several did focus on one and sometimes two of these areas of enquiry. Fortunately, there were so many similarities between the nationwide records from both England and Wales and those used in the thesis to suggest that my findings about the structure and nature of contribution collection remain workable.

Moreover, very few more details have emerged about the military figures and administrators who were analysed in the original study. I still contend that both sides were recruiting administrators from below the 'normal' levels of social engagement for county governance. Likewise I still think that the doubly-defeated royalists would, had they achieved victory by 1646 have held tenaciously to their elevated situations and changed the face of local government at some level.[11] Once the lacklustre activity of some of the region's noble families had been exposed, and taken into account when local government was recreated by a victorious king: changes might have been as dramatic as those created by the issuing of the Militia Ordinance of March 1642 when prominent families were forced out of positions of authority. However, the royalists were defeated and the reasons for that in this region which I set out in 1986 remain the case. In the royalist administration the conflict was perhaps less dramatic in terms of the sort of social dilution seen on parliamentarian committees, but it was present. The Hastings family were not able to command complete respect within the counties in which they had lands and political and administrative clout. The active younger son, Henry Hastings, even when Lord Loughborough, had to cope with constant sniping from gentry families in Leicestershire, Derbyshire and Staffordshire. Yet this was not the same as the political opposition to his father (and elder brother) in the pre-war years in the terms of families and factions. I and David Fleming both challenged the idea that wartime divisions in Leicestershire were effectively the extension of traditional rivalries, in the 1970s and 80s.[12] Yet come the war the cache of soft power which the Hastings family retained was not brought into play, largely because the two wartime heads of the family, Henry the fifth Earl of Huntingdon and Ferdinando the sixth earl refused to play any leading role in the war. Henry the younger son was not able to inspire such loyalty as might have been possible had the scions of the family acted forcefully. In many ways, Henry Hastings' experience of military and administrative command was similar to that of his father, and to a lesser extent his older brother's, experience of county government in the pre-war years. Leading members of the region's gentry' families, Leveson and the Bagots in Staffordshire, Lucas in Leicestershire challenged Hastings' authority throughout the First Civil War. At the very least the colonels used the failure to establish firm control and a schedule of authorities at the beginning of the war, to avoid obedience. It is also true that the disobedient colonels were able to play up potential, if not actual, confusion over the issuing of Hastings' commissions as both colonel general and later lieutenant general, although it has to be admitted we are still no clearer as to what his role in Staffordshire was exactly during the period after his appointment as lieutenant general of Leicestershire and Derbyshire by Newcastle in the autumn of 1643.

An issue that I paid little attention to in the thesis, because I thought of my work as being a largely a socio-political study, set against a revised narrative of war in the region, was the Military Revolution advocated in the 1950s by Michael Roberts and developed by Geoffrey Parker.[13] As I now work my way through a research project focussing on the Civil War generals, I am obliged to look back at my work in a new light. In terms of the appointments to command there is little that can be said of the regimental officers and their experience and training; there simply is not the information available to track their pre-Civil War military career at home or in the wars on the continent. Amongst Lord Loughborough's officers as well as those who were gentlemen and had held administrative offices in the counties there were virginal players, choristers and choirmasters, a composer, attorneys and attorneys' clerks, barristers, clerks of the peace, borough recorders, a butler and falconer, clerics, an iron-master, a glove seller and even a cow gelder. But few men like Sir Richard Bagot with a background of military service – which overrode family status when it came to command are evident. It may be that the veterans made up the non-commissioned officers and ordinary soldiers whose names are largely lost to us. Officers in this army if they had experience at all were men who had served in the trained bands rather than abroad. The more experienced of them had been in the Bishops' Wars, which in itself was not the best introduction to modern warfare. These men were thus very like Oliver Cromwell in that they would have to learn the trade 'on the hoof'. Here the Military Revolution provided the literary source material in the form of over 90 books written on the subject of warfare and training in the years before the conflict.[14]

Another consideration regarding the development of warfare and strategy I did touch on, but did not develop in the light of the Military Revolution, was the issue of the strategy raised by the establishment of a large number of both large and garrisons as mentioned above. It has been argued that dissipating forces around garrisons is strategically detrimental. Given that there was little in the way of *Trace Italienne* inherent in English fortifications and none in the midlands at the outset of the war it was not necessarily going to be a war of sieges, but the rapid establishment of garrisons and outposts would shape the nature of warfare. I pointed out that the army created by Hastings was reasonably large and that at certain times in the war, Hopton Heath, the relief of Newark for example this army was a sizeable presence within associated forces assembled for a campaign. However, the ability to use this army strategically was limited by the sheer number of garrisons that it maintained. It was the nature of the war post Turnham Green which caused this to be the case, rather than a well-thought-out strategic plan. The need to marshal resources across the country to replace the fragile funding systems which allowed for the creation of the first field armies in 1642, had resulted in a land grab and the establishment of bases from which to undertake this and then to maintain control. The need to manage those resources throughout the First Civil War led to the creation of the super-garrisons, Ashby-de-la-Zouch, Lichfield and most importantly Newark which all acted as major military bases and administrative centres. It is therefore legitimate to ask whether a more concentrated mobile army could have overawed the parliamentarian strongholds of Leicester, Stafford, Nottingham and Derby as effectively as the many large and small garrisons established by the royalists. It is possible that it might have done, as the concentration of the forces commanded by Hastings would certainly have outnumbered each and indeed at times all of the parliamentarian forces in the region before mid 1644 had they ventured outside their protective walls in any force. One has only to look at the quite pathetic attempts of the local and regional parliamentarians to prevent the passage of Generalissimo Queen Henrietta Maria in mid 1643 to understand the problems which the region's parliamentarians laboured under. In some ways this pattern of dissipation of resources is reflected nationally. On the other hand the major garrisons of Ashby-de-la-Zouch and to a greater extent, Newark, showed that they were formidable obstacles. Ashby was never seriously challenged at any point during the war and Newark resisted three sieges. At the end of the war Hastings used Ashby as a bargaining counter when seeking terms for ending his war career, as did the king with Newark. Moreover, as Cromwell predicted in autumn 1644, Newark tied up two large field armies for six months preventing them from undertaking field actions.

In conclusion the royalist war effort in the North Midlands counties demonstrated both the strengths and weaknesses of the royalist cause as a whole. The royalists could raise troops and create potent armies throughout the war and they could manage a war effort which supported these troops. It is also true that there was a real potential for a regional approach to the war to work as an effective means of such management. However, the failure to establish with firmness and weight a clear and effective command structure, which could weather defeat and change of personnel caused serious problems. Clear chains of authority and a lack of external interference with those chains, whether or it be by the king or other royalist figures could have overcome the competing personal ambitions amongst field officers. It could also have replaced the failure to mobilise effectively the caches of aristocratic power and influence which might normally be expected to bolster or sustain command. The retelling or reframing of the story of the war also demonstrates that we need to take the role of regional commanders more seriously, and none more so than that of Henry Hastings, Lord Loughborough.

Thesis Acknowledgements, 1986

First and foremost, I must thank my supervisor, Dr Marilyn Palmer, for her untiring confidence in my work, which first manifested itself in late 1980, when I was an aspiring undergraduate. Since then, her patience and good advice has contributed, in no small way, to the completion of this thesis. The following list of people who also deserve my thanks and praise is, in no way, in descending order of merit. The Staff of the Pilkington Library, Loughborough University and in particular the Inter Library Loan staff; The staff and Archivists of the Derbyshire County Records Office; The Leicestershire County Records Office; the Lincolnshire Archives Office; the Nottinghamshire County Records Office; the Staffordshire County Records Office; the William Salt Library, Stafford. I must also thank the Lichfield Cathedral Library; the Lichfield Joint Record Office; The Northamptonshire County Records Office and the Sussex County Records Office; and of course the staff of the Public Record Office, Chancery Lane, London and the British Library.

The Staff of the History Department at Loughborough University must also be thanked for their interest and enthusiasm which has encouraged me throughout the last eight years. Thanks are also due to Dr Ronald Hutton, Dr Peter Newman and Dr Malcolm Wanklyn for their friendship and advice over the last few years. It would be unfair of me not to thank my parents, Warwick and Hazel, for their patient forbearance of a son who preferred to live as a student instead of getting a 'proper job' for so long. I must thank Deborah Tyler for her encouragement and faith, despite the difficulties of pursuing her own academic career in the United States, and for accompanying me to English Civil War Society battles when I wanted to find out what it was really like.

It remains for me to absolve all the above from responsibility for any errors, technical or otherwise, in the following work.

Introduction

In the summer of 1642, the King created a field army which he led south and with which he fought the battle of Edgehill. In so doing, he drained the North Midlands counties of royalists and left the stage open for local parliamentarians to gain control of pockets of territory. In response, Charles, at the end of the year, dispatched several of his army officers home to their native counties to establish a royalist power base in the North Midlands. The result was that within six months, a royalist war effort was forged on a footing capable of creating a self-sufficient regional association on the five counties of Derbyshire, Leicestershire, Nottinghamshire, Rutland and Staffordshire.

This system was created and run by the returned officers along with the commissions of array, originally created to raise troops and funds in June, July and August of 1642. The resurrected commissions became primarily a financial administration which organised taxation levies and other sources of income throughout the region, aimed at paying for the growing army which the officers created by virtue of their personal commissions rather than through the now generally defunct military powers of the commissioners. The system reached its height in the first months of 1644, when domination of the five counties was almost complete. The defeat of the northern royalists at Selby and later Marston Moor plunged the North Midlands royalist war effort into a chaos from which it was unable to extract itself before it had lost large areas of territory. During the subsequent 18 months the royalists' ability to levy taxes shrunk as their territory contracted and, correspondingly, the size of the military forces declined rapidly. However, upon each of the three occasions when the King's Field Army was present in the region, the ensuing military strength enabled the North Midlands royalists to extend their taxation system over the areas where they had temporarily regained control. These episodes revealed the latent abilities still within the system, which, given good fortune, could come into effect.

This book examines, in depth, the regional structure of the royalist system in the North Midlands. At all times the area is seen as an integral unit and not as a collection of five quite separate counties. Studies which have hitherto envisaged the counties as islands unto themselves have, it is felt, obscured the true nature of the royalists' provincial war effort. Within the superstructure the nature and composition of the several commissions of array and their tax systems will be analysed with respect to their organisation and methodology. The social and familial status of the commissioners and the officers will also be studied and the results given in both tabular form during the course of the text, and in biographical form in the various appendices. It will be shown that whereas the commissioners, for the most part, were established county figures with some experience of local government, their military associates were not. In some cases this led to a conflict of interest between these two groups of royalist activists. Many of the officers were careerists and sought social advancement through their wartime activities, whilst the commissioners were, to a greater extent, intent upon preserving not only their communities, but also their hold upon them. The ensuing power struggle did not lead to the destruction of the royalist war effort, but it did nothing to strengthen it in the face of external military pressures.

As well as the examination of the financial administration, the army which the royalists built up in the area will be reconstructed, regiment by regiment, in order to redress the view of it which has hitherto been left to history. The impression left by the dependence upon largely hostile descriptions of the army, has been that the royalist regional commander, Henry Hastings, was merely a guerrilla leader in charge of various bands of land-locked pirates. This is a serious misrepresentation: the North Midlands Army was an army in every sense of the word, consisting of over 40 regiments. This high number of units was however its main drawback. All regiments were drastically undersized, and as a result, over staffed with officers, thereby proving a drain on resources.

The final section of the book consists of an analysis of the rise and fall of the royalist control over the five counties, from the frantic activity at the end of 1642 to the slow steady reduction of the royalist fortresses at the beginning of 1646. It will be shown here that the royalist hold on the region was never complete and that this weakness contributed to the collapse after the middle of 1644. It will also become evident that the continuous drain on resources and manpower imposed on the region by royalist commanders outside the North Midlands was another important factor in the decline. The effect that this decline had upon the royalist cause as a whole, is taken into account in the book's conclusion.

Some of the results of the research which went into the production of this book have appeared in several published articles written by the present author, namely:

Lord Loughborough, Ashby-de-la-Zouch and the English Civil War, Ashby Museum, Ashby, 1984.

'Henry Hastings and the Flying Army of Ashby-de-la-Zouch', *Transactions of the Leicestershire Archaeological and Historical Society*, vol. LVI, 1980–1981.

'Henry Hastings and the Royalist Cause in the East Midlands', M. Palmer (ed.), *The Aristocratic Estate: The Hastings Family in Leicestershire and South Derbyshire*, East Midlands Studies Unit, Loughborough, 1982.

'The Civil War Battle of Cotes', *The Leicestershire Historian*, vol. 3, No. 3, 1984–1985.

'Leicestershire's Royalist Officers and their War Effort in the County, 1642–1646', *Transactions of the Leicestershire Archaeological and Historical Society*, vol. LIX, 1984–1985.

'Contribution and Assessment: Financial Exactions in the English Civil War 1642–1646', *War and Society*, vol. 5, No. 1, 1986.

Chapter 1

The Royalist War Effort in the North Midlands: an Introduction

This book is the study of one group of counties formed into an association by the royalists in early 1643 and placed under the command of Henry Hastings, the second son of the Earl of Huntingdon. The counties concerned are Derbyshire, Leicestershire, Nottinghamshire, Rutland and Staffordshire. The part played by each of these counties in the Civil War has, to a greater or lesser extent, received some consideration from historians but they have not hitherto been treated as a group.

R.E. Sherwood's *Civil Strife in the Midlands*, though an honest attempt to see the Midlands as a whole, is concerned more to narrate events than to analyse the structure and organisation of either of the rival war efforts in the region.[15]

Regional participation in other areas of Britain during the Civil War has been studied and the results have provided both inspiration and guidance for the present work. Clive Holmes has furnished us with detailed work on the parliamentarian Eastern Association, whilst Ronald Hutton has analysed the royalist war effort in Wales and the west.[16] Peter Newman's work on the northern counties is, as yet, unpublished, but his thesis is a further example of a thorough and penetrating study of regional activity during the Civil War.[17] The North Midlands provided a vital link between the north and the west and both Newman and Hutton have indicated the value of a study of this area in contributing to an overall picture of the way in which the royalists fought the war.

In addition to considering the counties as a region this book will examine the personnel, the army officers and commissioners of array, who together operated the royalist war effort in the area. The social and familial status of the men involved will be considered along with their political, administrative and educative experience previous to the outbreak of hostilities in 1642. A comparison will be made between the two groups, administrators and soldiers, to see whether or not their backgrounds were similar. This may shed light on the difficulties which the two groups experienced in working together. More generally, such a study will, in tandem with Peter Newman's pioneering work on the analysis of royalist officers over the rank of captain, and with B.G. Blackwood's statistical survey of Lancashire's royalist officers, indicate from which social groups the King was able to draw support.[18] The structure of the parliamentarian administration will be briefly considered along similar lines so that the social origins and experience of the two rival groups can be compared.

The final section of this book will examine the effectiveness of the royalist administration and the royalist army in action by looking at the course of the First Civil War in the North Midlands. This will focus on the attempt first to win and then to maintain a position of domination in the region: a position they lost after the summer of 1644.

The remainder of this chapter will be concerned firstly with a review of the work already produced on the royalist war effort in the North Midlands, which will indicate why the further study undertaken here was thought necessary. Secondly, the chief sources used in this book will be reviewed and consideration given to their value and limitations. Finally, the aims of the book will be restated and an indication of the structure of the rest of the work will be given.

Previous Work

On the Royalist War Effort

The way in which the royalists ran their war effort has received recent attention in Joyce Malcolm's book *Caesar's Due: Loyalty and King, Charles*, produced in 1983.[19] Malcolm examined the diverse elements of the entire war effort, from the central and local administrations to the propaganda machine. Her conclusion was that it was an elitist organisation which suppressed local initiative and crushed the counties with harsh financial demands. The royalists neither wanted nor encouraged through their press the active participation of the lower orders of society in any other way than to provide generals with 'cannon fodder'. The result was, she maintains, a royalist army made up of Welsh, Irish and a large proportion of mercenaries. Undoubtedly this view owes much to her over-dependence on printed sources and Clarendon who certainly held the King's Army in no high esteem. Thus, though the work is an attempt at an overview it is highly coloured by its use of (hostile) parliamentarian propaganda. Dr Wanklyn and Peter Young point out in a rejoinder to Malcolm's article on Charles' recruitment drive in 1642, she is blinded by making 'little effort to compare or collate royalist and parliamentarian sources'[20]

Of more practical value is the factual study, by J. Ensberg, of royalist finances, written in 1966.[21] Ensberg analyses the upper echelons of the royalist financial management. He details the powers of the treasury over the local commissions and briefly refers to the methods by which money was collected within the counties. However, in this he only looks at the system employed in Oxfordshire and does not extend it to a wider sphere. His work, read in conjunction with F.C. Dietz's examination of the issues and receipts of the exchequer for the early Stuart period, remains useful as an introduction to the complexities of royalist financing.[22]

Ian Roy's study of the royalist army at Oxford, which predates Ensberg's work by three years, gives an excellent insight into the command structure at the royalist capital.[23] Roy explores the organisation of the military effort at Oxford and analyses the power of the Council of War.

He emphasises the difference between this which was at least semi-permanent and councils of war in the provinces which were perhaps irregular or ad hoc. Some generals, such as Rupert or Lord Goring rarely made use of a council. Roy's work was made possible by 70 sets of minutes from the Oxford Councils of War, which are still in existence, unlike any of the councils in the North Midlands, for which only fragments of their deliberations survive. In conjunction with Ensberg's brief work, Roy's study provides us with a comprehensive picture of how the royalist war effort functioned in the Oxford region but does little to indicate how royalists in other areas operated.

Indeed, in the counties little has been done on the operation of the royalist war effort. Within the North Midlands the chief studies of Nottinghamshire and Derbyshire are heavily weighted towards the parliamentarians and their war effort. Both theses on Derbyshire, those of A.M. Morton-Thorpe and Lynn Beats, are chiefly dependent upon parliamentarian source material though the former does examine the gentry of both sides.[24] Similarly, as Patricia Lloyd concentrates upon the personnel and politics of the town of Nottingham, the bias is obviously towards the parliamentarians who held the town throughout the war, rather than towards the royalists who were based at Newark.[25] On the other hand J.T. Pickles' study of Staffordshire does concentrate upon the royalists and how they fought the war in their county.[26] The problem with this thesis is that interpretation is restricted by acceptance of the confines of the county borders.

Peter Newman in his work on the Northern Army does not accept such rigid confines.[27] His as yet unpublished thesis takes into account not only one county's contribution to the war but that of a whole region. This regional slant is important; restriction to county studies can obscure intercounty relationships and thus distort impressions of the Civil War in the provinces. If a county outlook is maintained, then any appearance of a commander not from that county appears as an intrusion, as in the case of Henry Hastings' 'intervention' in Staffordshire and Derbyshire referred to in the works of Pickles and Beats, which will be further considered later. This was not how it would have been perceived in the First Civil War, when Hastings was given control of a region, not a county, and operated outside his actual base of Leicestershire. There were cases of external intervention in the North Midlands, but these were by Prince Rupert or other royalist commanders, not by the regional commander. We need to adopt a regional approach and cease to regard counties as islands in an hostile and foreign sea, a view which was much promoted by Alan Everett yet which ignores both links between counties and geographical barriers to county unity of the sort Ann Hughes has identified.[28] A County study may be of value in studying some aspects of county society but seems wholly inadequate when examining a national war.

By far the most extensive published study of the royalist war effort is the work of Ronald Hutton.[29] He examined the county groupings of the south-west and the Marcher counties and the way in which they were controlled by their various commanders-in-chief from the end of 1642. He treats the commanders in a semi-biographical manner and looks at their operation of the royalist administration with reference to the various forms of financial exaction, excise, sequestration and contribution. Hutton firmly believes that the way in which the war was fought reflects the view, held by the participants, of the part they played in society. Those who owned much of the counties were naturally unwilling to overburden them, and thereby themselves, with taxation and thus came into conflict with those of lesser social standing who had less to protect. He then asserts that revulsion against the war was a prime cause of Charles' defeat, but argues that this was not the revulsion against the King himself which Malcolm portrays, but dissatisfaction with the breakdown of the normal royalist or county administration. It is the high handedness of military necessity, practised by Lord Goring and Barnabus Scudamore, governor of Hereford, which are a chief cause of clubman risings or other examples of popular feeling. Hutton's work is of great importance as it breaks down county restrictions and views the royalist war effort on a much wider level, which is how it would have been seen at the time. In going further than the narrow geographical confines adopted by Ian Roy he extends our perception into the provinces where Oxford laws were tempered by local practicality.

Hutton includes Staffordshire in his study. His justification for this is that Rupert began exercising a form of military suzerainty over the county from the spring of 1644. It was, however, originally part of the North Midland Association, under Hastings. Thus Hutton's book *The Royalist War Effort* prompts a study of this association, both to link Hutton's chosen region to that of Peter Newman's and to reconsider the position of Staffordshire within the royalist war effort.

In the above section we have traced the development of studies concerning the royalist war effort from the work on Oxford and Oxfordshire through to the more recent examinations of provincial administrations which are separated by the North Midland counties. This book is intended to fill that gap in the literature.

Analysis of the Social Structure of the Royalist Activists

Identification of royalist officers began, in a serious way in the 1960s. Peter Young, who for years had collected information regarding these men, made his findings more generally available with the publication of his book *Edgehill*.[30] His subsequent works on the battles of Marston Moor and Naseby have formed supplements to this.[31] The latter, however, contains some basic factual errors regarding the names of parliamentarian officers, which may be an indication of the need to be wary when consulting Young's works. Young is also guilty of not fully documenting his Sources: nor does he make any attempt to analyse the officers in terms of social background and the like, being content to deal solely with their military careers. This type of work was left to others and it was around 10 years after the publication of *Edgehill* that studies of this kind began to appear.

B.G. Blackwood's study of Lancashire gentry included tables statistically analysing the county's royalists and parliamentarians. Blackwood looked at their social and familial status and their experience of education or central and local government.[32] J.T. Brighton likewise worked on the officers and administrators of both sides in Derbyshire as well as the county's neutrals.[33] Peter Newman, in his thesis, identified the Northern Army's officers, analysing them, firstly rank by rank and then as an entire group. His conclusions were that the royalist army he was dealing with was commanded chiefly by members of the gentry, rather than by the traditional military commanders, the aristocracy. He also indicated that the lower officer ranks contained members of the lower gentry and even elements from below gentry status. He said,

> 'It will be seen that in attempting to identify officers who had held local, national or court office, prior to 1642, or who had received university education, a remarkable lack of any such experience emerges.'[34]

Newman qualifies his statement somewhat by asserting that the absence of experience could be partially explained by the presence of a large proportion of Catholic officers, who would have been excluded from holding such offices. Even so in work derived not only from his thesis, but from his mammoth directory of royalist field officers,[35] Newman presses his point about the social status of the officer cadre,

> 'From the commencement of real warfare, mere gentry and lesser men were well represented at all levels of field command in the royal armies.'[36]

Apart from Brighton's work and the list of royalists in the Newark garrison compiled by the Royal Commission on Historical Monuments in their book on the town's siegeworks, nothing has been done to analyse the North Midlands officers.[37] This book will look at the officers of the North Midlands Army in the same terms as Newman examined those of the north to evaluate his judgement on the link between lack of an administratively experienced officer corps and the high proportion of Catholic officers. The proportion of Catholics in the North Midlands is accepted as being much lower per head of population than in the north and it will be seen if this has a significant effect on the analysis of the region's officer corp. A parallel study will be made of the commissioners of array appointed to the five counties in the area and comparisons made between the two bodies.

Works on the North Midlands

The geographical position of the North Midlands alone ensured that it would play a major part in the First Civil War. This point was not lost on the inhabitants of Leicestershire in 1642 when they petitioned the King from

> 'In the midst of your Kingdom of England, and in the midst of our great fears and apparent dangers ...'[38]

Nor has it been lost on J.P. Kenyon when he claims that Nottinghamshire, as well as other counties, were almost 'continuous war zones'[39] Yet there has previously been no work dedicated to the region, though it will be shown work has been done on individual counties within it. Nor have general works given full consideration to the region, concentrating rather on specific incidents like Prince Rupert's relief of Newark in 1644 or the siege of Leicester in 1645. C.V. Wedgwood refers to Hastings, the central figure of royalist authority in the area, in the following terms: 'that he maintained the Royalist cause with vigour and ferocity in Leicestershire'[40] Thereby, she chooses to mention only one of the five counties under his command! But she was following the example of Clarendon who, though also praising his vigour and effort, did not deal at length with this important Midlands general. To other historians, ranging from Woolrych to Young, Hastings and the Midlands shires generally only require a mention when he, or they, appear in the light of a more nationally known character, such as Rupert or Charles himself. Yet Hastings, his army and his command were constant celebrities in the Civil War newsbooks of both sides. To the royalists he was noble and gallant: to parliamentarians a notorious 'rob-carrier'. Use was made of these news books and some other contemporary sources by John Nichols when he compiled his *The History and Antiquities of the County of Leicestershire* at the end of the eighteenth century.[41] In his work Nichols provided a chronological sequence of documents and extracts of documents connected to each other by brief statements. No attempt was made to interpret the events mentioned within the sources, nor was the bias or origin of them commented on. The documents available to Nichols were chiefly of parliamentarian origin and thus presented a, naturally, jaundiced view of the royalists, which, as said, Nichols did not seek to balance. Other county studies contain brief reflections of the Civil War and, as with Nichols, refer to the pre-eminent families involved therein. Stebbing Shaw's *History and Antiquities of the County of Staffordshire* contains some reprinted Civil War letters and tract; references to which can be found later in this book. Stephen Glover's *History, Gazetteer and Directory of the County of Derby* contains the same selection along with two versions of the career of Sir John Gell, one of which is from the Gresley Manuscripts used extensively in this work.[42] Thoroton's *The Antiquities of Nottinghamshire* and Wright's *History and Antiquities of Rutland* are in the same vein, often reproducing the same information as the above histories and, like the others, carry details useful to the compilation of biographies of the participants of the war.[43] Also comparable with the above five county histories is *A History of the Antiquities of the Town and Church of Southwell...* which reprints documentary evidence of the Civil War including 'Coritani Lachrymantes, being an historical account of the Civil Wars in this and neighbouring counties by Mr Savage'. This is an interesting memoir of the war but the veracity of its information has to be checked against other sources.[44]

In the nineteenth century several North Midland counties received the attentions of historians with regard to their part in the Civil War. In 1840, J.F. Hollings wrote *The History of Leicestershire During the Great Civil War*.[45] This account, based on a lecture delivered to the Leicester Mechanics' Institute, does not include references to source material but it would appear to be heavily dependent upon the documentary evidence provided in Nichols' history. As an antiquarian work Hollings' article is unrivalled for its attention to detail and the work by Hensman in the present century referred to below, though shifting the emphasis onto Hastings' contribution, is really only a reworking of this.

The growth of county history societies during the last century contributed to the number of published articles regarding the Civil War. This is particularly true of Staffordshire and Derbyshire. No less than six such articles appeared in *Collections for a History of Staffordshire* and five in the *Derbyshire Archaeological Journal*, before 1900. Most of the Staffordshire work was done by Major General Wrottesley, who not only traced his own family's role in the war, but that of other prominent county families. In Derbyshire, J.C. Fox looked at sequestration in the county as well as county personalities. These articles, though useful in providing clues to source material regarding such individuals who attracted the attentions of historians, did not, as a whole, advance the understanding of the Civil War to any substantial degree. They were of interest to the devotee of purely county or family history, but of little other value.

This trend continued into this century with E.W. Hensman's two articles on the career of Henry Hastings.[46] Although they did bring Hastings into prominence, their dependence on the material supplied by Nichols limited their potential for saying anything original about the war in the area. Hastings thereby, remained very much in the role of a guerrilla leader, a role implied by the parliamentarian press' treatment of him three centuries earlier. Work on other counties did nothing materially to alter this view. Introspective as they were, the view of Hastings was very much that he was an outsider interfering in their county's affairs, thereby they assigned to him the position of an intruder and not that of regional military commander.

The most important relevant published county history of the Civil War period is A.C. Wood's *Nottinghamshire in the Civil War* written in the 1930s.[47] It is a well researched advance on the nineteenth century accounts. Wood examined the 'county community' before the appellation was in general usage. His relation of the war is more penetrating than previous work and a genuine attempt was made to see Nottinghamshire in relation to national events. That some of his conclusions and factual interpretation have now been superseded by further works does nothing to denigrate Wood's effort. Yet even he did not really place the county fully into a regional framework and again Hastings appears more as an outsider than a commander with responsibility for the county. Having said this, it must be pointed out that there is a little more justification in this case. The strength of the Newark garrison and its special relationship with Hastings' immediate superior, the Earl, later Marquis of Newcastle, and its subsequent relationship with Prince Rupert, tended to give the town's governors a great deal of influence, if not control, within the county. The mutual dependence of Hastings and the succession of governors of Newark will be explored in chapters 5 and 6.

The study of the county community during the Civil War began in earnest in the 1960s and produced the county portraits of Kent by Alan Everett, of Yorkshire by J.T. Cliffe and, during the ensuing decade, of Lancashire by

B.G. Blackwood.[48] It was hoped that the county studies would give some indication of the nature of the struggle revealed in the controversy generally known as the 'storm over the gentry'. Examination of the personnel of both factions, might reveal whether there was a significant economic decline amongst the aristocracy and an inverse rise in the wealth of the gentry. What did become apparent was the difficulty in making precise definitions between social groups and as a result the desired wide ranging conclusions were never reached. Instead the period saw a shift from the study of the gentry to the study of county society and thus the 'county community' came into prominence. Everett felt able to state, that when people

> 'spoke of their "country" they did not mean England, but Wiltshire or Kent, Leicestershire or Northamptonshire, Cumberland or Durham.'[49]

In turn, however, the concept of the county community came under critical examination in the 1970s by Clive Holmes and Ann Hughes, amongst others.[50] Whereas Everett saw the county almost as an island entire of itself and generally at odds with central government, Hughes and Holmes pointed out that there were social and economic ties, within or between counties, unrestricted by administrative boundaries. Some aspects of county life - intellectual and religious ones, for example - transcended, not only borders with neighbouring counties, but also regional boundaries. This would imply that the attempts at centralism, or at least regionalism, made during the Civil War were not wholly alien to the English counties of the seventeenth century in the way that county studies have generally sought to infer. Though this book is not concerned with the county community debate, the fact that rigid adherence to county borders is no longer regarded as necessary to the study of the Civil War in the provinces is important. The need to examine the regional effects of the war is given credence by these new views and thus there is no need to excuse the geographical scope of this book.

The county community debate left its mark on the North Midlands. Three of the five counties were the subject of such studies during the 1970s and early 1980s. Rutland alone was not subjected to any such work and Leicestershire was not dealt with in any major work, perhaps due to the expectation that Alan Everett might follow up his brief look at the county's community made in 1969:[51] this did not materialise. Instead, one of Everett's students at Leicester University's Department of English Local History presented him with a short dissertation which was later turned into an article.[52] In it David Fleming cast doubt on Clarendon's assertion that the political divisions amongst the county's gentry previous to the war were essentially continued unchanged into the war. These divisions, between supporters of the Grey family and those of the Hastings faction, did, argued Fleming, break down upon the advent of war, with prominent opponents of the Hastings family adopting the same royalist stance as their former enemies. Fleming also indicated that the county's royalist faction contained the majority of the administratively experienced and legally trained members of the community. This must be borne in mind when reading chapters 2, 3 and 4, when statistical analyses of the royalist activists and parliamentarian committeemen are made. Fleming's work can be read in conjunction with Gruenfelder's study of the Hastings' electoral influence, which gives a picture of gentry allegiances.[53]

Nottinghamshire has scarcely been more fortunate in the attentions it has received from historians. It was as recently as 1983 that Patricia Lloyd completed a master's thesis examining the politics of the county town between 1640 and 1688.[54] The study is limited by her deliberate concentration on Nottingham as opposed to the county, with the result that, with reference to the Civil War Lloyd's emphasis is on the parliamentarians rather than an over view of both sides. Though undoubtedly an advance on the analysis of the parliamentarian administration given by Wood, it was never intended to convey a general impression of even this one county at war.

Staffordshire received a greater share of attention. The useful reproduction of the county committee minute books by Pennington and Roots in 1957, was prefaced by comprehensive interpretation of the county's parliamentarian war effort. As a guideline it has been of invaluable use in the writing of Chapter 3. J.T. Pickles' thesis of 1968 provided this with a counterpoise by being concerned with the county's royalists.[55] Pickles made extensive use of Hastings' letters in the research for his work but still maintains the impression that he was an outsider rather than a regional commander. Pickles does, with some success, outline the quarrels between Hastings and the Staffordshire commanders but may be guilty of over-emphasising the harm this did to the royalist cause in the area.

Derbyshire has received more attention than the other counties. Articles much in the vein of Cox's nineteenth-century studies were written during the 1950s, but the 1970s saw two theses devoted to the county. In 1971 A.M. Morton-Thorpe produced an MA thesis on the county gentry.[56] He examined the major characters in a biographical manner and outlined the principal military events of the war in the county. In both, the study is limited in scope by its heavy reliance on parliamentarian sources and he reached very few conclusions about the nature of support for either side. A much more thorough and searching investigation of the county was made by Lynn Beats in 1978.[57] Beats was concerned with the county gentry and the rival war efforts during the First Civil War. She perceived that an inherent localism within the county was largely responsible for the collapse of the parliamentarian East Midlands Association under Lord Grey. This is in keeping with the general theme of the insular nature of Everett's county communities, yet the argument suffers from a major imbalance. As will become apparent in Chapter 2, there is little surviving evidence regarding the royalist war effort in the county; thus Beats was, like Morton-Thorpe before her, heavily dependent on parliamentarian source material. If she had not been restricted by her county centred approach the conclusions may have been different. With a much wider study it is possible to dovetail what evidence there is from Derbyshire into information gleaned from other parts of the region and thereby create a much more developed picture. The response of the county to royalist regional policy will become apparent in Chapter 2, where such an exercise is carried out. In addition, with regard to Derbyshire, there is the work by J.T. Brighton on the composition of the royalist and parliamentarian parties within the counties, as well as his narrative of the career of Sir John Gell.[58]

None of these county histories does anything to create an impression of the regionally operated war effort which was aimed at by both sides during the Civil War, though Beats goes as far as suggesting that such a system was defeated by localism. The present author believes that individual studies of counties cannot, by their very nature, be sufficient judges of regional activity and that this book is necessary to define the existence of a regional organisation. This study will also remove Hastings from his present role as a guerrilla leader and outsider and consider him as a regional commander faced with the problem of controlling his territory in the face of opposition from indigenous parliamentarians. This and the need for further study of royalist activists and their war effort, provide ample reasons for the pursuance of this book.

Sources

Just as it was impossible to present an examination of all the secondary sources, which have dealt with the geographical and historical area, it is likewise so for the primary sources which form the basis of this book. Instead, only a few will be looked at in any depth. These will be grouped into three sections – the war effort, the North Midlands Army and the course of the war itself. For details of the full range of the sources used the reader is referred to both the endnotes to each chapter and to the bibliography.

There is little evidence regarding the central policies of the royalist war effort and this is reflected in the localities as well. Lists of the members of commissions of array are available in the transcripts of Sir William Dugdale contained in the Finch-Hatton manuscripts and in the records of the Clerks of the Chancery, also transcribed by Dugdale and later printed, but not published, by W.H. Black.[59] These are not, however, complete lists. The Finch-Hatton manuscripts do not give details of every commission appointed and the Chancery papers do not give full details of the membership of all the commissions contained within. Other names can be gleaned from the papers of the Committee for Compounding and of the Committee for the Advance of Money. These latter contain cases of factual errors and should be used with care.[60] The period after the war was a time when local rivalries could be prosecuted thoroughly and false witness be borne against an unpopular neighbour, resulting in instances of unreliable evidence being presented to committees prosecuting royalists.

Whilst parliamentarian state papers can be found in great number in the relevant calendars as well as in the collections made by Rushworth (contemporary) or Firth and Rait (1911) no equivalent exists for the royalists. Apart from the far fewer royalist state papers in the calendars, instructions issued to the commissions – notably those for Northamptonshire and Worcestershire – do still survive. Only Rutland, of the North Midland counties has such a document in existence.[61] As a result, a lot of the evidence comes from the few remaining accounts of village constables and headboroughs, the minor officials faced with the awesome task of collecting the wartime taxes from the local communities. These, combined with the instructions issued from above which do survive, present a picture of the royalist war effort in the region. A full discussion of the constables' accounts is given in Chapter 2. On occasion, evidence from contemporary newsbooks can be utilised, with caution. Both sides' propaganda machines were designed to obscure facts as much as, if not more than, to present them. Only the barest details of potential validity can be gleaned. They can give details of where a group of commissioners, or committeemen, were at a particular time but the accounts of their activity is dependent upon the author's bias. Thus, depending on who wrote about whom, commissions or committees would be plundering and issuing unlawful warrants or receiving the bounty of a well affected county.

The parliamentarian war effort, examined for comparative purposes, can be perceived via the use of the central government sources cited above and also by the local evidence available. Only one of the region's committees left considerable details of its operations, that of Staffordshire. This has already been referred to in the form edited by Pennington and Roots. The original, held at the William Salt Library, Stafford, has also been consulted. The town council minutes of Nottingham and Leicester contain references to the activities of the respective committees; however the minutes of the committees have been lost.[62]

Evidence for the identification of activists can be gained from all the above sources. The newsbooks are again fraught with pitfalls. Names of officers or others contained within them can be distorted by having originated in hearsay or in some cases can be entirely fictional. Even the pamphlet containing the names of the officers in both armies in the early stages of the war produced in 1642 and subsequently edited by Peacock in the nineteenth century is full of inaccuracies.[63] As a general rule it is safe not to accept names from this list unless they can be corroborated by evidence from another source.

Commissioners' names can, of course, be found in the two Dugdale transcripts mentioned earlier, whilst there are two chief sources for the names of the officers also. The 'List of Officers Claiming to the Sixty Thousand Pounds Etc Granted by His Sacred Majesty for the Relief of his Truly Loyal and Indigent Party'[64] lists by regiment, with additional unregimented names at the back, the names of officers still alive in 1663 who had been reduced to penury by their service to Charles I. The list is not without flaws. In the case of the Earls of Lindsey no distinction is made between the regiments raised by the father and the son; similarly no distinction is made between regiments raised in the First Civil War and those raised subsequently. Details regarding individuals are scanty, simply rank, immediate superior, regimental commander and place of residence. In the case of the latter this may be recorded as London and Westminster, the place of residence whilst making the petition. Even when not so, it may not be the place of residence in 1642 which is necessary for this book.

The notebook kept by Richard Symonds, an officer of the King's Lifeguard, is very useful.[65] It contains a list of officers in Hastings' army during 1644. Symonds does not list all of the regiments, only those he has seen or heard of. That some of the information came to him by word of mouth is suggested by the spelling of some of the names. By combining these two sources with snippets of information gathered from other sources a list of 356 names was compiled for the North Midlands Army officer corps.

Identifying their social background involved a variety of source material. Personal documents were few and existed for only a minority of individuals. General sources such as heraldic visitations and lists of university and inns of Court entrants were consulted as were catalogues of the names of JPs and deputy lieutenants in the State Papers in the Public Record Office.[66]

Confusion of names is common in all of the sources used. This is particularly true when there are two or more people of the same name. In Derbyshire alone, there is quite often no distinction made between Sir John Harpur of Swarkestone and Sir John Harpur of Caulke or between Sir John Fitzherbert of Norbury and Sir John Fitzherbert of Tissington. In each case the former was an active royalist and the latter was not. Even Hastings is not free of such confusions. When enobled he became Baron Loughborough of Loughborough, but is often referred to as Lord Hastings of Loughborough or just as Lord Hastings. The latter is particularly problematic as Lord Hastings is the courtesy title given to the first son of the Earls of Huntingdon and therefore to Hastings' elder brother. Such errors have been continued into even recent secondary material. These instances all concern quite prominent figures and the potential for confusion is probably much greater when working with minor characters.

The presence of no less than three John Lowes in Derbyshire regiments is one such point. On limited evidence it would have been quite easy to assume that there was only one man of this name who had transferred from one regiment to another. However successive evidence revealed three quite separate individuals.

Problems occur when trying to place the royalist officers and commissioners into social groups, though with the latter it is often easier as some indication of rank is given along with their names in the commissions. In the greater number of cases the ascription of social rank is impossible. It would appear that they are either obscure lower gentry or were from the 'grey area' just below gentry status. At that level, obscurity is important: by the implication that they were lower gentry or below, Dr Morrill's assertion that,

> 'those at the tail end of the gentry are far less likely to have been involved in the Civil War than those at the top of the gentry.'[67]

is thrown into question. For those people who were in the ranks of the gentry, the distinctions between esquire and gentleman are made from the information gathered from a number of sources, both legal and personal. There is much of value in the various tests of gentry status put forward by Dr Wanklyn and others and summarised by Dr Morrill. This book in some way uses a combination of them all. Title is derived from the heraldic visitations, upon which J.T. Cliffe based his examinations and upon common usage as applied to individuals at the time as adopted by Dr Blackwood. Even with such a high proportion of officers with obscure origins, important points can be made regarding the nature of royalist support in the North Midlands and elsewhere as will be shown in Chapter 4.

For the final area covered by this book, the description of the role played by the North Midlands royalists and their war effort in the Civil War, a wide variety of sources, including many already cited, have been employed. Correspondence between the officers and the commissioners plays an important role. Some of these are contained, in printed form, in publications of the Historical Manuscripts Commission. The Hastings collection, the Portland Papers and the Rutland Manuscripts are three of the prominent ones.[68] Several of Hastings own letters, some of which appeared in Eliot Warburton's work on Prince Rupert and the cavaliers, are held at the William Salt Library and have been used extensively.[69] Individual, or collections of, letters can be found in the endnotes or listed in the bibliography. The parliamentarian Sir George Gresley's copybook kept at the Derbyshire Record Office also contains transcripts of Hastings' (captured) letters: in particular there is an amusing sequence between Gell and Hastings regarding the latter's capture of the mayor of Derby.[70]

Contemporary biographies, journals and diaries are also important source material, perhaps the best known being Lucy Hutchinson's life of her husband John.[71] Lucy was notoriously biased in her treatment of people she did not like, of which there appear to be many on both sides during the war. Fortunately she is sufficiently candid to make such feelings obvious, thus cutting down the chance of taking all of what she says at face value. Margaret, Duchess of Newcastle's, biography of her husband the former Earl and then Marquis of Newcastle, contains many useful references to the North Midlands as well as to the campaigns in the north. The diaries of both Sir Henry Slingsby and Sir William Dugdale have also been consulted.[72] Despite his being based in the south, Sir Samuel Luke's Journal contains many references to the situation in the Midlands as does the memoir of Colonel John Birch.[73] Clarendon too, although all too infrequently, found time to comment on the region.[74] All of the above are used in conjunction with each other and the various sources referred to earlier. Again the reader is recommended to consult both the endnotes and the bibliography for both specific and general details of the primary source material used.

The Book: Aims and Themes

The broad aims of this book have already been referred to. These are the study of royalist war effort and the examination of the people who played an active role in operating it. The geographical limits are also the organisational ones: that is, the counties of Derbyshire, Leicestershire, Nottinghamshire, Rutland, and Staffordshire, which were united under the command of Henry Hastings, Lord Loughborough. The need for studies of both more regional examples of royalist war effort and for a study of the North Midland counties in particular, have been shown above, as has the need for further investigation of the social nature of active royalist support. This book will embrace these three elements in an attempt to provide an insight into the operation of the royalist war machine, not only in the North Midlands but in the country as a whole, and will attempt to illuminate in particular the decline of royalist power after the middle of 1644. Hastings' command was directly involved both in the build up to the defeat at Marston Moor and in the aftermath of the battle which had dire consequences for the royalist cause as a whole. The parliamentarian victory outside York swept away a substantial and important area of royalist control, both south of the Yorkshire border as well as north of it. This book is concerned with that area south of Yorkshire and will show that, just as Peter Newman has argued for the possibility of the north being regained by the royalists had they mounted a convincing and sustained effort to that purpose, the North Midlands offered even more potential for a royalist resurgence.

This work is organised on the following lines. Chapter 2 is the examination of the wartime royalist administration; the main methods of royalist finance are analysed, as are the commissioners of array for the region. These latter will be examined on a social and familial basis, with their political, administrative and educational experience taken into account. The findings from this analysis will be presented in a statistical form; details regarding each individual are contained in Appendix I. Throughout the chapter, findings will, if possible, be related to statistics from other regions.

Chapter 3 will be a briefer, but similar, examination of the parliamentarian war effort, organised along the same lines. Information regarding individual committeemen can be found in Appendix II.

Throughout this chapter, comparisons will be made with the royalist system and personnel.

Chapter 4 is an analysis of the North Midlands Army. It is necessary at the beginning of the chapter actually to recreate the army in terms of its constituent regiments. It has rarely been considered an army as knowledge of its composition has been vague. Each regiment is examined with regard to size and evidence for inclusion in the army. As with the commissioners and committeemen, the officer corps are studied and findings presented statistically. Appendix III contains details about individual officers.

Chapter 5 is the first of the two chapters dealing with the part played by the associated counties in the war. It details the rise of the royalists in the region and how they came to dominate the area by the end of 1643. It will also show how their hold was, even at this time, never complete and that outside interference and, indeed, Hastings' own success was to work against him and flaw the royalist achievement. The final section of the chapter is concerned with the campaign culminating in the relief of Newark in March 1644. This action revealed both the strengths and the weaknesses of the North Midlands royalists, whilst at the same time advancing Prince Rupert's reputation to new heights.

Chapter 6 follows on with the critical period after Newark when the Yorkshire royalists were defeated at Selby and the Marquis of Newcastle was forced to take up refuge in York. The effects of this had dire consequences for the North Midlands and the subsequent defeat at Marston Moor was to shape the area's future until the end of the war.

Chapter 7 will draw together the elements contained within the previous five chapters. By doing so it will indicate how the story of the North Midlands royalist war effort contributes to our understanding of how the royalists fought the Civil War and, perhaps, of why they lost the struggle.

Chapter 2

The Royalist Administration in the North Midland Counties

The purpose of this chapter is to examine the nature of royalist administration during the First Civil War in the North Midlands. To do this, the chapter is divided into three sections. Firstly, the establishment of the commissions of array is placed within the context of the events of summer and autumn 1642 and the failure of the commissioners to mobilise effectively the military forces, with severe consequences for the King's attempted creation of an army, will be studied. Secondly the nature and composition of the active commissioners will be examined with reference to their social, familial and administrative status. The final section will be concerned with the transformation of the commissions from their primarily military role to a chiefly financial one. Their methods of gaining income from the region's communities will be analysed in some depth. This will provide the basis for Chapter 4, a study of the regiments raised by those in receipt of individual commissions and which were dependent upon the income raised in the region.

The Establishment of Commissions of Array: March to August 1642

The King's departure from London in January 1642 made government difficult for Parliament; without the King's signature they had no legal method of enacting laws. This was never more obvious than over the militia problem. Concerned by the dangers of the Irish Rebellion and by the possibility that the King might attempt to raise military forces upon the pretence of going over to fight in Ireland, Parliament desired control of the Trained Bands – England's semi-permanent militia. During February and early March protracted bargaining between Parliament, attempting to establish such a control, and the King, determined to resist any such form of emasculation, resulted in a series of proposals and counter proposals with little common ground. Exasperation drove Parliament into issuing their own Militia Bill as an ordinance, effective immediately, as if it were an act, but without the

King's signature.[75] Though they expected the King would agree later, they had in effect, by issuing the ordinance in the first place, established the method by which they would govern the country during the war.

With the Militia Ordinance, Parliament replaced the lords lieutenant in the English and Welsh counties with men of their own choosing. These crown officials had been in existence since the previous century and had chiefly, and originally, been commanders of the counties' militia. During the early seventeenth century their remit expanded to embrace powers normally incumbent upon the high sheriffs, the collection of recusancy fines and responsibility for vagrants. This, and other extensions of power, such as their responsibility for the collection of distraints of knighthood, caused resentment in the counties expressed most vehemently during the years following Charles' accession. A committee to examine the lieutenancy had, as a consequence, been established during the first session of the 'long' Parliament with a view to restricting their powers. Yet the Militia Ordinance did not alter the lieutenants' power over the militia; it simply changed the personnel involved.

Throughout England the ordinance produced little immediate response. Several of the sitting Lords Lieutenants were reluctant to travel to Westminster to rescind their commissions. Eventually, however, the changes were made and in some cases caused local tension: in the North Midlands, the changes were quite dramatic. In Derbyshire, the Earl of Rutland displaced the Cavendish family – long-standing incumbents of the office. In Nottinghamshire, the Pierrepoint family were ousted by the Earl of Clare. Only in Staffordshire, where the sitting lord lieutenant was the parliamentarian Earl of Essex, was there no change.[76] In Leicestershire at least, the changeover represented the culmination of a long-standing family rivalry. The joint Lieutenants the Earl of Huntingdon and his eldest son the Lord Hastings were ousted by the head of their great local political rivals, the Greys, in the person of the Earl of Stamford. Huntingdon and his son were also displaced from the lieutenancy of Rutland by the Earl of Exeter. In Leicestershire, the Grey family had long been attempting, with the alliance of several gentry families, to unseat Huntingdon.[77] The 1640 elections had seen the Hastings family going into political eclipse, despite having successfully fought off serious opposition to their parliamentary candidates during the 1620s. Stamford's appointment was very much the culmination of this power shift.[78]

Mistakes had been made. The Earl of Clare was not a man of action and it was soon clear that he was not able materially to assist Parliament's cause. The initiative was firmly with the old lieutenant, Lord Newark, and he was the King's man.[79] Dependable though he was, the Earl of Essex could not be everywhere at once. He appointed Walter Wrottesley as his vice lieutenant for Staffordshire. Wrottesley subsequently raised troops for the King and was probably an active commissioner of array.[80] It does not appear that the Earl of Exeter played any part in the raising or training of Trained Bands in Rutland. On the other hand the Earls of Rutland and Stamford were material in assembling and training the militia in the counties under their Lieutenancies.

During April and May, after the shock of Parliament's initiative had died down and both the King and Parliament attempted reconciliation, the latter tried to persuade the holders of the King's lieutenancy commissions to return them for cancellation. Charles meanwhile considered allowing Parliament's appointees to remain in office for one year. But then the King's humiliation at the hands of Sir John Hotham and the material disaster of the failure to secure the arsenal at Hull, convinced him of the need to prevent the execution of the Militia Ordinance.

On 28 May he expressly forbade compliance with the Ordinance.[81] But already, in the centre of England, men were complying with it. Lord Willoughby of Parham was raising Lincolnshire's militia by early June.[82] In Leicestershire, the Earl of Stamford was doing likewise by 4 June.[83] Clearly, Charles had to take more positive action. On 8 June the Leicestershire Trained Bands had even mustered in Parliament's name.[84] The situation had become dangerous for the King. The execution of the Militia Ordinance in the very heart of his kingdom was not only a threat to his prestige but also to his safety.

In response, Charles issued the first of the Commissions of Array on 23 June and directed it to Leicestershire. There was an important difference between the Commission and the Ordinance, despite both being designed to gain control of the counties' militia. The Militia Ordinance was permissive; it did not alter the structure of the militia system but only replaced the personnel whilst reaffirming the power of the lords lieutenant. The Commissions, on the other hand, were mandatory. They had the express purpose of calling out the Trained Bands in the near future with the intention of suppressing rebellion. Commissioners were to

> array and train our people, and to apportion and assess such persons who have estates and who are not able to bear arms to find arms for other men:

The arrayed people were to be organised into companies and regiments 'as convenient'.[85]

The commissioners of array were to have a quorum of three before orders for musters could be issued. The commissioners were personally responsible for organising such muster and for inspecting the soldiers at such events. It was not envisaged, even as late as 15 August, by which time all of the North Midland counties had received commissions, that the militia would be on permanent muster. Instead they were to be left at home until such time as they were called. This and the further instruction that there be no increase in the number of soldiers in the Trained Bands, was in order to keep costs down.[86]

The North Midlands

It is necessary to indicate which commissions of array fall within the boundaries of this study. Henry Hastings, second son to the Earl of Huntingdon, displaced from his Lieutenancy by the Militia Ordinance, was in the summer of 1642 appointed to the commissions for both Leicestershire and Derbyshire; as he was heavily involved in both counties during the following four years their inclusion needs no other explanation. His authority over Staffordshire, questioned by both Colonels Bagot and Leveson, was reaffirmed several times by the King right through until the end of 1645, and so therefore this county is included. The Rutland commission is included even though from early 1643 the county was supposedly under the command of the Earl of Kingston and the Lord Widdrington. The Rutland commissioners met first at Ashby-de-la-Zouch and then at Belvoir, both within Leicestershire, and the collections of taxes within Rutland was done by Belvoir-based regiments under Hastings' command. Thus as the income from the county was used by the North Midlands Army the county and its commission are a part of this study. The Nottinghamshire commission is also included as Hastings was placed in command of the county after the Earl of Newcastle had established the royalist garrison at Newark. Although a certain air of independence does seem to mark the county, even before Sir Charles Lucas took command of a large part of the county's horse in 1644, Nottinghamshire forces generally acted in concert with those of the other North Midland counties throughout the war. In addition, several units directly under Hastings' command were stationed at Newark during the war and collected taxation from the area as well as receiving their pay from such revenue. Lincolnshire is a different case. Originally it too was put under Hastings' control but was hived off to the Earl of Kingston's command in early 1643. Although Hastings' troops were often involved in actions in the county it appears that, unlike Rutland, he was never involved in the administration side of affairs and so this county is excluded.

The response of the men appointed to the commissions in the region was not one of unanimous action. In Leicestershire, neither the Earl of Huntingdon nor the Earl of Devonshire were involved in raising troops. As a result it was left to Huntingdon's second son, Henry Hastings, to undertake the work in the absence of the two men whose names had headed the commission. Four days after Hastings had received the commission, he instructed Leicestershire's Under Sheriff to issue the warrants necessary to summon the Trained Bands. At the same time three other commissioners attempted, but failed, to seize the county magazine.[87] During the ensuing few days plans were made to assemble the bandsmen on 22 June, but though the High Sheriff had initially concurred, he sought Stamford's advice and the latter contacted Parliament. The result of the discussion in Parliament on 18th June was the declaration of the commission's illegality and the issue of orders for the arrest of Hastings and the other commissioners.[88] High Sheriff Palmer reversed his earlier decision and whilst the town of Leicester attempted to remain neutral by accepting whichever of the two warrants, those of crown or Parliament, arrived first, Palmer arrested his under sheriff to prevent the issue of the warrants ordered by the commissioners.[89] The upshot was that the attempted muster of the 22nd had to be postponed until the next day. On the 23rd the Earl of Stamford fortified his house at Bradgate and Hastings gathered a force of his father's miners and the Trained Bandsmen from the north of the county at Loughborough. With these he marched to the appointed site of the muster at Leicester. The rendezvous at the Horse Fair Leas was a fiasco. Palmer and two representatives from

Parliament declared the commission illegal and attempted to arrest Hastings. The latter was rescued during a scuffle but the King's attempt to secure the county had failed. Despite Charles' hope that Stamford would be arrested, it was clear that the Earl held the upper hand.[90]

The King did not abandon the idea of a military coup in the Midlands. Staffordshire had received a Commission on 16 June, Derbyshire and Nottinghamshire on the 18th and Rutland on 2 July.[91] On 1 July, Hastings, having earlier returned to York, re-entered Leicestershire with the High Sheriff of Nottinghamshire, John Digby. They had both ammunition and cannon.[92] In addition Charles instructed the Derbyshire commissioners to raise their Trained Bands to aid Hastings.[93] Already, the North Midland counties were expected to work together. This cooperation, which appears to have lasted about seven days, did not result in the securing of the Leicestershire magazine which was now largely in the hands of the Earl of Stamford. In Nottingham too, Lord Newark failed to secure that county's magazine.[94]

Force was accompanied by coercion. In the face of these failures Charles abandoned his hopes of capturing Hull and entered the Midlands. He was at Nottingham on the 21st July and at Leicester on the following day. There he expressed his desire for peace and accommodation, but was met with demands for Hastings' arrest.[95] There were other problems: Dr Bastwick, the puritan who had suffered at the hands of the High Commission in the 1630s, was arrested in Leicester after trying to avoid the King's notice. Charles wanted him tried for treason but Justice Reeve convinced the King that no jury in Leicester would convict him. Instead Bastwick was carried away to York and thence to Knaresborough. In addition, 25 men had barricaded themselves in the county magazine with the portion of ammunition left there by Stamford. Either to appear pacific, or to cover for his lack of armed forces to attempt a forcible entry to the store, the King agreed to disperse the contents to the county hundreds.[96] He left the city having gained nothing.

Attempts by commissioners of other counties in the region also met with limited successes. In Derbyshire only one commissioner, Christopher Fullwood, appears to have made strenuous efforts to raise the militia. The nominal head of the commission, Devonshire, was as inactive in this county as he was in Leicestershire. At first the lead miners of the north of the shire were strongly supportive of Parliament's men, Sir John Gell and the Earl of Rutland. However, the King made concessions to them regarding dropping the lead tithe and this enabled the energetic Fullwood to raise up to 1,000 men and escort them to the King at Shrewsbury, in September.[97]

In Nottinghamshire, the bandsmen were mustered in the King's name by Lord Newark in July; however his subsequent failure to capture the county ammunition dented his authority. When the King was in the town during August, prior to raising the standard, only 30 bandsmen obeyed the initial summons to arms. Joyce Malcolm, in *Caesar's Due…*, cites this as a prime example of the lack of popular support for the King's cause. However, in the ensuing few days this was mediated by the appearance of at least 300 bandsmen and other volunteers.[98]

In Staffordshire, although some attempts were made by the commissioners of array to raise the militia, they met with little positive success. It devolved upon men like Lord Paget or Sir John Beaumont to use their personal commissions to raise troops within the county. On the whole the county was extremely reluctant to appear in arms for either side. This led to bi-party negotiations, as late as November, aimed at creating a third force to expel any protagonists who entered the county. In the case of Rutland, there is no evidence to suggest what attempts were made to raise the county's forces.[99]

By August, it was clear that the commissions of array had failed in their immediate aim - to raise an army for the King. Control of the Trained Bands had been impossible to attain and, in response, Charles began to issue commissions to individuals in order that they raise regiments of their own to support him. At the beginning of August, Hastings was empowered to form a regiment of 400 horse and by the middle of the month he had raised at least two troops.[100] It was, as Ronald Hutton argues, by these commissions that the King's Army was raised. Though some, at least, of the men so empowered, like Hastings, Sir John Harpur and Sir John Fitzherbert, both of Derbyshire, as well as others, were commissioners of array, it was their work as individuals, not as a part of the commissions, which created the royalist army within the Midlands shires.[101]

Though they had failed in their primary task, which resulted in the creation of the regiments studied in Chapter 4, the commissions of array did not disappear. Though they appear to have met only rarely, if at all, during the rest of the year and in some cases became involved in local negotiations with parliamentarians, they were still in existence the following spring. In February 1643, the region's commissions were instructed to work with their neighbouring counties and on February 23rd the counties of Derbyshire, Leicestershire, Nottinghamshire, Rutland and Lincolnshire were associated under the command of Henry Hastings. Within weeks Lincolnshire and perhaps Rutland were taken from his territory but Staffordshire was added to it.[102]

The role of the commissioners was now altered: there was less emphasis on their role as a military body and more on their part as a financial one whose function was to supply and maintain the forces raised in the region by the colonels, by means of taxation. Their methods of doing so are examined in the third section of this chapter. The next part is concerned with an examination of the individuals who remained active commissioners during late 1642 and became the figures responsible for the financial administration with which they were entrusted during 1643.

The Commissioners of Array

In order to assess the extent to which wartime local government was in the hands of the pre-war social elite and to deduce from which social groups the King was able to draw active support, it is necessary to analyse the commissioners of array. These are, of course, only one of the two groups of activists at the regional level and a study of the royalist officers, and how they reflect the social structure, will be made in a following chapter. The commissioners, and the officers in their turn, will be examined with reference to their social rank, their familial status and with regard to their experience of higher and/or legal education as well as their experience of central or local government.

Only commissioners deemed active, by light of available evidence, will be examined in the text, though all appointees will be covered in Appendix I. Within the text mention will be made of any differences to the proportions revealed in the tables, by the inclusion of statistics derived from examination of men deemed inactive because of their incapacitation, or simply through lack of evidence. This is because of the possibility of error brought about by the dearth of information regarding the activities of the commissions. At the close of the war commissioners, faced with the enquiry by the compounding committees as to their war record, were careful to destroy as much incriminating evidence as possible. This left the compounding committees a difficult task and has left the historian an even more problematic one.

The commissioners will be considered firstly county by county and then as an entire group. Comparison between them and the royalist officers will be made in Chapter 4, which deals with the officers themselves.[103]

The Derbyshire Commissioners of Array

A total of 23 men were appointed to the two commissions issued for Derbyshire, that of July 1642 and of December 1643. The only significant difference between the two commissions is that the Earl of Rutland, by that time overtly a parliamentarian, is excluded from the list of names. Similarly, Lord Deincourt is also left off the commission and the Marquis of Newcastle is added in their place. However it is pertinent to note that none of the nobles appointed to either of the commissions took an active part in their work. Newcastle was busy elsewhere, Devonshire avoided any connection with the commission and the Earl of Chesterfield had been captured before the commission really began to assert itself as a financial body.

Eleven of the nominees appear to have been activists. Along with Rutland, Sir Edward Leech and Sir John Coke were parliamentarians. Sir John Fitzherbert of Tissington died before the end of 1642 and four others, including Sir John Harpur of Caulke, high sheriff in 1642, seem to have avoided working on the commission. John Agard's case is a problem: although he appears to have been at Tutbury Castle in 1643 and was captured from there by the parliamentarians early in the year, he does not appear to have served as a commissioner and is not included in the following statistics.

The social composition is affected by this lack of active nobility; the one person included in the noble classification is Sir John Fitzherbert of Norbury, heir to Lord Norbury.

Social Status

Noble	Bart	Knight	Esq.	Gent.	Yeoman	Trade/ profession/ clergy	Unknown
1	2	3	5	0	0	0	0

Thus we can see that wartime county government was in the hands of the second rank of county society. No less than six of these commissioners were also colonels of regiments. Of the lower social ranks, Hastings and Fullwood were out of the commission by the time the second one was issued. This leaves the remaining nine even more heavily concentrated at the upper end of the gentry.

A similar concentration is in evidence in the familial status table.

Familial Status

Head	1st son	2nd son	Other son	Unknown
8	1	1	0	0

With eight actual and one potential heads of families we can see that in Derbyshire at least, the level of commitment in activists' families was very high. Committing the family head to a cause in such a way would entail grave financial consequences if that cause failed. Given the structure of the seventeenth century 'family' such a commitment of the head would entail the financial involvement not only of the nuclear but also the extended family. In addition active involvement may well have deprived the family of its spiritual, as well as its economic, leader for protracted periods.[104]

The Derbyshire group were possessed of a great deal of administrative experience gained in the years before the war which would serve them whilst on the commission. Only Sir Andrew Kniveton appears to have been without such experience.

Political, Administrative or Educational Experience

(MP = Member of Parliament; LL = Lord Lieutenant; DL = Deputy Lieutenant; HS = High Sheriff; JP = Justice of the Peace; Inn = attendance at one of the Inns of Court)

MP	LL	DL	HS	JP	University	Inn
2	0	4	4	5	6	3

As neither of the MPs had sat in the 'long' Parliament, they did not get summoned to the Oxford Parliament and thus were not removed from the commission for this purpose in 1644. Of the high sheriffs, two, John Milward of Snitterton and Sir John Harpur of Swarkestone, would have been involved in the collection of ship money: this was of value in respect to the gathering of taxation. All four of the deputy lieutenants had been involved in the raising of Trained Bands during the Scottish Wars. Of four of the six commissioners who had attended university, little is known of their actual educational experience. The other two gained MAs. Coupled with even the barest legal knowledge gained by the four who had attended one or other of the Inns of Court this makes the combined educational experience of the Derbyshire commission quite impressive.

More of the educational aspect of the commission will be said below. The presence of the five JPs is important. Appeals against aspects of royalist financial exactions would be made to this group, which gave the royalists' administration some impression of legality. This formed a major part in Charles' pretensions to be acting in respect of the English constitution'. This collective ability, coupled with the local knowledge and the social connections that such a group would have, indicate that the Derbyshire commissioners had formidable potential. With such a large proportion of colonels on the commission there would be little likelihood of factional rivalry between military and administration as happened in other counties.

There were no Catholics amongst either the active or non-active Derbyshire commissioners. Their exclusion from pre-war county government was reflected in the war-time equivalent; however there were Catholic officers from the county in the North Midlands Army.

The consequences of high familial commitment were eventually visited upon the county's activist families. Only in the case of Sir Edward Vernon of Sudbury is there no evidence of post-war fines. Fullwood's death did not deter the parliamentarians from confiscating the greater part of his estate, leaving one of his three daughters dependent upon charity. This emphasises the dire consequences, not only for the family but also for their posterity, of being an activist. Harper was also heavily prosecuted; the first assessment of a fine was over £4,500 and was only eventually reduced to £4,000. There is a large gap between Harpur's fine and the next largest figure – due, no doubt, to the fact that he was reputed to be the richest man in the county. John Milward and John Bullock of Darley suffered exactions of over £1,000. The rest paid sums less than this. Hastings and Kniveton were able to avoid crippling fines by judicious demands when surrendering their garrisons to the enemy. This does not of course take into account the costs paid out during the war from personal income. Hastings estimated that fighting the war cost him £10,000, a small amount compared to the £900,000 said to have been paid out by the Marquis of Newcastle, but great to a man with an estate said to be 'little or nothing of worth'. Just as the potential ability of the Derbyshire Commissioners was great, so was the price of their heavy commitment great.

The Leicestershire Commissioners of Array

Of the 31 nominees to both the commission of array of June 1642 and the commission of peace intended to assume some wartime duties as well as add legal weight to the administration, issued in 1644, only 13 appear to have been active. Three, two Earls of Huntingdon, father and son, and Edward Farnham of Quorn, may have at some time been involved in the operation of the war effort, but there is not enough evidence to fully include them as activists. The elder Earl appears to have left everything to his second son, his heir having dabbled with Parliament's cause to the extent of having been (briefly) at the battle of Edgehill. He may never have become involved in the administrative affairs conducted at Ashby-de-la-Zouch, to where he claimed to have fled to avoid parliamentarian harassment. Farnham left Ashby during the plague in 1645 and thus may conceivably have been embroiled in the war effort. Of the others deemed inactive, three were parliamentarians, one died without having been involved and two were royalist activists elsewhere.

View of the battlefield of Edgehill from Edgehill looking towards Kineton. (Photo: David Stowell)

As in the case of Derbyshire the social concentration is in the upper gentry bracket, titled gentry and the squirarchy. The sole noble is Sapcoat, Viscount Beaumont, added to the commission in 1644 although he may have been involved earlier unofficially. By that time Hastings was a baron in his own right, but as we are here only concerned with pre-war rank, he only figures as an esquire.

Social Status

Noble	Bart	Knight	Esq.	Gent.	Yeoman	Trade/ profession/ clergy	Unknown
1	2	4	5	1	0	0	0

The commissioner of lowest social rank was Richard Turpin of Knaptoft, whose commitment was to cost him dear in the aftermath of the war. Two of the commissioners were colonels (including Hastings) and six others had sons in the forces.

Again, following the pattern of the Derbyshire commission, familial commitment was high. This is not very surprising. As the commissioners were initially chosen perhaps with regard to their county standing, most would have been the leading figure within their own family to have achieved that standing in the first place.

Familial Status

Head	1st son	2nd son	Other son	Unknown
11	0	2	0	0

Again it can be perceived that the financial commitment was high. Nuclear and extended family fortunes as well as the activists' 'posterity', were risked in the heavy commitment which these men made to defending the position of the monarchy. Hastings and Turpin were the two second sons.

Only two activists, Beaumont and Sir Eusebius Pelsant appear not to have had any pre-war administrative experience to bring to bear on the work as commissioners. In neither case is this apparently due to age, i.e. they were too young to have held office previous to the war, nor due to religion: they were not ineligible due to being Catholics. This may be some indication of either the preparedness or necessity of going below the caucus of county families which normally provided county officials.

Political, Administrative or Educational Experience

MP	LL	DL	HS	JP	University	Inn
2	0	4	7	3	6	2

Of the MPs neither had served in the 'Long' Parliament so were not called upon to sit at Oxford. Had the Earls of Huntingdon been active they would have both figured in the lord lieutenant category. All four of the deputy lieutenants had been involved in the raising of the Trained Bands for the Scottish wars and had been engaged in the attempts to bring them on to the side of the King in the summer of 1642. Of the high sheriffs, only Sir Richard Roberts of Sutton Cheney and Sir Henry Skipwith of Cotes had actually been connected with the raising of ship money, but the collective experience of the seven sheriffs would be invaluable. In contrast to the members of the Derbyshire commission who had attended university, none of the Leicestershire men had gained degrees, though two did progress to the inns. These latter would join with the JPs to bring legal knowledge and an appeals body to the commission. Only one of the commissioners was specifically accused, though not guilty, of being a Catholic, despite it being widely asserted that Hastings was working hand in hand with papists from the outset of the war.

All the commissioners faced financial penalties at the end of the First Civil War, although in the majority of cases there are no numerical details. Sir John Pate of Sysonby was the greatest sufferer. In 1646 he was fined one sixth of the value of his estate, a sum of over £800. Later, perhaps due to some unrecorded involvement in the Second Civil War this was increased to over £4,000. Sir Richard Halford paid over £2,000 and Sir Erasmus de la Fontaine of Kirby Bellars, whose estate was used as a parliamentarian garrison, over £1,000. Turpin's burden was both financially and personally heavy. In addition to having to sell off his Knaptoft estate to pay his £900 fine, all of his sons were killed in the King's service.

This commission was in one way different to Derbyshire's. It was not dominated by the military, unless Hastings could hold it in his sway. It came into conflict with Colonel Gervase Lucas, governor of Belvoir Castle when he objected to their allotment of territory to his forces. But, on the other hand, both commissions could call upon a wide variety of administrative experience held by their members and both entailed a great deal of financial forfeit for the activists.

The Nottinghamshire Commissioners of Array

Out of the 35 nominees to the 1642 Nottinghamshire commission of array and to the county's representatives on the bi-county commission established with Lincolnshire in 1645, only nine are deemed active by this survey. This commission has left slightly more documentation regarding its structure than the others in the region, but even so it is still possible to have three cases of insufficient evidence to include them amongst the activists. Sir Matthew Palmer served in the north instead of working on the commission. Colonel William Stanton, despite being in the Newark garrison, does not appear to have sat in his capacity as commissioner of array and Robert Mellish also in Newark does not appear to have been active. Because of the presence of doubt in all of these cases they are referred to in the relevant appendix. Two would-be commissioners were captured early in 1643 and thereby kept out of the way and no less than eight nominees were actively to espouse the parliamentarian cause. Eight others were to serve the royalist cause outside the county, one of these being the Marquis of Newcastle whose absence from the Derbyshire commission has already been referred to. A further eight have left no evidence to suggest what they did during the war years. They were probably either passive royalists or determined neutrals. One, however, Robert Grieves, Nottingham town clerk, was deprived of his office by the resident parliamentarian committee who regarded his presence at Newark as indicative of royalist sympathy if not activity. There is evidence that Grieves was under arrest for at least part of his time in Newark.

There was one holder of a noble title on the commission, John Lord Chaworth of Armagh.

Social Status

Noble	Bart	Knight	Esq.	Gent.	Yeoman	Trade/ profession/ clergy	Unknown
1	1	2	4	0	0	0	1

For the first time there appears an individual whose social rank cannot be determined. However, unlike the large numbers of such cases in the statistics pertaining to the officer corps, Holder was not entirely obscure. He would appear to be from the gentry or at least to have pretensions of belonging to it – he signed the county's petition calling on its MPs to adhere to the King's side in spring 1642. Holder's origins do not affect the position too much. The concentration at the upper end of the gentry, though not higher, is still apparent.

This is likewise true of the familial position of the commissioners.

Familial Status

Head	1st son	2nd son	Other son	Unknown
7	0	0	1	1

It is Holder again who remains a mystery. Richard Byron of Strelley was a third son; both his elder brothers were active royalists. His eldest brother John had also been appointed to the commission but served out of the area for the whole of the war, at one stage being Field Marshal of Horse and Foot in Cheshire. Richard became the governor of Newark from early 1644 until his defeat at the battle of Denton undermined his authority and he was removed at the end of that year or early the next.

The Nottinghamshire commission did not have a high degree of collective experience. Four commissioners, Holder, Byron, Thomas Williamson of East Markham and John Digby of Mansfield, had no experience of county government before 1642. This is somewhat mitigated by the fact that Byron was from a family that had such experience behind it and Digby had been the high sheriff during summer 1642 and thus heavily involved in the early stages of the King's attempt to gain the Midlands' support.

Political, Administrative or Educational Experience

M.P.	L.L.	D.L.	H.S.	J.P.	University	Inn
3	0	1	0	1	4	1

Two MPs, Robert Sutton of Averham and Sir Gervase Clifton of Clifton, had sat in the 'Long' Parliament. Both appear to have attended the Oxford sessions at some time but were chiefly involved in the work of the commission. Sutton was also the sole deputy lieutenant; he had experience of mobilising the trained bands. The lack of any high sheriffs, particularly ones with experience of collecting ship money levies, may have caused initial difficulties with the financial system which cannot actually be discerned from the available evidence. There was also remarkably little legal experience on the commission and the presence of only one JP would present problems vis-à-vis the attempt to maintain an appearance of legality. However, the county's parliamentarians could only muster two JPs. Of the four who had attended university, only Clifton seems to have taken his degree.

The price of their commitment to the cause was, in some cases at least, high. Clifton was fined over £7,000, Williamson over three and Roger Cooper of Thurgarton, two. Byron, perhaps as a third son, may have possessed only a small estate as his fine appears to have only been £120.

The two chief points brought up in the two previous counties, is reflected again here. Firstly the commissioners are, in the main, drawn from the upper ranks of the gentry although not from the highest ranks of society, this due in part to two of the county's nobles serving elsewhere.

Secondly the activists are from the apex of their families' structure and are thereby committing them financially to the King's war effort.

The Rutland Commissioners of Array

Only 12 persons were nominated to the commission for the smallest county in England. Six appear to have been active on the commission and three were royalist activists elsewhere. Edward Heath of Cottesmore and Sir Christopher Hatton KB of Kirby, Northamptonshire, were both at Oxford. Robert Tredway of Ketton sat on the joint Nottinghamshire-Lincolnshire commission by right of his holding estates in the latter. Two of the three other non-activists died in early 1643.

Lord Camden died at Oxford in March, having earlier helped Gervase Lucas capture Belvoir Castle. His younger son Henry Noel died in imprisonment after Lord Grey captured him in February 1643. The third man, Thomas Levett, has left no clues to his part in the Civil War.

The representative of the nobility is Camden's eldest son Baptiste Noel, who succeeded to the title in March 1643, but is included here by virtue of his being an heir to the title on the outbreak of war.

Social Status

Noble	Bart	Knight	Esq.	Gent.	Yeoman	Trade/ profession/ clergy	Unknown
1	0	2	3	0	0	0	0

The commission is very much from the upper end of county society. This is reflected in the fact that all six were heads or potential heads of families.

Familial Status

Head	1st son	2nd son	Other son	Unknown
2	4	0	0	0

Only one of the activists had no experience of administration; the five who had were well versed in such affairs between them.

Political, Administrative or Educational Experience

MP	LL	DL	HS	JP	University	Inn
3	0	0	2	1	5	1

Two of the MPs were entitled to sit at Oxford and did so for some of the period of that Parliament's sitting. Neither of the high sheriffs had held office in the period when the ship money levies were made and no one had been involved in the mustering of Trained Bands. Two of those who had been students actually took degrees. The one JP was Sir Francis Bodenham of Wingfield who had attended Gray's Inn.

Financial consequences of the involvement in the war effort were high. Noel was fined over £11,000 for his part, the original assessment had been more than £20,000. Guy Palmes of Ashwell had to pay over £3,000. Bullingham's fine was much lower than these that was eventually reduced to £300. All of the commissioners had to pay some form of fine for their commitment to the royalist cause. Their posterity was again burdened with the consequences of their defeat.

The Staffordshire Commissioners of Array

Of 30 nominees to the commissions for Staffordshire, 14 seem to have been active. Walter Chetwynd of Rugeley who produced iron for the royalists and Thomas Crompton of Stone are both shrouded in uncertainty. Though in this instance Charles and his advisors picked no future parliamentarians, several of the commissioners were involved in the attempts to establish the third force in the county during late 1642. Three of the nominees served outside the county: Lord Paget and Sir Richard Shelton, the King's solicitor general, were at Oxford and Sir Henry Griffith of Whichnor served in the north. Six appointees played no role in the Civil War beyond passive royalism or trying to remain aloof from the conflict.

None of the nobility originally appointed to the commission was active upon it; this again included the Marquis of Newcastle. Thomas, Lord Cromwell, was appointed to the commission established in 1645 and was to crop up on minor ones concerned with the county during the final year of the war. As this book is chiefly concerned with those figures actively involved from the outset of the war, he does not figure in the statistics, nor do Sir Jacob Astley or Henry Hastings also appointed to Staffordshire commissions in 1645.

Social Status

Noble	Bart	Knight	Esq.	Gent.	Yeoman	Trade/ profession/ clergy	Unknown
0	7	2	5	0	0	0	0

With the high number of titled gentry, there is no doubt that this commission was composed of men who were, if not at the apex of county society, at the top of the gentry bracket within that county. Sir Simon Avery of Eggington, Derbyshire, was one of the county's commissioners as well as serving on that of his native county. It is highly probable that he was able to partake in work on both commissions and thus he is counted as being active for both, although in the final analysis of all the commissioners he will naturally be counted only once as will Hastings who also served on two bodies.

Only Sir Robert Wolseley was not a first son by birth; at the commencement of the Civil War his exact position in his family is unknown so he is counted here as a second son as he was at birth.

Familial Status

Head	1st son	2nd son	Other son	Unknown
13	0	1	0	0

The concentration is again, convincingly, at the top of the table. Again it must be recalled that in some way this is to be expected as to have reached a position of responsibility within the county the commissioners were more likely to have been the representatives of families of administrative experience.

Political, Administrative or Educational Experience

MP	LL	DL	HS	JP	University	Inn
7	0	2	4	6	9	5

Only one commissioner, Thomas Lane of Bentley, appears to have no pre-war experience in any of the above fields. Four of the M.1).s were entitled to sit at the Oxford Parliament and only one, Ralph Sneyd of Keele, did not attend at some time. Sneyd was heavily involved in attempts to raise troops in the north of the county during 1644 and this would have prevented him from going to Oxford. Both deputy lieutenants had raised the militia during the wars with the Scots and two of the high sheriffs had been involved with ship money. Of the nine men who had received higher education none appears to have taken their degree though five did progress to the inns. The presence of six JPs would be an important factor in maintaining a facade of legality as well as providing an inbuilt appeals body. Only two of the commissioners held a contemporaneous military rank: Sir Richard Leveson was operating in neighbouring Shropshire for much of the time and Sneyd was, it appears, largely unsuccessful at raising a regiment in the north of the county. Thus it does not appear strange that this commission had problematic relations with the county military personnel, Thomas Leveson in particular. Leveson continuously found fault with the commissioners' allocation of territory between the county garrisons especially with respect to, what he saw, as the excessive area allowed to Colonel Bagot, commander of the Lichfield garrison, son of one of the commissioners.

Their defeat cost the commissioners dear. Sir Richard Leveson was fined over £10,000 after the war on top of which his estate had been under sequestration during the conflict. Others who paid high fines include Sir Thomas Littleton who lost over £6,000, Sir Edward Seabright over £3,000 and Sneyd over £2,000.

The pattern established with the Derbyshire commissioners is carried through to their Staffordshire counterparts. Wartime county government was in the hands of a social elite, if not at the top of the social ladder then very near it. They were drawn chiefly from the upper gentry bracket; either from the squirarchy or the ranks of the titled gentry. They were not, for the most part, magnates with vast multi-county land holdings but were powerful within their home county and very often had played leading roles in their society by holding administrative office within it. This combined to give them not only practical knowledge to help them in their wartime task, but would also give them a desire to temper the rigours of war when dealing with what was essentially their or their associates' property, their source of both income and status.

Before moving on to the overall analysis of the commissioners it is necessary to look at two areas referred to in the preceding examination in more depth. These areas are education and religion.

Education

a) The Universities

As has been suggested throughout the relevant sections of the county by county analysis, very few of the commissioners who attended university left with degrees. University attendance in the seventeenth century was considered important not solely as a means of obtaining an education. The English universities were a place for the young members of the gentry to meet others of their ilk and thus make potentially advantageous social connections. It is the purpose of this section to explore the possibility that the commissioners of array made social connections during their respective times at university which stretch until the outbreak of war. Such connections, if made, may be an indicator of a shared basic ideology, although, of course, there is practically no hope of proving such a hypothesis.

Of the 28 commissioners who had received some amount of university education, only eight appear to have taken degrees. Given that Lawrence Stone has argued that the pre-war period was a time of an educational revolution as the numbers of entrants to the universities increased, the number of commissioners who went may seem low, being slightly over half the total number of activists. Stone also suggests that, due to deficiencies in the records kept of matriculants, up to a third more people may have attended Oxford or Cambridge than it is possible to prove. This rough estimate cannot, of course, be turned into meaningful figures for the group we are concerned with, and so we are left with only the 28 known cases. The point does remain however that 23 commissioners did not gain either the benefits of social alliances nor the recognisably necessary smattering of legal knowledge to survive in what were notoriously litigious times. As attendance at university was a mark of social standing we are, perhaps, reminded by these figures that the commissioners, though of high standing in their counties, were not all representatives of the apex of the social ladder.

There are no significant groupings of commissioners, during the time they spent at university, which suggest social or economic ties. The 13 who attended Cambridge went to eight different colleges, the highest number at any one college being three, at St John's. These men did not share a common time period and nor are there any significant time period groupings amongst any of the other commissioners regardless of college. Four of these Cambridge men attended what were considered 'puritan' colleges, though as we cannot say what their actual educational experiences were, no real conclusions can be drawn from this.

At Oxford, the 15 commissioners were again spread amongst eight colleges. There are no significant groupings either on a time or college basis. No Oxford commissioner attended a 'puritan' college.

Turning to the status of the undergraduate commissioners: only ten can be so judged, these all being Cambridge men. Seven were fellow commoners which meant that their families afforded the cost of their education. Two were pensioners also present at their families' expense, and one was a scholar who was there at the expense of the college, having proved himself to be of academic ability. There were no sizars or plebeians, the lower class of student, amongst the commissioners as there were amongst the royalist officers.

Whilst on the theme of comparing the two groups of activists there are practically no groupings of officers and commissioners at either university. At Oxford there were however three future commissioners and six future North Midlands royalist officers present in the year 1616–1617. At Cambridge only one commissioner was in attendance at the same time as any of the officers. The difference in age between the two groups can be noted at this point. The average age of the commissioners was 15 years older than the average age of the field officers (the only officers for whom any meaningful age statistics could be obtained). This is reflected in the university attendance. Whereas only three of the commissioners matriculated after 1625, only nine of the 36 officers who went to university matriculated before the same date.

There seems to be little or no ground for asserting that the commissioners made lasting connections with each other at university. The instances of any being at either establishment within the same time period are so few that connections could well have been re-enforcements of social links forged as a result of being a part of the same community. Therefore there are no grounds for suggesting that potential for common ideologies was formed at the universities.

b) The Inns of Court

As with the universities, there appear to be no links forged between the future commissioners who attended the Inns. On the question of time groupings, only four of the 11 commissioners were there within any acceptable number of years, in this instance 1611–1615. Three of these were at Greys and one at the Inner Temple. Though five in all attended Greys, only these three were there in anything like a significant time span. The Inns provided a useful legal training which, to gentry who were likely to spend some of there life in legal wrangles over land rights, would have been extremely useful. They were also used in much the same way as the universities, that is they were at once an expression of status, a place for making useful social contacts and also a base in the capital city from which to make forays into the court.

Presto in his work on the Stuart Inns came to the conclusion that there were strong regional ties revealed in the patterns of attendance at the inns. However the statistics revealed in the study of the North Midland commissioners of array do not easily fit into the picture which Prest gave. Greys, he stated, drew most of its men from the north, East Anglia and Kent. According to the findings regarding the commissioners it also drew on the North Midlands. This is also true of the Middle Temple hose bias was supposedly towards the south-west and Northamptonshire and of the Inner Temple; the latter but not the former would accord with Prest's theory. Also in accordance with Prest is the fact that none of the commissioners went to Lincoln's Inn. The numbers in this instance are too small for any valid critique of Prest's finding to be made, but the regional question will be referred to again as the sample gets larger when firstly the parliamentarian committeemen are added and finally the royalist officers are examined.[105]

Religion

Though four of the commissioners were, at some time during the war, accused of being papists it is not likely that any of them were, unless they were successfully covert crypto-Catholics. Appointing Catholics to administrative posts at such an early stage of the war when the first commissions were drawn up was potentially dangerous. The dislike, if not fear, of papacy would ensure a high rate of disregard for the commissions of array in the provinces had they actually contained Catholic members. The problems of appointing Catholics to the administration even at a late stage in the war were revealed when the placing of the Earl of Shrewsbury to head the Marcher Association provoked the Worcestershire 'clubmen' to issue the Woodbury Declaration. Thus, though allowing Catholics into the army was a successful method of tapping their financial wealth, the inclusion of them in commissions of array would have been counter productive. This may explain the exclusion of the Catholic Thomas Leveson from the Staffordshire commission, an exclusion which certainly rankled with him.

Certainly in one case out of the four, that of Sir Richard Dyott of Lichfield, there were very spurious grounds for labelling him a Catholic. Whilst a barrister at the Inner Temple, he had been a furious opponent of the puritans at the Inn, an antipathy he may well have kept up whilst Chancellor of the Palatinate of Durham. Incidentally, the only other commissioner to have apparently strong religious views was Christopher Fullwood, who had opposed the puritan element at Grey's Inn.[106] As it appears that there were no Catholics on any of the commissions, we are dealing with an area closed to them, just as pre-war administration was, in general, closed to them. Thus the only positive outlet for royalist Catholic activists was the army. Their presence in the North Midlands Army will be examined in Chapter 4.

The Commissioners: An Overview

To commence the study of the commissioners as a single body a table of the total number is presented. Once those people who held dual or even triple membership are taken into account, there were 128 men nominated to commissions in the five counties with which we are concerned. The breakdown is as follows:

Activists	51	39.8%
Cases for which it is not possible to ascertain their behaviour	9	7.0%
Non-Activists		
a) Dead or captured before April 1643	7	5.5%
b) Activists outside the county	16	12.5%
c) Parliamentarians	15	11.8%
d) Passive royalists or neutrals	30	23.4%
TOTAL	128	

It is at once obvious that, at York, grave errors of judgement were made regarding the expected support for the King in the counties. Only 58 percent of those seen as potential activists actually became so, and this includes those who became active outside their own counties. No less than 15 men were active supporters of Parliament. There are also 30 individuals whose part in the war was so small as to be untraceable. They were, it would seem, either passive supporters of the royalists or neutrals. Neutralism was not recognised by either side and 14 were fined or at any rate assessed for fines by the victorious Parliament.

Thus we are left with 51 active commissioners and the possibility that a further nine may have been involved in the work with them. It is to the 51 men that we now turn; if any significant difference to the findings is made by the inclusion of the nine others, mention will be made in the text.

The pattern which emerged in the examination of individual counties is made clear when the group is considered as a whole.

Social Rank

	Noble	Bart	Knight	Esq.	Gent.	Yeoman	Trade/ profession/ clergy	Unknown
	4	11	13	22	1	0	0	1
% of whole	7.7%	21.2%	25.0%	42.3%	1.92%			1.92%
% of whole	7.8%	21.6%	25.5%	43.1%	1.6%			

The overwhelming majority of commissioners who were active royalists derive from the ranks of the titled gentry and the squirarchy rather than the nobility. It is evident that the local communities under royalist control were in the hands of the gentry just as much as the Northern Army, according to Peter Newman. If the nobility who died before April 1643 and those included in the nine uncertain cases are taken into account, the numbers of the aristocracy are increased to eight thus achieving a proportion of 15.8 percent. This does not materially alter the fact that the nobility were not the dominant group in the counties. Equally, despite the large proportion of esquires active on the commissions, the actual numbers were not high.

The lack of information regarding the thoughts of these men regarding their choice, either between sides or between activity or passivity, means that no sound judgements can be made regarding their motivation. In the cases of some, particularly amongst the nobility, it may be that exclusion from the court played some role in this. But Huntingdon was a court appointed Lieutenant and did nothing, perhaps due to age or as part of his long-term policy of the avoidance of central politics.[107] Yet Newark from a similar family, and likewise a Lieutenant, did become active. Devonshire, another Lieutenant, was a passive royalist whilst Chaworth, with seemingly no court connections, became an activist. With others it may have been opposition to the King's policies during the 1630s which guided their view of the Civil War, but Erasmus de la Fontaine, fined for depopulation in the 1630s, was an active royalist; additionally some commissioners had been fined for distraint of knighthood. There are no easy-to-apply rules regarding fealty to Charles in the war years, and it is beyond this book to try to establish these: it is concerned with a mere identification of the groups from which loyalty did come, not with a psycho-historical analysis of why.

On the other hand those who did commit themselves to the cause were risking not only themselves in doing so, they committed their families too.

Familial Status

	Head	1st son	2nd son	Other son	Unknown
	40	5	4	1	1
% of whole	76.9%	11.5%	7.7%	1.92%	1.92%
% of whole	78.4%	11.8%	7.8%	1.96%	

The proportion of heads of families remains high, even when the nine cases of uncertainty are taken into consideration. It is clear that the King aimed to have his war effort run by men of certain status. If he failed to galvanise the majority of them, those left were still from essentially the same groups as is shown by the fact that they were at the head of their families. The willingness of these activists to get involved did cost them and their thus embroiled families dear. The 25 activists whose precise fines are known paid out over £160,000 between them for their 'delinquency'.

The committed group were also to some extent an experienced group of administrators. Over half of the commissioners had received higher education and over a quarter had served as high sheriffs and a quarter as MPs, and this is important. The range of experience stretched from the collection of ship money to the representation of grievances in the House of Commons. In addition, although the numbers may appear small, there were representatives of peace time law in the commissions. Therefore they had the entire range of abilities necessary for the running of a system geared to the collection of finance, the arbitration of disputes over tax assessments and, if necessary, the representation of the region's grievances in the Oxford Parliament.

Political, Administrative and Educational Experience

MP	LL	DL	HS	JP	University	Inns
15	0	10	18	14	28	11
29.0%		19.6%	35.3%	27.4%	51.9%	21.6%

On the whole many of these men had been at the forefront of their county's government at both local and national level. There are thus several possible conclusions to be drawn. One is that Charles was simply lucky in that the activists just happened to be the most experienced men amongst those he had chosen to conduct the royalist war effort. Another, more probable, conclusion is that the upper and governing ranks of county society were more conservative in their view of the constitution and saw the King's cause as the one most akin to their own beliefs. Thirdly, and this may well tie in with the last point, the existing county governors saw that holding on to control of the counties themselves was the best method of preserving the communities intact and alleviating the burdens of war. Certainly by being in charge of regional finance during the war, they would be in a position to do just that. It is with this idea in mind that we now turn to the examination of the ways in which the commissioners did run the finances of the royalist war effort in the North Midlands shires.

The Work of the Commissions of Array

Evidence of the running of the war effort is not abundant. Many royalists were careful to destroy incriminating documents which would give dumb testimony to their activity on behalf of the King. Hutton, in his book on the war effort, says that there are few general sources.[108] There are the Chancery records of the commissions issued by the King to individuals or groups of individuals during the war and Dugdale's record of the commissions created in 1642 and 1643.[109] More specific documents are the papers of the Worcestershire Commission of Array and the minute book of the Glamorgan Commission. No equivalent of the latter two sources exists for any of the commissions in the North Midlands.

In the absence of such material the royalist war effort in the area has to be built up from a diverse variety of material and where possible related to information regarding other war efforts, such as those mentioned above. There are letters of the commissioners of Staffordshire to and from the King and Prince Rupert as well as to Hastings, in the Salt collection at the William Salt Library. These are useful for their references to the relationship between the commissioners and the military.[110] The sets of accounts kept by the Lichfield garrison in the two years 1643 and 1645 are of immense importance, as are the letters in the HMC report on the Hastings manuscripts.[111] However the chief source for the collection of contribution, possibly the most viable means of income for the war effort, does not emanate from the authors of the system. Nor does it come from the propagandist newsbooks produced by either side. Dr Stephen Porter has depended heavily upon the latter for his interpretation of the financial systems of both sides during the war. Using such material, Porter saw the collection of taxes as a form of extortion racket similar to the German *Brandtschatzung*, burning money, whereby villages were forced into payments to troops by the threat of destruction of property.[112] Instead, this present book has made extensive use of the accounts kept by constables, headboroughs and thirdboroughs. As a source these accounts have several strengths. They are not propaganda, aimed at encouraging or discouraging the reader, nor are they the plans of central or regional government which would be subject to mutation during their application to the communities. These are records of what was, and in some cases, what was not, paid by these communities into the royalist (or parliamentarian) coffers. By relating the evidence that they offer to that provided by private correspondence, official letters and other sources cited above, a reasonably comprehensive picture of this aspect of royalist administration can be obtained.

The five commissions were, to some extent, peripatetic in the same way as Kent's county committee.[113] Leicestershire's commission sat variously at Ashby-de-la-Zouch – its main base – Belvoir Castle, Melton Mowbray and Loughborough.[114] The Rutland commission, as mentioned above, was sitting at Ashby-de-la-Zouch in May 1643, though it appears chiefly to have met at Belvoir Castle. Members of it ended up at Newark at the end of the war.[115] Derbyshire's commissioners also may have met at some time at Ashby during early 1643, whilst Gell was dominant in their county; certainly two members, Hastings and Harpur, were there at the time. The commission later sat variously at Ashbourne, and Chesterfield. It spent the last years of the war ensconced in Tutbury Castle.[116] Both Nottinghamshire's and Staffordshire's commissions were more static. The latter was based at Lichfield as early as the end of 1642 and apart from the time up until May 1643 when it met at Stafford, and its occasional meeting at Uttoxeter, Lichfield was where it remained.[117] The former was established at Newark at the beginning of 1643 and remained there for the duration.[118]

Each commission had to deal with the difficult problems of finance: how to balance the needs of war with a desire to preserve the local economy. The chief ways in which the royalists gained money were: contribution – a regularly collected property tax; sequestration – the exploitation of enemy estates and excise – a tax on home produced goods. Oxford also imposed an additional levy to be raised on gentry estates and collected by the high sheriffs independent of the commissions of which they were a part; Sir John Pate had this task in Leicestershire.[119] By 1644 the Oxford Parliament had become sufficiently perturbed by the potential, if not actual, abuse of the taxation systems in the counties to establish committees of accounts in each of those under its contro1.[120] Parliament, too, ran a system very similar to this. Sequestration and excise were important sources of income to their treasuries. The parliamentarian version of the contribution – known as the weekly assessment – was collected on a property basis in the manner of ship money. An examination of Parliament's financial exactions is undertaken in the following chapter.

The three main sources of income – excise, sequestration and contribution – will be examined in turn. For the first two, there is little evidence either direct or otherwise, and thus their prominence may suffer unduly due to the relative wealth of information regarding contribution.

The Excise

John Pym had first proposed the imposition of an excise to aid Parliament's finances as early as May 1643, but it was not until the following July that the first ordinance establishing an excise was passed at Westminster. By then it was necessary for the payment of the armed forces and to cover debts already incurred in the first 11 months of the war. The excise was to prove Parliament's second largest source of income after the weekly assessment. However it did not cover the amounts borrowed from the city of London on the strength of its expected bounty.[121]

The royalists followed suit when the Oxford Parliament passed a similar excise aimed at bringing income to the central treasury. London had established a group of eight commissioners responsible to the Committee for the Advance of Money and created sub-offices in the major towns under Parliament's control. The royalists appointed three man commissions in each of its counties along with separate commissions for Worcester and Bristol. There were regional variations, with some areas having commissioners of array serving on the excise commissions, but as Hutton says, there is no evidence to suggest why these variations existed.[122]

For the North Midlands, there is only evidence of the creation of one excise commission, that of Staffordshire. James Povey, Elias Ashmole and John Hill, none of whom had been on any other commission, were appointed in May 1644. The commission was renewed one year later, when Povey was replaced by Elias Pydall.[123] On each occasion, the commission was established to be in operation for one year, or until the London excise was stopped, which ever was the shorter period. This is part and parcel of the King's attempt to make Parliament look the innovator and portray himself as being forced to take unconstitutional measures purely as a makeshift response. The appearance of Povey, Ashmole, Hill and Pydall is in itself interesting. They were not of the same social calibre as the commissioners of array; thus in some way they may be an example of the form of social dilution which was, by this time, supposedly occurring in Parliament's minor committees. If they are, they may be an indication that there was an element of 'new men' amongst the royalist administrators as well as amongst their enemy's. However the lack of substantial evidence means that no hard case can be made for this assertion, but the suggestion does remain.

The excise rates, established at Oxford for 1645, do not include levies on beef or pork to which Parliament extended its tax that year. This extension was the direct cause of civil unrest in Derby.[124] Sir John Gell was powerless, or unwilling, to prevent attacks on the excise commissioners or the accompanying riots.[125] The royalist excise did cause problems in Cheshire, but there is no evidence of it causing problems in the North Midlands, although this may be just a reflection of the general lack of evidence. Rioting such as that experienced at Derby was noteworthy and certainly of excellent value to the propaganda orientated press; given this, if any problems did occur it is surprising that they were not seized upon. It is therefore reasonable to conclude either that there were none or that they were of a minor nature.

However, because of the lack of evidence regarding the royalist excise, little can be deduced about the application or success of the system. This is regrettable given that, for Parliament, the excise was such a valuable source of income. It may be that in the North Midlands the returns from the levy were small. The commissions were not issued until May 1644, by which time the North Midlands royalists were within two months of losing their mastery of the region. The potential of the excise as a source of income would decline from July of that year even if it had begun well in May. In addition, the chief market towns of the region were always in the hands of Parliament. Though the royalists were able to curtail severely the trading at these places for much of the war, it is unlikely that they were able to establish successfully alternative venues in the towns they controlled. This would be a serious hindrance to the collection of an excise tax, dependent as it was on the market place.

Sequestration

The royalists moved slowly into the adoption of a system of taking over and exploiting the income of enemies' estates. There were incidents of pragmatic raids upon the homes of 'delinquents' within the Midlands. On 28 August Hastings and Prince Rupert led such an attack on the home of the Earl of Stamford at Bradgate Park.[126] In March 1643 the Oxford Council of War issued instructions to the Oxfordshire commissioners of array regarding estates of 'delinquents'. These instructions contained a comprehensive definition of who was to be regarded as a delinquent. The list gave not only obvious categories such as those actually in arms or acting as administrators for Parliament but also tenants whose rents had been seized by Parliament. This was a rather harsh definition not mirrored by Parliament's equivalent legislation. Royalist sequestration procedure, as outlined in these instructions, required high sheriffs to seize the property of suspected delinquents and hold them until the case was proved or otherwise. If the person was judged delinquent, then the estate could be sold to prosecute the war. It would appear that this was an unsatisfactory system as land sales would hardly be easy to effect in a situation as uncertain as a Civil War. Potential purchasers would have had to be convinced of the likelihood of royalist victory, as this would be the only guarantee of the permanence of the sale. Even in such a case, any spirit of, or political necessity for, reconciliation may well have negated the sale once the war was over.

Instead, it seems more likely that in many cases the income from the estate was used as a form of constant revenue. This was more in the manner of Parliament's sequestration method, and, although admittedly from limited evidence, seems to be the case in the North Midlands.

Parliament's legislation came into being in April 1643 and was similarly designed to exploit estates to increase funds.[127] The same month, royalists to the north and west of Hastings' command, a command which now included Staffordshire but not Lincolnshire, were sequestering the estates of parliamentarians. Likewise, Leicestershire was quick off the mark when its commissioners began sequestering the estates of the county's leading parliamentarian, Lord Grey, at Groby. Derbyshire's commissioners were to sequester Sir George Gresley's estates in the south of the county throughout 1644, having begun to do so in late 1643. The Rutland commissioners were sequestering the Earl of Rutland's county estates by January 1644 at the latest from their base at Belvoir Castle.[128]

No evidence of the official structure of the royalist sequestration process in the region for the early part of the war has come to light.

Sir Edward Seabright, a commissioner for Staffordshire, was appointed to a committee to investigate enemy estates in Worcestershire during late 1643, and may have held a similar post in Staffordshire. In December 1645 Hastings, along with Lords Aston and Astley, was ordered to investigate the collection of sequestration money in Staffordshire and the Marcher counties.[129] By this time, except for one Staffordshire Hundred, the royalists' hold on the area was minima1.[130] The commission directed to Hastings stated that the income from sequestration was to be used in, and for, the county of origin. It is likely that this was no new departure. Though such income had originally been intended to benefit central coffers, the Marcher Association had, in 1644, been granted the right to use this money. The income at Oxford from Sequestration amounted to only £1,225 in 1644, while there appears to have been none in any other year. It would seem that the concession to the Marcher counties was a recognition of fact, rather than a new departure. Royalist counties, as well as their parliamentarian counterparts, were using the income from sequestration for themselves rather than sending it to Oxford.[131]

It is perhaps the case that in the North Midlands sequestration revenue was not very high despite the presence of large 'delinquent' estates. What revenue there was would decline after the battle of Marston Moor. Thus Aston, Astley and Hastings would not have been daunted by their task in late 1645. On the other hand, one piece of evidence regarding royalist sequestration shows that Sir George Gresley's estates were being subjected to some form of sequestration at the end of 1644, and the Earl of Rutland's castle at Belvoir was a royalist garrison until February 1646. In addition, some parliamentarians would own property in their enemy's garrison towns, which would be used to quarter commissioners, officers and soldiers, another form of sequestration.

The Contribution

The contribution can be examined in more detail than the other sources of income for the royalists in the North Midlands. As with excise and sequestration, evidence regarding the superstructure of the system is limited beyond the names and instructions issued to some commissioners. However there are some sources which shed light on the actual allotment and collection of the tax. This relative wealth of source material may give contribution a higher profile in this book than it deserves; however, Parliament's equivalent, the weekly assessment, was their largest source of income, and so it may be that this prominence is somewhat justified.[132]

Contribution was collected for the use of the county soldiery by commissioners' warrants, after they and the garrison commanders had conferred as to the amounts desirable. It is probable that both Oxford, in the county by county allotment, and the commissioners, in their division of the amount between their county's communities, used ship money as a guide.[133] The amounts requested from individual communities are similar to those collected by Parliament who did use the much hated tax of the 1630s as a basis for their wartime levies. This makes the assumption credible. The presence of high sheriffs who had experience of collecting the ship tax on three of the commissions will also be recalled. A conflict of interest was apparent within the royalist war effort, between the largely civilian commissions of array and the military, for whom the contribution was generally destined. In the counties of Nottinghamshire, Derbyshire, Leicestershire and Rutland, this potential conflict would be reduced due to the inclusion of several prominent colonels of county regiments on the commissions. Even so in Leicestershire the exclusion of Gervase Lucas, led to his dissenting from the commission's decisions. In Staffordshire, where Colonel Thomas Leveson was excluded, the problems were, if not more severe, then at least of longer duration than those of Leicestershire; the problem was exacerbated by his being created high sheriff. Instead of bringing him into the administration it allowed him to act independently under the authority of his own position.

At the discussions between the administration and the colonels (whether formal or not cannot be divined) the counties were divided up between the various garrisons on, if possible, a hundredal basis. In Derbyshire, Scarsdale Hundred was the province of Bolsover Castle during 1643 and 1644, though after the castle fell the area was used by the garrison of Welbeck during the short period of its second occupation by royalists in 1645.[134] Tutbury Castle, though itself in Staffordshire, appears to have been allocated Moreleston and Litchurch Hundred in Derbyshire right until the end of the war. This would be in part based on the fact that the area was the Honour of Tutbury and thus traditionally bound up with the castle. Tutbury may also have had control over parts of Repton and Gresley Hundred.[135] The other three of the county's hundreds cannot be so definitely allocated: Wingfield garrison may have been in charge of levying taxes upon Wirksworth Hundred, High Peak under the control of the smaller garrisons along the north-west border of the county, and Appletree under the garrisons at Tissington and Ashbourne. Leicestershire was for most of the time split up between the two main and often only garrisons of Belvoir and Ashby; the latter being a very large garrison may have also shared Repton and Gresley in Derbyshire with Tutbury. In addition it would have the levies from Sparkenhoe, Gartre, Guthlaxton, West Goscote and perhaps until the quarrels between Lucas and Hastings, East Goscote as well. There is some evidence that Ashby also gained contribution from parts of Warwickshire. Belvoir garrison gained contribution from Framland Hundred, the whole of which it annexed in late 1643 and later from East Goscote as well as parts of Lincolnshire and Rutland.[136] In Nottinghamshire, Newark and its satellite garrison at Shelford House were collecting contribution from Broxton wapentake and Newark alone, from bide and Newark wapentakes; it would share Thurgarton wapentake with the satellite garrison at Thurgarton itself.[137] The two southern wapentakes, Rushcliffe and Bingham, may also have been under Newark's control. Bassetlaw and Oswardbeck would probably be under the Welbeck garrison. In addition Newark could at favourable times collect contribution from large areas of Lincolnshire. Together, in the summer of 1645, Welbeck and Newark were gaining contribution from no less than four counties, Yorkshire, Nottinghamshire, Derbyshire and Lincolnshire.[138] Rutland would be the province of the Belvoir forces after the royalist garrison at Burleigh House had been forced out in late 1643; however, earlier in the year, it appears that it may have been at least partially responsible to Ashby.[139] Lichfield garrison in Staffordshire was assigned Offlow Hundred for its income as soon as the town was recaptured by the royalists in April 1643. It is probable that the financial problems experienced by the governor, Richard Bagot, in the last weeks of that year necessitated the extension of its territory to Totmansloe

Ashby de la Zouch Castle. To the right is the Kitchen Tower and to the right the Hastings Tower – the central defence work built by Lord Hastings. The Buildings in the centre are the original manor house building, several centuries old by the civil war. (Photo: author's collection)

Hundred and Pirehill. The former it would have to share with Tutbury and the latter had until August been under Eccleshall, now held for Parliament.

Lichfield could still gain income from parts of these hundreds in December 1645.[140] Bagot had lost parts of Offlow to Tutbury Castle and Rushall Hall in 1643, and as compensation had received areas of Warwickshire. This in a way contributed to his problems as Leveson of the Dudley garrison was to dispute the Warwickshire allotment in April 1644.[141] As well as parts of Warwickshire and Worcestershire, the Dudley garrison was assigned Staffordshire's Seisdon Hundred during 1643 and 1644.[142] Cuttlestone Hundred may also have been responsible to Dudley as there was a satellite garrison established at Lapley House in the hundred.[143]

Tutbury shared Pirehill, Offlow and Totmansloe with Lichfield, in addition to the areas of Derbyshire from where it could collect contribution.[144]

At this level, the county boundary was not allowed to inhibit the royalist organisation. The garrisons of Tutbury, Belvoir, Dudley, Lichfield, Newark and Ashby-de-la-Zouch, collected income from counties other than those in which they were situated. This would have been a response to their geographical positions since all were near to county borders. The sub-county boundaries appear to have been adhered to; the division of counties on an hundredal basis shows this.

Up to this point the county administration has been shown to be in the hands of bodies alien to peace time local government. From this level downwards strenuous efforts were made to utilise officials and methods more common to provincial administration. Once the allotment of financial and geographical divisions had been made between the garrisons, the commissioners sought to conduct operations through the normal offices of county life. Many of the country's commissions of array incorporated the relevant county's high sheriff; others had been deprived of one by the incumbent's parliamentarianism. Leicestershire's had Hastings, picked after the commission was made, Nottinghamshire had the energetic John Digby, Staffordshire's Sir Harvey Bagot, Derbyshire's had the non-active royalist, Sir John Harpur of Caulke, and later John Pate, but Rutland did not have the current high sheriff amongst its commissioners.[145] Therefore, within the Midlands, most of the warrants for tax levies could be sent out in the name of the current high sheriff – an appearance of legality or at least normality as this was the usual way of authorising financial collections. More often than not the levies would be ordered in the name of the sheriff and members of the commission but sometimes they may just have been sent out in the name of the requisite three members of the commission's quorum. By utilising the sheriffs it was hoped to give the warrants some form of recognisable legality, an objective that the parliamentarian war effort sought by similar means to achieve – this resulted in cases of counties having a dual shrievalty.

Warrants for contribution, as the levy was known at a central level, were passed on to the constables, headboroughs or thirdboroughs by whichever name the communities' officials were known. It is from the records of these village officials that we are able to learn more about a fundamental part of the royalist administration of the North Midland counties. The office of constable was an elective post – he was chosen from amongst the freeholders of the community by his peers. Once elected for his year of office, he became responsible for the licensing of ale houses, the removing of 'strangers', the supervision of the village's contribution to the Trained Bands, looking after the village weaponry and keeping the parish bull. He may also, in the absence of overseers of the poor, have administered the poor rate and undertaken the apprenticing of orphans. More pertinent to the present work, he was responsible for collecting and even allocating the fiscal levies which were passed on to him by county government. In the 1630s this had meant ship money; in the 1640s it was on his shoulders that the onus of collecting war taxes fell.

During the early part of the century constables were not obliged to keep records of their financial dealing. Most did not. Some used, and then lost, loose papers of records; others kept scant or cryptic accounts. The constable of Rugeley in Staffordshire, for the year 1643–1644, watched his house burn down, taking with it his accounts for his term of office.[146] Other constables may have used the war as an excuse for not keeping accounts. The note:

> 'The mighty accounts in the years 1642, 1643 and 1644, between this town of Edwinstowe and Miles Oldham constable that because of the war could not be then or now counted.'[147]

fills an otherwise blank page in the Edwinstowe accounts – a one sentence substitute for three years of financial administration. For Derbyshire, Leicestershire, Nottinghamshire, Rutland and Staffordshire, there are only 21 sets of constables' accounts surviving out of a potential number of about 800.

Of these only 11 offer reasonably continuous records of financial transactions; three of them alone give week by week accounts for periods longer than a year. There is one other important shortfall; there are no relevant detailed accounts for Derbyshire which exhibit any continuity in their compilation. Despite this paucity, there are enough links and similarities amongst the surviving 28 sets of accounts to enable a substantial picture of this aspect of royalist administration in the region to be built up.

The constables of Offlow Hundred seem to have been involved in the royalist financial system as early as November 1642, when the commissioners at Lichfield summoned them to a meeting.[148] This was before there was a coherent royalist party in the county of Staffordshire and, indeed, was at the time when there was a distinct possibility of the county adopting armed neutrality.[149] Also at this time, local taxes were only adopted as temporary expedients. The system of loans at eight percent interest on the public faith would not, and voluntary donations from the landed magnates could not, finance the war effort once it became clear, on the field of Edgehill, that the war was to be more than a short term problem. By February, Nottinghamshire's commissioners had established monthly meetings for the constables at Newark in order to allocate and co-ordinate levies. During the same period, the royalist commissioners now at Stafford, were calling in Staffordshire's constables in the sheriff's name.[150] The constables of the region's other three counties would probably be likewise summoned to meetings for the same purpose. By May the Staffordshire commission had assessed the county for a primary levy of £2,000 and appointed collectors for each of the county's hundreds.[151] Derbyshire's commission was conducting its financial system on a regular basis by June 1643 at the latest.[152] By this time the pragmatic approach had clearly been shed with governors prevented from issuing warrants and commissioners ordered to supply accounts to Oxford.[153] Contribution collection began to take on an aspect of regularity.

However, it is clear from the constables' records that not all of these officials were attending the meetings held by the commissioners. There would be many reasons for this. Firstly, the geographical location of many of the commissions' meetings made it difficult for some men to attend. For example, Ashby-de-la-Zouch is on the border between north-west Leicestershire and south Derbyshire. Both of the relevant county towns were held by the enemy and were between Ashby and large sections of the two counties' communities. This, coupled with the sheer distance from the headquarters of these commissions, would have been prohibitive to the attendance of a large proportion of constables. Secondly, there was the distinct possibility of retribution by Parliament's committees in the counties. Constables who were guilty of cooperation with the royalists could be regarded as enemies and therefore be liable to arrest and displacement from office – though few instances of this appear to have occurred.[154] Thirdly, during the early months of the war, some desire for neutralism or at least avoidance of responsibility may have pervaded some constables. Fourthly, there was also the probability that some of the constables would have political motives for ignoring the royalists' summonses to county meetings. As a result some of the constables who did attend the meetings had to carry warrants to their absentee neighbours' constablewicks, whilst others had to administer several constablewicks for some periods of the war.[155] Also once the organisations had established themselves, constables would only have to travel as far as their nearest garrison and as royalist collectors often coursed the villages minimal movement was required.

However a constable received the warrants, he probably had to pay for his own copy – usually 4d or 2d a time.[156] It was then up to him to allot the individual amounts that went to make up the levy amongst his fellow property owners in the village. This was probably done at a meeting of what were often termed 'his neighbours', either at his house or at a local inn of convenient size.[157] The allotments were made in the form of a property tax, suggesting that they, like the parliamentarian equivalent, were following the pattern established by ship money. When the villages were incorporated into parliamentarian territory, either permanently or temporarily, there was little alteration in the size of the levy made on it – again an indication of the validity of the assumption about ship money being used as a guideline.[158]

At Stathern in Leicestershire, the allotment of the levy was made on the following terms:- 8d per acre of land, 8d per score of sheep, and 4d per pasture beast. This was in 1643. At Waltham on the Wolds in the same county, the levy appears to have been, one shilling per yardland and 3d per cow in the same year.[159] At Coddington in Nottinghamshire, the 1643 rates for the levy were: 2d per acre, 2d per score of sheep, 1d per beast and a penny for a dwelling or perhaps an outbuilding. Here, by the following year, these amounts had all doubled except for the levy on beasts when the amount went up to one shilling. Similar increases are evident elsewhere indicating that the burden was increasing.[160]

The regularity with which the constable collected, or at least allotted the portions of the levy, appears to vary slightly. The best recorded levies are those given for Waltham on the Wolds between October 1644 and the following August:[161]

29th October (1644)	£7-0s-0d
30th December	£14-0s-0d
21st February (1645)	£27-4-0
5th June	£27-4-0
16th August	£27-2-0
Total	£102-10-0

There are two possibilities regarding the sudden fluctuation in the amounts; either the incoming constable reduced the number of individual collections made in the year, thus increasing the amount of money collected each time, or the constablewick simply had to face demands for more money from Belvoir in the way that the village of Coddington had to provide Newark with more money at about the same time. If the latter is the case then the increase was in the region of 25 percent. At Branston in Leicestershire, the constable collected four levies during the same time period as the Waltham constable made five.[162] At Stathern there was no regular series of collections; varying amounts were collected sporadically. At Coddington, only three such levies were made in 1643. Elsewhere there are no complete series of levies recorded. It appears then that there was considerable variation in the ways that the constables operated within the region.

In some cases these levies of the individual amounts represented the end of the constables' duty regarding contribution. The garrisons to which it was payable often collected the village levies from them. This was done usually at weekly or fortnightly intervals, wherever possible by a quartermaster of a regiment of Horse stationed in the garrison concerned. Thus at Waltham on the Wolds, Quartermaster Power of Captain Mason's troop collected the contribution from the constable. Mason was one of the captains in Gervase Lucas' Regiment of Horse and was described as the 'commander of the fen robbers', indicating that his regiment may have been involved in collecting contribution from Lincolnshire as well. Power called at fortnightly intervals from December 1643 until at least October 1644, when the new constable kept less detailed accounts. Nevertheless, it appears that Mason's troop was responsible for this area around Belvoir until November 1645. Branston too, was visited by Mason's troop on a weekly basis during 1644.[163] In the Staffordshire community of Mavesyn Ridware the three constables in office between 1642 and 1645 made fortnightly trips to pay money to Captain Jeffry Glasier, the Lichfield treasurer and captain in Richard Bagot's Regiment of Foot.[164] Constables in Seisdon Hundred in Staffordshire also appear to have travelled to their nearest garrison, in this case Dudley Castle, to pay their levies. The garrison treasurer, Captain Lieutenant John Birch of Thomas Leveson's Regiment of Horse, may have on occasion arranged to have the money collected from the communities.[165] In Nottinghamshire, Upton's constables were paying money to Newark at weekly intervals. It is not, however, clear if they had to make the journey to the garrison themselves. As there are no complete accounts for Derbyshire or Rutland we cannot be certain of the pattern of events in either county. It is most likely that the former fell into the same pattern established in Staffordshire, at least in the sections administered from Tutbury. As for the latter, we can assume that the system there operated in the same way as the rest of the territory administered by the Belvoir garrison.

Not all the contribution was collected in the form of cash. It was much easier for the royalists to take some of it in the form of provisions, as this prevented the necessity of returning to the various communities in order to purchase goods. Villages provided the garrison with their own specialities. Stathern sent peas and barley to Belvoir Castle; Branston sent oats, beer, veal and cheese.[166] Mavesyn Ridware provided Lichfield with coal, hay and all embracing provisions as part of its contribution.[167] The same pattern is followed in Nottinghamshire where towns responsible to Newark sent hay and provisions to the garrison.[168] It is probable that this shipment of goods followed pre-war trade patterns. In return for these provisions, a receipt was issued to the constable (for which he had, naturally, to pay) in order to prevent confusion when the value of the goods came to be deducted from the contribution total. These receipts would be copies of the ones kept by the garrison treasurers.

The cost to the communities of the constant collection of contribution would be high. At Mavesyn Ridware, where the accounts are most complete, the yearly totals for 1643, 1644 and 1645 are given: these amounts are broken down into details, with respect to cash and provisions. Individual fortnightly payments in this period vary from £9-6s-8d in November 1643 to £1-18s-6d in cash and £0-18s-6d in goods paid over in June 1644. The more usual total sums are in the region of £4-10s. The annual sums are thus:[169]

1642–1643 (October to October)	£30-13s-7d
1643–1644 (In addition to £47-5s-0d to Parliament)	£144-17s-4d
1644–1645 (In addition to £87-7s-9d to Parliament)	£128-13s-3d
Total	£304-2s-2d

In other parts of Staffordshire, amounts paid to the royalists (or indeed the parliamentarians) are not so easy to find. Uttoxeter probably made over a total of £200 to the Tutbury garrison in 1645. In Leicestershire, Branston paid Belvoir £50 in 1645 whilst paying £90 to the parliamentarians. Had it only had to pay one side the amount would appear to have been around £100–£120 per annum. Waltham on the Wolds paid £99-16s-4d in 1643–1644 and £103-8s-3d in the following year to Belvoir.[170] In Nottinghamshire, Thorpe sent approximately £75 to Newark in 1644, whilst Upton paid out over £170 in the following year. Some of the latter money went in sporadic payments to the parliamentarians whilst the majority went to Newark.[171] As for individual amounts paid by constablewicks in Derbyshire we can say nothing.

Scarsdale Hundred owed around £100 at the garrison's second surrender, in November 1645; it seems likely that this represented four weeks' contribution.[172] For purposes of comparison, Lichfield received approximately £48 a month from Offlow Hundred in 1643 and over £300 from the same area, along with an additional 12 constablewicks, in October to December 1645.[173] As it would seem from these figures the sums expected from Derbyshire at the end of the war were reasonably similar to those expected elsewhere, it is probable that this was true throughout the periods when the royalists were able to tax the county.

There is little possibility of assessing how much of an additional expense the war entailed for villages, however, especially when concurrent payments to Parliament are taken into consideration, the burden on the communities appears to have been very high. There are few accounts which cover both pre- and post-war periods in any detail. Belton in Leicestershire does provide a useful exception:[174]

1638	£ 9-11s-8d (ship money period)
1639	£14-15s-9d (First Scots War)
1640	£14 -9s-10d (Second Scots War)
1641	£ 8-18s-11d
1644	£34-4s-5d
1646	£17-6s-3d

From these figures we can see that in 1638 and 1641, when there were no 'foreign' wars to drain the village's finances, the annual outlay was in the region of £8–£10, whilst at the height of the war the sum was over three and a half times higher. The majority, if not all, of the 1644 sum would go to Ashby-de-la-Zouch. At Biddulph in Staffordshire, the proportional difference is quite similar, with a rise from £8-9s-7d in 1640 to £26-12s-6d in 1645, a threefold increase.[175] Edwinstowe in Nottinghamshire in 1641–1642 had an expenditure of £8-4s-4d which increased to £23-0s-7d in 1646, a year when Belton amongst other places paid less than in other war years. Again, this is almost three times the normal sum.[176] The amount collected there in 1648 was only £2-2s-2d, indicating that the war was already a burden by 1642 or the village had become impoverished by 1648. At Rugeley in Staffordshire, accounts not destroyed in the fire at Robert Burton's house show that peace time disbursements totalled around £17, whilst in 1644–1645 they reached £43-13s-9d (perhaps paid to both sides). This is once more a threefold increase.[177] From these few figures we can say that for those villages which did pay contribution on a regular basis the war was an expensive business, involving a proportional increase of around three times the normal village outlay. The fact that these figures come from three separate counties adds weight to this assumption.

Due to the lack of information no real estimate can be made of the total income that the royalists gained from each of these counties; we can only use regional sums as a guideline. Two, the £100 owed to Welbeck by Scarsdale in 1645, and the £100 per month paid in the same year to Lichfield, have been mentioned. To these must be added the claim, made by Henry Hastings, that Belvoir Castle was claiming £200 a week from its allotted areas in 1644.[178] In 1645, Richard Symonds claimed that the Leicestershire royalists were claiming 'four score and seventeen thousand pounds' per annum from the county.[179] If true this would entail an average annual sum collected from the communities of £340. The highest sum we have come across in the region was the £174 paid by Upton to Newark. In Leicestershire, the highest figure is Branston's £140 split between both sides. As we have also seen, many villages paid considerably less. If the Branston sum were taken as the average figure for the county and simply multiplied by the number of parishes, the annual outlay would only be £34,580. If the highest county sum paid to the royalists alone is so multiplied (Waltham's £103) the annual sum would thus be £25,441. The highest figure which can be derived from the Leicestershire statistics is gained by assuming that the £200 that the Belvoir garrison was claiming came from only 100 in the county. This gives us an annual total of £71,800. As this entails the unlikely possibility that the royalists were able to collect money from the whole county when their power was on the wane, it seems that Symonds was wildly overestimating. These rough estimates made for Leicestershire, if extended to the other counties, suggest that around £30,000 per annum could be gained from each of the larger counties, Rutland being the exception.[180]

Though it is probable that many of the constablewicks fell at some time or other into arrears, there is amongst the constables' papers little evidence for this. Only at Mavesyn Ridware does the constable mention arrears and then only twice: he cites no figures. Both instances occurred in 1645.[181] To check the performance of the constables it is possible that the garrison commanders and their treasurers called them in from time to time. Many visits to the garrisons are referred to in the account books and in at least one such instance recorded at Mavesyn the purpose was to go over the accounts. Arrears must have occurred more frequently than there is evidence for. The decline in the size of the North Midlands Army after the middle of 1644 cannot be solely due to the results of military action. The increasing hold over the region established by the parliamentarians will have reduced the income of the royalist war effort. This would have had undoubted effects on the commanders' ability to pay their men, thus possibly leading to desertions.

From the evidence presented by the constables' accounts it is clear that the royalist war effort was run, not on an ad hoc basis, but as a systematic yet flexible organisation. There is strong evidence from villages such as Mavesyn Ridware, Branston and Upton that they were paying a regularly collected property tax rather than a seventeenth century version of protection money. Yet it has recently been suggested by Stephen Porter that the legitimate method of collecting contribution was the method of collection by threat. Porter saw contribution as a form of *Brandschatzung* – burning money – the form of protection racket operated by commanders in the current continental wars. This would involve explicit or implicit violence being a part of the collection of contribution. The majority of Porter's evidence for such a theory is derived from parliamentarian sources when dealing with contribution, and royalist ones when referring to Parliament's assessment. Thus the picture he gives, especially in the light of the more objective sources used in this book, would appear to be of suspect value. Indeed to infer that contribution was an English equivalent of *Brandschatzung* is erroneous.[182] Problems over non-payment were sorted out by discussion and possible readjustment. In extreme cases constables could be arrested and deprived of office but this was a resort to law not to the sword. In any case a war effort required a constant income not sporadic bouts of plunder. A system consisting of violent extortion would have caused a public reaction and the war effort been less successful. Not only would large numbers of troops been necessary to enforce payments but villages could have withheld supplies. There is no reference to contribution in the terms of a fine or by any other names than tax levy or assessment. There were payments made to troops specifically to prevent plundering, but these come under an entirely different category and involved small payments such as a shilling or two. These would appear to be payments to a few deserters or stragglers, not to representatives of the royalist or parliamentarian war efforts.[183]

It remains difficult to assess how much of the region was incorporated into the royalist war effort. It is probable that at the end of 1643 Derbyshire, Leicestershire and Nottinghamshire were, with the exception of the county towns, firmly in the grip of the commissioners' system. The Leicester committee and the London press asserted that assessment in the county could not be collected; nor could parliamentarians collect their own rents; the county was blocked up, cut off from trade and communication with London.[184] Derbyshire was likewise cut off from the south and had the Marquis of Newcastle's army in residence as well as the indigenous royalists under Hastings. Nottingham parliamentarians were on the defensive and attempts were made to capture the town in November and the following January. The fall of Eccleshall must have dented royalist control of Staffordshire in late summer 1643, but the county was described, by the parliamentarian press, as being in great distress after Lapley House fell to the Dudley garrison in the following December. Lichfield's hold on large parts of the county continued throughout the war and still were able to dominate one hundred at the end of 1645.[185] In the period following the battle of Marston Moor, the local parliamentarians were, with outside help, able to assert control over large parts of the North Midlands; however, we are left with the conclusion that until such a time the royalists were able for some months to extend their control and gain contribution from the vast majority of the region's communities. The obvious exceptions were, of course, the county towns. Due to the lack of evidence regarding the income from any of the chief royalist sources of income, excise, sequestration or contribution, no assessment of their relative input to the royalist war effort can be made. Thus no fiscal value can be placed on the cost of the loss of these major towns to the royalist financial system.

Additional Levies

Unfortunately for the various communities, contribution was not the only levy imposed by the local garrisons. Whilst food for men and horses were covered by this property tax other goods, it would seem, were not.

In October 1644 £3 worth of beds and bedding were sent from Waltham on the Wolds to Belvoir Castle. Likewise Upton sent such items to Newark, Mavesyn Ridware to Lichfield during the same and following years.[186] Also, labourers were often supplied upon warranted demand to work on the defensive structures at the garrisons, either to build or repair earthworks. Such labourers were required of Stathern by Belvoir, of Upton by Newark and of Mavesyn Ridware by Lichfield in 1644 and 1645.[187] These men were paid their wages by their home community. The additional cost was not docked from the contribution but the constable may have included such a possibility when he assessed the individual contributions within his village.

What was probably more burdensome to the villages was the presence of another royalist army in their area on top of the local forces. Henrietta Maria's Army was an additional drain on Upton's resources in June 1643 for example. The most difficult period was the time in May 1644 when the Northern Horse under Goring was based in the north of the region prior to joining Rupert's army for the march to York. The effects of this were felt right through the North Midlands and the dire effects of Goring's presence are discussed in Chapter 6. The march of the King's own field army through the area in May 1645 was also financially a burden to the villages on the route. The unification of the elements of the North Midlands Army when it was engaged on a particular project also caused an increase in the financial burden. Thus Upton and other places in the area were faced with the cost of regiments not normally based there, during March 1644 after the relief of Newark.[188]

Military Expenditure

Having deduced how the money necessary to the war effort in the North Midlands was collected, it is now intended to give a brief indication of the way in which that money was spent by the royalists. Evidence for the expenditure side of the accounts book is even harder to find than for the income section.

Food and fodder have already been dealt with as they generally were part and parcel of the contribution. There would also be cash payments to the troops, though their food and quarter was deducted from their pay. This would form the most constant drain on the royalists' resources. The wages laid down at Oxford, were four shillings a week for a foot soldier and 12 shillings a week for a horse soldier (this includes the food and quarter allowance as well as that for the stabling charges incurred by the trooper). A rough estimate based on the size of the North Midlands Army indicates a wage bill of over £1,200 a week, or £64,480 per annum inclusive of allowances.[189] It is probable that in many cases wages were often paid irregularly. However at Lichfield, where the accounts are the most detailed, the soldiers were paid regularly until the end of 1643 when the decrease in the garrison's allotted area due to Leveson's encroachment and the establishment of the garrison at Rushall, prevented this and mutiny threatened.[190] Yet by the end of 1645 the garrison, which had in 1644 gained concessions of territory, was still able to pay the soldiers regularly. At the end of September 1644, Tutbury's governor, Sir Andrew Kniveton, was 'very much distressed' for money to pay his soldiers at a time when Parliament's power in the county was growing. In this case and in the case of Lichfield in 1643 temporary expedients were made by the provision of 'loans' by the county gentry.[191]

Weapons and gunpowder had to be bought either at Oxford or elsewhere from manufacturers. There could also be arrangements to exchange goods between regions. Captain Dupont of the Ashby garrison suggested that Richard Bagot send saltpetre he was producing at Lichfield to Oxford, where there was a shortage, and in return he would receive the equivalent weight of gunpowder, the finished product.[192] Iron and other necessities were obtained from local suppliers if possible. Colonel Leveson at Dudley was in the heart of what was, already, a burgeoning proto industrial area and obtained his iron from nearby.[193] Lichfield was supplied with the same by Walter Chetwynd of Rugeley.[194] There was, of course, the cheaper expedient of seizing the enemy's stocks as they passed through the region.

Bagot's accounts for 1643 give a useful insight into what else funds were used for. During the nine months following his installation as governor of Lichfield in April, he rebuilt the town defences and added to those already in existence. To enable the town to become self-sufficient, he built a corn mill and a gunpowder mill. He had the facilities to produce brass cannon and had his own saltpetre furnace. These were on top of the numbers of skilled workmen constantly in his pay to produce the goods in each of these works and skilled arms manufacturers.[195] Though there is no evidence of any other garrison possessing such operations it is unlikely that the larger garrisons like Dudley and Tutbury and especially Ashby and Newark would be without the ability to produce their own weaponry to some extent.

The Royalist Administration: A Conclusion

From what has been discussed above, it may be concluded that there were two factors which produced the system that the royalists used to finance their operations. Firstly the commissioners of array who ran it had an established stake in the region over which they presided. They were not great magnates who had large estates in other counties: their primary holdings were within the county or regional boundaries of the North Midlands, and these they sought to protect. Also they would not wish to aggravate the populace, which included their own tenantry upon whose work they depended, or the freeholders, whose votes they needed to keep their men or even themselves in Parliament. In addition these men were familiar with the mechanics of the system which they were to use in the war. They had served in the various offices of county government and respected its traditions and values. Thus they sought to graft wartime government of necessity onto the peace time government of stability.

Secondly, it made military sense not to destroy the area in which they were living and hopefully going to be living and maintaining an armed force in for some time. To threaten and to carry out the threat of military retribution and violent extraction of funding from the town or village communities would not be conducive to long-term military presence and strategy.

For these reasons the system here described was gradually developed. It was essentially dependent on the collection of a weekly collected property tax akin to that which had been utilised earlier in order to raise ship money. This system, with its pseudo-legal appearance, would cause relatively little confusion as it resembled so closely that which had been applied recently and as it was conducted through the traditional channels of county governance and was also often carried out by the same individuals. Only the amounts of money, which have been shown in some cases to have been treble the normal annual outlay of a village, broke greatly with tradition. This is an important point. The long-term imposition of these sums which were collected by armed men would ensure that everyone realised a war was in progress. There could be no surprised ploughmen in the Midlands. If the term 'total war' implies the utilisation of all a country's resources, then the English Civil War was no simple collection of disconnected localised incidents: this war in the bowels of England was a seventeenth century version of Total War.

To assess the effectiveness of the royalist war effort we must turn to its performance; this will be illustrated in later chapters in detail but a brief outline of which is given here. Throughout 1643 the system supported a growing army: the conquest of Derbyshire by the Marquis of Newcastle created a well defined area of royalist control in which the small pockets of parliamentarians grouped in the county towns could only enact a kind of guerrilla warfare. Very little else was needed. The counties were secure enough for outside royalist forces to pass through and draw support from the indigenous garrisons. As an area between two great regions of royalist domination – the south and west, and the north – the Midlands had only to be kept stable. In this the system was a success having, in effect, provided the royalist cause with a self-sufficient regional base.

Failure only came with the full onslaught of parliamentarian incursion after the battle of Marston Moor in July 1644. Had the financial system been run differently the result would have been the same: the commissioners of array were not to blame for the military defeat in the north. As it was their system ensured that there was not defeat from within. A harsher operation may have evoked popular reaction, as was in evidence in other areas, which would have damaged the effectiveness of the system and made it unworkable, had civil control been weak and the military 'swordsmen' been correspondingly stronger. That this does not occur indicates two things. Firstly that the commissioners of array were able to some extent to run successfully a potentially oppressive system through normal channels and secondly that the royalists were not defeated because their financial organisation was at fault.

Chapter 3

The Parliamentarian War Effort in the North Midlands; a Comparative Analysis

This chapter is intended only as a brief survey of the topic; for detailed work on the parliamentarian war effort the reader is referred to the works by Pennington and Roots and by Everett, which are mentioned in this text and in the bibliography at the end of this book. This chapter's purpose is twofold. Firstly it is to present a more balanced picture of the region in order that the royalist war effort does not appear in isolation. Secondly, throughout this analysis of the rival administration, points of comparison with the royalists will be presented thereby placing the findings of the bulk of this book within context.

Unlike the royalist war effort, the parliamentarian equivalent is well documented at the central level. Ordinances for the creation of county committees and for the establishment of excise, sequestration and assessment levies, along with their respective attendant committees, are contained within works by John Rushworth and that by Firth and Rait.[196] Secondary sources include works by Alan Everett and Clive Holmes which have presented us with detailed examinations of several individual county committees, and James Wheeler, who has illuminated the methods employed by, and the success of, the parliamentarian war machine.[197] At the local level there is less evidence to work on, but the sources used will become apparent in the later section dealing with the regional operations.

This chapter is divided into four main sections. Firstly the establishment of the committees and their history up until the middle of 1643 will be examined. Secondly the membership will be studied in a manner similar to that employed in the previous chapter when examining the commissioners of array. Following this the three main sources of revenue will be taken into consideration. Finally the way in which the committees within the region worked in unison will be explored.

The Establishment of the County Committees

From December 1642 Parliament began to establish committees in counties over which it had some control. By the following February it instituted such committees for counties over which it was, for the time being, powerless. Devon and Yorkshire were amongst those counties which received a committee-in-waiting. In the North Midlands, Derbyshire, Leicestershire, Nottinghamshire and Rutland all received committees before the end of 1642; Staffordshire appears not to have received one until the new year. The first one recorded seems to have been issued in February by which time the county had been placed under the command of Lord Brooke who was marching north to seize military control from the growing royalist party within the county.[198] In Derbyshire and Nottinghamshire, the committees were formed around the leading parliamentarians who had been instrumental in securing the county towns in the absence of royalist activists. When the King moved west to Shrewsbury and then south towards London, he drained the North Midlands of prominent royalist figures such as Hastings, giving active parliamentarians a free hand.[199] Accordingly Sir John Gell, a noted lessee of lead mines and ex-high sheriff, aided by troops supplied by Sir John Hotham at Hull, took Derby. John Hutchinson, eldest son of the respected owner of Owthorpe in Nottinghamshire, who had become prominent earlier in the year when he prevented Lord Newark from seizing the county magazine for the King, likewise took control of Nottingham.[200] It was, given their obvious zeal, a practical idea to centre the committees around men such as these. In Leicestershire, since the Earl of Stamford, the parliamentarian lord lieutenant, had become embroiled in the war in the south-west, the committee was formed around Stamford's son Lord Grey of Groby.[201] Within the same month as these committees were formed, they and their counties were grouped into an association along with Rutland, Northamptonshire, Huntingdonshire, Bedfordshire and Buckinghamshire; Lord Grey was placed in military command over them.[202]

Within the first half of 1643 the committee system in the North Midland counties was developed. By February all of the five counties covered by this book had committees responsible for the raising and training of military forces. The means of raising income had progressed from the dependence on loans at eight percent interest, to measures more suited to a long-term prosecution of the war. The chief source of income was the collection of a weekly tax, the Assessment, established by an ordinance in late February.[203] By the end of the following month the sequestration of enemy estates was provided for.[204] For both of these measures a committee was established, the membership of each being drawn from the personnel of the militia committees established earlier. The same was true of the contemporaneous committees for 'punishing scandalous ministers'. By utilising the same corps of men Parliament aimed at preventing the possibility of conflict between rival organs of government. It is to an examination of the composition of these committees that we now turn. As with the study of the commissioners of array, these men will be examined in the light of their social standing, their familial status and their experiences of education, local or national government.

The County Committees

The counties dealt with here are the same as those with which the previous chapter was concerned, Derbyshire, Leicestershire, Nottinghamshire, Rutland and Staffordshire. In each county we will be taking into account the nominees to all the committees created in the county, but only those deemed to have been active on the committees will be included in the statistical analyses. Any significant difference to the findings of the tables produced by the addition of statistics from a group excluded from the main analysis, will, as in the previous chapter, be dealt with in the text. The statistics only take note of titles or offices held before the issue of the Militia Ordinance in March 1642. As with the previous chapter, each county will be examined in turn and then the committeemen will be considered as a whole. Throughout this analysis reference will be made to comparable statistics from the last chapter.

Derbyshire's Committeemen[205]

It would appear that a total of 30 men were appointed to committees within Derbyshire between December 1642 and the end of 1645. Of these, only four did not play an active role in the county administration. One of these was captured at the beginning of the war, two were possible neutrals and one falls into that category where there is not enough evidence to indicate clearly whether or not he was an activist. This leaves 26 known activists whose social breakdown is as follows:

Social Rank

Noble	Bart	Knight	Esq.	Gent.	Yeoman	Trade/ profession/ clergy	Unknown
0	4	2	5	10	1	0	4

Though there are six men from the titled gentry, it is immediately obvious that right from the outset Parliament, whether from necessity or not, was willing to appoint men of lesser social standing than were the royalists. Though in the nominees to the commissions of array there are men termed simply as 'gentlemen' there are very few of them and they certainly never come near to forming the largest single group. The one yeoman was appointed after 1644, when it was evident in many counties that there was an element of social dilution occurring in the parliamentarian county administration. The appointment of even just one yeoman is significant especially when notice is taken of the four men in the unknown category. These too would come from either the low obscure tail of the gentry or even like the yeoman, from below the identifiable rank of gentleman altogether, indicating that the parliamentarian war administration was an agent of social mobility. These figures also show that parliamentarian administration was chiefly composed of men from the lower end of the gentry spectrum or below. It has been argued that social dilution occurred during the war, that committees became, as the war progressed, increasingly reliant upon men of low status. Here, it is suggested that an element of such men was apparent from the outset.

Familial Status

Head	1st son	2nd son	Other son	Unknown
11	8	1	3	3

With regard to familial status, it can be seen that a large number of activists came from the upper end of the family scale. The commitment is similar to that shown by the royalist commissioners. Involvement of the heads of families was in effect the committal of the families' wealth and future to the cause. The risk was no less great than that undertaken by royalist families. It is only with the benefit of hindsight that we know which side won the First Civil War and were thus not faced with financial penalties.

Despite the apparent lack of social standing amongst the committeemen there was quite a high degree of experience on the committee, but compared with the county's commissioners there is a much higher proportion who had no political or administrative experience at all (10 out of the 26 as opposed to one out of 11). However a larger proportion of committeemen did attend places of legal and higher education. There was also one man with town government experience – an element missing from the commissions. This can be partly explained by the location of the committees in the county towns. Gell was not enamoured with Derby's council as a whole; when Hastings captured the mayor and offered to return him, Gell suggested sending Hastings the rest of the council as he found them an obstruction.[206]

Political, Administrative or Educational Experience

MP	LL	DL	HS	JP	University	Inn	Town Govt
2	0	2	5	4	13	10	1

Derbyshire's committee was drawn from a broader social base than the county's commission of array. On a familial level there is the same pattern shown: a concentration at the upper end of the family scale with the same consequent embroiling of the families' wealth. Though a large number of the committeemen received some form of education, administrative experience is confined, as might be expected, to those at the upper end of the gentry spectrum.

Leicestershire's Committeemen

Forty-nine men were appointed to the committees handling Parliament's affairs in Leicestershire. Of these the high number of 34 seem to have played at least some part in the working of the committees. Four men left insufficient evidence for their part to be accurately assessed, one man was a passive supporter or neutral, three were activists elsewhere and seven were royalists.

The social breakdown is as follows:

Social Rank

Noble	Bart	Knight	Esq.	Gent.	Yeoman	Trade/ profession/ clergy	Unknown
1	0	3	16	5	9	0	9

A slightly higher proportion of these committeemen came from the upper gentry (esquires and above) than did their Derbyshire counterparts. However the large number of 'unknowns' indicates that there was still a significant proportion of lower gentry or even elements from below the gentry. Of the 10 appointed after 1644, only two were esquires; the others were of low or implied low gentry status. The petition, presented to Parliament by Leicestershire's 'well affected' in late 1644, indicated that the county committee were already perceived as being created of lesser men with no estates in the county.[207] This fear of social dilution would not be stilled by the post 1644 additions to the committees. The claim that some of the committee had no Leicestershire estates, is not true: all had estates in the county, but some were not very substantial.

Despite the large number whose exact familial status cannot be discerned, we still have a group dominated by those from the upper end of the family scale. However there is a noticeable proportion of men who are not. There is no reason why the 'unknown' group should not follow the pattern established by the others.

Familial Status

Head	1st son	2nd son	Other son	Unknown
12	6	3	2	11

There is still evidence of the apparent willingness to commit the family to the cause shown by the great number of the heads and potential heads of families present in the statistics.

Only 15 of the committeemen appear to have had pre-war experience of education or administration. This is quite different to the situation in Derbyshire and compares poorly with the county's commissioners. The number who had had some experience of higher education, is also low, being only a third of the total. We are left to conclude that the petitioners of 1644 may have had grounds upon which to base their fears of the committee's suitability to administer the county.

Political, Administrative or Educational Experience

MP	LL	DL	HS	JP	University	Inn	Town Govt
0	0	0	0	1	12	6	3

We do again see an element of men with experience of town government present on the committee.

On the whole Leicestershire's committeemen appear to be, and were perceived to be at the time, of low social standing and experience. Though there is a slightly higher proportion of upper gentry than is present in Derbyshire the general lack of social standing is not, as in Derbyshire, compensated for by an impressive amount of political, administrative and educational experience. We see again Parliament's willingness to call upon lower social groups to control its local affairs.

Nottinghamshire's Committeemen

Of the 29 men appointed to the Nottinghamshire committees before 1646, only four appear not to have played a part in their activities. Three were either passive parliamentarians or neutrals and one, William Drury, was thrown off the committee for suspected royalist sympathies and compliance in royalist attempts to capture the town.

Social Rank

Noble	Bart	Knight	Esq.	Gent.	Yeoman	Trade/ profession/ clergy	Unknown
0	1	2	11	6	0	2	3

The two men in the 'Trade…' category were both of professional status with, perhaps, claims to urban gentility; one was a physician and the other a lawyer. Two of the 'unknowns' were probably involved in trade and were both involved in town government, therefore they may well have been in the same group as the aforementioned urban gentry. Despite the firm anchor in the upper ranks of the gentry where over half of the committee men had their origins, it is clearly shown that Parliament's cause utilised men of lower social standing in the administration than the royalists were willing to do. Dr Huntingdon Plumtree, the committeeman, was not considered for the royalist commission probably due to his low social standing: his parliamentarianism owed a lot to force of circumstance, living as he did in Nottingham.

Familial Status

Head	1st son	2nd son	Other son	Unknown
5	5	3	2	10

Though the large number of 'unknowns' is disconcerting it would appear again that the Nottinghamshire committeemen are from the upper end of the family spectrum and could be expected to hold or to succeed to the family's financial reins. Though their social obscurity clouds the issue in 10 cases it may be possible that these prospective lower gentry had something to make them eligible for consideration as candidates for committee post. That may well have been their familial position, thus it is possible that they were heads of their (obscure) families.

This may be born out by the fact that it was obviously not their proven skills as administrators which won them their place. Only 11 of the committeemen had had such experience and they were from the upper end of the social ladder.

Political, Administrative or Educational Experience

MP	LL	DL	HS	JP	University	Inn	Town Govt
0	0	1	1	2	8	5	2

It will be remembered that the county's commissioners were not particularly well versed in the relevant experiences tabulated here either. The committee's Sir Francis Thornhaugh did have experience of ship money collection in the 1630s. This would be of no small value given that Parliament's assessment was based on this much hated tax.

Nottinghamshire's committees were, it has been shown, composed of men drawn from a broad gentry spectrum but were not made up of men of proven administrative worth. Yet the social elite and the experienced administrators of seventeenth century life were represented on the committee, where their presence would add weight to both its appearance and its performance.

Rutland's Committeemen

The 14 active members of the Rutland committees came from a total of 15 nominees: the one absentee was in London for the duration. The social pattern is similar to those of the committees seen above. The two gentlemen were appointed after 1644 when social dilution was becoming evident. However this is offset by the fact that the one noble, Lord Grey, was also a post 1644 appointee. The two 'unknowns' were however nominated before 1644, and were probably mere gentlemen.

Social Rank

Noble	Bart	Knight	Esq.	Gent.	Yeoman	Trade/ profession/ clergy	Unknown
1	1	0	8	2	0	0	2

On a familial basis the pattern set by the other committees is mirrored in Rutland.

Familial Status

Head	1st son	2nd son	Other son	Unknown
5	3	0	1	5

The issue is again clouded by the large number of 'unknowns' in the table, yet social obscurity does not automatically imply that these men were from lower ranks of the family tree.

Only seven of the committeemen had any of the forms of experience relevant to this study.

Political, Administrative or Educational Experience

MP	LL	DL	HS	JP	University	Inn	Town Govt
0	0	0	4	1	5	2	0

In this respect they compare badly with the commissioners of array as, despite the committee being twice the size of the commission, there are only two more men of experience on it. The strength of the committee would lie in its possession of four ex-high sheriffs, three with experience of ship money collection.

Rutland's committee had, like the others seen so far, a firm anchor in the upper gentry but not the highest elements of society. It also drew men from much lower down the social spectrum. This is reflected in the fact that only half of them had had either higher education or a hand in pre-war county government.

Staffordshire's Committeemen

The Staffordshire committeemen are exceptional cases for several reasons. Firstly there were considerably more nominees to the committees – a total of 52. Secondly, unlike any other of the North Midland county committees, they left behind a series of minutes of their activities. Thirdly, and leading on from the last point, it is easier to assess which members were active. The numbers given here are similar to those in the analysis by Pennington and Roots, though they are not entirely the same.[208] The number deemed active is judged to be 19. Two appointees were to be royalists, five to be active elsewhere for Parliament, and no less than 26 appear to have remained aloof in one way or another. This could indicate one of two things. It may be that the relative wealth of information regarding these committees has enabled a more accurate picture of the level of activism to be made, thereby indicating that the numbers of activists given for the other counties is an overestimate. Or secondly, that the powerful tendency towards neutralism, shown by the county's attempt to raise a 'third force' as late as December 1642, led to wide-scale avoidance of involvement with the war effort. However it must be remembered that with regard to the Staffordshire commissioners of array the proportion of activists was not wildly different from other commissions in the way that the Staffordshire committee figures are different from other counties' committees. It is probable that a combination of the two above propositions is the explanation and a work dedicated to the full examination of the parliamentarian war effort, unlike this present book, would be more able to pursue this point. It does remain true that the county relied heavily upon outsiders for a lot of its initiative. Hastings was the driving force behind the royalists, at least in the early stages of the war. Sir William Brereton was the impetus behind the parliamentarian counter measures once the other outsiders – Brooke's – initiative petered out. By late 1643 it was to be the Earl of Denbigh who was to influence the parliamentarians of the county, often in opposition of Cheshire's Brereton. Denbigh was an informal presence on the committee with two others who formed part of his faction: none of these three is covered by this analysis.

The 19 activists were not of the highest social standing and in many ways form a contrast to the other committees studied. Over half of them were below the rank of esquire without including the 'unknowns'. The commissioners it will be recalled were of quite high social standing. Given this and the assertion above regarding neutralism this may be an example of what Morrill meant by his argument that fear made some men royalists and others neutrals. We may be witnessing proof here that this was the case in Staffordshire. Fear amongst the ruling county groups of the shire over the potential for social revolution drove some into active royalism, which they saw as a means of preserving their county, but, at the same time it drove more of the same group into neutralism. This left Parliament with the necessity of drawing active support from lower social groups.

Social Rank

Noble	Bart	Knight	Esq.	Gent.	Yeoman	Trade/ profession/ clergy	Unknown
0	1	0	4	6	0	2	6

If we assume that the six 'unknowns' are unidentifiable because of their social obscurity then it is clear that the Staffordshire committee is drawn heavily from the lower gentry ranks. The two men in the 'Trade…' bracket were both described as ironmongers but one had served as mayor for Stafford and thus one or both of them may have claim to 'urban gentility'. The obvious lack of social status on the committee does not entail a parallel shift down the familial scale.

Familial Status

Head	1st son	2nd son	Other son	Unknown
3	8	1	0	7

Again this may reflect the point that there must be some identifying factor which made these men out to be potential nominees. At the time the majority were chosen the war was still in its infancy and it is therefore unlikely that it was evidence of their talents in prosecuting the cause that made them candidates for committees. Probably the only mark of standing they would possess would have been their position at the top of a family hierarchy.

It was not, in all but eight cases, evidence of pre-war administrative experience which made them candidates for the committees.

Political, Administrative or Educational Experience

MP	LL	DL	HS	JP	University	Inn	Town Govt
0	0	0	0	6	4	1	

Not one of the committeemen had experience of governing Staffordshire or representing it in Parliament; the one MP was Brereton and he had represented Cheshire. This may well have had serious repercussions on the committee's ability to manage the county and will go some way towards explaining the dependence upon outsiders. It may also explain why the royalists were able to maintain control of large portions of the county right up until the end of the war.

The Staffordshire committee had the least number of members with administrative experience of the five county committees and was certainly the one composed of the lowest number of men from the higher gentry ranks and the largest proportion from the tail of the gentry and below. It shows that there may well be validity in Morrill's assertion about the fear of social disruption and revolution; the large-scale avoidance of involvement in either cause as shown in this county is reflected in the others but not to the same degree.

Before progressing to the study of the committeemen as a whole it is proposed to take the educational aspect separately. As in the case of the commissioners this will enable us to detect social connections made between the future parliamentarians and reveal any grounds for the formation of any common ideology within the group.

Education

a) The Universities

Forty-three of the committeemen deemed active went to university; 36.75 percent. This is a smaller proportion than is true of the commissioners. There may be several reasons for this. Stone mentions the possibility that there were decreasing opportunities for men of lower status to enter the universities, though this is in dispute and may not account for the lack of committeemen who had been to university. However we are concerned with a large group of lower and non-gentry and these may be a group which could not afford to attend university unless they achieved a scholarship or undertook work whilst in attendance or a group to whom university attendance was still alien and not yet accepted as part of the normal pattern of life. Whatever the cause we are faced with the fact that in what has been termed a time of 'educational revolution' a large portion of Parliament's county governors had not attended university.[209]

In the cases of those committeemen who attended Oxford, there are no significant groupings by either college or time period. Only in the years 1610–1611 were there any more than three students who were later to become committeemen present; none were at the same college. Only Magdalen had more than three student committeemen – none contemporaneously.

At Cambridge, in both 1621 and 1624, there were four men destined to become North Midland committeemen. Two of those present in 1621 were in the same college and both served on Leicestershire's committee. In 1624 three of the four contemporaries were to serve on the Nottinghamshire committee, though none was at the same college. Too much must not be read into these seeming connections. Though it is true that university was regarded as a place to establish social and economic links to be of service in later life, Cambridge may not have been the catalyst. These men were from the same counties and broadly speaking, from the same social circles, thus the university may only have been responsible for the furtherance of connections already made.

There is again little evidence to suggest the status of the student committeemen. There are only 16 cases where such a definition is possible, only one of them from Oxford. The majority, 15, were pensioners and commoners and thus financially supported by their families indicating that the majority of those who attended university were derived from committeemen at the upper end of the social scale. One was a sizar supplementing his subsistence by doing work later to be performed by the college servants. Only one, William Bendy, was registered as being of plebeian status. As in the case of the commissioners there are no scholars, men who as a result of their proven ability, were supported at the expense of the university. It was argued at the time and later by Lawrence Stone that many scholarships were being given to members of the upper gentry for favours rather than for merit. Thus it was, and is argued, that less of them were available for the lower, impecunious gentry.

It is impossible to suggest that common ideologies were formed at university, ideologies which would bind the committeemen, in later life, to the cause for which they risked themselves and their families for in the 1640s.

b) Inns of Court

Some degree of legal knowledge was considered very useful to the landowners of the seventeenth century, given that part of their life would be spent in legal wrangles over land holdings. To one involved in county government such knowledge would be of enhanced value, preventing the likelihood of falling into the pitfalls of office holding. The committeemen of the North Midlands counties were not on the whole well versed in legal knowledge. Though three of them were barristers before their appointment to the committees, only 27 (23 percent) appear to have attended the Inns of Court.

As with the study of the university experience there is little evidence to suggest that social, political or economic ties were forged at the Inns. Only in 1619 was there a group of more than three committeemen present – two each in Gray's and the Inner Temple. These may be suggestions of links being made but this is only conjecture. As with the other examinations of educational aspects of the North Midland activists, it is beyond the scope of this book to trace extra-regional connections between future royalists or parliamentarians.

Turning again to Prest's regional argument, we once more find Gray's, which he claims had a heavy northern bias, taking the largest single proportion of committeemen (10) which was also true in the case of the commissioners. Lincoln's which according to Prest would be less likely to have any members from this region – a point confirmed with regard to the commissioners – took six men who were later to become committeemen. Middle Temple with its supposed southern bias took four and Inner Temple with its Midlands bias had seven.[210]

The Committeemen of the North Midlands Counties: An Overview

Activists	117*	67.2%
Cases for which it is not possible to ascertain their behaviour	5	2.8%
Non-Activists		
a) Dead or captured before April 1643	2+	1.1%
b) Activists outside the area	11	6.2%
c) Royalists	10	5.7%
d) Passive parliamentarians or neutrals	29	16.6%
TOTAL	174	

* This allows for Lord Grey with a position on two committees.
+ This figure includes the one member thrown off a committee.

In the previous chapter it was indicated that the King made serious errors of judgement when selecting prospective commissioners of array. Parliament should have had more success; by the time the first committees were named the war had been in progress for three months and the lines of division had been drawn. Therefore, it might be expected that Parliament would be able to draw upon men who had already shown their commitment to the cause. This was, in a way, evinced when Parliament formed its Derbyshire and Nottinghamshire committees around the activists Sir John Gell and John Hutchinson. It is, at first sight, borne out by the above figures which show that 67 percent of the nominees did become activists in the area. With the addition of the activists outside the area the total is 73.4 percent as compared with only 58 percent in the case of the commissioners. The number of passive supporters or neutrals remains high at 16.6 percent but is lower than the 23.4 percent in the case of the King's nominees. Given what was said in the Staffordshire section about the possibility that the activist numbers for the other four counties may be overestimates, the number of neutrals given here may correspondingly be an underestimate. On second glance the figures do not suggest that the Parliament was as successful as it could have been in selecting its supporters; no less than 10 did become royalists. But it does remain true that Parliament's war effort was run by a larger number of people than the royalist equivalent and thus it may have, in its execution, represented a wider spectrum of views, both social and economic.

Social Rank

	Noble	Bart	Knight	Esq.	Gent.	Yeoman	Trade/ profession/ clergy	Unknown
	1	7	7	44	29	1	4	24
% of whole	0.8%	6%	6%	38%	24.8%	0.8%	3.4%	20.5%
% of known	1%	7.5%	7.5%	47%	31%	1%	4.3%	

Only just over a half of the committeemen (50.8 percent) were from the ranks of the upper gentry (esquires and above) and nobility. This contrasts with the 96.2 percent of the commissioners in the same groups. In both cases the esquire category accounts for the single largest group and also in both it is in the region of 40 percent. But with the commissioners this was, with one known exception and one 'unknown' exception, the bottom group, whereas with the committeemen there are at least 29 percent and a possible 49.5 percent below the rank of esquire. The war was something that inspired the English squirarchy into action even if it did not galvanise a like proportion of their social betters.

Returning to the committeemen, we do see that the parliamentarian war effort was staffed by men drawn from a wider social spectrum than was the royalists': either it was more attractive to, or more dependant upon, such a wider group. The royalists sought to promote the impression that they were composed of the country's natural governors – yet the statistics given in the last chapter place serious limitations of the validity of this assumption. It still remains clear that the royalists had a higher proportion of the upper strata of county society but smaller administrative bodies, perhaps as a result of the reluctance to go below the squirarchy. The membership of the committees is as far as social rank is concerned more akin to the royalist officer cadre than to the royalist administrators. This will be demonstrated in the following chapter. With respect to age, the committeemen were, on average, nine years younger than the royalist commissioners, a reversal of the position in the House of Commons and six years older than the royalist officers.

The connections between the royalist officer corps and the committeemen does not extend to familial status. There is a far greater tendency for the committeemen to be heads of families than there was for the royalist officers.

Familial Status

	Head	1st son	2nd son	Other son	Unknown
	36	29	7	8	37
% of whole	30.8%	24.8%	5.9%	6.8%	31.6%
% of whole	45%	36.25%	8.7%	10%	

If the pattern established by the identified committeemen is carried on through to the 'unknown' bracket then the propensity to be head or potential head of a family is the same in both the commissioners' and the committeemen's cases. This indicates, again, the level of commitment shown by both sides' active administrators to their respective causes. We must not let hindsight, and the knowledge that the parliamentarians won in 1646, cloud our judgement of their risk that these families were involved in when their head or first son became a committeeman.

Fifty-seven of the committeemen (48.7 percent) had some form of political, administrative or educational experience behind them when they took up their positions.

Political, Administrative and Educational Experience

	MP	LL	DL	HS	JP	University	Inn	Town Govt
	5	0	2	9	7	43	27	4
% of whole	4.3%		1.7%	7.7%	6%	36.7%	23%	3.4%

This compares poorly with the 86.5% of commissioners who had similar experience. This is not surprising given that, as has clearly been shown, the parliamentarians were drawn from a broader social spectrum thus embracing social groups which were normally barred from participation in county government. In terms of numbers, the North Midland royalists had more MPs, deputy lieutenants, high sheriffs and JPs working on their smaller commissions and proportionately more people who had attended the universities or Inns of Court. Thus we see reflected here the point that status, education and trust go hand in hand. This lack of status and experience may well have led to shortfalls in the running of the parliamentarian financial system other than those consequent upon military failures. However elements of all the forms of experience covered in this study were available to the committees, though admittedly in fewer numbers than in the case of the royalists.

The larger size of the committees would allow for a greater participation in county affairs bringing perhaps new light on the matter of local government. These two points combined suggest that the social and other deficiencies evident on the committees would not automatically make them incapable of performing their allotted task; after all, once the royalist military domination of the region was broken these very committees were able to extend their financial system to areas once the domain of the royalists.

It is to a study of their financial system that we now turn.

The Work of the Committees 1643–1646

Like the commissions of array, the county committees of the North Midlands were generally static. That of Nottinghamshire remained firmly ensconced in Nottingham Castle once the town proved to be vulnerable to royalist attacks. Derbyshire's committee stayed usually within the county town though it did sit at Chesterfield at some time. Leicestershire's likewise remained at Leicester and Staffordshire's in Stafford after the town fell to Parliament in late Spring 1643. The Rutland committee probably sat at Leicester, perhaps as an adjunct of the Leicestershire committee, until Burleigh House in Rutland was captured by Colonel Waite. In the four cases where the committees met in the county towns this grew mainly from necessity. The towns were all, to some extent, fortified and for a substantial period represented the parliamentarian's only hold on the region. It was also dangerous to venture out. Part of the Leicestershire committee was captured whilst engaged on a peripatetic session at Melton Mowbray and the same happened to part of the Derbyshire committee whilst it was at Wingerworth.[211]

The committees, like the commissions, had to deal with three main forms of revenue – excise, sequestration and assessment. There were, in addition, other financial collections of a minor nature to be dealt with. These were the levy aimed at financing the war against the Catholic rebels in Ireland and the levy towards the pay of the Scots Army once it had entered the war in January 1644. Only the major three levies will be considered here.

The Excise

For Parliament this was the second largest source of income. The first ordinance establishing the excise passed through the Lords on 22 July 1643 and came into force three days later. A central committee was established in London to which the accounts of the excise committees established in the counties were sent quarterly.[212]

The major towns where the excise was to be collected and over which Parliament had military power, were each given an excise office, open each weekday for the registration of excise goods. A register of all buyers, sellers and manufacturers of goods upon which excise was due would be held at these offices. Registration was supposed to be undertaken voluntarily by the manufacturers etc., but by September 1643 it was clear that there was, if not hostility, then certainly antipathy to doing so. A second excise ordinance was therefore passed empowering sheriffs and constables to take the registrations and collect the sums due.[213]

As was found with the royalist excise, there is little local evidence to suggest how the system operated in the North Midlands. The royalists did their best to upset markets and fairs where excise could be collected, even in the period marked by their military decline.[214] Thus receipts from the area may not have been high. However the parliamentarians did possess the four major county towns and would be able to divert several county markets to these places as the Marquis of Newcastle did at York. Certainly in Stafford, provision was made for the traders in the town's military regulations, indicating that markets were still held with some frequency.[215] It is not known how successful the parliamentarians were at holding these markets, though in Derbyshire, at least, the markets were reported to be recovering from 1644, but no trade figures are available.[216]

On a national level, though excise brought in at least £697,000 between September 1643 and February 1645, it did not cover the amounts that Parliament had borrowed, from the London merchants, on the strength of its expected income. As a result the list of goods on which excise was liable was increased to include beef, mutton, pork and veal.[217] It was these changes which provoked the anti excise riots in Derby in April 1645. During the riots, led by women, an excise commissioner was chained to the Bull Ring. Gell was unwilling or unable to prevent the rioting. Instead, seeing potential advantages, he supported the townspeople. As a result the excise was suspended for several months.[218] Gell's motive was that he required the tax for use in the county to supplement assessment revenue. By July he had therefore secured a major victory when Parliament in an attempt to quell the disturbances allowed the county to retain half of the excise income for its own use.[219] This did not, as might be expected, appease the town where antagonism to the tax remained high. The Derby incident is important; it is, apparently, the only occasion in the North Midlands that popular revulsion towards wartime financial systems ran to the extent of public demonstration. The aims of the protesters were far more specific and limited than the demands of the clubmen of the south Midlands. Their only quarrel was with the excise tax and then chiefly to its extension to meats. Regular taxation of rural property provoked no such problems in the region during the First Civil War. So it may be assumed that propertied groups within society and rural elements which possessed a limited amount of livestock on common land and thus a hedge against such extensions of excise, were content to pay their lot. On the other hand, urban groups with little or no means of supplying a part of their own food stocks were harder hit by the extension of the excise to meat and were, correspondingly, more liable to respond in the manner such as occurred in Derby. If a detailed study could be made of the Derby rioters, we would be able to say more about the link between rural passivity and urban activity. If the Derby rioters were not property owners or those who only had a limited property stake, then it would identify them as the social group most hostile to wartime taxation. Those manufacturers whose produce had been assessed for the excise and had only registered passive opposition to the tax, by their reluctance to register voluntarily, had, by their subsequent acquiescence, revealed that they were capable of bearing the expense. The rioters were, it appears, therefore, a different group and a different case.

Unfortunately, as indicated, we cannot discern the financial success or otherwise of the excise system. Clearly it cannot have been as provident as it was in the counties of East Anglia or Kent which were dominated by Parliament throughout the First Civil War. However, income from the tax would have increased and gone on increasing from mid 1644, despite royalist attempts to hinder the markets. Even though nationally it proved to be an important source of income for Parliament, excise proved in the North Midlands that it was a potential cause of discontent far and above either contribution or assessment, or even both.

Sequestration

Towards the end of March 1643 Parliament formalised the seizure of estates and incomes of those whom it regarded as delinquent.[220] First on their list came the bishops and they were followed by anyone in arms against Parliament or who had, or were to, contribute money to the King's forces. Also included were those involved in royalist tax collection. This was a less comprehensive statement of requisites of delinquency than the royalist sequestration order discussed in the previous chapter. It did not, for example, consider as delinquent tenants who had handed their rents to royalist sequestrators, unlike the royalists who would have done so had the tenants handed money to parliamentarian sequestrators.[221] Money from the sequestration of estates – which involved the confiscation of lands, property and rents, minus a subsistence allowance to delinquents' families – was to go straight to the London coffers for the finance of the army. The ordinance named a committee of sequestrators, with a quorum of only two, for each county. The membership was, in general, derived from the membership of the committees already established within those counties. Nationally the committees for sequestration only appear to have been of limited success.

The regulations regarding their operations were tightened up in May 1644, particularly with respect to the percentage of the income which committees were allowed to rake off, to cover expenses.[222] Wheeler estimates that the national income from Sequestration was around £200,000 per annum.[223] Unfortunately there are no specific figures relating to the North Midlands.

Not all the sequestration money reached London – counties used some of the money to finance their own needs. In many counties this was eventually recognised as legitimate by London. Composition, the fine paid by delinquents who agreed to abide by the rules of Parliament to have their estates freed from sequestration, was also intended to be paid to London. Initially, compounders were expected to travel to London to settle the composition fee. Nevertheless, in some cases, composition was settled in the counties and fines collected and used in the county. Staffordshire was a case in point – the composition book still survives.[224] In it details are given of the sums paid by prominent North Midlands royalists such as (Colonel) Rowland Eyre, Walter Wrottesley and the Bagot family.

Within the North Midland counties, the ability of the parliamentarians to collect sequestration would follow a pattern inverse to that of the royalists. That is to say their ability to sequestrate would have been at its lowest ebb in late 1643 and early 1644. Then as royalist power declined the parliamentarians would be able to begin a more comprehensive sequestration of royalist estates. By the conclusion of the war the estates of at least 130 royalist activists within the North Midlands were under sequestration. In addition there were far greater numbers of neutrals or passive royalists whose estates were also under sequestration. Some of the royalist activists managed to free their estates from devastating sequestration in return for surrendering garrisons; Hastings himself was one example.[225]

Despite the general lack of information regarding the day to day running of the parliamentarian sequestration procedure, some details can be ascertained. Derbyshire's sequestrators were operating in April 1644 and were hoping to collect money from the estates of Francis Revell despite the fact that one of his estates was close to the royalist garrison at Wingfield Manor.[226]

With the estate of Robert Waring at Clapton Hill in Nottinghamshire, the sequestrators were in receipt of the rents as they were being paid to Gervase Clifton, one of the Sequestration committee, in 1644.[227] Lists of those who compounded are contained in the Calendars of the Committee for Compounding as referred to in a previous endnote. Administration of sequestration in Staffordshire formed, in the words of Pennington and Roots, 'one of the most arduous duties of the Committee and its officials'.[228] The order book in the William Salt Library, clearly indicates that a committee had to accept, in some cases, that rents could not be collected from sequestered estates even by August 1644.[229] Occasionally they were able, as were the Derby committee, to gain the rents from the majority of a royalist's tenants as was the case with Sir Charles Cavendish's estates at Barleston.[230] It is probable that in the other counties of the region it would be as true as it was in the case of Staffordshire, that the establishment of the Committee of Compounding at Goldsmiths' Hall in London would deprive the counties of income they

Wingfield Manor, held by the royalists in Derbyshire from 1643 until 1644. (By Pahazzard. Own work, CC BY-SA 3.0 <https://commons.wikimedia.org/w/index.php?curid=15024698>)

had come to expect and depend upon, from their indigenous delinquent population. This would not, in the estimation of Pennington and Roots, be fully ameliorated by the agreements made with Goldsmiths' for the retention of a portion of the composition fine. As Staffordshire was only allowed to retain £3,000 of such money and the 25 commissioners of array for the region whose precise composition fines are known paid around £16,000 between them, the loss to the local parliamentarians can be gauged as substantia1.[231]

Weekly Assessment

Originally conceived and passed by Parliament as a temporary expedient subject to renewal, the weekly assessment became the largest source of income which Parliament had. Over £1,100,000 was collected as weekly pay between February 1643 and October 1646. For the last 20 months the tax was known as the Monthly Tax and had yielded the largest part of the total sum. The Monthly Tax was aimed at covering the costs of the new Model Army, and its collection indicates Parliament's growing control over the counties.[232]

In February 1643 the weekly assessment for the five North Midland counties was listed as follows; Derbyshire, £175; Nottinghamshire, £187-10s; Leicestershire, £187-10s; Rutland, £62-10s; and Staffordshire, £212-10s.

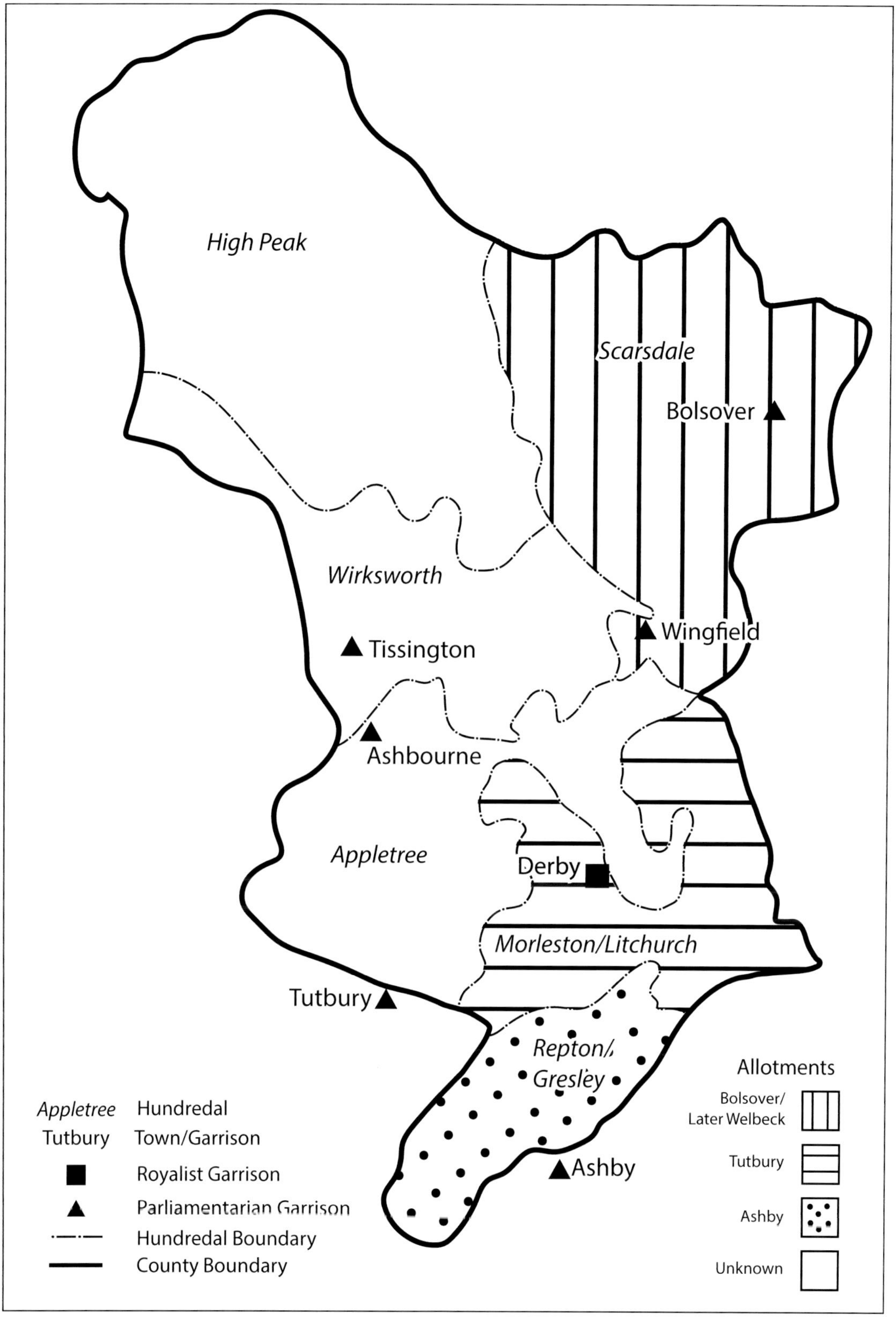

Map 1 Hundredal Allotment of Contribution in Derbyshire.

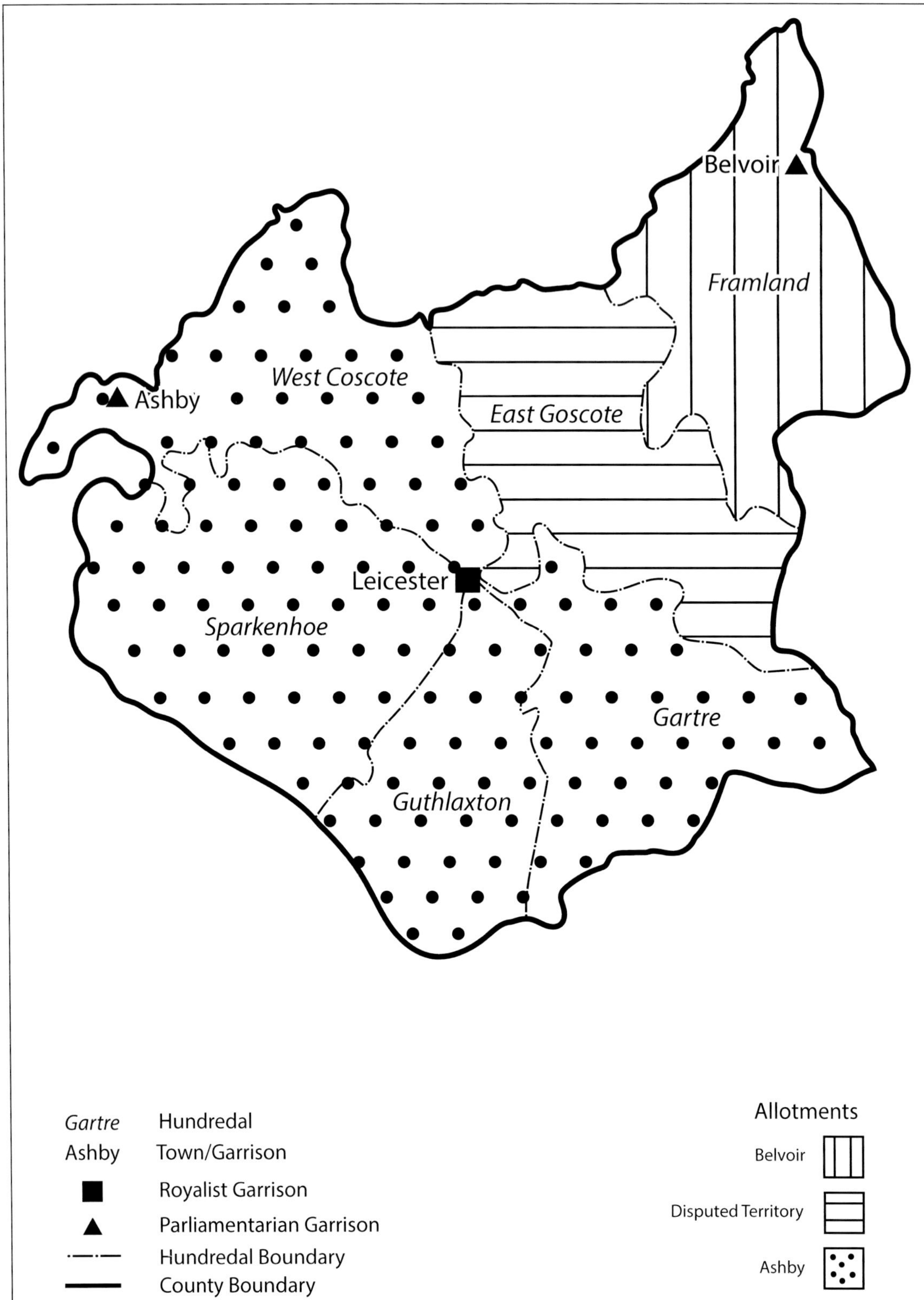

Map 2 Hundredal Allotment of Contribution in Leicestershire.

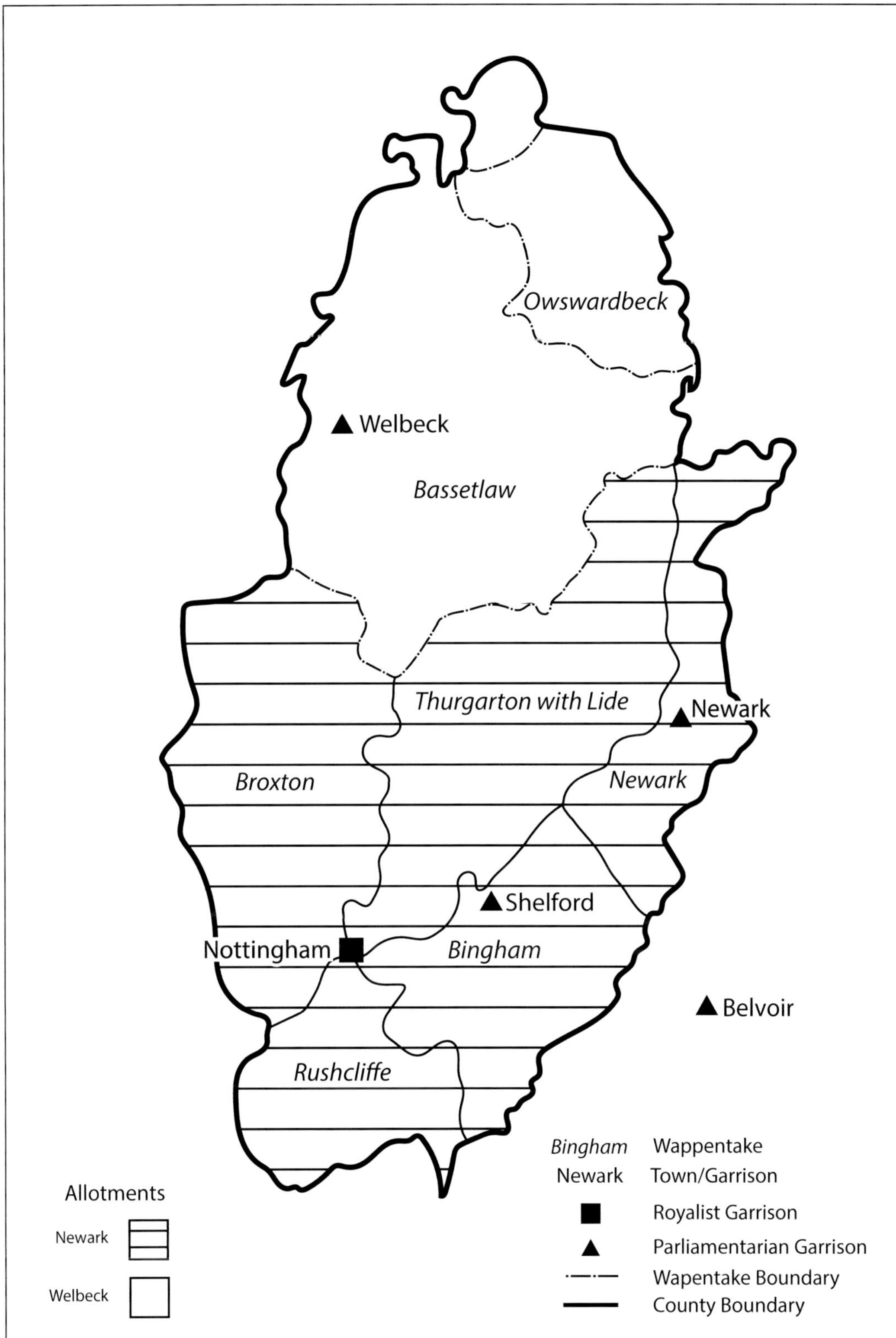

Map 3 Hundredal/Wapentake Allotment of Contribution in Nottinghamshire.

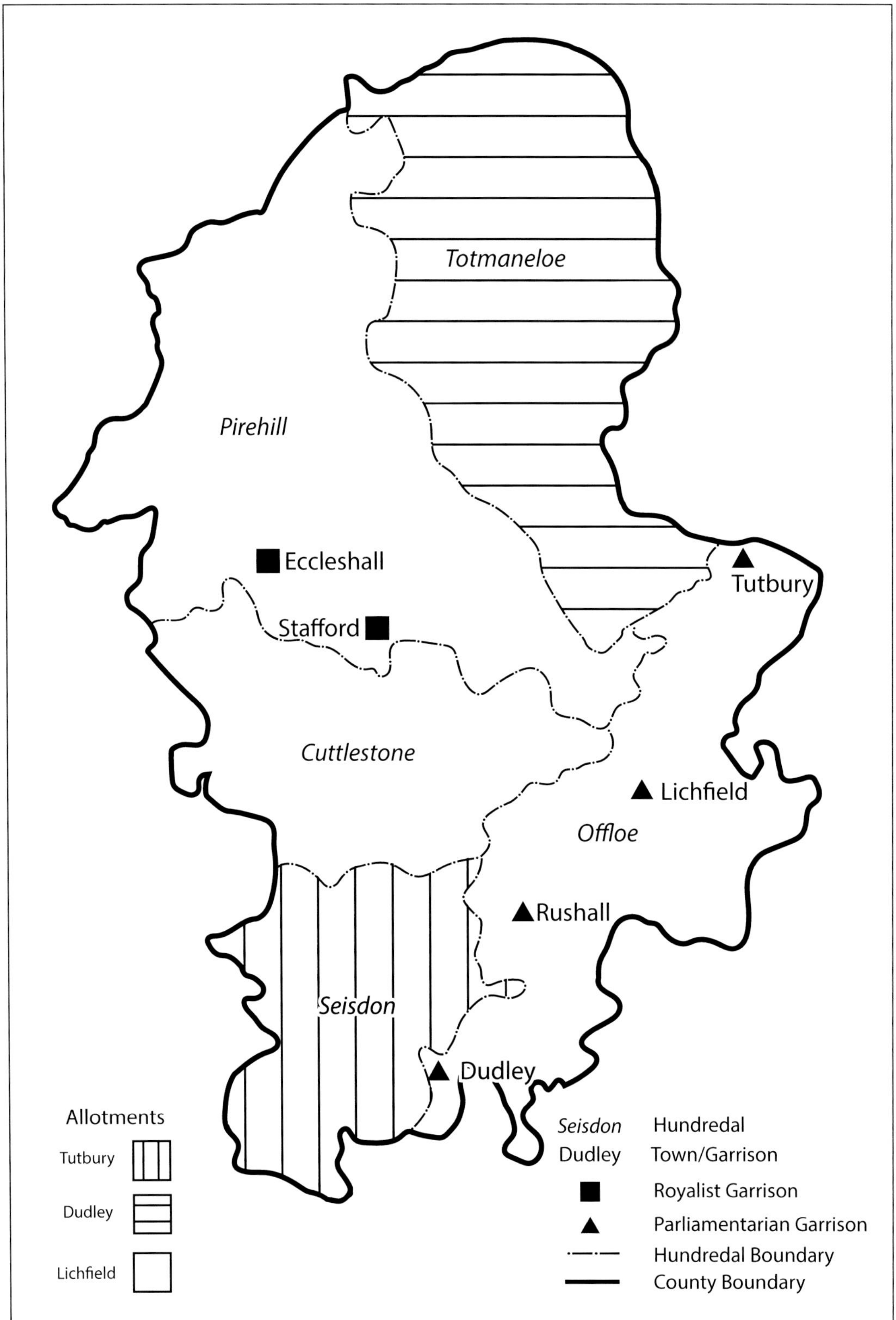

Map 4 Hundredal Allotment of Contribution in Staffordshire.

None of these sums was particularly high; Devon, for example, was charged with £1,800 a week, Shropshire with £375 and Warwickshire with £562-10s.[233] These values were based on an earlier general assessment aimed at raising £400,000 nationally. In the case of Derbyshire the sum represented three times the annual sum collected for ship money in the 1630s.[234] The setting of an overall rate for the counties left the responsibility for dividing the counties into districts and appointing collectors for the levy up to the Sequestration committees created in the ordinance.

As with the royalist case, the exact methods involved in the process of assessment collection at county level are hard to define. Again the constables' accounts are of great value especially when used alongside the Staffordshire order book – the most detailed document regarding administration in the North Midlands. Central government had indicated the items upon which the assessment levy was to be based: these included property such as plate, cattle and land and income such as rents annuities and tithes. It was therefore a combination of an income tax and a property tax similar to that which the royalists were collecting.

Basically, the system of collection operated by Parliament was the same as that used by the royalists. Constables, called to meetings with the committees, or in receipt of warrants from them, were to assess the individual contributions of the inhabitants of their communities. Again, as described in the previous chapter, this would be done at meetings of 'neighbours'. It is probable that in cases where the village was already paying to the royalists the parliamentarians would charge approximately the same amount. This is evident in many of the sets of constables' accounts still in existence and may be true elsewhere.

Parliament enabled committees to divide counties into sections to facilitate collections. In practice this seems to have followed the same pattern as the royalists used: that is, making indigenous garrisons responsible for assessment collections within their own area. The small garrison at Lapley House, whilst it was in parliamentarian hands, was to collect the £8-13s-7d from the four villages and parishes surrounding it. However the garrison was to deduct its own requirements from this and send the residue with receipts to Stafford. Similarly, the 40- strong garrison at Carswell House was collecting the local assessment and, in the case of non-payment, was empowered to distrain cattle.[235] Organisation in Staffordshire reached, in theory, an advanced stage with Totmansloe being assigned to Colonel Bowyer, Cuttlestone and Pirehill Hundreds' assessments to be used solely for the pay of the county's foot and Seisdon and Offlow Hundreds' for the horse.[236] The degree to which the royalists were prepared to ignore county boundaries in ascribing contribution allocations was only, it would appear, achieved temporarily by their enemies in Staffordshire. In 1644, parts of Offlow Hundred had been given to Warwickshire commanders, but the Earl of Denbigh and the Staffordshire committee revoked the agreement in the October of the same year.[237] Pennington and Roots have correctly detected that the system in the county was not as sound in practice as it appeared. Denbigh interfered with the allocations of territory made before his arrival in the county just as Charles tinkered with the royalists' allocations. Thus some garrisons were left unpaid or in arrears like the forces at Leek: this necessitated the collection of supplementary assessments.[238] Royalist domination of large parts of the county, outlined in the last chapter, would make the above ascriptions of hundredal allotments mere wishful thinking for a significant part of the war.

By mid 1644 the parliamentarians were, in many places, beginning to make incursions into royalist areas. At Waltham on the Wolds in Leicestershire, 'Lord Grey's tax' was first paid in mid 1644: £4-6s-0d was collected towards an annual total of £68.[239] It was paid sporadically from then until the following year when payments became more regular. The same is true of Branston also in Leicestershire, where in mid 1644 the constable was summoned to Melton Mowbray to meet members of the committee and learn of the assessment charges. After this occasion, the tax became steadily more regular until by the end of 1645 the majority, though not all, of the village's tax payments were made to the parliamentarians. In both these cases, the communities were contributing to both war efforts until the close of 1645.[240] From mid 1644 to the end of the following year, the village's constable had to collect payments for both sides from his neighbours. In Staffordshire the classic example of assessment collection is Mavesyn Ridware. Here Henry Lowe, the constable, was faced with collections of taxes for both sides for a period of six months beginning in February 1644. In this case the assessment is clearly shown as being collected both as cash and as receipted goods. The amounts of both were slightly lower than the royalist contribution payments Lowe was making. The period's totals are, £46-11s-0d for the contribution and £41-3s-10d for the assessment. This small disparity reveals that the figures given by Joyce Malcolm suggesting that the sums levied on counties by royalists were up to 74 percent higher than those charged by Parliament, conceal a large number of disparities and thus obscure the true state of affairs.[241] Parliament was not able to control fully the region until the last of the royalist garrisons had surrendered. Places like Uttoxeter were still paying money to the royalists on a sporadic basis until the very last weeks of the war.[242]

Though there is less evidence of parliamentary taxation contained in the constables' accounts for the region and therefore no chance of judging the county totals for figures contained therein, other clues do exist – at least for Staffordshire. Pennington and Roots show that the county's treasurer, Robert Wilmot, only recorded the receipt of £1,321-6s-5d from county assessment. The vast majority was being spent in situ by the garrison commanders without the money ever passing through the hands of the county committee. Captain Foxal, whose company was based at Stafford, himself collected £2,840-12s-10d in assessments from villages allotted to him. His disbursements and short fall in his company's pay exceeded this sum by £404-10s-10d.[243] From this example alone it is easy to see why Wilmot only received what he did and why Staffordshire and Nottinghamshire were excluded from the original New Model ordinance which established the Monthly Pay. Income from such counties excluded because of the impossibility of guaranteeing an income from them, was to be used to pay debts already incurred by Parliament. This policy was an attempt to base the New Model's pay on a firm and dependable source in order to secure regular payment of the soldiers.[244]

Weekly Assessment or the Monthly Pay which succeeded it was, in concept and practice, similar to the royalists' contribution. Both were essentially property taxes and both were collected by constables – traditional elements of county government. In addition both taxes were collected initially by local garrisons for their own use, within an overall framework based upon hundredal or wapentakal boundaries. As contribution collection declined it was superseded by the expansion of the assessment collection. It may be as true for assessment as it was for the contribution that though it was a major source of income, it failed to cover fully the cost of the war.

The Association of Counties

Parliament associated four of the North Midlands counties – Derbyshire, Nottinghamshire, Leicestershire and Rutland – with Northamptonshire, Bedfordshire, Buckinghamshire and Huntingdonshire, on 15 December, 1642. Staffordshire was associated with Warwickshire on 31 December. The former association was under Lord Grey, the latter under Lord Brooke.[245] As to the military operations in the counties, these are covered in chapters 5 and 6 and there is little need to go into detail here; only a brief outline is necessary.

Brooke's attempt to gain military control over the counties he commanded came to an end with his death at the siege of Lichfield in March 1643 after he had conquered Warwickshire. Even his success in that county was to be short lived. The Earl of Northampton's march through the county, on his way to help Hastings recoup his losses in Staffordshire, saw the abandonment of many of the garrisons established by Brooke. As a result of work by Hastings with help from Northampton and then Rupert, Staffordshire was generally under royalist control from this period until the decline of royalist power throughout the region after the middle of 1644. The gains made by the parliamentarians within the county, the capture of Stafford, Eccleshall and other minor garrisons, were due to the intervention of Sir William Brereton and his Cheshire/Lancashire forces, not through the county's association with Warwickshire.

The association was given new life with the appointment of Lord Denbigh in mid 1643; but due to his being investigated for suspected royalism, he was not able to take the field until March 1644. His command also included Shropshire and Worcestershire.[246] Denbigh's military intervention did not see a wholesale conquest of Staffordshire and indeed it led to division within the county committee.[247] The struggle for control of Stafford between Brereton and Denbigh continued even after Denbigh left the county's military affairs in July 1644. It is covered in detail by Pennington and Roots and by R.N. Dore in his edition of Brereton's letters. For the purpose of this book suffice to say that though Denbigh continued to interfere in county affairs it was Brereton who became the dominant figure.[248] It was to Brereton that the major garrisons of Tutbury, Lichfield and Dudley fell in 1646. Thus Staffordshire's history in the First Civil War is dominated not by its ties with counties in the south Midlands, with which it was formally associated, but by the military prominence of Brereton and his forces from Cheshire and the west Midlands.

The first test for Lord Grey's association was the abortive siege of Ashby in January 1643. Grey's abandonment of the siege prompted the Derbyshire faction to accuse him of being a faintheart. This was simply a reflection of their dissatisfaction with the result of the campaign, as Hastings based at Ashby was a very potent threat to south Derbyshire over which he had already, temporarily, been able to assert some control and was likely to be capable of doing so again.[249] In the following months the two failures to capture Newark and the Association's inability to prevent the march of the Queen's army through the region on its way southward, led to the decline of Grey's authority. Sir John Meldrum, the Scots professional soldier, became the effective leader of the Association's soldiers until his and their defeat at Newark in March 1644. Grey's nominal command was finally at an end and the Association broke up, when Nottinghamshire and Derbyshire were added to the Northern Association after Marston Moor and the Leicestershire area became subject to Rossiter's command in Lincolnshire. Even so, it was both Leicestershire and Derbyshire forces which together attacked and captured Wilne Ferry in July 1644 and the committees of the two counties who jointly established the garrison at Coleorton to watch Ashby-de-la-Zouch in November 1644.[250]

Cooperation between Derby's and Nottingham's committees was evident from the very commencement of the war. It was with Gell's help that John Hutchinson was able to establish Nottingham as a parliamentarian garrison. Gell's troops were also responsible for saving Nottingham from the pressure of Newark's attempt to establish a permanent garrison on the Trent, only a mile from the town.[251] However relations were not always cordial. As early as January 1644, the Nottinghamshire committee accused their Derbyshire colleagues of collecting horses from the Stapleford area. Derby replied, being in 'wonder of men making title to wisdom' as to why such an accusation could be made in the knowledge that Nottingham troops were quartered in Derbyshire and collecting horses from there. Gell, Gresley and the rest of the committee quite rightly suggested that Hutchinson confine himself to fighting the Newark royalists. The dispute resurfaced in the late summer when the Nottinghamshire committee again accused the Derbyshire men of levying horses in the Mansfield area.[252] It can be said, that between the parliamentarian administrators there was as much rivalry and conflict as there was amongst their royalist counterparts – largely due to Grey's ineffective leadership and the resultant lack of positive direction to the Association.

Strange Bedfellows: The Two Administrations

For the entire period of the First Civil War the rival administrations worked side by side. The general pattern of royalist supremacy and subsequent decline and the parliamentarians' struggle to achieve their own supremacy and victory will be explored in detail later. As the royalists lost the ability to gain regular taxes from the communities the parliamentarians were able to take them over. For a time in many cases both sides obtained income from the same place. There must have been some element of 'turning a blind eye'. It cannot be true that either side remained ignorant of the constables' duplicity in the double taxed communities. Constables were arrested or displaced. Hastings arrested one at Lutterworth and the committee at Stafford arrested several during the war. However it may be that in these instances the constables were politically motivated, guilty of not only handling enemy warrants and tax, but also of neglecting to put into effect those that Hastings or the committee wanted them to. For the others their ability to handle both levies meant survival – of sorts. The office of constable was made onerous by the Civil War and, like that of sheriff, one to be avoided if possible. It is no surprise that the constable of Branston for 1645, John Worsdale, wrote at the end of the accounts for his year of office:

> Mount not up to the place of honour for prosperity is more dangerous than adversity and more perish at the right hand of prosperity than on the right hand of low and poor degree.'[253]

However, there are excellent examples of a live and let live approach to the matter of coexistence. In 1644, the inhabitants of the Nottinghamshire portion of the Vale of Belvoir petitioned the Newark royalists and the Nottingham parliamentarians regarding the number of horses that each side was taking from the area. In reply, both parties made some attempt to agree on a joint policy on horse collection. Nottingham suggested that no more than one horse in four or five be taken from its owner. The bilateral agreement was never finalised due to mutual distrust when planning the necessary joint meeting - however, the very fact that it was considered is important in itself.[254]

When the royalist garrison at Welbeck surrendered in November 1645, after Colonel Freshville had held it for some months, the garrison was in arrears. In recognition of this the Derbyshire committee agreed, as part of the surrender terms, that the contribution due to the garrison from Scarsdale Hundred, be collected and paid over by Lieutenant Colonel Thomas Gell.[255]

What the incidents illustrate is part and parcel of the attitude which the commissioners of array, and to some extent the committeemen, had towards their communities. The two bodies appear to have been reluctant to overburden the counties in which they after all had some stake. Thus it may be seen that the leisurely approach to prosecuting the war, evidenced in ignoring the fact that constables were playing a double game, attempting to make bilateral agreements and paying enemy arrears even when their own soldiers were underpaid and when victory was certain, is just an extension of this. It is a recognition perhaps of the fact that the war was not being fought in some foreign country which could be left, after the war, to sort out its own problems as the combatants returned home. In the Midlands, at least, the conduct of the war seems to have been tempered by the desire to protect the homelands. In this region and perhaps in other parts of England, it was not a war fought as Ian Roy and others may suggest, in the manner of the war on the Continent. It was not a case of England turned Germany.[256]

The Parliamentarian War Effort: A Conclusion

The system was very similar to that employed by the region's royalists. However, it was run by men of a markedly lower social status and of lower administrative experience. These factors partially explain the committees' inability to exercise their system in late 1643 and early 1644. It is the royalists' overwhelming military supremacy during this period which is the overriding factor in this. By the end of the war Parliament's system was being run as efficiently, if not more so, as the royalists had run theirs. The parliamentarian war effort in this area was dependant upon outside military intervention. Though Gell, Hutchinson, Waite and to some extent Lord Grey and his successors at Leicester, were indefatigable in their attempts to maintain pockets of resistance, their eventual victory was due to outside help. Gell lost Derbyshire during 1643; it was returned to him by the Earl of Manchester in the summer of 1644. When the King entered the county in the summer of the following year, Gell was unable to prevent the royalists resurrecting part of their financial administration. Hutchinson never conquered Nottinghamshire: this was left to first Manchester and then to the Scots. Royalist Staffordshire fell to Brereton, not to the forces of the county committee. Leicestershire was plagued by royalists right up until the end of the war despite the committee being able to take advantage in their enemy's internal strife. The failure of the royalists, shown in chapters 5 and 6, to capture any of the county towns before 1645, left the hardy parliamentarians with bases from which to run their war effort once the tide had turned. Therefore we must conclude that the parliamentarian war effort could only be established and run, with any measure of success, when military supremacy was achieved. It does not appear that, in the North Midlands, Parliament was capable of making such an achievement possible in the way that the royalist war effort had done.

Chapter 4

The North Midlands Army

In recent years there has been growing interest in the composition of the royalist armies of the First Civil War. The Oxford Field Army has been examined by Ian Roy, the army in the west by Malcolm Wanklyn and the Northern Army by Peter Newman.[257] The armies involved in various campaigns have been noted and studied in many published monographs.[258] The personnel of the officer corps of several armies have been listed in some of the above; biographies of major characters have been produced and the biographical dictionary of over 1,600 royalist field officers has been a welcome addition to the subject area.[259] The officer corps have also been subjected to statistical analyses by Peter Newman and others, notably Dr D.G. Blackwood who incorporated his study in his work on Lancashire.[260] Until now none of this treatment has been accorded to the North Midlands Army, though most of its field officers were covered in the biographical dictionary and other work by Newman.[261] Indeed, apart from some brief acknowledgements, its existence as an army is largely ignored. Ian Roy referred to it as a 'Flying Army' in his work on the royalist ordnance papers and Peter Young has occasionally referred to Hastings' army in passing. In general, however, works dealing with specific geographical areas have skirted around this region.[262] Ronald Hutton deals with Staffordshire, considering it as an appendage of the Marcher counties, and Peter Newman establishes that 'they are North Midland shires and few of their regiments played any part in the Civil War in the six northern counties', thus they play no part in his thesis.[263] On the other hand officers of the Derbyshire regiments have been identified by J.T. Brighton, but this is a work concerned with that county alone and mentions this 'ephemeral' army only in passing.[264] It is a major contention of this book that such an army did exist and that it played an important role in the war. References to it and some of its officers, do appear in general works when it, and they, played a part in what are considered central events'. But doing so was only part of its role, a role which is fully dealt with in chapters 5 and 6. In order that it be allowed to take its place amongst the other royalist armies which have been studied, it is necessary to recreate it with a regiment by regiment study; these regiments will be analysed if possible with respect to their size, their military record and their eligibility for inclusion in this army. Following the regimental breakdown, the officer corps will be analysed along the lines adopted for the commissioners and committeemen. This will not be a list of officers – such is left to Appendix III.

It is hoped that by the conclusion of this chapter the character of the North Midlands Army will be established. It will be seen that for a major part of the war it was not simply a collection of isolated guerrilla bands as it appears to be in several of the works referred to in Chapter 1. Instead it will be shown that from spring 1643, but particularly from the following Autumn, until October 1644, it was more a sort of field army, which embodied Napoleon's maxim of a century and a half later that an army should divide up to survive, yet unite to fight. Its division into various garrisons enabled it to live off local resources gathered in the manner described in Chapter 2, but occasionally some or all of it could and would unite to participate in several major field operations.

The Regiments of the North Midlands Army

In order that the structure of the regiments described below can be seen in relation to general military establishments common in seventeenth century England, it is necessary to look briefly at the sizes of various forms of regiments.

Foot Regiments

Ideally these would be composed of 1,300 men. Each regiment would be divided into 10 companies not of equal strength. The three field officers in a regiment each had companies which, in their absence, were commanded by captains lieutenant. The colonel's company was 200 strong, the lieutenant colonel's 150, and the (sergeant) major's 140. The seven captains each had companies of 100 men. Regiments would, in addition, have a surgeon, a chaplain, a quartermaster and other individuals. Foot regiments in the North Midlands Army did not, as will be seen below, reach full strength.

Horse Regiments

Regiments would, in theory, consist of around 500 men, in six troops, each troop having around 60 troopers and several officers. The field officers again each commanded troops, looked after in their absence by captains lieutenant; these troops were the same size as those of the captains'. Though regiments in the North Midlands Army consisted of six, seven or even eight troops these were often undersize, in some cases with as few as 20 men.

Dragoon Regiments

These tended to vary in size but were organised along the same lines as the foot, being in companies. Dragoons suffered from the stringencies of the times. In good times they had mounts – though not usually of the highest calibre. In bad, they marched and fought as foot; they were in any case simply mounted foot soldiers and thus accorded less pay than horse soldiers. It is probable that in the North Midlands Army as in Hopton's forces in the south-west, dragoon regiments were in effect the size of a single troop and attached to regiments of Horse.

Artillery

Unfortunately no substantial information regarding the artillery used by the North Midlands Army has come to light. Certainly nothing is known of its organisation or numbers. As a result it cannot be dealt with in this chapter. When the numbers of guns for a specific period are known, they are dealt with in the relevant parts of chapters 5 and 6.

The regiments belonging to this army are here listed by county of origin; they will be examined in turn in this order.

Colonel	Type(s) of Regiments Commanded		
Leicestershire			
Henry Hastings (Lord Loughborough's)	Horse	Foot	Dragoons
William Nevill	Horse	Foot	
John Pate	Horse		
Derbyshire			
Rowland Eyre	Horse	Foot	Dragoons
Sir John Fitzherbert	Horse	Foot	
John Freshville	Horse	Foot	
Sir John Harpur	Horse	Foot	Dragoons
John Milward/John Shalcross	Horse	Foot	
Sir Andrew Kniveton	Horse	Foot	
Roger Molyneux (also raised in Notts. and Lincs.)	Horse	Foot	
Ferdinando Stanhope/John Barnard (also raised in Notts.)	Horse	Foot	
Nottinghamshire			
Isham Parkins	Horse	Foot	
Staffordshire			
Richard/Harvey Bagot	Horse	Foot	Dragoons
John Lane	Horse		
Thomas Leveson	Horse	Foot	
Devereaux Wolseley	Horse	Foot	
Lincolnshire			
Gervase Lucas (also raised in Leics.)	Horse	Foot	
Regiments which are associated with the North Midlands and which may have been a part of the army			
Sir John Corbet		Foot	
Francis Wortley/Dud Dudley			Dragoons
Christopher Roper (may only be part of Hastings')		Foot	

Though some of these regiments were raised by commissioners of array, Hastings', Fitzherbert's and Harpur's being examples, they were not generally, with perhaps the exception of both Eyre's and Stanhope's foot, men raised as a result of the work of the commissions. Instead, they were raised as outlined in Chapter 2, by virtue of commissions issued to the colonels as individuals once it became clear that the commissions of array were largely unsuccessful at what had been their primary task. Any soldiers raised by these bodies after the beginning of 1643 were incorporated into the regiments already in existence.

Henry Hastings' (Lord Loughborough's) Regiments of Horse, Foot and Dragoons

The Horse was originally raised in August 1642 by virtue of a warrant to raise 400 men.[265] They were reputed to have fought at Powick Bridge and Edgehill; parliamentarian observers suggest that there were eight troops including that of the colonel. This estimate may in part be fanciful as only two of the officers named in the estimation appear subsequently as officers in the regiment.[266] Hastings led the regiment north from Oxford with the power to raise a further 500 dragoons.[267] During December 1642, he was recruiting in Worcestershire and Shropshire; these recruits and those he had raised earlier may have given him around 300 horse by the end of the month.[268] However, during the siege of Ashby in January 1643, Hastings was reported to have 500 horse and foot in the castle and may have sent some out of the way before the siege began. By February he could muster 700 horse, in 15 troops. Some of these troops could have been the embryo regiments of Pate, Harpur or Wolseley.[269] There may also have been dragoons counted amongst these numbers for in Cheshire later that month Hastings certainly had some dragoons.[270] Therefore Hastings' own regiment was potentially a full-size unit during 1643 and part of 1644. Certainly no less than thirty-one troop captains can be traced as having served, or claimed to have served, in the regiment at some time during the war.

After the middle of 1644 the size of the regiment appears to have declined. Only 100 men from it were attached to the King's field army in May 1645, although as Symonds indicated that this represented only three troops it is possible that this was only a portion of the regiment.[271] At the surrender of Ashby in February 1646, there were three of the troop commanders present whilst the lieutenant colonel was absent with 100 men and there were also sections of the regiment still stationed at Newark.[272] As there is only one captain's name which can be traced for the dragoons, it is possible that this unit was of troop size and generally attached to the horse.

The foot regiment was also, perhaps, recruited in Worcestershire and Shropshire as well as in Leicestershire. Hastings was provided with munitions for musketeers before he left Oxford in December 1642.[273] Gell heard that there were 300 foot in the castle at Ashby by the end of the year.[274] The names of 12 captains can be traced for the regiment. It is possible that there were as many as seven of them serving at any one time. There appear to have been two majors, Robert Bonney who was transferred and promoted to lieutenant colonel of Milward's Foot and Christopher Roper who replaced him in late 1643. Roper appears to have been promoted to a colonelcy by the end of the war; this may have involved his assuming command over part of Hastings' regiment. The estimate of 400 men which Hastings was said to have at his attempted relief of Eccleshall Castle, along with soldiers he may have had to leave at Ashby, would seem to suggest that the regiment was around 500 strong, about the usual size of a large royalist regiment.[275]

It is certain that Hastings' regiments were amongst the largest in this army. It would appear that these regiments acted as a kind of training school for officers as a number of men like Major Barnabas Scudamore, who became a colonel and later governor of Hereford, and Captain Sigismund Beeton, who also reached the rank of colonel and governed Welbeck, were to progress to high command. Many sections of the regiments served in other garrisons or became small garrisons away from Ashby. Major Hacker and Captains Gregory and Archer took their troops to Newark in 1644. These probably formed the garrison on the river Trent set up a mile from Nottingham on two occasions, with Hacker as governor. At least one and probably two of the Captains Robinson were, with their companies, stationed at one of the small forts established on the river Trent; there were three companies in all at the Wilne Ferry garrison – a total of 70 men.[276]

It was an experienced trio of regiment. Parts of them had fought at Powick Bridge, Edgehill, Hopton Heath, the capture of Lichfield, the relief of Eccleshall, the battle of Cotes, the relief of Newark and the capture of Leicester in addition to the numerous small skirmishes around the region.

William Nevill's Regiments of Horse and Foot

On 28 December 1642, Henry Nevill of Holt began to raise soldiers to defend the south Leicestershire/Northamptonshire area from the local parliamentarians.[277] Within three weeks he had fortified his house at Holt and established his regiments as a garrison. On or about 21 January it was attacked by Lord Grey; Nevill was captured and sent as prisoner to London.[278] Evidently parts of the regiments had escaped and were taken over by Nevill's eldest son William with the second son Thomas as lieutenant colonel. One of the brothers had served as a captain in Hastings' Horse in the summer of 1642. The regiments were with Hastings' forces when they were seen by Richard Symonds, yet it may be that they served at Belvoir and/or Newark at some time during the war. At the surrender of Ashby Castle the regiment of horse was present.[279] The officers of the regiments came from the three counties of Northamptonshire, Lincolnshire and Leicestershire and may thereby reflect the area in which the soldiers were recruited. There are no known figures regarding the size of the regiments. However, there appears to have been one major, one captain and two captains lieutenant, which incorporating the brothers Nevill gives a total of four troops. If these were small units as were other troops of horse in the army, there may have been only around 100 to 120 troopers. There may have been as many as five companies of foot, perhaps a maximum of 200 men.

John Pate's Regiment of Horse

Pate's regiment was probably raised in 1642, though as Hastings' lieutenant colonel William Bale was transferred to Pate's it may have been younger than Hastings' horse. However the transfer of Bale cannot be dated; it thus may have been in 1643 when Pate's regiment served at Belvoir. Hastings apparently used Bale as a form of spy to watch over Lucas at Belvoir whom he did not trust. When Symonds made his list of the regiment there were seven troops, but only one of the four captains appears on the list of indigent officers.[280] As with the previous regiments no numerical evidence is given. With seven troops it was probably between 140 and 200 strong if its troop sizes were similar to other North Midland Army regiments. The men like their officers were possibly raised in Leicestershire and Lincolnshire. This regiment may have formed part of the large number of horse with which Hastings is accredited in early 1643. One of the captains was at the surrender of Ashby but as it would appear the regiment had been at the surrender of Belvoir, four weeks earlier) the regiment was not usually stationed there. Pate himself seems to have gone straight on to Lichfield from Belvoir.[281]

Rowland Eyre's Regiments of Horse, Foot and Dragoons

Eyre was one of the six colonels commanding the Derbyshire forces in the Autumn of 1643, and the regiments were raised then and during the early part of the following year.[282] The regiments formed the garrisons of Chatsworth House and Hassop. Milward's regiments were also at Chatsworth. It is possible that the foot of both colonels was raised by the county's commission of array; Hastings described them as array men and believed that, as such, they were unreliable. Eyre's foot may have had as many as five companies but each only numbering around 20 men. When he and Milward led their men north in 1644 they only had 220 men between them; Milward appears to have had six companies.[283] It is possible that Eyre's foot were severely mauled at Marston Moor and the regiment may not have been reformed afterwards.

The horse seems to have had five troops and were perhaps about the same strength. On the field at Marston Moor they were teamed up with Milward's horse. Unlike the foot they would have had some measure of success at the battle and may have escaped reasonably intact. But on their return most of the regiment was captured at Boyleston in August 1644. Eyre and those that remained made their home at Newark and were part of the Newark Horse at Naseby. Nevertheless the regiments were included by Symonds in his list of Hastings' army in 1644. The dragoons appear to have been in one troop under Captain Tunstead.

Sir John Fitzherbert's Regiments of Horse and Foot

When Symonds listed these regiments there appeared to be little of them in existence, but by which time they had spawned Kniveton's regiments.[284] Formed as early as 1642 the regiments made up part of the royalist presence in Stafford during February 1643.[285] Later they formed the garrison at Tissington and part of that of Wingfield Manor where soldiers from them threatened mutiny. When Wingfield fell and Derbyshire was dominated by the parliamentarians, the regiments moved on to Tutbury where they may have stayed up until Kniveton's replacement as governor in 1646. The regiment of horse may have been fairly large: there were 10 captains at some time or another, but again no numbers are known. The regiment was always a scattered force; parts served at Ashby, and Lichfield as well as Tutbury. There may have been seven troops each of 20 men.

The foot appears to have had about half a dozen companies and was perhaps about 150 strong.

John Freshville's Regiments of Horse and Foot

The horse were formed in 1642 and served in the Edgehill campaign. From then until the following year the regiment was part of the Oxford forces and fought at the battle of Newbury in September 1642. Freshville then returned to Derbyshire to become one of the Marquis of Newcastle's six colonels. In the Marston Moor campaign Freshville had eight troops each of approximately 20 men. It is possible to trace six captain's names. By the Marston Moor campaign, either John Eyre had transferred to Fitzherbert's or Gervase Pole had been killed thus leaving the eight troop commanders (including the three field officers) present at the battle.[286] The horse which survived the battle went on to serve at Newark and may have fought at Naseby. In July 1645 Freshville captured and garrisoned Welbeck, holding it for four months before returning to Newark.[287]

In March 1644 the foot numbered as many as 300 men, though only 100 or so appear at Marston Moor.[288] Thereafter there is no specific mention of them, and their Major Jammot may have transferred to the horse. They were a pair of experienced regiments having between them fought at Edgehill, Marston Moor, Newbury, Cotes, the relief of Newark and possibly Naseby.[289]

Sir John Harpur's Regiments of Horse, Foot and Dragoons

These regiments were raised in early 1643 after Hastings had been invited to intervene in south Derbyshire. After being driven from Swarkestone in January of that year they were based at Ashby until the Queen's Army captured Burton-on-Trent in July and they were then installed as the garrison. On 6 January 1644, the regiments were attacked at Burton. Harpur and Lieutenant Colonel Bullock were in the north of the county attending the councils of war at Chesterfield. In the fight which led to the capture of the town by the parliamentarians, as many as six captains and a major were captured.[290]

Whilst forming the garrison the two regiments had totalled 500 men, but it is unlikely that Bullock and Harpur did not have some part of the horse with them at Chesterfield. If we assume that there was only one troop of dragoons under Captain Corbet, and assume that it was about 20 to 30 strong, we could have a strength of around 220 for the other two units. Symonds lists five troops of horse and five companies of foot.[291] If the regiments were of equal size then each troop and each company would be about 40 men strong. At least one troop, that of Captain Sykes, was present at the siege of Leicester. Many of the officers, including Bullock and Harpur, had laid down their arms by the end of 1645.[292]

John Milward's/John Shalcross' Regiments of Horse and Foot

Milward formed the regiments in late 1643, possibly as part of his role as a commissioner of array. Shalcross was his lieutenant colonel. The regiments were based at Chatsworth with Eyre's. Both the regiments went north with Eyre in the campaign which culminated with Marston Moor. The foot with Eyre's and perhaps Freshville's are suspected to be the unit which de Gomme left untitled on his map of the battle.[293]

The horse seems to have been a small regiment, with, as its nucleus, the troop of Captain Vernon, transferred from Hastings' regiment. The regiment as a whole was perhaps only 100 strong, with the foot being about the same size.

Milward submitted to Parliament in the panic which followed Marston Moor when Freshville was thinking along the same lines. Shalcross took over the regiment of horse, but it may be that the foot, damaged or destroyed at Marston Moor, had, as a regiment, ceased to exist. Shalcross and the horse were absorbed into the Northern Horse, and he signed the petition of the Northern Horse desiring to return northwards from Oxford in 1645. As a result the regiments were sent on the dazzling mission which led to the relief of Pontefract in March 1645. However it is probable that Shalcross was captured in this campaign.[294]

Sir Andrew Kniveton's Regiments of Horse and Foot

Little information regarding the foot can be found. Symonds appears not to have seen them when he drew up his list of the army, though he does indicate that the field officers of the horse held, as was common, dual commands in both regiments. If Symonds is referring specifically to units involved in the relief of Newark then we can assume that the foot were on garrison duty at Tutbury at the time. Even so no regimental officers come to light later.

The horse had five troops when Symonds listed them. At the time one of the captains had just been killed. He was replaced by either Captain Merry or Brough who seem to appear after Symonds drew up his list.[295] No evidence remains regarding the size of the regiment, though going by the size of others it was about 100 to 120 strong. Kniveton had first been Fitzherbert's lieutenant colonel and it is likely that the regiment was formed around his troop in Fitzherbert's. Though Sir Andrew was present at the surrender of Ashby, after his replacement by Blakiston at Tutbury, the regiments were still at Tutbury when it surrendered in April. Sir Andrew's brother and lieutenant colonel, Peter Kniveton, was involved in the negotiations.

There may have been a dragoon regiment. A letter from Kniveton to Hastings in September 1644 mentions the capture of a Lieutenant Smith 'that belonged to the dragoons'. There is no corroborative evidence, though it is probable that any dragoon unit would be the size of one small troop.[296]

Roger Molyneux's Regiments of Horse and Foot

Molyneux's two regiments appear to have been raised in Nottinghamshire and Leicestershire as well as in Derbyshire. The first seem to have come under Hastings' command when they are established as the garrison of Wingfield Manor in December 1643. It is likely that there were five companies of foot and a small number of horse. Nevertheless in August 1644 the only horse units present in the garrison were those of Sir John Fitzherbert.[297] Molyneux's Major Fiennes and Captain Wilkinson of the horse were present in the garrison at the time they do not appear to have been accompanied by their troops. It is possible that as the garrison was under siege, most of the horse had been evacuated.[298] After the garrison surrendered, Major Fiennes disappears from the scene and Thomas Eyre, who hitherto may have been major of the foot, only assumed the post of major of horse. The foot regiment may have disintegrated after the siege, but the horse moved on to Newark. At Naseby the regiment was part of the Newark Horse and Eyre was mortally wounded. No figures are available for the size of either regiment. Molyneux seems to have commanded five troops when he captured part of the Derbyshire committee in February 1645; this may indicate that both units were of similar size, perhaps 100 men each.[299]

Isham Parkins' (Parkyns') Regiments of Horse and Foot

Symonds does not mention Parkyns' Horse but a Captain Geoffrey Trease (Trees) of Nottinghamshire claimed, in 1663, to have been a part of such a body. Symonds only names two captains of foot, which suggests that the regiment was very small.[300] It appears to have been raised in 1644 in Nottinghamshire and Leicestershire. Their position in the North Midlands Army is confirmed by their role as part of the garrison at Ashby-de-la-Zouch where Parkyns was governor.[301] Both regiments may have been between 20 and 50 strong.

Ferdinando Stanhope's/John Barnard's Regiments of Horse and Foot

These regiments would have their origins in the garrison which the Earl of Chesterfield established at Bretby in late 1642, and then led to Lichfield. Having gone into a form of voluntary captivity at the surrender of Lichfield to Gell in March 1643, Chesterfield left the regiments to his fourth son

The Battle of Hopton Heath and death of the Earl of Northampton. (Steel engraving by J.T. Willmore, after George Cattermole (1800–1868). (Public domain)

Ferdinando who had brought a troop of horse with him from Oxford at the end of 1642.[302] The horse were present at Hopton Heath in March 1643; Stanhope was wounded and a cornet was captured during the battle.[303] By the end of that year there were at least 120 men, divided into four companies, in the foot. In November 1644, Stanhope was killed at a skirmish near Nottingham. The man who Symonds noted as being the major, John Barnard, appears then to have assumed command of the regiment, yet he had already been called colonel a year earlier – this may indicate that he was either the lieutenant colonel by this date, or that he had his own forces.[304] Whatever the situation Barnard's regiment or part of the regiment, which had officers from Stanhope's regiments, went south before Stanhope's death, thus effectively leaving the North Midlands Army. Barnard served as temporary governor of Hereford before Scudamore, Hastings' old major of horse, was given the position. Barnard's forces then became the garrison of Abbey Cwm Hyr which they surrendered in January 1645. In the following July he and the regiment were massacred at Canon Frome when the Scots stormed the garrison.[305]

Richard/Harvey Bagot's Regiments of Horse, Foot and Dragoons

Both the Bagots were company commanders in Lord Paget's, later Sir Richard Bolles' Regiment of Foot, raised in Staffordshire.[306] They had, as early as March 1643, returned to their native county, perhaps as part of the King's initiative aimed at securing the North Midlands. They served under Hastings in the campaign of Hopton Heath.[307] When Lichfield was recaptured by Hastings and Rupert, Richard was made governor and a colonel with Harvey as his lieutenant colonel. He not only developed the foot companies that he and his brother had, but began to raise a regiment of horse. By the end of the year there may have been as few as three troops of horse.[308] The 1644 recruitment drive, which led to quarrels with Leveson, resulted in the creation of a regiment of seven or eight troops by the time that Symonds listed the officers.[309] By 1645 the regiment of horse was probably 300 to 400 strong. At Naseby there were 200 present in Sir Thomas Howard's brigade; Richard Bagot was mortally wounded in the battle.[310] When at the end of 1645 Sir William Vaughan's royalist force was destroyed, the horse, now with Harvey as colonel, were probably involved. This would account for their not being included in the Lichfield accounts for the months of October, November and December 1645.[311] It would appear that there was only one troop of dragoons, attached, perhaps to the regiment of horse.

The regiment of foot had seven companies and 300 men by the end of 1643.[312] A year later there were 400.[313] At the end of 1645, there were a total of 489 men in seven companies and a part time citizen company raised in the town of Lichfield had been established.

Thus it can be seen that even as royalist power in the region was declining, the regiment was growing in size. The regularity with which the regiment was being paid was undoubtedly a factor in this, since at this time even the new model was falling into arrears. No doubt Bagot's regiments were attracting soldiers from disbanded or destroyed regiments.[314] Its initial size and its continued growth made the foot regiment, like the horse, one of the largest regiments in the North Midland Army.

During its existence the regiments would have fought at Hopton Heath, Cotes, the relief of Newark, Marston Moor and Naseby as well as numerous actions in the Marcher counties and Lancashire, making it very much a field regiment.

John Lane's Regiment of Horse

Lane's regiment was probably formed from the troop Lane commanded in Lord Digby's regiment at Edgehill.[315] It either returned to Staffordshire as part of the King's attempts to secure the county or as part of Rupert's forces sent to help Hastings recapture Lichfield in April 1643. At the end of the month it formed the garrison of Stafford Castle.[316] After the fall of Stafford it became the garrison of Rushall House. The total garrison was 200 strong. Lane's Horse were 50 strong at the time. The foot at the house may possibly have been Lane's, but were more likely to be part of Bagot's Foot or Hastings' Foot. When Rushall fell to Denbigh in 1645, the horses were lost as part of the terms.[317] These must have been replaced as there is evidence to suggest that the regiment served in later parts of the war at both Lichfield and Ashby. Lane and two of his captains surrendered at Ashby-de-la-Zouch.[318]

Thomas Leveson's Regiments of Horse and Foot

Leveson was empowered to raise 1,500 foot in May 1643.[319] His regiment would not have been anything like this size. There were 200 present at the relief of Newark; with those left in the garrison the total would be near to 300 men. By 1646 actions during the war had reduced its size to about 150; Naseby would have caused a great decline in numbers. The horse was probably about the same size. At Newark there were 100 troopers present; at Marston Moor, 200. At the battle of Naseby the three troops totalled 150 men.[320] There appear to have been five troops, thus indicating that the forces left at Dudley, under Lieutenant Colonel Beaumont, numbered on this occasion two troops.[321]

The majority of the officers in these regiments were, like the colonel, Roman Catholics, generally coming from the south of Staffordshire which had a high concentration of Roman Catholics.[322] Leveson was adept at ignoring Hastings and arguing with Bagot. This led to his attempting, where possible, to withhold his units from the North Midlands Army.[323] In the Newark campaign he strategically appended his forces to those of Prince Rupert rather than join them to the gathering forces at Ashby in the preceding days. Symonds includes his regiments under Hastings' forces when he drew up the list, and indeed the King pointedly indicated to Leveson that he was under Hastings' command.[324] A full discussion of this problem will be given in the following two chapters.

Devereaux Wolseley's Regiments of Horse and Foot

These regiments formed the garrison of Bagworth Park, from early 1643 until the following October. From that time onwards, they were probably attached to the forces at Ashby-de-la-Zouch.[325] The regiment of foot may have had six companies when Symonds drew up his list though he did not note its size. The horse may only have had three troops, that of the colonel, Lieutenant Colonel Knapper's and that of the only person claiming to have belonged to that body in the list of indigent officers, Captain Walter Hastings. The latter was a transfer from Hastings' Horse; he may have brought his troop with him to form the embryo of Wolseley's regiment.[326] The strengths for the regiments would be in the region of 150 foot and about 50 horse. The remains of the regiments were at Ashby-de-la-Zouch when the castle surrendered.[327]

Gervase Lucas' Regiments of Horse and Foot

When Lucas, Lord Camden and his eldest son Baptiste Noel captured Belvoir Castle at the end of January 1643, they established a base for the Rutland Commission of Array and for Lucas' soldiers.[328] The regiment of horse which Symonds later listed had seven troops, yet may have been numerically small. When Hastings drew up his complaints against Lucas in 1645, he asserted that Lucas had only 30 horse and 100 foot, and claimed that Lucas was collecting contribution on the basis that he had twice as many soldiers as that.[329] Lucas' regiments were often involved in working with the forces from Newark, especially in Lincolnshire. After Newcastle went into voluntary exile, Lucas did his best not to cooperate with Hastings, and though Symonds indicates that William Bale was the lieutenant colonel, it is more probable that Bale was still in Pate's regiment and was in Belvoir to keep an eye on Lucas.[330] This is borne out by the fact that at the end of 1643, when Lucas was attending the councils of war at Chesterfield and Bolsover, he left Captain Lucas in charge, not Bale. These latter two men were then involved in a dispute in Gervase Lucas' absence. Lucas' claim that Bale was disruptive suggests that he was rightly suspicious of Bale's role in the castle.[331]

Lucas' Horse were involved in Major General Porter's disastrous intervention into south Yorkshire in March 1644. The regiments were, between them, involved in the relief of Newark and the catastrophic defeat at Denton in October 1644.

The above are the regiments which positively appear to be a part of the North Midlands Army. There are several others which were associated either with the army or with the area: Sir John Corbet's Foot (and Horse?), Francis Wortley's Dragoons and Christopher Roper's Foot. Roper had one man claiming to have served in his foot regiment in 1663.

However, as pointed out earlier, the 300 foot he led to Chester may have been a part of Hastings' regiment over which he was possibly given a colonelcy. Corbet had been a captain in Hastings' Horse; perhaps his troop formed the embryo of his regiment. In 1663, one man claimed to have served in Corbet's Foot. Corbet's forces seem to have been detached from the North Midlands Army and sent to serve in the Marcher counties.[332] Wortley, son of Sir Francis whose dragoons had been the only royalist presence in the North Midlands during the Edgehill campaign, may have been the colonel of the regiment which included Major Dud Dudley. It is not certain whether this regiment was a formal part of the North Midlands Army, though Wortley surrendered at Ashby in 1646. There may have been some form of regiment under Ralph Sneyd. If he did succeed in his attempts in raising troops in 1644 he may only have served in Cheshire and the Marcher counties.[333]

It is unfortunate that there exist only scanty references to the use of impressment in the North Midlands. In Staffordshire the responsibility for levying impressment befell Thomas Leveson in his role of high sheriff, but also to the commissioners of array. A quorum of three was necessary to enact any levy, thus the power to raise troops did not go to Leveson alone. At the end of 1643 Leveson had tried to use his power to collect *posse comitatus* – in effect conscripts – in defiance of Hastings. By involving both him and the commissioners in impressment, the King sought to prevent any repeat of the problems caused by this matter. In March 1644, Leveson and the commissioners were empowered to raise 67 men in Staffordshire. Due to this lack of information it is impossible to estimate the number of conscripts that were in the North Midlands Army or how many men were sent out of the region for service elsewhere.[334] It may be that the men in Eyre's and Milward's foot regiments whom Hastings referred to as 'array men' were impressed men. It is clear that the commissioners were still allowed some power over the raising of troops though it was no longer their main function. There are very few references to impressment in the constables' accounts indicating that conscription was never a permanent feature of the war in the region. This point bears on the relationship between clubmen risings and the administration of the counties. In some regions impressment formed a major grievance of the clubmen petitions.

The possible total numbers, based on the above discussion, is given in tabular form below. The regiments dealt with in the last paragraph are not included.

Arm	Number of Regiments	Possible Maximum Strength
Horse	17	2,575
Foot	15	2,520
Dragoons	4 (troop size only)	90
TOTALS	36	5,130

This would accord with the estimate Symonds gives at the end of lists of Hastings' regiments.[335] It would appear that Symonds suggests that there were 5,000 men of Hastings' forces present at the relief of Newark in March 1644. However, there were only 3,000 of Hastings' army in the field during the campaign. The total of 5,000 is perhaps nearer the mark if the numbers of men left in the garrisons during the campaign is included. Given that the regiments at Dudley and Lichfield left between a third and a half of their strengths in the garrison, whilst the rest were in the field, this proposition has some value. There is the probability that some of the smaller garrisons like Tissington, Ashbourne, Hassop and Staveley, were temporarily abandoned during the campaign.[336] This and the possibility that some of the regiments listed above may have been derived from sections of other regiments and therefore has resulted in some double counting, would suggest that the possible maximum strength is a slight overestimate. Even so, we are dealing here with an army adjudged to be between 4,000 and 5,000 strong.

Hastings himself estimated that in the summer of 1643 he had 2,000 men under arms and could, if given the weapons, arm a further 1,000.[337] During the ensuing months the conquest of Derbyshire resulted in the creation and addition of the regiments of Eyre, Freshville, Milward and possibly Molyneux – a potential increase of nearly 1,000 men. Other regiments, following Bagot's example, would be recruiting at what was a very favourable time for the royalists. Thus we see that the period when the campaign of Newark was being fought saw the North Midlands Army at its strongest. There were, at this time, a number of units from this army serving under Sir Charles Lucas in the north.

Decline was rapid. As indicated above, Marston Moor probably saw the destruction of Freshville's, Eyre's and Milward's foot regiments. Though their horse would, given their greater mobility, have suffered markedly less, the combined losses could have been as high as 500. The disastrous summer, which saw Derbyshire change hands and resulted in the collapse of several garrisons, would also have witnessed the gradual drift of men from the royalist armed forces in addition to losses incurred through death and casualties. On top of this there were the defeats at Burton in August and at Denton which would have further contributed to the decline. By May 1645, Symonds reckoned on there being 1,500 royalist soldiers in the region.[338] Following this there were instances of plague at both Tutbury and Ashby - the natural consequence of large unhygienic collections of soldiers, as well as the casualties of Naseby, to contend with.[339]

Decrease in size was accompanied by the increasing fragmentation of the army. The regiments of four of the Derbyshire colonels drifted into, and became part of, the Newark garrison, serving with it at Naseby. As early as the end of 1644, local parliamentarians began to establish small garrisons between the royalists' major ones. The intention was to interrupt as much as possible the day to day running of the royalists' system and to disrupt communications between the various garrisons.

The success of these attempts is questionable, given the good state of affairs with Lichfield's exercising of the contribution collection in late 1645, and Ashby's ability to operate once the plague cleared up in November 1645. Further damage was done by the royalist high command when they continued their policy of hiving off parts of the North Midlands Army for service elsewhere. In mid to late 1645 the Staffordshire units served first with Sir William Vaughan and later, with Ashby units, under Lord Astley.

Another point about the numerical composition of the North Midlands Army, apart from its size removing from it the label of 'guerrilla band', is the way in which it epitomised the problems concerning the strengths of the royalist regiments, perceived by the Oxford Parliament.[340] There were too many small regiments which, given the disproportionate balance between officers and men, would entail unnecessary expense. Had all the regiments in this army been full strength the total numbers of soldiers would have been 8,500 horse and no less than 19,500 foot.[341] As it is there was, in numbers, the equivalent of only five regiments of horse and less than two of foot. Such a force should only require seven colonels, at the most – with duality of commands there need only have been five – yet there were 23. A rough estimate of the number of all officers required by these seven regiments would suggest somewhat less than 150; there were, throughout the First Civil War, a total of 356 officers in the army; not all, of course serving at the same time: some were killed, others moved into regiments from other areas, or simply gave up the fight. Such an over proportion of officers created a drain on resources which the Oxford Parliament sought and failed to rectify. Reasons for this failure sprang from the same root as the problem. The failure of the commissioners of array to raise men in the summer of 1642, had resulted in the proliferation of commissions given to individuals, each with the power to appoint their own officers. The inability of these officers to recruit fully their commands, be they troops or companies, resulted in the existence of this large collection of small units. The independency which the individual commissions had given, not only to the persons to whom they were originally directed, but also to their appointees, meant that any attempt to reduce their numbers would involve the destruction of a whole collection of almost autonomous units. This, given the status inherent in the position, and the following discussion of how the army provided a social ladder to various groups in Stuart society, would be opposed vigorously by those in danger of being thus 'paid off'.

The Officer Corps

Having in the above section 'created' this army it remains to examine the social status of the officer corps along the same lines as the commissioners were examined in order to round out our picture of the committed royalist activists and to help us further identify the social groups from which the King was able to draw support. There are many and varied sources for this study; several of them have been discussed in Chapter 1. The main ones for providing the names of the officers are the 'List of Officers Claiming to the Sixty Thousand Pounds etc Granted by His Sacred Majesty for the Relief of his Truly Loyal and Indigent Party' which contains lists of regiments and their officers and the Notebook kept by Richard Symonds. The former has many limitations as a source which were thoroughly rehearsed in the first chapter. Obviously it does not contain lists of officers killed during the war unless they are named by one of the claimants. Though attempts were made during its compilation no distinction is made between the regiment(s) raised by Sir Francis Wortley and that (or those) raised by his son. Just as that problem is pertinent to this study so is the problem over regional origin which the 'List…' throws up. Many of those who gave their address as London and Westminster were only living there whilst making their claim to the money. There is also the point that those officers who are mentioned by those who served under them, but did not register their own names, are only accorded the scantiest of details, usually just their rank and surname. Despite these important deficiencies the 'List…' provides a valuable source for those wishing to recreate royalist regiments.[342]

Symonds saw the North Midlands Army some time in 1645, or so it would seem as he refers as if in retrospect to its size in March 1644. It therefore is probable that the list drawn up was either done as he saw units in May 1645 whilst the King's Army was in Leicestershire, or he compiled his list from information provided to him at the time and thus included units which were by this time elsewhere. Alternatively, the list was actually compiled in March 1644, and comments were added later regarding its decrease in size. In any event Symonds did not include all the units of the army. Nor does he name any officer below the rank of captain lieutenant. But this notebook is very important, providing as it does the only list drawn up of the army still in existence and giving clues as to the size and composition of some of the regiments.[343]

Other main sources include the Calendar of State Papers, Domestic Series as well as many of the papers themselves held in the Public Records Office, the Calendar of the Committee for Compounding and that of the Committee of Advance of Money. The first gives occasional references to the names of some officers in the army. The compounding papers do, on the other hand, give the war records of several of those attempting to sue for composition. These and the Committee for Advance of Money's papers also provide useful information about the estates of the officers. This has to be treated with caution, as the royalists were, naturally, unwilling to provide the committees with a full account of their property, as this would lead to higher fines than they wished to pay. Nor did other witnesses always provide accurate information, particularly if they had a grudge against the compoundee.

The docquets of the Clerks of the Chancery, referred to in Chapter 2, with reference to the commissioners of array, can also provide details of the commissions, and their scope, issued to several of the North Midlands Army colonels. Black's printed, but unpublished, version of these docquets also provides such, and other, information.[344]

Names given in the various newsbooks and papers can be very misleading. In some cases they were even invented, and many times the reported name is a misspelling of a name gained by hearsay. In these cases and that of the *Catalogue of … the King's Marching Army* it is best to accept the names as a positive identification only if they can be verified by another source.[345] Modern examinations of the royalist officers which were referred to in Chapter 1 have also been consulted and mention of their findings is given in the text and the endnotes.[346]

When Dr Blackwood identified the status of the officers of Lancashire, he included a category named 'gentry?' With this study the number of men who simply cannot be identified, by use of the heraldic visitation or even calendars of probate inventories, is very large. Thus in this case the 'gentry?' status has had to be abandoned. Where plebeian status can be positively identified, it has been done but the category

unknown' contains not only doubtful gentry, but also men below the rank of gentry who have left little or no evidence of their status behind them. In other cases, status is taken as that accorded before March 1642. Evidence for this comes from a variety of sources including the visits of heralds, both before and after the war. Official sources which refer status are invaluable and give perhaps a more 'up to date' (in seventeenth-century eyes) outlook upon how men were perceived and how they perceived themselves than do the heraldic visitations which used dated terms of reference. It must be remembered that this is not a gentry study in itself, but an attempt to identify the status of a given number of royalist officers and, in Chapter 2, other royalist activists. In this case, the fact that many of the men are unidentifiable as far as status is concerned is very important as it indicates that active royalist support came from social groups with which the royalist high command did not identify. Modern works which give means of judging social rank are used in this part of the chapter and reference is made to other studies of royalist armies.[347]

The officers will be studied rank by rank after the colonels. Officers of horse were generally of a higher status than their colleagues in the foot and therefore these two groups are taken separately. At various stages the officers will be considered in larger groups; for instance the field officers and the regimental officers will be taken together as a whole. After the rank by rank study the format reverts to that used in the previous two chapters, with education being looked at as well as religion. One general difference between this and the previous two chapters is the attention paid to regional origins. In the cases of the commissioners and the committeemen regional origin was easy to ascribe, as to qualify for selection for these bodies, in the first place, residence in the county, or at least major estate holdings within it, was essential. In the case of the officers, there was no such formal tie, although it was more likely that a colonel would pick people he knew from the same area as himself to be his officers. But as will be shown below there were a number of officers from other regions in the North Midlands Army.

The ranks which are covered by this analysis are, in descending order, colonels, lieutenant colonels, majors, captains, captain lieutenants, lieutenants, cornets and ensigns. Quartermasters, of which there was one per foot regiment and one per troop of horse, are not included; unfortunately, the information regarding these men is so limited that making any valid assumptions about them is impossible. This is regretted as a study of these men, who would be below gentry status for the most part, and who would have a difficult task during the war, could be of very great value.

The numbers of men in each of the ranks under consideration is given here.

Arm	Field Officers			
	Colonels	Lieutenant Colonels	Majors	All
Horse	-	13	22	35
Foot/Dragoons*	-	7	8	15
TOTALS	23	20	30	73

* These are those field officers that do not seem to have held dual commands and only held rank in the foot regiments

Arm	Regimental Officers					
	Captains	Captain Lieutenants	Lieutenants	Cornets	Ensigns	All
Horse	92	12	35	39	-	178
Foot/Dragoons	52	4	24	-	25	105
TOTALS	144	16	59	39	25	283

This gives a total of 356 officers. In the analyses which follow it will be noted that when descending through the ranks, the number of officers who can be identified becomes fewer. For instance it is impossible to create a pattern of mortality rates amongst the officers as the deaths of officers below the rank of major were rarely recorded. As lower ranking officers in the foot regiments were more vulnerable, having no horses upon which to escape danger, their mortality rate would be higher. However, due to the dearth of relevant information, the only evidence for this in the North Midlands Army is the relative lack of foot captains. Exceptions to this pit of obscurity occur when individual officers gained notoriety for themselves by some actual, or imagined, act in either the royalist or parliamentarian press.

Colonels (Horse, Foot and Dragoons)[348]

As most of these officers were the commanders of regiments of two or three arms of the army they are considered as a single group. The pattern followed in this section is that established in the studies in the previous chapter with the noted exception of the regional question, and will be followed in the studies of other ranks. There were twenty-three men who served as colonels in the North Midlands Army. Their social rank is broken down as follows.

Social Rank

Noble	Bart	Knight	Esq.	Gent.	Yeoman	Trade/ profession/ clergy	Unknown
1	2	0	17	1	0	0	2

It can be seen that although the group undoubtedly are strongly based in the gentry, there are very few titled gentry and only Sir John Fitzherbert represents the nobility by being heir to a title. Hastings of course, though counted as an esquire in the above table, was the younger son of an earl, as was Stanhope. It is clear that the main social group are the esquires. Both the 'unknowns', Roper and Barnard, are at least gentry and may well be esquires. The one identified gentleman is Gervase Lucas who won his colonelcy and then a baronetcy through his capture and retention of Belvoir Castle. Of the six who definitely possessed colonels' ranks before April 1643, Fitzherbert is one, Hastings and Stanhope were a further two, one other was a baronet, leaving two esquires. This may indicate that the influx of gentry into the colonelcy followed an initial period during which the King appointed men of more established status to command his regiments. Men like Leveson, Bagot, Lucas and Lane, became colonels later, having already proved their worth to the royalist cause. Three of the colonels were the owners of lead mine leases in Derbyshire and represented, along with Hastings who had coal mines in north-west Leicestershire, the only industrial interests amongst the colonels.

Familial Status

Head	1st son	2nd son	Other son	Unknown
7	8	5	1	2
(30.4%)	(34.7%)	(26%)		

Though a large number of the colonels were heads or potential heads of families, a significant proportion were not. Three of the colonels appointed early in the war were amongst this latter group. As shown in the previous two chapters the commitment of the head of a family to a cause was a major step. Such action not only deprived a family of its nucleus and its spiritual, moral and economic patriarch, but effectively gambled, not only the nuclear, but also the extended family's fortunes and future. Any retribution exacted by the victor of the conflict could be expected to involve some financial penalty – a probability of which none of the activists could have been unaware.[349] The presence of six men who were not in, or likely to be in, the position of head of the family, does indicate that even in the early stages there were difficulties in finding men of the highest status to fight for the cause. Hastings was undoubtedly a substitute, not only for his inactive father, but also for his parliamentarian elder brother; either of these would have brought more status to the cause than could Henry.

By examining the political, administrative and educational experiences of the colonels, and later other officers, one can determine their importance within their social class by seeing how much trust their peers and betters reposed in them previous to the war. Also, as many such roles would involve them in working with, guiding and commanding other men, lessers and equals, we can judge how much experience of leadership they brought with them into military command.

Political, Administrative or Educational Experience

MP	LL	DL	HS	JP	University	Inn
2	0	4	5	3	7	3

Ten of the colonels do not appear to have been involved in any of the areas covered by this analysis. Only one of these, Wolseley, was one of the original colonels. It may be possible that Christopher Roper was the man elected as MP for Dingle in Munster for the 1640 Irish Parliament. This then would give us three MPs and only nine with no experience of office or higher education.[350] Even so, the proportion we are left with of men who had some form of experience or at least education, is not very high. In addition only seven men had pre-war military experience. However, eight did rise in rank to a colonelcy during the war; three of these latter are not included in the latter table, and therefore had had practice in handling groups of men before assuming regimental command. We do see that a large number of colonels had not been recipients of society's trust previous to the war, and yet during it, North Midlands society was subject to their military commands.

As indicated above, defeat was potentially a financial disaster. However only 16 of the colonels have left evidence of their financial plight brought on by their losing the war.[351] Only one of them had died before the war ended so that has left six who did not seem to have been fined. Some like Kniveton and Lucas may have ameliorated their plight by negotiating judicious terms when surrendering their garrisons; Hastings himself was the outstanding example of this tendency. But this does not account for many of the colonels. The highest fine paid was £4,583, reduced to £4,000 later, paid by Sir John Harpur.[352] This was a small amount when compared with some of the commissioners; Baptiste Noel, second Lord Camden, was fined over £19,000 for his role on the commission and raising troops for the King.[353] Harpur did no less and in a way his small fine is surprisingly low given that he was reputed to be the richest man in Derbyshire. This high incidence of low or non-payments indicates that we are dealing with a group of men many of whom had, like Hastings, estates describable as being 'little or nothing of worth'.[354] Some of those who did not pay fines based on their estates would therefore have little property on which to base such a fine.

Only four of the colonels did not live, or have major estates, in the five counties under study in this book. Gervase Lucas was a Lincolnshire man. His county was temporarily under Hastings' control, and the castle in which he established himself was on that county's border with Leicestershire. Of the others, two served in regiments emanating in the five counties before rising to the command of a regiment. This leaves only Francis Wortley esquire of Yorkshire, who may have entered the army with the rank of colonel.

Lieutenant Colonels of Horse

This category also includes men who held the same rank in regiments of foot. Out of the 12, three cannot be ascribed social rank. It is unlikely that they were of below gentry status.

Social Rank

Noble	Bart	Knight	Esq.	Gent.	Yeoman	Trade/ profession/ clergy	Unknown
0	0	0	10	0	0	0	3

As all the identified officers were esquires, this confirms that the untitled ranks of the gentry were those from which the North Midlands Army field officers were, in general, drawn.

Familial Status

Head	1st son	2nd son	Other son	Unknown
0	6	4	1	3

There is an indication that the lieutenant colonels were more likely to come from lower down the social scale than full colonels. Two of them were men serving as their brothers' second in command.

The lieutenant colonels had no experience of office holding though several had attended universities and or Inns of Court.

Political, Administrative or Educational Experience

MP	LL	DL	HS	JP	University	Inn
0	0	0	5	4		

This does indicate that previous to the war these men had very limited, if any, experience of man management, although some may have served in minor office such as constable, thirdborough or headborough. None of them had any pre-Civil War military experience. This poses the question as to why the colonels chose them as their seconds in command in the first place? It is probable that the answer is related to social position, family and/or economic ties and possibly even simply friendship rather than in proven ability.

Only seven of the lieutenant colonels paid estate based fines for their part in the war. The highest amount recorded is only £1,458.[355] Thus it would seem that these officers came from the same social group as their colonels.

Not only did they come from the same social group but also from the same region. All of the 11 whose origins can be traced served in a regiment raised in their own home county or one adjacent to it. This would support the notion that there were social, familial or reason of friendship behind their appointments, although it is difficult to prove as there are so few personal papers existent for any of the groups of royalist activists.

Lieutenant Colonels of Foot

Of this small group little can be said. Of the seven, four cannot be ascribed a precise social rank. The others fit into the broad general category of gentry, one being a knight and the other two gentlemen. Though little can be assumed from such a small group it is interesting to note that despite their high rank and potential responsibility, they could serve as temporary governors in their commander's absence and take on other charges; no less than four have left so little evidence behind them as to remain largely anonymous. Equally only one can be given a familial role and he was a first son. As for experience, only one had any form of those noted in this survey. Sir Arthur Gorges, Hastings' lieutenant colonel, had attended Oxford University. Further confirmation of their lack of status is the point that only two left evidence of paying composition. Gorges' fine was the highest at £806–5s-Od, later reduced to £512.[356]

Regionally, three are untraceable. Two, Gorges and Tamworth Reresby came from outside the region, hailing from London and Yorkshire respectively. As for the other two, one served in a regiment raised in his home county and the other in one raised in a county adjacent to his own.

Majors of Horse

This group although larger, also contains a high proportion of officers about whom we can only find the scantiest of information.

Social Rank

Noble	Bart	Knight	Esq.	Gent.	Yeoman	Trade/ profession/ clergy	Unknown
0	0	0	7	2	0	2	11

Most of those, if not all, in the 'unknown' category will be from the gentry. Those who can be identified are all from the broad untitled gentry with the exception of William Warner who was a clerk and Cecil Cooper who was an apprentice and may have been a younger son of a gentleman. The presence of Cooper and Warner and the large number of unidentified officers suggests that the majors are from lower down the social scale than their commanders.

Familial Status

Head	1st son	2nd son	Other son	Unknown
0	2	3	2	15

Not only are these men of a lower social status but they may also be of lower familial status. This cannot be said for certain, the large numbers of 'unknowns' present tending to obscure the picture.

Though Hugh Calverley had been a high sheriff, he was the only major of horse to have such experience of office. He and two others did attend universities and one man, Major John Bannington, went to Gray's Inn. Of the 22, only six have left evidence of having paid composition fines; the highest sum paid was £1,855.357. On a regional basis these majors follow, for the most part, the pattern established earlier. Of the 14 men who came from Midlands counties all but one served in a regiment raised in his own or an adjacent county. Two of the men from other areas may have been recruited in Hastings' drives in the autumn of 1642. Calverley and Scudamore, both of Midlands counties but not from the North Midlands, would certainly have come into the 'army' in this early period, the former perhaps as late as February 1643 when Hastings entered Calverley's home county of Cheshire.

With the majors it appears that we are witnessing a downward shift in social status despite the importance of the rank. Majors would be responsible for the regimental administration and were often in charge of military operations and involved in minor actions. The potential importance and attendant ability of the majors was high – it was Christopher Heveningham who captured Lapley House in 1643, and it was Rowland Hacker who commanded the Trent Bridge fort in 1644.[358] The men who held these posts in the North Midlands Army were not of very high social standing, nor were they men in whom society had placed much trust previous to 1642.

Majors of Foot

The small group of majors who only held the rank in foot regiments confirm the above. Only two can be ascribed social rank. One was a yeoman and one a gentleman, the other six remain 'unknown'. With the one yeoman who may not even be a member of this social bracket – he was described as a cow gelder at the time – we have proof that the field ranks of the royalist army were open to those of below gentry status. Thus the six 'unknowns' may well be from the 'shady' area below gentry status and may contain other yeomen or men from below this rank. Only two can be traced as to their familial rank. One was a second son, the other illegitimate. Likewise, only two appear to have been fined. One was Dud Dudley, the illegitimate son of Lord Dudley and iron master who produced weapons for the royalist forces as well as serving as a major of dragoons. His estate was confiscated after he had been sentenced to death for his activities in and after the Second Civil War.[359] None of them had any administrative, political or educational experience. Of the eight, one of them remains of unknown regional origin. One, John Jammot of Freshville's Foot, was a Walloon and one was from Scotland. The four who came from the Midlands all served in regiments raised in their own or an adjacent county.

It would appear that what has been said about the majors of horse was equally if not more true of these majors. It is suggested that they were of genuine rather than accidental obscurity. That is, their obscurity is not solely due to evidence being lost in the years since the Civil War but is due to the fact that they were socially obscure at the time.

Field Officers

As there has appeared to be little discernible difference between the officers of horse and foot in the terms of this examination, the field officers will be considered together in this brief overall analysis.

The colonels are demonstrably derived from the upper echelons of the gentry. With but one exception they came from the esquire class and above. However, it is noticeable that they are not, in general, from the upper strata of national or even county society. There are only three men from noble families and only one who was actually heir to a title. In Peter Newman's study of the Northern Army the proportion of baronets and knights balance the number of esquires – a phenomenon not apparent in this present case where the esquires dominate the field ranks. The familial status of the North Midlands Army colonels is similar to those of the Northern Army but a smaller number of them had political, administrative or educational experiences.[360] Amongst Blackwood's Lancashire royalist officers, the proportion of esquires to titled gentry is similar to the field officers in this study; that is to say that in both cases the squirarchy is the dominant group.[361] This is not true of the Northern Army even when all the field officers are taken as a whole. Thus the North Midlands royalist officers are, with regard to the field officers, more akin to those in Lancashire than to those in Yorkshire and the north. However all three studies have established that the royalist armies were led by the gentry as opposed to the aristocracy and that the field ranks were open not only to the untitled gentry and lower gentry but also to those below gentry status.

In the case of familial status we can see a decline in the tendency for North Midlands field officers to be heads, or potential heads, of families as we descend through the ranks. This is only partly explained by the fact that some of these officers were serving in elder brothers' regiments. It must be assumed that service as an officer in the royalist army was seen as a potentially rewarding career move by younger sons.

Thus active royalism must not simply be seen as an expression of loyalty to the King, although this would play some role in the choosing of sides. This assertion is supported by the obscurity from which so many of the field officers emerged when becoming officers and into which they returned having failed to consolidate their new social position by winning the war.

The statement about their obscurity is made plainer by the fact that even the colonels were not particularly well versed in either higher education or administration previous to their appointment to the commands of regiments. This dearth is more evident as one descends through the military ranks. Overall the majority of field officers had no such pre-war experiences.

Even so, the 43.5 percent of the field officers who compounded for their estates is above the 34 percent of all the country's royalist field officers that Peter Newman has traced as having compounded.[362] Given this, the fact that 56 percent of the field officers did not compound for estates is still significant. Taking into account that some papers will have been lost, some men may have escaped paying fines through having made use of social or familial connections and there will be others who have slipped either through the nets of the compounding committees or the modern historian.

We are dealing with a field officer corps composed for the most part of men with little estate. Their lack of property and wealth may be due either to their low familial status or to their social obscurity. Of those who did compound, over half of the 18 who left record of the final sum paid less than £500.

The regional examination has revealed that there is little evidence of geographical mobility amongst the field officers. Military service seems to have been largely determined by regional ties; the majority of these men served in regiments raised in their own county or in a county adjacent to that of their home. This is not really surprising as even if these men were socially obscure to the twentieth century historian, their faces would be better known then – an aid to recruitment in their home area, but not elsewhere. So, despite the distinct possibility that the army was seen as a social ladder, it appears that for these men it was not so great an inducement as to entice them far. This is compounded by the point that these regiments were, for the most part and for the largest part of the time, acting in the regional sphere of the North Midlands.

Captains of Horse

With the lower field ranks the lack of available evidence for identifying the individuals became noticeable; with the 92 captains, it becomes dramatic.

Social Rank

Noble	Bart	Knight	Esq.	Gent.	Yeoman	Trade/ profession/ clergy	Unknown
0	0	1	6	21	1	5	58 (61.5%)

Over half of the men of this rank are unidentifiable beyond their military rank and regional origins. For those that are identifiable the concentration is from the gentry. The 'unknowns' may well be from the lowest ranks of those of gentle birth and from the 'shady' area beneath. Only one man is identified as being a yeoman by his contemporaries, suggesting that the majority of the 'unknowns' may well be of some form of (lower) gentry status. Two of those in the 'trade…' category were 'preacher', one was an attorney and another sold gloves.[363] We are left to assume that though the rank of captain was open to men involved in working for a living, the majority of the posts, like the ranks, were held by men whose income was largely derived from the ownership of land, although the captains were not either the richest or the leading members.

Within their own families, these men were of more importance.

Familial Status

Head	1st son	2nd son	Other son	Unknown
1	23	5	2	61

The vast majority of those whose familial status can be traced were potential or actual heads of families. Remembering that this involved potential risk of the nuclear and extended family economy we can see that a great number of families, or at least their heads, saw the risk as worth taking. This may be a further indication that the career of royalist officer was seen as a social ladder.

None of the captains of horse had been involved in politics or county administration previous to 1642. Eight men had been to university and five went to Inns of Court. Unlike other statistics in this section, these are more likely to be the final figures as they are taken from the registers of the organisations concerned and are not dependent upon attempts to find information from each individual. This, of course, has its own limitations which have been dealt with in the education sections of the previous two chapters and will be referred to below. As education was an expensive luxury, it may be this cost factor which prevented the vast majority of these officers being part of the 'educational revolution'. Only one of the captains appears to have had any sort of military career previous to the war. The fact that for only 34 percent does any composition evidence exist does not in any way denigrate the point that these men seem to have been of low status. For most of the compounders no figures are available, possibly because not all of them were capable of paying a property and income based fine. Of those who did pay, only one was fined over £1,000 whilst others paid as little as £40.[364]

The regional examination has revealed that the captains follow the pattern established by the field officers. All but 19 of the 92 can be traced regionally. Twelve only were from outside the Midlands as a whole and of the remaining 61, only five were not from the North Midlands. Out of the 61 Midlanders, only three men did not serve in regiments raised in a county neither their own nor adjacent to their own. There were a few exceptional cases. Captains George and Edward Fitzrandolph and Robert Moore were all from Surrey and all served in Fitzherbert's Horse. Why and how they came to do so cannot be satisfactorily explained. They may simply have been reformadoes or may have held untraced Derbyshire estates. The regional ties which appear to have influenced the majority of officers' military service limits any notion that these men, who may well have had an eye to the social potential of service in the King's armies, might have been simply mercenaries.

Captains of Foot

In the period when the number of foot officers per regiment was higher than the number of officers in a regiment of horse, the relative dearth of North Midlands foot captains indicates two things. Firstly we are dealing with an army of undersized regiments. Secondly even if foot regiments had full complements of officers, if not men, the post of captain was infinitely more vulnerable than his counterpart in the horse. Encumbered by back and breast plates and perhaps by the awkward leg guards – tassetts – and armed or hindered by a partisan, the captain was not, in defeat, an agile creature. Unless a captain achieved notoriety – and tax gathering, a sure way of coming to the attention of hostile press, was the province of horse captains – the death of a captain, his body thrown into the common pit, often went un-noted. Only 52 names of foot captains have come to light.

Social Rank

Noble	Bart	Knight	Esq.	Gent.	Yeoman	Trade/ profession/ clergy	Unknown
0	0	0	1	5	0	5	41

The vast majority remain unidentified; the remainder suggest that the captains of foot were not of high social status. Of the five in the 'Trade...' category, two were shoemakers, one an apothecary, one a tailor and the other a barrister. The first four were from groups more associated with the parliamentarian armed forces than those of the royalists by historians and by the royalists themselves.[365] Even so, the majority of the remaining men, the 'unknowns', may well be of the landed, if not armigerous, classes.

Little can be deduced from the familial status as only eight individuals can be so ascribed. Of these, six were first sons, one a second son and another a third. Only five of these men attended university and two Inns of Court. None of them had any other relevant form of experience, though two had seen military service before the war. Nine alone have left evidence of having paid composition fines. Not all the others will have been without estates upon which to base fines. Apart from lost papers some captains would have escaped through pulling familial or social strings. There is, however, the strong possibility that a large number of these captains would, at the cessation of hostilities, have owned little or no property of their own. Of those who did, and were fined accordingly, only one paid over £500 and this was a sum reduced from only £1,395.[366]

The captains' regional origins trace the same pattern followed by captains of horse and established by the field officers. Of the 32 from Midlands counties, only one captain served in a regiment that was not raised in his own county or one adjacent to it. Six alone came from outside the Midlands; 15 cannot be regionally placed.

This group of officers come from fairly low on the social scale though the majority were still probably from the landed classes. The greater number preferred only to practise their royalism within the region in which they were born – though they were not content to let this simply be their home county.

Captain Lieutenants of Horse

Eight of the 12 men for whom this was the highest rank achieved during the First Civil War cannot be identified. The four who can were all gentlemen. Three of them were first sons and went to university, one attended the Inner

Temple. Only one appears to have compounded. Beyond this, little can be said with so small a base number and tables are unnecessary. The four identified men fit into the pattern established earlier; they are lower gentry with some education but no experience of administration. The regional origins of these officers also follow the pattern set by other groups, that is they tended to serve in regiments from their own or adjacent counties.

Captain Lieutenants of Foot

All four of these men remain unidentified. It is possible that Ralph Smith of Bagot's Foot attended Oxford but it is by no means conclusive. Only one appears to have been fined – a sum of £171-10s-0d was paid by Timothy Startin – his estate was later confiscated in the third Confiscation Act of 1652.[367]

Lieutenants of Horse

Twenty-nine of the 35 lieutenants cannot be ascribed social rank. Of the six who can be so identified, five were gentlemen and one was a vintner. With regard to familial status, five were first sons and three were younger sons. Only one attended university and only two compounded. On a regional basis 10 came from non-Midlands counties, two from Midlands counties other than the five under study in this book; the rest were all from the North Midlands. Of these 23, all served in regiments raised in their own or adjacent counties. Thus it would appear that right down to the junior ranks, men derived from the tail end of the gentry and below, military service was, to a large extent, determined by regional origins.

Lieutenants of Foot

Only two of the 24 lieutenants of foot can be ascribed social rank. One was described as a composer and may have had some claim to gentility, the other was a yeoman. The others, notable neither for their talent nor their status, must have come from the tail of the gentry or the ranks of society with pretensions to gentility. Two were first sons (the yeoman was one) and as might be expected none had any political, administrative or educational experience. Only one has left evidence of having compounded. Again, these men, at least those whose regional origins can be traced, were for the most part restricted in their military service by their place of residence.

Cornets

Of the 39 cornets, 33 cannot be identified to any significant degree. Of the six who can, five were gentlemen and one described as a lead miner – he may have been a gentleman with commercial interests in mining. Four of these six were first sons and two were younger sons. Only one of the gentlemen had attended university and none of them had any political or administrative experience. One man compounded and the lead miner's property was seized during the war.[368] Some of the cornets were serving in their elders regiments or troops. Their regional origins follow the established pattern.

Ensigns of Foot and Cornets of Dragoons

The final group are all unidentified. One, Jeffery Dudley, was however related to Dud Dudley, his major, and had married Dud's sister, but his exact social status is unknown. Another man is definitely known to have been a younger son and one may have gone to university. It may be that the Phillip Draycott who compounded for his estates was Leveson's lieutenant colonel's ensign, but this possible identification is not assured.[369] The regional pattern as far as it can be traced follows the established pattern of the majority serving in regiments raised in their home or adjacent counties.

Regimental Officers

As a whole this group of officers are remarkable for the lack of evidence regarding them as individual officers. Undeniably these men came from, in general, a lower social group than their superior officers.

Where they were drawn from the same backgrounds then they were from lower down the social scale. There are a few exceptions, such as Sir Richard Astley, but these men were appointed earlier in the war when there were fewer posts available. Yet, on the other hand, the large number of the officers who came from the lesser ranks of the gentry or below and yet were from high up the familial scale, indicates that there was a great deal of commitment shown to the cause, both by these individuals and by their broad social group. This along with the smallness of the fines, when indeed any were paid, indicates what a risk these minor families were taking with their small stake in the counties they were defending. Those who could afford a modest fine would have little to fall back on after the war, and those who could not may well have exhausted their meagre finances during the war. The high numbers of men who do not appear to have compounded, indicates a number of things. Some officers, through social, familial or economic ties, may have been able to elude compounding. Papers relating to some cases may have been wilfully or negligently lost. In some instances absence of papers for an officer who does not appear to have subscribed to the list of indigent officers or does not crop up in any post-war documentation, may indicate an unrecorded wartime death, or that the officer died in the period between the war and the restoration and is not discernible from any source. But it must be true that these will only account for the minority of the 78 percent of regimental officers who have left no trace of composition or any other property based fine. The majority would appear to have no estates, real or personal, upon which to base such a fine. This is borne out by the fact that those who did pay fines were only, for the most part, charged comparatively small amounts.

Thus it must be asserted that the vast majority of regimental officers came from either the tail end of the gentry or from various social groups below the gentry. The financially enforced obscurity, which had excluded these men and their families from previous political or administrative office and higher education, did not, it would seem, prevent them from believing that they had a role to play in their region's affairs during the war. The involvement at a high familial level, with all the attendant risks referred to in this and the previous two chapters, would seem to indicate that some individuals, if not families, may have seen active involvement being a gamble, the possible returns being an increased peace time role in their region's affairs.

Few served in a regiment raised far from their home county but many were not restricted to serving in regiments raised in their immediate locality. The adherence to area is a regional phenomenon rather than a county one.

As in the previous chapters educational aspects of the officer's backgrounds will be taken into consideration separately. The purposes of this are to assess the possibility that the future officers made social contacts at the universities and the Inns which may have served them in some way, such as the selection of junior officers in their later life during the Civil War period.

Education

a) The Universities

The highest proportion of the officers who attended university were from the ranks of field officer. Sixteen of the 73 field officers attended one of the universities whilst only 20 of the 283 regimental officers did so. As indicated earlier the gaining of a degree was not the sole, or even the chief, aim of attending such an institution. Only 10 of the officers did take a first degree: seven of these progressed to a Master's degree, two became fellows.[370] As the universities could be a vehicle for the forging or enhancing of social contacts it is worth studying the periods and college locations of the 36 North Midlands officers in such a light. It must be remembered that in both the previous cases, the royalist commissioners and the parliamentarian committeemen, there were few, if any, grounds for asserting that there were any social connections founded or political ideologies developed and shared between those from each group who attended either of the universities.

At Cambridge there were three major groupings of students on the basis of time, 1627–8, 1635 and 1638–9. In the first of these, there were three future officers at the university, Hastings and one of his captains being two; both of them were at Queen's. In 1635 there were four officers at the university, two of Harpur's field officers and two of Bagot's officers. In the final period the two men from Harpur's were still at the university as were three other men, two of whom were later to serve as captains in Hastings' Horse. On a college basis there is only the instance cited above of Hastings and one of his officers at Queen's and another instance where two otherwise unconnected officers were in St John's at the same time.

At Oxford there are again three time period groupings of officers, 1616–7, 1631–2 and 1635–6. In the first there were five officers present; Rowland Eyre and his future lieutenant colonel were amongst them. As the latter was Rowland's brother this is obviously no indication of a social connection either forged or compounded! Two of Hastings' future officers were also amongst these five. In the grouping of 1631–2 none of the officers was to serve in the same regiment, and of the final group only two were later to serve in the same unit. On a college basis, two future officers were contemporaneous at each of the three colleges of Trinity, Brasenose and Lincoln. Of these only the latter two served in the same regiment. With reference to the commissioners, at Oxford in the first time grouping as the officers, there were also three commissioners present, whilst at Cambridge there was only one occasion when a future commissioner was present at the same time as a future officer.

Such are the significant groupings of future royalist activists. Any assumptions about potential influence on later military service are purely conjectural as none of the people involved left diaries of any form from which such possibilities could be ascertained. There is, with the officers, more potential for these groupings to have witnessed the forming or advancement of social connections than there was in the cases of either the commissioners or the committeemen. The incidences of contemporaneous students who then served as officers of the same regiment would suggest this. But as the number of cases is small it only goes a little way to explaining the command structures of North Midlands royalist regiments.

The status of only 13 of the officers, whilst at university, can be traced. None of them was admitted as a scholar, which would have offered evidence of ability not wealth. Scholars were funded by the universities and could potentially come from social groups normally excluded from admission by the cost element. Instead most of these men were pensioners or commoners, who would be financed by their families. There was one sizar who like other sizars would probably supplement his income by performing the menial tasks later ascribed to college servants. Three men were, however, admitted as plebeians. This rank normally included yeoman stock or those from a trading background. In this present case two of the plebeians remain unidentified as to their status, other than the ascription of 'plebeian' at admission. The other however is Sir Robert Harding, described as having an impoverished estate at the end of hostilities. It was considered at the time that the opportunities for those of lower status to get into university were on the decline due to the tendency for scholarships to be offered to sons of men well able to afford the cost in order that dons might secure patronage.[371] Whether or not this was so, and there is some doubt, the small number of officers who had attended university, even allowing that as many as a third again of the numbers here may be added to compensate for the inaccuracies of the registers as suggested by Professor Stone, would indicate that opportunities for those of low gentry or common status, as many of these officers undoubtedly were, were very limited.[372]

b) Inns of Court

Training in the basic precepts of law was, in the seventeenth century, essential to the landowner, who would spend some part of his landholding life involved in legal battles. The inns did not however offer concessions on fees – there were no scholarships and no sizars. As the fees and associated costs were high, entrance was prohibited to the impecunious gentry.[373] Thus it is not surprising, given the assertions made earlier regarding the social standing of many of the officers, that only 15 had attended the inns. The inns were as much a social venue as the universities, with the added attraction of the proximity of the royal court with its ability to make and break careers and fortunes. Therefore attendance at the inns is examined in the same way as the universities. However, there was only one significant time grouping, 1636–7, when four officers were present – two at Gray's. There were no other groupings by individual inn and none of the contemporaries served in the same regiments.

On the regional question raised by Prest and referred to extensively in the previous chapters little light can be shed, except to say that Gray's with its supposed bias towards men from the north, Kent and East Anglia, again drew the most significant proportion of North Midlands activists to itself.

With so few connections between the officers as individuals and as a group in relation to the commissioners, no assertions of value can be drawn about the exploitation of the inns as a place for forging useful social connections.

Religion

Whereas the commissioners of array did not have Catholics amongst them, perhaps for political reasons, the army had several Catholic officers in it; in many ways it represented the only outlet for Catholic activism. The proportion of Catholic officers in the North Midlands Army was not as high as it was in the Northern Army. As may be expected the most accurate figures available are for the field officers and, as a result, the most accurate estimates regarding proportions of Catholics can be made for them only. Even so, of the seventy-three field officers 32 cannot be definitely categorised on the lines of Protestant or Catholic. Of the 41 who can, 11 were Catholics. This is a proportion of 26.8 percent. Given that Catholic officers were singled out by the parliamentarian media and the sequestration and other committees, the vast majority if not all of the thirty-two 'unidentified' men were Protestant. At the extreme this would reduce the proportion of Catholics to 15.1 percent. We are, therefore, dealing with a proportion between 15.1 percent and 26.8 percent. In either extreme this is not near the proportion of 36 percent of Catholic field officers in the Northern Army.[374] As the familial status of four of the 11 Catholic officers in the North Midlands Army cannot be traced, little can be said about the commitment of North Midland Catholic families. Certainly for the five of the remaining seven who were heads of families or first sons, the familial commitment was very high.

Of the regimental officers much less can be said. Only 59 can be identified in sufficient detail to ascertain their religious convictions; of these 20 were Catholics, a proportion of 34 percent. At first sight this matches Newman's figures for Northern Army field officers quite well. But for the reasons in the above paragraph it is safe to assume that the vast majority of the 'unidentified' officers were Protestants. It is therefore likely that the actual proportion was similar to that witnessed in the case of the North Midlands Army field officers, that is less than 26.8 percent.

The highest concentration of Catholic officers is in Thomas Leveson's regiments raised in south Staffordshire. Almost all the officers serving in his horse were Catholics as was Leveson himself, and most of the officers in his foot were Catholic also.[375] This gravitation towards a Catholic commander is understandable. Suspicion of the value of the employment of Catholics would make many Protestant commanders shy away from offering them commissions. Nor is it surprising that this large group under Leveson came from south Staffordshire as the area was known for its Catholic population. Derbyshire also provided a large number of Catholic officers, many serving in the regiments of Rowland Eyre or Sir John Fitzherbert. Despite these two counties having higher proportions of Catholics than other areas of the North Midlands, the proportion of Catholic activists in the North Midlands Army is greater than that of Catholics indigenous in the counties. This supports the findings of Peter Newman which indicate that the same is true in Yorkshire, though perhaps to an even higher degree than is shown here. However, this proportion is not sufficiently high to explain the lack of administrative or political experience shown by the officer group as a whole as Newman asserts may be the case in the Northern Army. The explanation must, in the North Midlands Army at least, lie in the general low social status and seeming low financial position of the officer corps as a whole.[376]

The Officer Corps of the North Midlands Army: Conclusion

As has been shown, for both the field officers and the regimental officers, the social status was not particularly high. No title holding noble held any commission in it and only four titled gentry held rank within it. The majority of officers whose status can be traced were esquires or gentlemen, though a significant number were demonstrably below this class.

Social Rank

	Noble	Bart	Knight	Esq.	Gent.	Yeoman	Trade/ profession/ clergy	Unknown
	1	2	2	40	45	3	15	247
% of all	0.03%	0.05%	0.05%	11%	12.7%	0.08%	4.2%	69.6%
% of known	0.9%	1.8%	1.8%	36.7%	41.2%	2.7%	13.8%	-

The vast numbers of unidentified men, the majority of whom were from the regimental officer group, can only indicate that these men came from socially obscure families, though they were perhaps derived from landowning groups with pretensions to, if not possession of, gentry status, at least in the eyes of the College of Heralds. This leads to several conclusions. Firstly, the King's attempts to galvanise the upper strata of society failed in the North Midlands. Whether this was due to dissatisfaction with his government or not we cannot tell, but the fact remains that the North Midlands Army was led by the gentry under the overall command of the second son of a declining aristocratic family. Secondly, the army was commanded by men who, because of their low status during the pre-war years, had been excluded by wealth and standing from the conducting of county government. Only four deputy lieutenants, six high sheriffs, three JPs and two MPs served in the army. Thus Hastings had under him a large collection of men with no experience of administering anything beyond their parish and their (possibly meagre) estates. Thirdly, these two last factors indicate that these men who had so little grip on seventeenth century affairs may well have seen the war as a means of social advancement on a scale normally closed to them. Thus they were exploiting the multiple dysfunction of society to further their own ends, whether or not they had a deep political commitment to the royalist cause. Their defeat meant that the door to social progress remained closed; the financial hardship caused by their espousal of the losing side, whether the result of fines or by the outlay of money during the fighting, resulted in the door being locked and bolted. This hypothesis supports the work done by other historians, particularly Peter Newman, with regard to royalist officers in other areas).[377]

Very few of the ex North Midland Officers did gain by their part in the war after the restoration. Gervase Lucas became the governor of Bombay but he was one of the few exceptions. Hastings, Lord Loughborough since 1643, merely took over the lieutenancy of Leicestershire which was his family's prerogative anyway. It is unlikely that his pension or his income from concessions on the cattle trade ever compensated his financial outlay of £10,000 during the war.[378]

Field Officers and Commissioners: A Comparative Analysis

Both groups emerge from a similar social spectrum, that is the nobility to the lower gentry. In both cases esquires are the largest single group, consisting of about 40 percent of the whole. However the field officers differ in one crucial respect: their membership extends much further down the social ladder. In the group of commissioners, with one exception, the esquires form the baseline; among the field officers, with only four exceptions, the esquires are the highest social group from which they were recruited. The fact that such a large proportion of the field officers are unidentified is further indication of their social inferiority, although some gained advancement as a result of military service. It is a similar case with familial status; there is a far greater tendency for the officers to be younger sons than for the commissioners to be so.

Officers, it is evident from the administrative tables, had not the same administrative experience as the commissioners of array. This would, no doubt, affect the way in which each group saw their communities in wartime. Officers may not have had the same desire to manage the war effort using the traditional methods, of which they had little experience. They also had less of a material hold on the communities in which they were waging war. Only around 42 percent of the field officers appear to have paid property based fines or assessments, compared with almost all the commissioners having done so. With less ties and less experience of government in the counties their attitudes to them may not have resembled the careful handling of the commissioners who often had major estates in the same shires. But with the commissioners acting as a brake on them, the officers were not able to act in a way which would have invoked a popular reaction. This would be a major contribution to the maintenance of a system which provoked no clubmen reactions in the North Midlands. On the other hand, when colonels did act out of concert with the commissioners, the opposite was the case. When Gervase Lucas disobeyed Hastings and the Leicestershire commissioners and, on the instigation of the King, annexed Framland Hundred, petitions were collected in protest. When Hastings' ex-major Barnabus Scudamore pressed for more taxation in Herefordshire, he in no small way contributed to the provocation of the populace which led to the massive Herefordshire clubmen risings.

Chapter 5

The Establishment of Royalist Control of the North Midland Counties

In chapters 2 and 4 the machinery of both aspects of the royalist war effort, financial and military, have been examined. It remains the province of this and the following chapter, to analyse the military control of the counties upon which the financial system depended and, indeed, paid for. In this present chapter, the period dating from Charles' raising of the standard until the relief of Newark in March 1644 will be studied. It is the purpose of this chapter to show that during this period the royalist war effort in this region became so effective that by the end of 1643 the royalists had established sufficient control of the area for the map of territorial depositions for that period to be redrawn in their favour. The course of this rise was not smooth and, more importantly, the achievement was not flawless. Hastings faced two problems, which will be considered in this chapter. Firstly, because he had to constantly provide military aid to neighbouring royalists, he could never concentrate his full efforts on his own region. Secondly, and partly as a result of the latter, he could not muster enough strength on his own, or inveigle any outside help, to enable him to destroy the pockets of parliamentarian resistance established in the region's county towns. Two further themes, the constant unhelpful interference of the King and others and the internal wrangles between commissioners and commanders, are left until the following chapter. The difficulties thrown up by these two problems were to have a greater impact on the latter part of the story of the North Midlands. Throughout this chapter, an analysis of the composition of Hastings' forces on particular occasions is given, if at all possible, to support the assertions made in the previous chapter concerning Hastings' army being more than a collection of guerrilla bands.

In Chapter 2, the discussion of the consequences of the Militia Ordinance, and the issue of commissions of array, involved a description of events leading up to the King's raising of the standard at Nottingham in August 1642. This chapter will therefore commence with the events in the North Midlands which occurred that month.

August 1642 to the Battle of Edgehill

The early period of the conflict, both prior and subsequent to the raising of the standard, saw a definite approach to the imminent struggle by the royalists, which could be described as a 'field army mentality'. It appears that both sides expected a brief clash of arms to decide the issue. As a result of this the forces which Charles empowered his nominated colonels to raise were intended for a marching army and not for the establishment of local power bases. This was to have serious consequences as it deprived the North Midlands of royalist activists who could seize strongpoints from which to establish regional control.

Hastings' Horse, which he had been empowered to raise on 4 August, within 11 days consisted of at least two troops, though no indication of its numerical strength can be found. This might indicate, given the small amount of time between the two troops appearing and their commission, that in this case at least, Hastings' appointment as colonel may have recognised his already established position as a commander of armed forces. Hastings and his troops were ordered into Warwickshire to join local royalists in an attempt to wrest the county from the grip of Lord Brooke's successful recruitment campaign.[379] The extension of this attempt was the unification of the forces under Hastings, Sir Nicholas Byron and the Earl of Northampton under the King himself, in an attempt to seize Coventry from an hostile populace and a small parliamentarian garrison. The failure to coerce the town into submission and thus to obtain the county munitions contained therein, saw some of the first hostile shots of the war being fired. Because of this, the raising of the standard several days later was a recognition of, rather than the declaration of, a state of war.

In the three weeks following the King's acknowledgement of the war, the royalist horse was stationed in Leicestershire. On 26 August Hastings and Prince Rupert, commander of the horse, attacked Bradgate Park in an effort to seize the ammunition which the Earl of Stamford had taken there from Leicester.[380] On 6 September, Rupert, in the King's name but without his approval, issued a demand for £2,000 from Leicester and threatened to bring forces to the town if it was not cooperative. The King, realising that such an act was unlikely to warm the region to his cause, wrote to Leicester to 'utterley disavow' the demand. It was a signal both to the commanders and the towns themselves that communities were not to be treated to peremptory demands for money. The King did, however, keep the £500 the town had already sent to him, indicating that he himself was pressed for money.[381]

On the 12th, Charles began his march west from Nottingham, to join the regiments raised by Sir John Beaumont and Lord Paget and to enable him to link up with the Welsh recruitment programme.[382] The horse followed a parallel course to the south of the King's foot forces which marched through Nottinghamshire and Derbyshire. On its progress the horse encamped on the property of two future North Midlands Army colonels, Isham Parkyns at Bunny and Sir John Harpur at Swarkestone. Whilst the King was at Stafford, the horse were at Field, the property of the Bagot family which provided three activists for the royalist cause: Richard and Harvey were already in

Paget's Foot.[383] When the King established himself at Shrewsbury,[384] Rupert took the horse south towards Worcester to meet a convoy of plate, on its way north from Oxford University.[385]

The fight at Powick Bridge, which ensued when Rupert drove off a would-be ambush on the convoy, blooded at least two of the units which would later be a part of the North Midlands Army. Freshville's Horse and Hastings' Horse were both involved.[386] As the King moved south from Shrewsbury on 10 October, he left the Marcher counties secured by garrisons at Bridgnorth, Shrewsbury and Wrexham. He had not secured the North Midlands in the same way, nor had he left any local activists of the calibre of Hastings behind him.[387]

As a result, Sir John Gell, the parliamentarian leadmine owner from Derbyshire, was able to enter his county with the foot troops he had been given by Sir John Hotham at Hull. With these he drove the only remaining royalist unit, the Yorkshireman Sir Francis Wortley's Dragoons, out of the county. By the time Edgehill had been fought, and its uncertain conclusion had destroyed the myth of a short war, a large part of the North Midlands had been lost by the royalists.[388] The King now had to reverse his policy of denuding the region of its activists, which the creation of the field army had achieved, and reinject these men into the shires to forge a royalist powerbase.

Edgehill to Lichfield: Breaking Parliament's Grip

In the period from October 1642 until April 1643, the royalists in the North Midlands had an uphill struggle. They were faced with the task of regaining territorial losses and asserting themselves in the face of concerted opposition. This they did, both at the King's instigation and by local initiative. However, despite being able to build up their forces they were unable to assert themselves fully without recourse to outside intervention. Sir John Gell received his first horse unit in November from Nottinghamshire. On the 11th, Sir Francis Wortley attempted to re-enter Derbyshire but a sharp engagement at Dale saw him worsted.[389] Staffordshire did not want Wortley's forces either and the county's gentry decided, at a special Sessions of the Peace in mid November, to raise a force to repel any such incursion of troops from either side.[390] It was to this potentially dangerous situation that the King turned to after the Battle of Brentford.

To deal with the Staffordshire problem he ordered the high sheriff to garrison the county and, with Wortley, to secure the county town.[391] At the same time Thomas Leveson was to garrison Wolverhampton.[392] Hastings was sent from Oxford with his regiment of horse, a commission to raise a regiment of dragoons and ammunition for a regiment of foot.[393] Hastings was, moreover, to establish a base from which to control Leicestershire. Also sent home from Oxford was Ferdinando Stanhope, the Earl of Chesterfield's fourth son. He was to join his father's small garrison at Bretby in Derbyshire, with his troop of horse.[394] Nottinghamshire was to be seized with help from the Earl of Newcastle, by the high sheriff John Digby, another man sent from Oxford.[395]

Such was Charles' response to the problem of parliamentarian control over the North Midlands. It was not a complete success. By mid December, Sir John Henderson, a Scots professional soldier sent down by Newcastle, and Digby had established themselves at Newark, but Nottingham was already fortified by the parliamentarian John Hutchinson with help from Gell. In Derbyshire, the situation was worse for the royalists than in Nottinghamshire. Early that month, Gell had cleared his county of the puny forces at Bretby thus enabling him to help his Nottinghamshire colleagues. In the middle of the month, Hastings, who had decided to recruit an army before entering the region, was beating the drum in Worcester and Shrewsbury.[396] Gell heard that Hastings had 300 horse and 400 foot by the end of December. When the latter did arrive in his native county, Henry Nevill of Holt began the establishment of a royalist garrison at Holt in the south of the county with the help of his two sons, one of whom appears to have led a troop of horse in Hastings' regiment.[397] Thus by the end of the year, the royalists had established garrisons at Ashby-de-la-Zouch and Holt in Leicestershire, Wolverhampton, Stafford and Lichfield in Staffordshire and Newark in Nottinghamshire.

Nevertheless, they were far behind their adversaries who not only had garrisons but had designed a structured local government to manage them. In mid December, Parliament had created county committees of local gentry to administer their war effort.[398] In addition the counties themselves were grouped into associations in order that they work together in an attempt to pursue the war more effectively. Nottinghamshire, Leicestershire, Derbyshire and Rutland were associated with Northamptonshire, Buckinghamshire and Bedfordshire and placed under the command of the young Lord Grey, heir to the Earl of Stamford.[399] Staffordshire was associated with Warwickshire under Lord Brooke.[400]

Though the royalists in the Midlands had been asked to work together as early as June 1642, the relationship was not formalised until the following February. In that month the counties were associated under Hastings. This was in many ways to be a recognition of the work which he and other local royalists had already achieved rather than a central initiative.

In December 1642, the royalists and parliamentarians in Nottinghamshire and Derbyshire attempted to hold bilateral talks, perhaps to emulate the events in Staffordshire. It may be possible that in both cases the initiative came from the royalists as a ruse to gain time. In view of the poor standing of the royalists in these two counties during the period, such attempts could only be advantageous. In both instances the talks came to nothing. In Nottinghamshire, John Hutchinson and his colleagues were suspicious of the royalist motives and refused to attend the meeting. In response to Digby's recruitment of forces at Newark, Hutchinson and his brother George put Nottingham in a state of defence.[401] In Derbyshire, the meeting took place between the royalists and Gell's brother Thomas along with other Derby parliamentarians. The royalists present demanded that Gell disgarrison Derby. It was a hollow demand as, since the fall of Bretby, the royalists had no armed forces in the county with which to coerce Gell into agreement.[402] Whether either side could have achieved a neutrality pact, even if the attempts were genuine, is debatable. Both King and Parliament had declared against neutrality, Parliament as early as October.[403] Even the Staffordshire attempt had failed to produce the promised third force. The establishment of royalist garrisons at Wolverhampton and the other places had met with no armed opposition despite these being a direct affront to the proclaimed neutralism of the county.

The impetus for concerted royalist action now came from within the counties. The Derbyshire royalists, realising the futility of their threats, appealed to Hastings for aid. Sir John Harpur of Swarkestone, with help from Hastings, began to garrison his house.[404] The ground for Hastings intervention was well prepared. Harpur had primed the local community into drawing up a formal protest concerning Gell, and directed to the Mayor of Derby. Fourteen south Derbyshire communities subscribed to the protest which denounced the expulsion of the Earl of Chesterfield from Bretby and thanked the King for sending Hastings to their aid.[405] It was a threat that Gell could not ignore. The villages concerned were all within eight miles of Derby itself, and Swarkestone, where Harpur was establishing his garrison, was only six miles away. There were further considerations. The bridge over the Trent at Swarkestone was the main route from the south of the county to the markets at Derby. Hastings himself declared publicly that his aim was to prevent the unwarranted taxation which the county petition had complained of and to protect those who wished to use the markets of Leicestershire as an alternative to Derby, due to the disruption caused by Gell.[406]

The threat was answered two ways. The Derbyshire committee issued a counter declaration accusing Hastings of destroying the bridge at Swarkestone and blocking trade routes to Derby. They also suggested that Hastings was exacting just the sort of illegal taxation that he had accused them of levying.[407] On January 3rd, the second reply took the form of an attack on Swarkestone Bridge. Though the royalists survived the first day, a renewed attack on the 6th drove Hastings and Harpur out of the village and back across the Trent.[408] It would appear that Hastings had not committed his full strength to the struggle as *Mercurius Aulicus*, the royalist newspaper, suggested that he only had 100 horse at the bridge though Gell's accounts infer that there were 300 horse and 400 foot. Even allowing that *Mercurius* probably deliberately underestimated Hastings numbers, Hastings would not wish to commit much more than half his forces at such a difficult stage.

The flight of Harpur and Hastings to Ashby-de-la-Zouch was seen by all local parliamentarians as the opportunity to crush local royalism in the bud. Lord Grey exercised his command and ordered a general assault on Ashby. With aid from Sir William Brereton, whom Parliament had dispatched to his native Cheshire with a regiment of horse, the North Midland parliamentarians could concentrate around 2,000 men. Their preliminary attack was a success. The 500 men Hastings had at Ashby were forced, from their outer defences in the town, to the castle itself, the fortified church and the school. Though the allied parliamentarians possessed cannon, it was of too small a calibre to breach the walls of the fifteenth-century manor house and they hoped to starve Hastings into submission instead. Yet Hastings had informed Prince Rupert of his predicament on 17 January. Already Hastings was recognised, at Oxford, as the mainspring of royalism in the North Midlands and five days later the Prince was at Brackley in Northamptonshire, heading for Leicester with five regiments of horse and foot. However, Lord Grey had already been informed of Rupert's coming to Hastings' aid after the Prince had reached Banbury, and had abandoned the siege.[409]

Perhaps in an effort to fend off expected criticism for such a hasty withdrawal, Grey turned on the smaller garrison at Holt and captured it on 23 January. Henry Nevill was taken prisoner, and sent (eventually) to London; his two sons, William and Thomas, assumed command of their father's regiments in order to continue the fight.[410] Grey's move south would also have placed him on the Prince's line of march and was, perhaps, designed as a deliberate attempt to fight the Prince's forces. However, Grey had not been as successful in dealing with his critics as he had been with Nevill's garrison. The Derbyshire contingent of his command were considerably rankled by the undue conclusion of the siege; possibly they felt Hastings more of a threat than Grey did. Both of the accounts of Gell's military career accuse Grey of being prey to rumours, suggesting that there never was a threat from Rupert.[411] This is without foundation, as the letter from Rupert to Hastings on the 22nd announcing his imminent arrival proves.[412] After Grey withdrew from Ashby, the Prince, confident of Hastings' ability to fend for himself, turned from his northward march at Daventry and moved west into Warwickshire.[413]

For Sir William Brereton the end of the siege was not such a problem. Freed from Grey's command he was able to turn to Cheshire where he had been heading when Grey embroiled him in the attempt on Ashby. He was, however, by this time too late to prevent Orlando Bridgeman garrisoning Chester with 1,000 men. Before the end of January Brereton did manage to defeat Sir Thomas Aston's forces and establish a garrison at Nantwich.[414]

Elsewhere in the North Midlands, royalist forces began to establish themselves. At Bolsover in the north of Derbyshire and Welbeck in Nottinghamshire, the royalist garrisons had begun to effect a local tax. At the end of January, Gervase Lucas established a second major Leicestershire garrison when he captured Belvoir Castle. This base was to be an intrinsic part of the royalists' attempts to exercise control over Lincolnshire.[415]

As early as November 1642, the Moorlanders, inhabitants of the scarcely populated areas north-east of Stafford, had been offended by the presence of royalist forces, namely those of Sir Francis Wortley. Parliamentarian successes had given the Moorlanders impetus and Gell and Brereton both encouraged them in their opposition to the royalists. With the provision of arms and ammunition the Moorlanders transformed their antipathy into action and went on the offensive, aiming at the capture of Stafford. The high sheriff, William Comberford, sent an urgent request for help to Hastings from the county town on 2 February.[416] The Moorlanders' attack the following day seems to have been fended off by Comberford, largely by means of negotiation. This respite was only temporary and Hastings was asked 'For God's sake [to] send what forces you can spare with what speed you can.'[417] Hastings was still short of men and had asked the King for reinforcements; it was clear he could not be everywhere at once. Comberford's request travelled via Rugeley and the Earl of Chesterfield at Lichfield before finding

Bolsover Castle. This bastion of the North Midlands fell to Parliament in the wake of Marston Moor but was briefly reoccupied by Sir John Freschville's troops in 1645. (Photo: Stephen G. Taylor, CC BY-SA 2.0 <https://commons.wikimedia.org/w/index.php?curid=9306088>)

Hastings and his forces in the Vale of Belvoir, where he was preventing a parliamentarian attack on the new garrison in the castle.[418] It is apparent that by the 9th he still had not been able to send aid to Stafford and the town had faced attacks on two consecutive days by that date. Though on each occasion the Moorlanders had been repulsed, it had been a close run thing. Sir John Fitzherbert's regiments had been involved, with Sir John himself narrowly escaping capture during one of the assaults. Some of Hastings' forces had by the 8th been in the Yoxall area, and this had, to the eyes of the Lichfield garrison, weakened the Moorlanders' resolve.[419] At the same time the forces at Newark heard a rumour that Skippon's parliamentarian forces were heading northward and desired that Hastings join them in case Skippon attacked. Hastings had delayed long enough and ignoring Newark's request, turned west to help Comberford.

By 15 February, Stafford was secured and Comberford was able to take his forces into south Cheshire to recruit. On the 18th Hastings was at Stafford himself, with as many as 700 horse in 15 troops.[420] On the 21st these forces captured Rushall House, south of Lichfield, and established a garrison.[421] Secretary Nicholas confirmed, on that same day, that Skippon had no intention of marching north, leaving Hastings free to establish garrisons at Tamworth in the south-east of Staffordshire, Eccleshall in the west and Tutbury, on the edge of the Moorlanders' territory.[422] The threat from the latter was now checked; with a new cache of arms from Oxford, Hastings was able to press on into Cheshire confident that Staffordshire was secure and north Leicestershire, south Derbyshire and Nottinghamshire were stable.[423] But with parliamentarian garrisons established by Brereton at Northwich and Nantwich, it was unlikely that Hastings could make much progress in Cheshire, despite the presence of the energetic Sir Nicholas Byron who was in command of the county's forces. Trouble was about to make a twofold appearance. A two pronged parliamentarian initiative, one of local origin and one of external invention, diverted Hastings from his Cheshire offensive.

The local venture was the gathering of combined parliamentarian forces from Derbyshire, Nottinghamshire and Lincolnshire to undertake an assault on Newark. With aid from the Earl of Newcastle, Henderson's garrison had grown considerably, so much so that Hutchinson at Nottingham realised that an attempt to capture the town had to be launched soon. In order to do this Hutchinson and others assembled an army from troops from Derbyshire, Nottinghamshire and Leicestershire at Nottingham and arranged to join forces with Lincolnshire regiments under Major General Ballard to attack Newark. On 27 February and 28th these combined forces attempted to storm the town. However, due probably to Ballard's incompetence and possible reluctance, they failed in their task. As a result the prestige and security of the tenuous, but increasing, royalist hold on the region received another boost.[424]

At about the same time, Lord Grey again used his forces to try and limit royalist encroachment in south Leicestershire and stormed another small garrison. This time it was the turn of Lord Camden's second son, Henry Noel, to suffer at Langham. Henry was captured and sent to London where, within a few months, he died. Camden and his heir, Baptiste Noel, were at Newark at the time of the attack.[425]

The more important externally inspired attack on the growing royalist presence in the region was directed at Staffordshire whilst local parliamentarians busied themselves at Newark. Lord Brooke, commander of Parliament's associated counties of Staffordshire and Warwickshire, had established partial control of the latter by the 27th February when he reached Coventry and had established garrisons at Stratford on Avon and Maxstoke Castle.[426] On the 28th, he was at Coleshill and ready to move into Staffordshire. Passing between the small garrisons of Rushall and Tamworth, he invested Lichfield at the end of the month. On March 2nd, Brooke was killed by a shot fired from the cathedral, the close of which constituted Chesterfield's garrison.[427] The siege was taken over by Sir John Gell, who had hitherto been engaged in preventing Hastings getting help to the Earl of Chesterfield's forces. Within two days of Brooke's death, Lichfield fell to Gell.[428]

Despite his possession of a small army, Hastings was not capable of conducting a siege operation unaided. Instead he and his forces circled the parliamentarians at Lichfield whilst waiting for aid from the Earl of Northampton whose forces were moving almost unopposed through Warwickshire. Hastings himself had around 1,000 foot as well as the 700 horse with which he had entered Cheshire. Stationing these at Stafford, Rushall, Tamworth and Ashby, he proposed to prevent any relief force reaching the increasingly beleaguered forces in Lichfield.[429] The effectiveness of the embryo North Midlands Army is in question as only half of the foot in Staffordshire appear to have been fully armed. The horse would consist of Hastings' own horse and dragoons, Fitzherbert's, Stanhope's, Leveson's, John Lane's, Devereaux Wolseley's, Harpur's and perhaps, Sir Francis Wortley's. Amongst the foot would be a section of his own regiment and perhaps the companies of Richard and Harvey Bagot. Inside Lichfield, Gell's force consisted of between 700 and 1,000 regular foot and 300 Moorlanders of

Lichfield Cathedral. It was from one of these towers that a sniper shot and killed Lord Brooke during the 1643 siege. (Photo: Bs0u10e01 – own work, CC BY-SA 4.0, <https://commons.wikimedia.org/w/index.php?curid=67319434>)

whom only half were armed. There were also six small troops of horse.[430] By the 8th, four days after the surrender of Lichfield, Northampton was moving north from Henley-in-Arden. Hastings suggested a rendezvous at Tamworth, the garrison held by Hastings' Major Scudamore. After the two forces joined, the royalists pressed on to Coleshill on 16 or 17 March.[431]

Gell, in order to secure the hold on Staffordshire and complete Brooke's task, intended to capture the county town. In order to do this he planned to link up with forces under Sir William Brereton. In the meantime Hastings and Northampton quartered in and around Stafford itself. On the 19th March, upon hearing that Gell was mustering his forces on Hopton Heath, the two royalist commanders gathered their regiments to face the threat.[432]

The battle has been extensively covered elsewhere and details of it are not necessary here. The account by J.T. Brighton deserves particular mention, and should be consulted for tactical information.[433] In the case of the present book, it is only relevant to indicate which units comprise Hastings' forces at the battle in order to substantiate the claim that there was an embryonic form of the North Midlands Army in existence at this stage of the Civil War.

Upon their arrival on Hopton Heath, the royalist forces numbered between 1,000 – a royalist eyewitness' estimate – and the 1,200 that *Mercurius Aulicus* reported.[434] Most of these men were horse troops; only 100 foot appear to have actually made it to the battle. It is possible that these latter were the companies of Paget's Foot which the Bagot brothers had brought from Oxford earlier in the year. The horse comprised of 25 troops of which nine were from Northampton's army: six of the Prince of Wales' Horse and three of Northampton's own regiment. The other 16 were from the army which Hastings had formally commanded since the end of February, with some possible additions from Shropshire. Hastings' regiments were probably Fitzherbert's, which had served in Staffordshire for some weeks, Stanhope's as he was wounded in battle, Nevill's (seemingly based at Ashby) and elements of Leveson's forces from Wolverhampton. The dragoons, of which there were 300 at the battle, would probably have been an amalgam of Hastings', Harpur's and Wortley's. Though the latter had been offered the chance to return north to his native Yorkshire, at the end of February, his dragoons were still in Staffordshire after the fall of Lichfield to Gell.[435] According to Brereton, some of the horse and dragoons were from Shropshire. For some reason, Peter Young in his article on the battle claimed that the Shropshire horse were Bagot's. This is unlikely, as Bagot's Horse were firstly a Staffordshire regiment and secondly was at most 60 men strong at the time, whereas Brereton asserted that the Shropshire forces were a 'greate addition' to the royalist army.[436] Despite the fact that there was a Shropshire element of indeterminate size, it is clear that the majority of forces present at the battle were derived from Hastings' army. This army he commanded by virtue of his appointment as Colonel General of the forces raised and to be raised in the North Midland counties, on 25 February, 1643.[437] Several other regiments under Hastings' direct command would still have been in the Stafford environs on the day of the battle due to their being too widely scattered into quarters on the previous night. Thus the North Midlands Army was already capable of acting as a field force by March 1643, as its contribution to the royalist victory at Hopton Heath proves.

The royalist forces faced around 1,400 parliamentarians brought together by Gell and Brereton in strong positions on the Heath. The battle consisted of a dragoon skirmish which resulted in some of the parliamentarians giving ground, and then a series of furious charges by the royalist horse. In the second of these, the Earl of Northampton was killed. The third charge did not meet with any great success, unlike the previous two, and Hastings could not gather sufficient of the now scattered forces for a fourth. It was clear however that the parliamentarians were beaten and they began to retreat. The royalist pursuit floundered in the dark when they ran into ground holed by coal pits but they captured no less than eight cannon.

Though the battle had taken the immediate pressure off Stafford, Hastings was still in no position to make an attempt on Lichfield unaided. He was able, however, to isolate further the garrison in the town and during the ensuing fortnight circled Lichfield with his forces in order both to do so and to assess the strengths and weaknesses of the town.[438]

On 29 March Prince Rupert was sent north by the King to give Hastings the support he needed to retake Lichfield. By 5 April Rupert was at Cannock, where he had expected to find Hastings. However, the Midlands general was at Belvoir Castle, working with the Newark and Belvoir forces who were establishing their hold on Lincolnshire.[439] On their return to Staffordshire,

Hastings' forces numbered 1,000 horse, 800 musketeers and 200 pikemen, three heavy guns and eight drakes – presumably those taken at Hopton Heath. The regiments involved in the renewed Staffordshire campaign were perhaps the same ones present at Hopton Heath, including both Northampton's regiment and that of the Prince of Wales. Rupert brought with him an additional 1,200 horse and 700 foot. On 10 April, their combined forces invested Lichfield. Two days later a body of miners from the Hastings' coalfields arrived and began to dig a mine under the town walls.[440] On the 15th, an attempt to bridge the surrounding ditch was made using faggots, and on the following day, royalists tried to scale the town walls. These latter two attempts failed.[441] On the same day, the King, worried by the success of the parliamentarian general William Waller in the West Midlands and Wales, ordered Rupert to return to Oxford as soon as he could.[442] This meant that the second part of Hastings' and Rupert's plans, the destruction of all the forces of Gell and Brereton, was postponed. It was an expensive mistake.

On 20 April, the mine at Lichfield was exploded and the town walls thereby breached.[443] Fierce fighting on that day resulted in the town's surrender on that following, once the royalists had forced their way into the cathedral close. Hastings conducted the negotiations.[444] Richard Bagot was appointed governor and elevated to the rank of colonel; his elder brother, Harvey, became his lieutenant colone1.[445] This was an appointment made on the basis of experience not on familial status. Staffordshire was thought secure with the re-establishment of a royalist garrison at Lichfield.[446] Rupert, in accordance with his uncle's wishes, returned south where he was sorely needed. On the 25th Waller had captured Hereford.[447]

Hastings' presence at Belvoir, in early April, may not have been wholly welcome. On the 19th, he was asked by Secretary Nicholas to leave Lincolnshire to its own devices and concentrate his efforts elsewhere.[448] Now that royalist garrisons were established in all five counties under Hastings' command, the King felt confident that Hastings could handle the North Midlands without assistance, despite it being obvious that the Midlands general had not sufficient forces of his own to mount a siege. This was an important shortcoming, given that Gell and Hutchinson were ensconced in the county towns of two of the shires in Hastings' charge. Although Lord Grey had served with Essex's army in the south whilst Hastings had been in Staffordshire, thus leaving Hastings' rear well secured, Leicester had thrown itself firmly into the parliamentarian camp.[449] Though Hastings estimated that each of the three local parliamentarian leaders only had 400 men apiece, all were locked into county towns with some form of defensive works. Even if these works were dated and of little strength, Hastings had not the manpower nor the money to conduct and finance a siege alone.[450]

Summer and Autumn 1643: Consolidation

Nevertheless, the recapture of Lichfield marked a watershed in the region's royalists' fortunes. They now had a collection of major garrisons from which to extend their control of the counties. This enabled them to put into effect the financial system outlined in Chapter 2. Within these garrisons Hastings had 2,000 men and he believed he could, with the necessary weaponry, recruit another 1,000. In the counties under his command he had garrisons at Ashby, Belvoir, Newark, Stafford, Tutbury, Lichfield, Dudley and Wolverhampton, as well as the garrisons at Bolsover and Welbeck, properties of the Earl of Newcastle, who administered them directly. There were, in addition, smaller outposts at Wiverton Hall, Bagworth Park, Tamworth, Rushall and Eccleshall Castle. Hastings also had fortified crossing points on the River Trent and perhaps Derwent in Derbyshire. To the west of his territory, Lord Capel was engaged in establishing royalist control of Shropshire and the Marcher counties. On his eastern flank, Sir Charles Cavendish was making inroads into Lincolnshire. To the north was the Earl of Newcastle and to the south was the King. His financial system, as shown above, was beginning to operate well. On the other hand, there were still the indigenous garrisons of parliamentarians and Rupert's march south had left Brereton's forces free to intrude upon north Staffordshire. Two thousand forces could not, like their commander, be everywhere at once.

Lieutenant General Charles Cavendish, accompanied the Queen from York to Newark. He was killed at the Battle of Gainsborough. (Unknown Artist)

At the beginning of May, ammunition purchased by the Queen in the Low Countries, was sent from York to Oxford. From its entry into the North Midlands until it reached Banbury, the ammunition was escorted by Colonel General Hastings and Sir Charles Cavendish.[451] Hastings had expected to receive some of this much needed consignment himself so that he could increase the size of the North Midland forces, but he was to be disappointed. The King, as he was often disposed to do, listened to the advice of those nearest to him, regardless of merit, and the Oxford commanders received the weaponry.[452] In Hastings' absence Lord Grey attacked some of his men at Loughborough, on 4 May, preparatory to his proposed joining of forces with Hutchinson, Gell and Sir John Hotham – recently appointed Parliament's commander of Lincolnshire forces, and Colonel Cromwell, sent into Lincolnshire as part of the effort to curb Cavendish's success. The point of this projected alliance had been to prevent the munitions convoy that Hastings was guarding going south. However, despite his success at Loughborough, Grey did not leave Leicestershire and when Cromwell and Hotham joined forces at Sleaford on 9 May, the convoy had reached Banbury! Cromwell and Hotham marched to Newark and faced the town on the 13th, but were attacked at Grantham as they attempted to withdraw to Lincoln. This fight at Grantham was heralded by S.R. Gardiner as being a foretaste of what was to come – for the first time Cromwell's horse displayed their tactical superiority. Whatever Cromwell's personal success, the parliamentarians continued their retreat to Lincoln.[453]

In the west, Brereton had entered Staffordshire and attacked the county town. The governor, Colonel Lane, had expressed his need of supplies as early as 20 April, and complained that the castle was too small for his garrison.[454] By 16 May the town had fallen and was in Brereton's hands and Lane, with his 300 men, was forced to take refuge in the small castle. Brereton's men then bypassed Lichfield and drove the small royalist garrison out of Wolverhampton.

Hastings had been powerless to prevent these occurrences whilst doing the escort duty imposed upon him by the Queen, and in addition, Bagworth Park, Ashby's satellite garrison under Colonel Wolseley, was also attacked by Grey.[455] Even more pressing was the serious threat to Newark. Cromwell and Hotham had, by the 24th, joined forces with Hutchinson, Gell and Grey at Nottingham. To combat this, the royalists mustered no less than 38 troops of horse at Newark. This would be a composite force of the Newark regiments, Cavendish's units from Lincolnshire and the North Midlands Army horse.

The size of the royalist opposition, the behaviour of Hotham, who was playing a double game, and the commander's inability to decide whether or not to march into Yorkshire to help the Fairfaxes, seem to have prevented the parliamentarians from launching their attack on Newark.

Lord Grey did lead an attack on the satellite garrison at Wiverton, with 5,000 men, but was repulsed. Nor did the allied commanders seem disposed towards marching north to aid the Lord Fairfax's forces in Yorkshire. Lord Grey in particular was edgy about venturing far from Leicestershire.[456] The Earl of Essex was already angry over the lack of cooperation displayed by the Midlands parliamentarians over the convoy incident, and to him their activities at the end of May must have displayed no improvement.[457]

On 4 June Queen Henrietta Maria, with her own army of 4,500, left York having already requested that Colonel General Hastings join his forces to hers during her march once south of Newark.[458] Two weeks later, she arrived at the town and the combined royalist forces went on the offensive. On either the 21st or 23rd of the month, this force attacked Nottingham. Though they did not take the town, the fact that they did attack it whilst it contained Grey's large army, indicates that the parliamentarians, far from thinking in terms of capturing Newark to prevent the Queen's progress, were firmly on the defensive.[459] Within a few days the parliamentarians responded to the royalist pressure and divided their forces, each to return to their own area. All they had achieved by their concentration at Nottingham was the unmasking of Hotham, who Essex ordered be arrested, and the revelation that Grey was not capable of exercising high command. The Nottinghamshire parliamentarians in particular were very much on the defensive and a similar pressure by the royalists could have created the same effect in Derbyshire.

On 3 July, the Queen left Newark and she and her army progressed to Ashby-de-la-Zouch. On the 7th, her army, along with Hastings', attacked and defeated the parliamentarian garrison at established when Gell held Lichfield. Now Hastings and his army could be masters of Derbyshire's southern section and its stretch of the Trent. Sir John Harpur was appointed governor and his regiments installed as its garrison.[460] Brereton's forces left the Stafford area leaving only a small garrison behind, and Sir William called off his siege of Eccleshall Castle.[461] Grey abandoned his home county and was heading south to join forces with the Earl of Essex.[462] But the royalists again failed to pursue a complete strategy and the Queen left the area and went south to join Rupert's forces which had been hovering on Leicestershire's southern borders. On the 13th the armies of Rupert, the Queen and the King joined on the field of Edgehill, and went on to Oxford.[463] Hastings was left alone with only a slightly improved position.

The Nottinghamshire parliamentarian forces were, by July 1643, reduced to only 300 men when Sir John Meldrum, recently appointed to command the county's forces by Essex, led men into Lincolnshire to retake Gainsborough.[464] Those in Leicestershire and Derbyshire each numbered about the same. In the latter county, the royalists had controlled the two large hundreds in the north since June and with the seizure of Burton-on-Trent, Hastings' ability to gather taxation in the southern hundreds was increasing.[465] To combat this, Gell mounted a concerted attack designed to capture Tutbury Castle at the end of July.[466] Hastings' forces managed to protect the castle but at the expense of not being able to assist Henderson and Cavendish in Lincolnshire where Meldrum and Cromwell were on the offensive. On the 20th the parliamentarian commander of the county, Lord Willoughby, had defeated the Earl of Kingston, his nominal counterpart, when he captured Gainsborough.[467] Four days later, Cromwell captured Stamford and then sought to supply Willoughby at Gainsborough. On the 28th he and Meldrum defeated Cavendish's forces outside the town; Cavendish was killed. But when the parliamentarians sought to fend off a renewed royalist attack, by what they thought was a small force, they found themselves confronted by all of the Earl of Newcastle's army, which had marched south after its victory over Lord Fairfax at Adwalton Moor in Yorkshire. Gainsborough fell after three days, Cromwell withdrew south, and Willoughby abandoned Lincoln after his retreat from Gainsborough. Lincolnshire, and thereby Hastings' east flank, was secure. Sir William Widdrington replaced Kingston and Cavendish as commander of the county.[468]

Sir John Meldrum, commander of Parliament's forces. He besieged Newark from February to March 1644, but was defeated by Prince Rupert and Lord Loughborough. (Public domain)

In the west Stafford Castle was finally abandoned by Lane despite aid from Hastings having reached him.[469] Throughout August, the North Midlands Army was free to deal with Leicestershire and Staffordshire. In the middle of the month, Hastings attempted and failed to persuade Leicester to capitulate, just as Newcastle failed to persuade Nottingham to do so.[470] Capel's forces failed to capture Nantwich in Cheshire despite Brereton's absence. The latter had joined forces with Sir Thomas Myddleton, who had been sent with a small force to aid in the destruction of Capel's command. The two parliamentarians opened a second siege of Eccleshall without immediate success. Then on 27 August, Hastings himself marched to relieve the garrison. The regiments he took with him included his own horse and foot, the latter numbering around 400, the former possibly as many as 800. It may be that the 800 horse Hastings had with him included some of Bagot's and William Nevill's. On top of the 800 there were also the regiments of Sir John Harpur and Sir John Fitzherbert. The North Midlands Army appears to have managed to force their way through the besieging army and to have reached the castle where Hastings may have installed a new governor, an unidentified Dane. In the process the royalists were forced finally to withdraw towards Tutbury. Two days later the garrison, supposedly unwilling to serve under the foreigner, surrendered. The captain responsible, be he the Dane or not, was to be brought to trial at the insistence of the King.[471] As Brereton had earlier captured Chillington House near Wolverhampton, one of Dudley Castle's satellites, the west of Staffordshire was free of royalists. Brereton had also taken Tamworth in the east of the county.[472] It is probable that the loss of this territory prompted the King to assign parts of Warwickshire to Dudley for the purpose of taxation. This was to have repercussions later on.

During September, with Brereton and Myddleton in Shropshire, Hastings' control of Leicestershire became more pronounced. The garrison at Leicester did manage to effect a cattle raid on Ashby whilst Hastings was at Tutbury, but this was its only success.[473] By the end of the month, the royalist commissioners of array had completed a circuit of the county, sitting at Loughborough in the north on the 25th, Hinckley in the south on the 26th, Market Harborough and the eastern town of Melton Mowbray on the 27th. Only at the latter were they challenged by parliamentarian forces. One thousand men of the North Midlands Army successfully drove the Leicester forces off. By the end of the month, *Mercurius Aulicus* reported that in the county, Parliament's assessments had dried up. In this instance it does not appear that the paper was exaggerating.[474]

The Earl of Newcastle from his position at the siege of Hull desired that Henderson with the Newark forces and Hastings with the North Midlands Army enter Lincolnshire to aid Widdrington who was being threatened by Willoughby and Cromwell in mid September.[475] It seems that both Hastings and Henderson saw Nottingham as a more rewarding prospect. On the 18th, they attacked the town and drove the garrison into the castle. They stayed for five days and before they left set up a fort on the River Trent, commanded by Hastings' Major Hacker.[476]

They had been wrong not to aid Widdrington earlier. On the 11th of October he was defeated at Winceby and the royalists abandoned Gainsborough. Even as Widdrington wrote to Hastings for help, the latter and Henderson were at Horncastle.[477] But Secretary Nicholas ordered Hastings to help Capel, who it appears was already using some of the North Midlands Army – namely sections from Dudley and Lichfield. Hastings wanted these forces back to protect his rear whilst he was operating in Lincolnshire, baling out forces he had earlier been instructed to leave to themselves'.[478] As a result of this necessity for the North Midlands Army forces to divide in two, and fight in areas outside its own territory, local parliamentarians could act unhindered. The Leicester garrison captured Bagworth Park which had bothered them all year, and the Nottingham garrison, with help from Gell, drove Hacker from the Trent Bridge fort in the week preceding the 23rd October.[479]

in Lincolnshire. His replacement was Richard Byron, brother of John, Lord Byron, active in Cheshire. Byron had attended the councils of war with Newcastle and the North Midland Army officers during the winter. He lost no time in reminding Hastings of his promise, made at Bolsover, to help the garrison at Newark whenever the need arose.[516] Even though the garrison was, in practice, out of Hastings jurisdiction, defence of it was important. Integral to the geography of the North Midlands, Hastings could not afford to be denuded of this important royalist stronghold. Important it was too, for the royalist cause as a whole. With Lord Byron's failure to defeat Brereton and secure Cheshire, communications with Newcastle's northern territory from Oxford via the west was all but closed. With the fall of King's Mills on the Trent communications via Derbyshire were liable to interruption. Thereby Newark, at the point where Fosse Way crossed the Trent) was an essential town as far as royalist communications were concerned.

The parliamentarian army surrounding the town consisted of between 6,000 and 7,000 men. In it were elements of Lord Willoughby of Farnham's Lincolnshire army, which were grouped chiefly to the south of the town while forces from the North Midlands were grouped to the north.[517] Inside Byron had less than 2,000 men; 1,200 foot and six troops of horse. The rest of the Newark horse were initially on the island in the Trent to the north of the town under the command of Major General Porter. Having 2,000 horse the parliamentarian army could keep an adequate guard on the surrounding districts to prevent small scale relief projects. Such an attempt made by the Belvoir garrison, with parts of the Newark horse quartered in the Vale of Belvoir, was driven off a week after the siege had begun.

Prior to his surrounding the town Meldrum had attacked the island in the Trent across which the Fosse Way left the north side of the town. On the island were George Porter and the Newark Horse and Gervase Holles' Regiment of Foot. Porter and the horse evacuated the island just before the attack began, leaving the foot behind. The regiment was, as a result, severely mauled when the island was stormed and captured by anything up to 3,000 men.[518]

Hastings' army was the nearest force of any size. Charles Lucas, who had until recently been as near as Doncaster, where he fortified the town in order that it be used as a communications route from north to south, had by this time gone further north.[519] Freshville at Staveley and Bolsover projected a relief project on March 3rd. Hastings was to bring elements of the forces he had recently had in Cheshire, with Prince Rupert, to Mansfield, from where the attack could be launched. For some reason the plan was never executed, probably due to the strength of the opposition.[520] Even with the help of Porter's horse and foot stationed at Tuxford, Meldrum's army would still be larger than the North Midlands Army. Hastings moved the forces he had had with him in Cheshire to Ashby and remained there as outlying units gravitated towards his headquarters.[521] The help of Prince Rupert was solicited by the Newark garrison before 7 March by J. Thorold, possibly a servant to Robert Sutton, one of the Nottinghamshire commissioners of array, based at Newark. Rupert replied that he would need a month to prepare such a project.[522] Thorold, witness to the opening stages of the siege, reckoned that the town could last no longer than 20 days. By the 9th, Rupert asked Hastings and/or Porter to provide him with 700 horses upon which to mount musketeers to facilitate the rapid march east.[523] Despite his desire to organise the western counties it appears that the idea of such a march was firmly in the Prince's mind. By the 12th, whilst he was at Chester, he was reported to be gathering forces with which to undertake the task.[524] This he did not make obvious. His movements to Shrewsbury on the 14th and Bridgnorth on the 15th, may have been an attempt to disguise the fact and indeed successfully did so.'[525] By the 12th, whether the Prince had decided to relieve the town of his own volition or not, the King wrote to urge him to do so.[526]

At Ashby-de-la-Zouch, Hastings had gathered his field force of 1,500 horse and 1,200 musketeers. He also had alerted Leveson's regiments and they attached themselves directly to the Prince's army.[527] The regiments of horse present at Ashby were Hastings', Freshville's, Eyre's, Bagot's, Milward's and Nevin's. Fitzherbert's and Kniveton's were probably also present.[528] Units of the Newark Horse which had gone into the Vale of Belvoir instead of north with Porter, were probably those units of the North Midlands Army, Hacker's troop and Archer's troop, both of Hastings' Horse, which were stationed at Newark, as they were incorporated into the force at Ashby without being apparent as separate units. The foot at Ashby would comprise the regiments belonging to the colonels who provided the horse. In all, including Leveson's regiments, the North Midlands Army fielded 3,000 men.

Before Hastings had informed Rupert of his preparedness, the Prince asked the Midlands general to demolish hedges and fences between Ashby and Newark to facilitate a cross country rapid march.[529] On the 15th, Hastings had probed the parliamentarian garrison at Leicester to investigate its readiness to assist the leaguer at Newark. After firing at the town walls the small royalist force retired along the line of the river Soar towards Loughborough. They halted for the night at Mountsorrel.

The parliamentarians at Newark were determined to prevent a combined army of royalists attacking them. However, it appears that they were primarily concerned to stop Porter joining Hastings rather than contemplating any attack made with the aid of Prince Rupert. Meldrum several days later still believed that the approach of Prince Rupert was only a rumour. Sir Edward Hartopp, the commander of the North Midland contingent at Newark, with most or all of the parliamentarian horse, went into Leicestershire to prevent the junction of Porter and Hastings. On the 16th, he and his force of 2,000 clashed with the royalist forces at Mountsorrel. Colonel Thornhaugh's Nottinghamshire regiment forced their way across the Soar bridge and into the town before the royalists were aware of Hartopp's presence. For some reason Hartopp refused to back up Thornhaugh's attack and, despite the latter being able to fortify himself in the town, he was ordered to withdraw. This gave the royalists time to organise and counter-attack. Thornhaugh's resultant extrication was difficult and costly in terms of casualties. Hartopp compounded this by withdrawing his entire force north towards the crossing point at Cotes just to the east of Loughborough. The royalists followed on the opposite bank.[530]

Hastings had fortified his own house, Burleigh Hall, to the west of Loughborough. From here, soldiers joined by the forces from Mountsorrel, moved on the bridge at Cotes where, on the 17th, they constructed fortifications, watched but unhindered by Hartopp. The bridge at Cotes was the route by which Porter would reach Hastings and thus was important in this respect alone, but it was also the route by which Rupert and Hastings intended to approach Newark. During the day of the 17th, forces from Leicester, three companies of foot and two cannon led by Colonel Grey, arrived at the eastern end of the bridge where Hartopp was stationed.

Hastings' report concerning the state of affairs at Cotes to Prince Rupert said that he would have 1,200 men at the bridge by the morning of the 18th.[531] A.C. Wood in his book on Nottinghamshire in the Civil War, asserts that it was Porter's forces which were present at Cotes on the 17th and this may have been the case, but it is highly likely that Porter was still north of the Soar on that day. If Hartopp was trying to prevent Porter joining Hastings he would clearly have failed already if Porter were at Cotes. On the 18th, Hartopp attacked the royalists on the bridge. The two cannon were used to good effect and appear to have caused a great deal of damage to the royalist foot. It seems that the royalists had five regiments of foot present on the east bank along with an unspecified number of horse. If Porter had been present the royalist numbers would have been in excess of 2,000. Hartopp had 2,000 horse and perhaps as many as 500 foot. After the artillery had 'softened up' the royalists, a concerted attack was made on the bridge. After their foot had cleared the way, the parliamentarian horse rode across it and attacked their royalist counterparts, which certainly included Freshville's

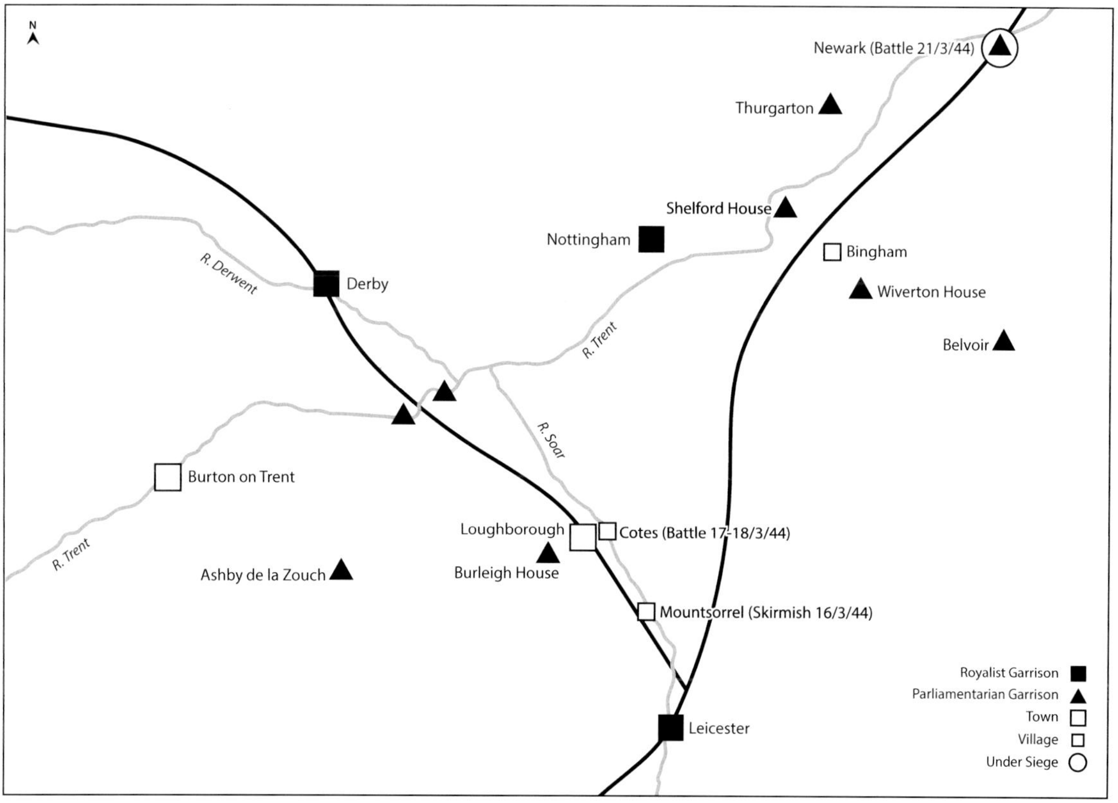

Map 5 The Relief of Newark, March 1644.

regiment. The royalist horse, after a fight of unknown duration, retreated through Loughborough to Burleigh Hall, whilst the parliamentarian horse pursued them as far as the town. Hartopp's forces were now in possession of the bridge as royalist foot retired from the Great Meadow, by the Soar, into the cultivated lands north of Loughborough. Thornhaugh's regiment of horse had not been involved in the attack; they were stationed on Stanford Hill, to the north of the battle site. From this promontory they would have an excellent view of the battle, but more importantly, they would be able to observe the movement of any troops in Hartopp's rear. This tends to support the idea that Porter's force had not joined Hastings and was still in Nottinghamshire, north of Hartopp's position.[532]

It is possible that more of the North Midlands Army began to approach the area as Hartopp withdrew his horse from the town by nightfall. Prince Rupert had, during the day, marched his forces from Lichfield to Ashby-de-la-Zouch.[533] It is still unclear whether Hartopp was fully ignorant of the proximity of Rupert's forces; it is probable that he still discounted the possibility of his being present. At any rate the arrival of the entire North Midlands Army was not something he felt able to face – especially as Porter was probably still between him and Newark. As a result of these considerations, the entire parliamentarian army retreated from the bridge and Hartopp marched towards Nottingham. Colonel Grey and the Leicester forces returned to their garrison. The three royalist forces could now unite unhindered.

Rupert brought with him three regiments of foot, numbering 1,120 men, two regiments of horse and his own lifeguard, numbering 700 – a total of 1,820 men, which he added to Hastings' 3,000. On the 19th he crossed the Soar and, using the route Hastings had, as asked, cleared of hedges and enclosures and reached Rempstone on that night.[534] On the following day the Prince's forces united with all of the North Midlands Army, some of which appears to have gone ahead after Hartopp, perhaps to complete the clearance of impediments to the route, and with Porter's 1,600 men at Bingham. At 2:00 a.m. on the 21st, the army marched to Newark and occupied Beacon Hill having made their approach via Balderton. Meldrum, now aware of the Prince's presence, concentrated his forces at the ruined hospice near Newark on the Spitta1.[535]

As with Hopton Heath, this brief battle has been dealt with, in sufficient detail for our present purposes, by secondary sources – this was not the case with the incident at Cotes.[536] Rupert's horse swept down from the hill and clashed with two bodies of parliamentarians under Colonel Rossiter on the left, and Thornhaugh on the right. The first charge was inconclusive, but the second saw the parliamentarians begin a retreat which may have become a rout, on to the island in the Trent. Meldrum probably hoped to retreat across the island and make his retreat via the bridge at Muskham. However Richard Byron and the Newark garrison sallied out and surrounded the fort erected at the bridge, preventing Meldrum's passage. When the small force in the fort fled during the night, Meldrum's escape was ruled out entirely and Rupert planned to starve him into surrender. On the morning of the 22nd,

Meldrum and his forces surrendered all their arms, ammunition and cannon to the royalists.

It was a masterpiece of strategy on Rupert's part but it was no less of a triumph for Hastings. The army which he had constructed in the previous 16 months had, despite having lost men to other forces, fielded no less than 3,000 men whilst at the same time maintaining men in several major garrisons. It had been achieved because of the financial system described in Chapter 2. It was indeed the zenith of its career. Rupert, like Newcastle in the winter, did not stay to complete the conquest of the counties. Though the jubilant commissioners of array did threaten Nottingham with Prince Rupert's army, the Prince did not linger. Lincoln was abandoned by the parliamentarians on the 23rd, but six days later, the Prince was at Ashby, heading west.[537] Parliamentarians in the North Midlands were shaken and defeated but not destroyed. The Earl of Denbigh, appointed the previous year by Parliament to take charge of several counties, including Staffordshire, had at last freed himself of the accusation of being a royalist sympathiser and had taken up his military task. By the time the Newark campaign reached its conclusion Denbigh had arrived at Leicester. At the same time, in response to Rupert's intervention and the fall of Lincoln, the Earl of Manchester, commander of Parliament's Eastern Association army, began to gather the forces in south Lincolnshire in order to march north.[538]

In the period covered by this chapter, the North Midland counties had become, at least superficially, a unified area of royalist territory. It could provide the manpower and finances for a field army and maintain major and minor garrisons. Even if the parliamentarians were in possession of four major garrisons in the area the royalists could maintain a reasonable degree of stability in the face of what amounted to guerrilla warfare. Yet it was and is still obvious that the North Midlands Army could not mount a sustained campaign, even within its own territory, without recourse to outside aid. The failure of the army to capture any of the county towns and its inability to secure Newark alone, give evidence of that. However, when it is remembered that for much of the time Hastings' army was working in entire or in part, in other areas, aiding Lord Byron, Lord Capel or Sir Charles Lucas, this is perhaps understandable. Moreover the success of Hastings' forces is shown by the fact that of all the commanders north of Oxford, with the exception of Newcastle, he was the only one appointed in late 1642 who was still in actual command of his region.

Nevertheless within the North Midlands, seeds of destruction were already sown, above and beyond the problems with the indigenous parliamentarians. The command system was not unified and its relations with the civil administration were strained. On top of this, Hastings' own success was to count against him for it opened the North Midland forces and resources to use and abuse by the royalists at Oxford and elsewhere. It is to these problems and the subsequent history of the royalist war effort in the North Midlands that this book now turns.

Chapter 6

Nemesis: The Breakdown and Defeat of the North Midlands Royalist War Effort

In the previous chapter the rise of the royalist war effort was examined. It was concluded that by the end of 1643 the royalists had established a firm grip upon the region and were able to operate the financial system outlined in Chapter 2. As indicated at the beginning of the previous chapter this present section will deal with the internal problems within the system and with the interference of the King which did not help Hastings to maintain his authority, but the bulk of this chapter will deal with the way in which the North Midlands slipped from the royalist grasp. The problem, established in Chapter 5, that Hastings was frequently forced to supply troops to other royalist commanders, will be seen to recur in the months following March 1644. It will also be shown that this played no small part in its downfall.

The royalists in the North Midland counties had quite a strong military hold on their territory at the beginning of April 1644. They had nine major garrisons and at least 15 minor ones, both from which to operate their financial system and in which to base their soldiers. In Derbyshire, the garrisons of major importance were Bolsover, which guarded the northern part of the county and provided a stopping place for northward movement of troops, and Wingfield Manor which, being within nine miles of Derby, was an important check on the town; in addition there were five minor garrisons in Derbyshire. In Leicestershire the major garrisons were Belvoir and Ashby-de-la-Zouch. The former, under Gervase Lucas, was Hastings' outpost on the Lincolnshire border and a place from where collections of contributions in that county could be administered and from where military initiatives were launched. Ashby-de-la-Zouch was probably a large garrison second only in size to Newark, with a force, in its vicinity, of over 1,000 men. In Nottinghamshire the chief garrison was, of course, Newark, the largest in the region with over 2,000 men stationed in it. Newark had a chain of outposts between it and Nottingham as well as having soldiers based, whenever the opportunity arose, at Grantham in Lincolnshire. In the north of Nottinghamshire was Welbeck garrison, one of the Marquis of Newcastle's

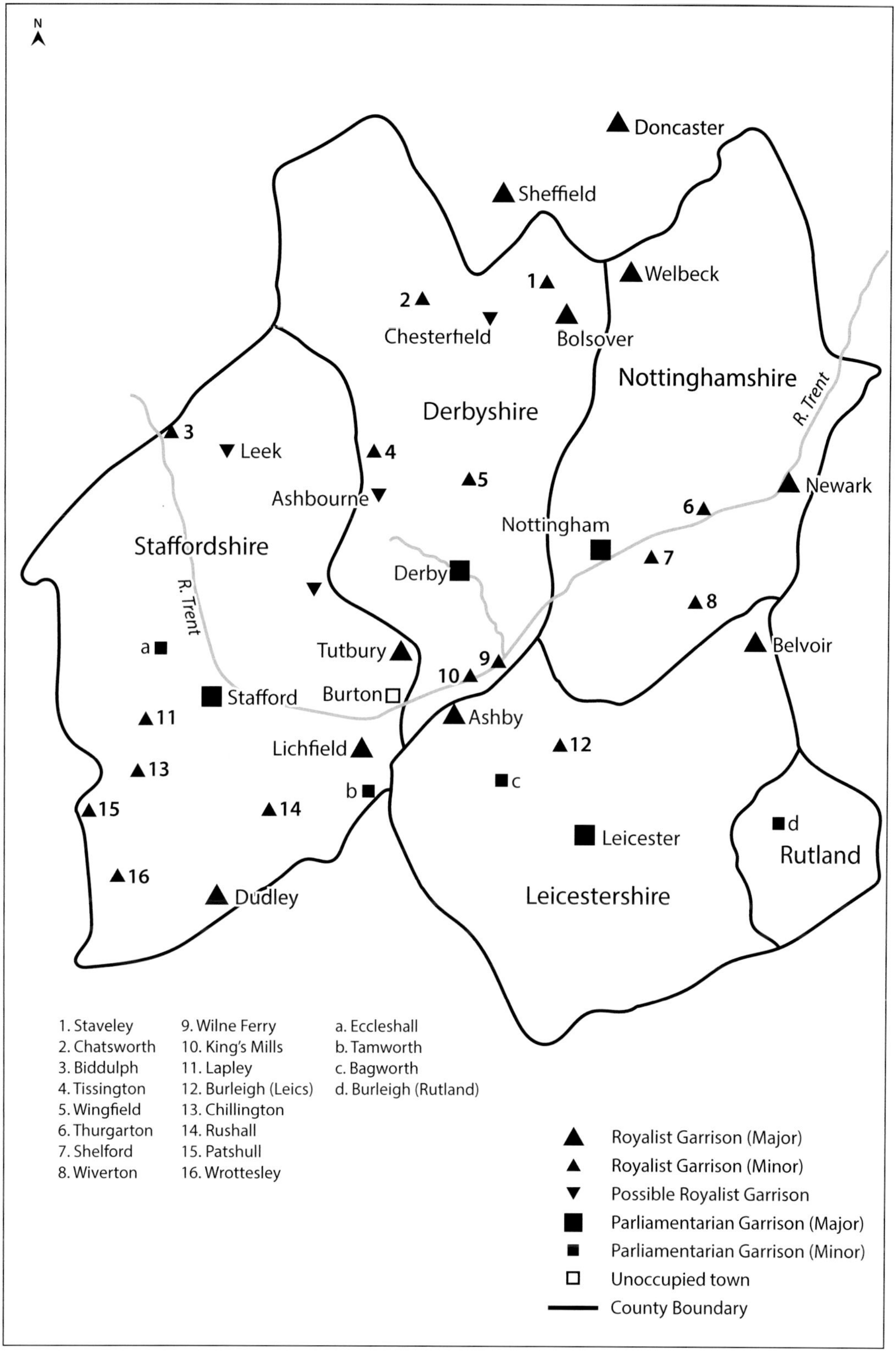

Map 6 North Midland Garrisons 1644,

houses. In Staffordshire there were the three major garrisons of Dudley, Lichfield and Tutbury and several minor garrisons. Dudley was in actual fact part of Worcestershire in an island of that county inside Staffordshire. Ronald Hutton in his book states that Dudley was [technically] thus divorced from Hastings' command.[539] Technically this may be so but in practice Leveson, whether he liked it or not – and he did not – was part of the North Midlands Army under Hastings. The King reminded him of this in October 1643 and he reluctantly acknowledged it was so a few days later,[540] although he had to be reminded again in January. All the garrisons mentioned here were, with the exception of Newark and its satellites and perhaps Bolsover, under Hastings' command. It appears that Welbeck in Nottinghamshire may well have been under Hastings too as its governor was Sigismund Beeton the shoemaker ex-captain of Hastings' Foot.[541] However, it is possible that this garrison like the other Nottinghamshire garrisons and Bolsover, were directly under the command of the Marquis of Newcastle (both Bolsover and Welbeck were the property of Newcastle[542]). Each garrison commander was, as Hutton asserts with reference to Lichfield, allowed autonomy in daily action subject to the work of the commissioners in financial matters and to Hastings' military needs.[543] It appears that Hastings' ability to assert his authority over a few of his colonels was limited and this helps to account for the internal strife which the North Midlands Association was to suffer in late 1643 and early 1644. This was a problem which was not eradicated either then or subsequently.

The first major difficulty arose when the King allocated parts of Staffordshire to the Dudley garrison.[544] This would initially seem sensible for, despite its presence in the Worcestershire island, Dudley was within Staffordshire and had been garrisoned by Leveson as an extension of his hold on the south county, whilst he was governor of Wolverhampton. However firstly, this was an example of Charles' interference with the local administrators who had already dealt with territorial allocation, and secondly, as a result, the allocation trespassed on territory previously assigned to Lichfield. These had already been reduced when Tutbury garrison began collecting contributions from Tolmansloe Hundred and parts of Offlow Hundred. This had cut down the area from which Lichfield was able to levy contributions. Rushall garrison also gained contribution from Offlow.[545] As a result in autumn 1643 Leveson and Bagot entered into a vicious argument with troops from each respective garrison fighting amongst themselves. Central government at Oxford appear to have realised their error and passed the buck on to Hastings.[546] He could not get the commanders to accept his decisions and the dispute dragged on throughout November 1643.[547] By the 10th December Hastings had decided to let his immediate superior, the Marquis of Newcastle, decide the argument, presumably at one of the councils of war held at Bolsover and Chesterfield.[548] The result was not in Bagot's favour. Leveson was considered to be very important by the King and Hastings had been reminded of this by Nicholas earlier and thus was probably swayed in his judgement. Bagot in early January 1643 insinuated to Hastings that not only was he short of money as a result, but that his soldiers would mutiny. His income was only around one eighth of his expenditure at the time. Moreover a large part of this income

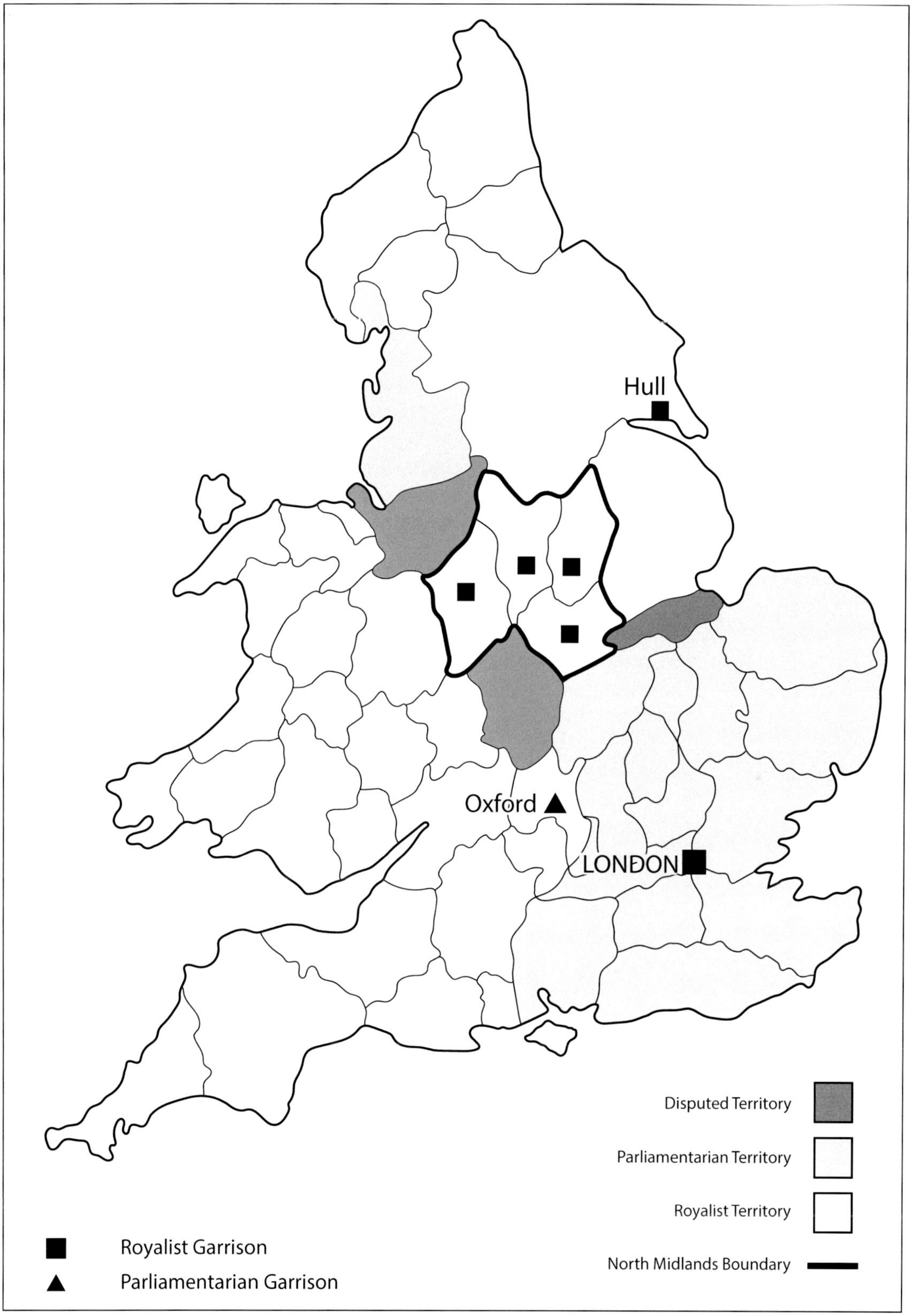

Map 7 England and Wales December 1643.

came from the sale of plate and not from contribution collections. Bagot was able to exist, hand to mouth, on loans from the gentry in the surrounding area until Prince Rupert, whose command of the Marcher counties had been expanded to cover Staffordshire, entered the region in February and dealt with the matter at one of his councils of war. Bagot and Leveson reputedly came to a mutual agreement.[549]

The problems were not over. Leveson was brought into the civil government of Staffordshire, when the King appointed him as high sheriff. This gave him, he assumed, the right of *posse comitatus* – the ability to raise soldiers. This he could do, he told Hastings, 'without acquainting you'. Whilst the same letter of 7 February expressed Leveson's hope that he and Hastings could maintain a working relationship, he adopted a quite different tone with Prince Rupert the following day. Hastings, he claimed, had prevented the execution of the warrants for the *posse comitatus* and this coupled with the local parliamentarians preventative measures had cost the King 1,000 recruits.[550] Hastings was right to be outraged: again the King had meddled directly in the affairs of the North Midlands to the detriment of the royalist cause. Bagot, upon whose territory Leveson's *posse comitatus* was also being levied, was now being deprived of manpower as well as money.

Powerless to prevent the King's actions in the first instance, Hastings turned to the Oxford Parliament. Despite being under attack from some elements in the Houses for allegedly demanding exorbitant sums from Staffordshire, Hastings succeeded in having Parliament remove Leveson's power of *comitatus*.[551] With Rupert's intervention in the financial matters and the parliamentary decision, Hastings had achieved a form of victory, but the victory, like the problem itself, was the result of outside intervention. Problems could have been eased if Leveson had been incorporated earlier into the civil and administration structure by the commissioners themselves. At Dudley, he was geographically as well as actually, isolated from the administration based at Lichfield. In part this isolation would be due to his Catholicism, which would seem to have excluded him from the commissions of array, as well as to his personal abrasiveness. His desire for military independence may well have grown out of this isolation. It certainly was not eased by the further fragmentation of the North Midland command structure, which Rupert's authority over Staffordshire represented. In effect this divided Hastings' command in a way similar to the independent status held by the garrison at Newark.

Although by the end of February Staffordshire was relatively stable, Hastings had two other problems within his command. Firstly, there was a practical military problem in Derbyshire. Sir John Fitzherbert, who had been a loyal colonel under Hastings since early in the war, seems to have felt that he had been unfairly treated in the later months of 1643. His lieutenant colonel, Sir Andrew Kniveton, had been promoted and given the governorship of Tutbury, yet Sir John only had command of the minor garrison, Tissington Hall, his cousin's house near Ashbourne. Furthermore, when Wingfield Manor was captured by the Marquis of Newcastle, Colonel Roger Molyneux had been installed as governor. Molyneux, though put under the command of Hastings, appears to have been an outsider at the time of his appointment. Alongside this, parts of Fitzherbert's regiments were stationed at Wingfield under Molyneux's command. Sir John petitioned Newcastle with a view to having the Marquis replace Molyneux with himself, but it would appear that Hastings and Newcastle agreed to leave things as they were.[552] Fitzherbert's men at Wingfield mutinied in January in support of Sir John and Molyneux requested permission to return them to Tissington. However, although the immediate outcome is unclear, some of Fitzherbert's Horse were in Wingfield during August 1644. We are left to assume that Sir John himself and perhaps his regiment accepted the decision of the high command. This suggests that, left to its own devices, the North Midlands royalists, with their overall commander, Newcastle, were capable of sorting out some of their problems, but not the problem of interference from Oxford.[553]

This last point, the interference from Oxford, is reinforced by the second problem which involved territory closer to Hastings' home base. Since the loss of large areas of Lincolnshire and Rutland during autumn 1643, the Belvoir garrison had experienced financial difficulty. To compensate, the Leicestershire commissioners assigned to the garrison the whole of Framland Hundred for a period of two months. By January 1644, the two months had elapsed and the situation in Lincolnshire had become easier, for the royalists and other units, probably those at Ashby, were being paid from the contribution income from Framland. However, in January, the King took it upon himself to assign Framland to Belvoir on a permanent basis, possibly as the result of a plea by Gervase Lucas, the castle's governor.[554] Though Charles did acknowledge that such arrangements were up to Hastings and the commissioners, and that this decision was subject to their approval, he did so after giving Lucas the territory, thus making reversal difficult. The effect of this dispute was not serious in the short term, but resurfaced a year later, when Lucas refused to recognise Hastings as his superior officer, and absented himself from the general's council of war.[555] Lucas clearly regarded himself as independent of Hastings, perhaps in the same way that the garrison of Newark was. He had been in the Newark garrison before his seizure of Belvoir and had participated in many of the military actions into Lincolnshire.[556] This has led several historians to assume that Belvoir was a satellite garrison of Newark, in the same way that Wiverton was. However it is clear that both Hastings and the King saw Belvoir very much as part of the North Midlands Association and, thereby, directly under Hastings' command.[557]

Despite the seeming stability of the North Midlands command achieved by the Newark campaign, the internal problems were largely unresolved and they remained so during the subsequent part of the war.

Yet it is not safe to assume that the internal wrangles were a major cause in the ensuing collapse of the regional command. Though many of the settlements were to prove transient, the disputes in themselves were not sufficient to wreck the system.

The Crisis: April–July 1644

During the two and a half months following the Scottish invasion of northern England, the military situation in the north had deteriorated and the effects of this were to have an adverse effect on the North Midlands in the subsequent period. Newcastle, unable to bring the Scots' Army to battle, was forced into a steady retreat before them. In the south of his command he had left John Belasyse in command at York with around 5,000 men. Belasyse had the onerous task of dealing with the Fairfaxes, father and son, who were ranging over the south of Yorkshire. Units of parliamentarians had raided deep into the East and North Ridings, capturing Bridlington and Whitby in the process. In the West Riding, during March, Bradford was occupied by parliamentarians, who fought off attempts to dislodge them.[558]

It appears that Newcastle first ordered Hastings to aid the Yorkshire royalists as early as March 1644, but no documentary evidence seems to exist. However the North Midlands Army's preoccupation with Newark precluded any such aid going north. Immediately after the relief of the town George Porter was sent into Yorkshire with the horse he commanded from Newark and some North Midlands Army horse, including Gervase Lucas' regiment. Porter and his forces were involved in Belasyse's second attempt to reoccupy Bradford, on March 25th, only four days after the relief of Newark. According to Peter Newman, Porter's horse failed Belasyse in the same way that they failed Holles' Foot and had also failed Rupert at Newark on 21 March.[559] Porter immediately returned to Nottinghamshire with his forces, and sought Rupert's permission to stay and recruit.[560]

Despite urgent appeals from York seeking his help, Hastings was concerned over the practicality of venturing north. Fairfax was between him and York with 3,000 and men, a force equivalent to the North Midlands Army, and the army of the Eastern Association under Manchester was active on his eastern flank.[561] By 8 April, Hastings had ordered Porter to go north again, whilst he intended to follow as soon as he had amalgamated his army units.[562] But Porter had still not moved out of Nottinghamshire by the 11th, when Belasyse's army was destroyed at the Battle of Selby. It was a portentous defeat. Newcastle, realising that York was about to come under siege and that his rear was exposed to the victorious Fairfaxes, turned his anger both on Porter and, perhaps with less justification, on Hastings.[563]

Despite the King's assertion that all was secure in the North Midlands, all was not.[564] Moorlanders, ever opportunists, had been attempting to push Ralph Sneyd's headquarters out of Uttoxeter and Hastings had been forced to commit 400 horse to preventing this from occurring.[565] Bagot's Horse were, according to their colonel, unable to go north because of high casualties suffered in the Newark campaign. Bagot had 80 troopers without horses, and collection of replacements was impossible without the section of the regiment that Hastings had at Ashby. In addition Leveson appears to have reneged on his promises and was encroaching on Bagot's territory, an encroachment which involved the collection of horses.[566]

In addition to the renewed internal problems there was the more dangerous threat posed by the Earl of Manchester. Though Hastings suspected that the Earl intended to march to Yorkshire at some time, the presence of the Eastern Association Army at Stamford made it impossible for Hastings to leave his region unprotected. As the Earl remained within striking distance of the

Leicestershire border for a further month, any possibility of going northward in strength was crippled.[567]

The Marquis of Newcastle, upon hearing of the defeat at Selby, marched his army rapidly to York. Shortly before his arrival at the city on 16 April, he sent George Goring and the horse south to prevent them from being trapped in York. Hastings knew of this arrangement as early as the 13th.[568] The King expressly ordered Hastings to take his forces north with Goring once the latter had entered the Midlands.[569] Goring was in Nottinghamshire by the 21st and Hastings duly dispatched some forces to join him. However, few units from Staffordshire appear to have been with Hastings, who was now at Uttoxeter securing the town against attack; thus a significant element of the army could not be dispatched to join Goring. Though it appears that within a few days Bagot's soldiers themselves were ready to march, he was awaiting the arrival of some of Leveson's regiment, and there was no sign of them arriving.[570] Bagot then informed Hastings that Leveson claimed Rupert had ordered him to stay put and not to go into the north. The shortage of horses in the area was still a major problem. The Staffordshire markets could only supply thin and wasted horses, thus again limiting the ability of the county's units being able to join Goring. Nevertheless, Hastings was able to dispatch Derbyshire regiments to Goring who was by this time based at Newark.[571] At least three of the Derbyshire colonels, Eyre, Milward and Freshville, joined the northern commander there.[572] Goring was not however satisfied; he chided Hastings for his lack of assistance and the Oxford royalists also condemned Hastings' seeming inactivity.[573] But despite the problem of manpower, the North Midlands were managing to feed and supply the forces Goring had brought with him. Freshville told Hastings that it was becoming increasingly difficult to do so, and that the northern commander expected too much.[574]

The presence of Manchester still preyed on Hastings' mind and especially as Lincoln had fallen to the Earl on 6 May. On the western flank, as Rupert, who was raising forces in order that he could march north, reached Shrewsbury, Leveson's regiments from Dudley joined him,[575] and as they did so, the Earl of Denbigh's army moved into south Staffordshire and lodged themselves around Tamworth.[576] It was clear that not all of the North Midlands Army could go north, either with the Prince or Goring.

With Denbigh in the south and Manchester in the east, the North Midlands were under as much of a threat as the north itself.

It was within these weeks that the North Midlands were stretched to their limits: horse flesh was in short supply; Hastings' own forces were in a poor state and were divided between two outside armies; the counties' financial structure was supplying both Rupert's and Goring's forces as well as catering for their own needs. The parliamentarian paper, *Kingdome's Weekly Intelligencer*, of 21–28 May, was unlikely to be far wrong when it stated that the 'condition of Leicestershire is much lamented'.[577] Given this and Freshville's comments in his letter to Hastings on 5 May, it is apparent that the North Midlands were in a sorry state. Though the newspaper, referred to above, suggested that Manchester dare not enter Leicestershire with his 4,000 foot and 1,200 horse (over 3,000 horse had gone north under Cromwell to join with the Fairfaxes), the same was not true of Denbigh, who had marched through Staffordshire and was at Eccleshall by 23 May. Rupert at this time was in Cheshire.[578] On the 24th Denbigh's army, back in the east of Staffordshire, attacked and captured Rushall, the garrison of Colonel Lane; Hastings had, a bare fortnight earlier, refused to disgarrison and level the Hall. As a result it was garrisoned by Parliament and became a constant thorn in Lichfield's side.[579]

When Rupert and Goring joined forces on 30 May, they had armies fed and paid out of the North Midlands' resources and at least 1,000 men from the region's army.[580] This left Hastings' command potentially incapable of resisting incursions by external forces and disruptions caused by indigenous parliamentarians. In such circumstances a victory in the north was essential to the survival of the North Midlands war effort.

Though by 3 June, Manchester's army was at York and thus out of Hastings' way, Denbigh was besieging Dudley Castle, denuded, like the region as a whole, of a large portion of its military forces. Dudley was left to suffer Denbigh's siege for over a week. Inside, Lieutenant Colonel Beaumont was in command of probably less than 200 men. There are no surviving letters to, or from, Hastings during this month so his actions against the threats within the region cannot be ascertained. The local parliamentarians were determined to make the most of the absence of a large proportion of the royalist regiments by going onto the offensive. In Derbyshire where, like south Staffordshire, the absence of royalists was felt most keenly, Gell proposed the unification of Derbyshire and Leicestershire forces to attack Hastings' garrison at Wilne Ferry.[581]

South of Hastings' command, the King was in danger of being trapped at Oxford by the armies of Sir William Waller and the Earl of Essex. On 3 June, the King left his wartime capital and on the 6th arrived at Worcester, with Essex and Waller following from there. Lord Wilmot, with the Oxford Field Army horse marched northward, and on the 10th, relieved Dudley Castle. Two days later Wilmot failed to defeat Denbigh at Tipton Green.[582] Denbigh moved south and linked up with Essex's army and remained in Worcestershire until the King made his dash from Worcester on the 16th. Then the Earl crossed Staffordshire and with Mytton stormed Oswestry before entering Cheshire, where he helped Myddleton take over the south of the county. Despite the predictions of *Perfect Occurrences* on 17 June that a second siege of Dudley Castle was imminent, Denbigh's military role in the North Midlands was at an end and he shortly returned to London.[583]

In the north, the worst possible event, from the North Midlands' royalists' point of view, occurred. On 1 July Rupert dazzled friend and foe alike when he relieved York as his enemies drew away from the city in a vain attempt to prevent his approach. On the next day his army and the forces of the Marquis of Newcastle were attacked whilst at supper on the field of Marston Moor. In the royalist army that day, several regiments from the North Midlands were startled by the sudden attack of the parliamentarian army.[584]

Prince Rupert's marching army contained Leveson's Horse, under their colonel himself. On the field of battle, Leveson's regiment was on Rupert's right wing, the cavalry force commanded by Lord Byron. According to de Gomme's map, the regiment was in the second line at the left hand end of the body next to Tyldesley's Horse. With Goring's marching army were the regiments of Eyre, Milward and Freshville. The first two and perhaps the latter, had taken both horse and foot. On de Gomme's plan, the Derbyshire foot may have been the unnamed unit marked 'S'. It is possible that all the foot were gathered here. Peter Young reckoned that the total number of Derbyshire foot was around 220, this being the number that Gell said that Milward and Eyre took out of the county.[585] If Freshville had taken his foot, there may have been a further 100 or so in the body, though Gell's report to the Committee of Both Kingdoms suggests that Freshville himself did not take many foot. The combined unit stood in the second line of foot regiments at the left hand end, between the regiments of Henry Cheater to the right and Edward Chisnell to their left. The three colonels' horse regiments were placed in the front line of Goring's wing on the royalist left. There were 500 musketeers interspersed with this wing; some may have been Derbyshire forces. These North Midlands Army regiments would have numbered between 800 and 1,000 men between them. However this was probably not the whole number of soldiers from the North Midlands Association. Behind Eyre's Horse stood Sir Charles Lucas' Brigade, a unit which, as we have seen, was composed in part of forces which he had taken from the North Midlands Army.[586] Thus it is possible that there were in excess of 1,000 men from Hastings' own forces as well as Newark regiments (Anthony Eyre's, for example) present on the field on 2 July 1644.

If, as Peter Newman asserts, Lord Byron plunged his front rank into disorder when he led them across the broken ground and the ditch which should have protected them, then it is equally true that Leveson's Horse would be amongst those attempting to stem the tide of Cromwell's advance. It was a vain attempt: the wing collapsed and Leveson's men would have fled to within sight of York's walls. On the other flank, where Goring was successful in defeating the horse under Sir Thomas Fairfax, Eyre's and Freshville's Horse would have been in the charges which swept the opposition off the field and exposed the parliamentarian foot's right flank. However, when matched against Cromwell's horse which had circled the battle between the foot regiments of both sides, Goring's outnumbered forces could not, despite fighting hard, hold their ground. Under cover of nightfall, they were forced to leave the field. In the centre, where the foot had slogged it out for over three hours, the regiments of the three Derbyshire colonels would have been instrumental in pushing back the parliamentarian regiments pitted against them. But when Sir Charles Lucas' horse repeatedly failed to make any impression on the Scottish foot, the tide began to turn. When Lucas was captured, his brigade broke up and the parliamentarian foot began to gain ground from their opponents. Slingsby wrote, 'Our Foot… although a great while they maintained the fight yet at last they were cut down and most part either taken or killed'.[587] Amongst them were the regiments of Eyre and Milward, composed of men raised by the commissioners of array in late 1643, of whom Hastings had said, 'I have no faith in them'.[588] He had been wrong.

In the North Midlands, there was brief optimism following the battle. Plans were made for the advance of a second composite force to join Rupert who, it was asserted, had just fought 'an Edgehill battle' (it was earlier thought to have been a victory). Hastings, unfettered by Denbigh's army and with no threatening forces on his eastern flank, was preparing an army of 1,800 men taken from the North Midlands Army, Newark and Pontefract, to join with Rupert near Doncaster.[589] But by the 8th, doubt as to the nature of events in the north was beginning to set in. Rupert's silence was ominous. Furthermore, it was rumoured that Waller was to lead his army north to aid Manchester, Fairfax and the Scots. If this was the case, Byron, at Newark, argued that the Midlands army should wait until Waller had passed, and then to follow him, to prevent being trapped between him and the other parliamentarian armies in the north. The resolve to go north had, it seems, by this time become less pronounced. Though Byron was actively planning to gain horses on which to mount musketeers, he was also pondering remaining in the Midlands where, he told Hastings, 'we shall be master of the field.'[590]

By 19 July, not only had Hastings learned of the defeat at Marston Moor, but also of the fall of York. Closer to home the loss of the fort at Wilne Ferry had lost him his remaining crossing point on the Trent, which had been the point of rendezvous with Byron.[591] Wilne had been captured, by the forces of Gell and Leicester, from Captain Thomas Robinson and parts of Hastings' own regiments. Two days earlier Derbyshire forces, with help from Nottingham, had established a leaguer around Wingfield Manor, Molyneux's garrison in central Derbyshire.[592] Clearly the defeat of Rupert at Marston Moor would give further impetus to the local parliamentary initiatives, begun when royalist forces by Rupert and Goring marched north. On the other hand, Dudley forces, free of any threat from Denbigh, were able to gain supplies from Birmingham.[593]

Hastings' plan for bringing together the North Midlands Army was preserved, but in order now to act within its own territory and rescue Molyneux. Bagot and the Lichfield forces were to meet Hastings at Burton-on-Trent and if possible, link up with Colonel Eyre's Horse, which had arrived in the area with Prince Rupert around 25 July. Eyre, Freshville and Leveson had returned via Lancashire with the Prince, whilst Milward's Regiment of Horse was with the Northern Horse and probably already led by the former lieutenant colonel, John Shallcross (henceforth the regiment will be referred to as Shallcross'). The Northern Horse were marching in the Yorkshire/ Lancashire border region.[594]

The planned meeting failed miserably. Eyre's regiment, presumably tired and careless, was captured in its entirety as it slumbered in the church at Boyleston in Derbyshire, without a shot being fired.[595] When Bagot's men arrived at Burton-on-Trent they found parliamentarians waiting for them, and so they withdrew into Staffordshire. The following day they were attacked and although they drove the parliamentarians off, Bagot was forced to retreat to Lichfield.[596] A desperate plea for help made by Molyneux to Hastings, caused the general to postulate another rescue attempt at the end of July, but it came to nothing.[597]

Since the end of March, when the North Midlands Army had been at the height of its power, and the counties where it had been raised had been relatively stable, the situation had declined dramatically. Staffordshire, part of Newcastle's territory during 1643, had, since April at the latest, been part of Rupert's command, thus giving Hastings two masters and Leveson the

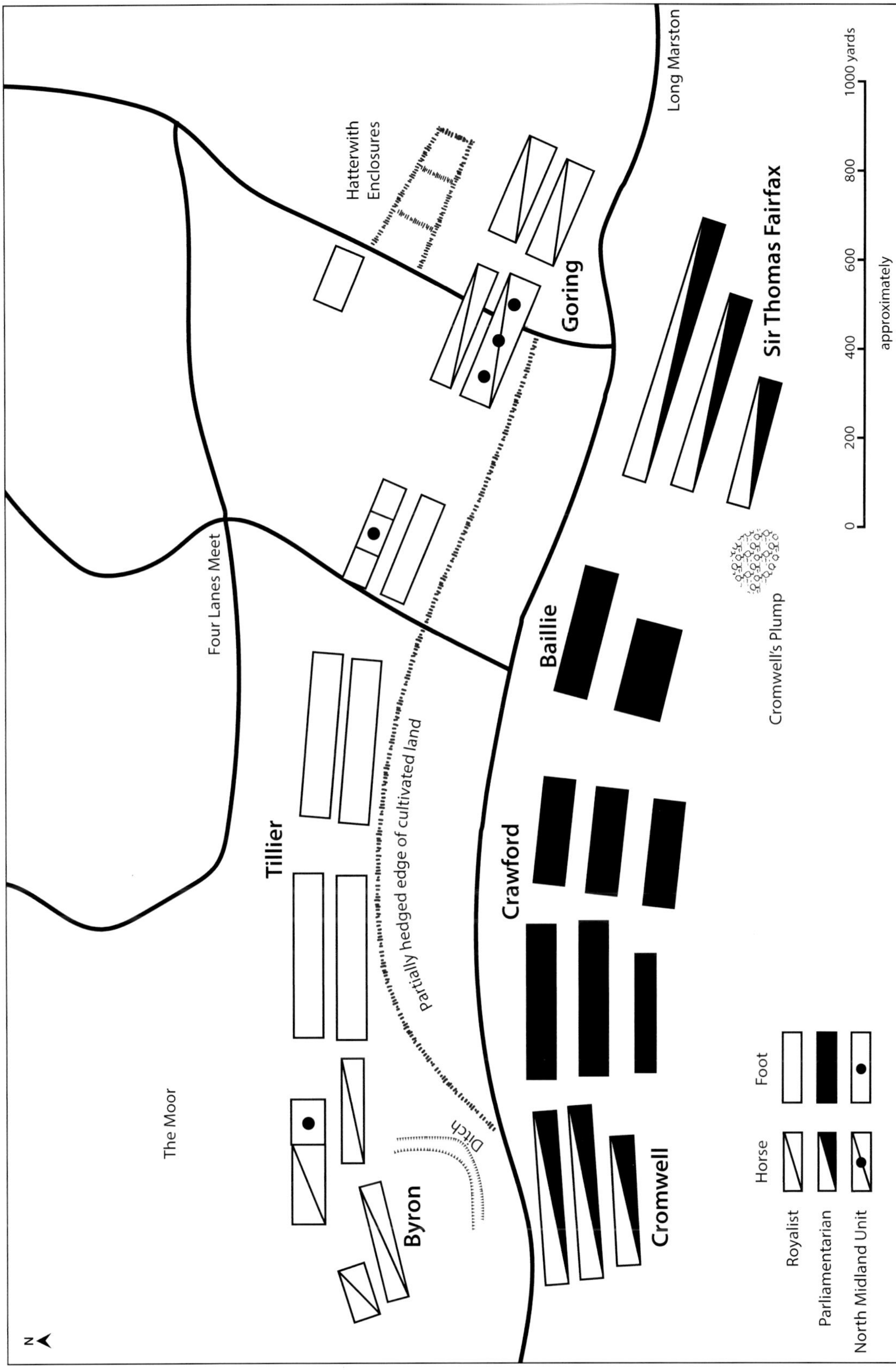

Map 8 The North Midlands Army at Marston Moor.

opportunity to break away from Hastings' control even more.[598] The drastic situation in the north had presented many problems to the Lieutenant General. From his territory food, horses and men had been invested in what had turned out to be a defeat. Three of the active Derbyshire colonels had, with their regiments, been taken north, leaving their county open to the parliamentarian initiative which deprived Hastings of a small garrison and would soon deprive him of the whole county after it had received outside help. The whole region, as a result of supplying the northward march of Rupert and Goring, had been drained of resources. For this sacrifice of resources and men, Hastings received small thanks – he was still blamed for the defeat at Selby. Moreover, the strategic position of his territory had changed. Hitherto the region had been the link between the royalist north and the royalist south and west. Now at the end of July, it was the front line – a front line with large numbers of men and resources wasted in other regions.

August, September and October, 1644: Decline

On 1 August, Welbeck was summoned by the Earl of Manchester's army. On the following day it surrendered and Manchester moved across the county border into Derbyshire to Bolsover.[599] Freshville had by this time returned to his garrisoned house at Staveley. But the colonel was, it seems, seized with the same panic which made Milward leave off his command and he offered to hand Staveley to the enemy and lay down his arms. On the 12th August, the day that Molyneux sallied out of Wingfield and attacked the besiegers, Freshville surrendered Staveley.[600] That same day Bolsover fell to Manchester and Hastings' northern garrisons were gone.[601] Elements of Manchester's army, under Major General Crawford, moved down to Wingfield with heavy artillery and began to destroy the walls of the manor. On the 17th, unable to hold out any longer, Molyneux surrendered.[602] In less than three weeks, northern and central Derbyshire had fallen to parliamentarians. Whilst enthusiastic London newspapers confidently predicted that Hastings would soon be under siege himself, Manchester's forces left the North Midlands area.[603] They set up headquarters in Lincoln where, in the words of Clive Holmes, Manchester 'dithered … until… early September'. Hastings was given a breathing space to protect what territory and income he still had.[604] Whilst the Belvoir forces successfully tackled the Rutland parliamentarians, based at the once royalist garrison of Burleigh House, Hastings was still able to collect contribution from within sight of Leicester.[605] The parliamentarians in the county town were now reduced to a small garrison under Colonel Henry Grey. Lord Grey of Groby's role in the region was almost at an end. Though the East Midlands Association was not dismantled until October, his commission, as *Mercurius Aulicus* pointed out, had been a hollow title since the middle of the previous year when parts of the region's forces had been hived off to other commands. In the resurgence of local parliamentarianism, Lord Grey was to play no part.[606]

By mid September, Hastings' fortunes had ebbed so low that the Leicester committee was now able to claim that it had bottled Belvoir and Ashby up and that they were fighting each other. There was some truth in this.[607] Lucas was disputing not only Hastings' right to command over him. Lucas' argument was that as Hastings' commission had been granted by the Marquis of Newcastle, the Marquis' voluntary exile made the commission extinct.[608] It does not appear that Hastings was as bottled up as Leicester claimed, or would have liked, him to be. Regiments of horse from Ashby were able to operate just south of Nottingham in late September, when Colonel Stanhope was killed and his regiment passed to John Barnard, who led it south[609] (for a full discussion of Barnard and the regiment see the previous chapter).

At Tutbury, Sir Andrew Kniveton was deprived of much of his Derbyshire contribution. This appears to have been a result of the deprivations of May 1644 whilst Rupert and Goring were in the area as much as the result of the collapse of royalist control in the county. Kniveton, like Bagot before him, was forced to supplement his income with loans from sympathetic gentry. Normality, of a sort, was resumed within a few weeks as the castle appears to have been able to collect contribution from Repton and Gresley Hundred.[610] In Leicestershire, a petition was organised by the 'well affected' and delivered to Parliament. The petitioners claimed that the raids of the garrisons of Belvoir and Ashby were becoming more frequent. The blame for this was put firmly on the shoulders of the Leicestershire committee which was accused of embezzling county funds and of having 'little or no estates amongst us'. The solution, according to the petitioners, was the recall of Lord Grey and the re-establishment of his command. Given the proven abilities of the noble lord this solution would have suited the royalists far more than the parliamentarians. It is possible that what worried the petitioners, was that the royalist forces were increasingly pragmatic in their tax collection. To suggest that the royalists were a more potent force in late 1644, when their power was definitely on the decline, than in late 1643 when they controlled virtually the whole county, is certainly spurious. However, the evidence cited in Chapter 2 suggests strongly that in certain parts of the county contribution was proceeding normally. Thus the actual fears expressed in this petition may well be less important, being of doubtful validity, than the desire that that committee do something to further the decline of royalist power. After all in Derbyshire, the major royalist garrisons had been eradicated but in Leicestershire they were both still present and potent.[611]

Following the departure of the Earl of Manchester with the major part of his army from Lincolnshire, the Belvoir and Newark forces went on the offensive. Units from Belvoir seized Crowland in early October. Such a nuisance did this small outpost prove to be, that Lincolnshire parliamentarians made immediate attempts to recapture the town.

Manchester was forced to send aid to Edward Rossiter and Thomas Rainsborough, the two colonels he had left in the county. By the end of the month Crowland was cut off and in need of aid. Hastings and Byron undertook the construction of a relief force from the North Midlands Army and the Newark garrison in order to rescue the garrison at Crowland.

Accordingly a rendezvous at Belvoir was arranged. The Newark forces contained Roger Molyneux's Regiment of Horse which had gravitated to the garrison after the fall of Wingfield. It is possible that other units of the North Midlands Army were also included in the Newark contingent. Also present were the Belvoir forces and elements of the Ashby garrison. In total the Midlands relief force totalled 1,500 horse and 500 foot. On the night of 29 October, regiments of Lincolnshire parliamentarians met at Denton, to the east of Belvoir. Another force of parliamentarians from Derbyshire, Nottinghamshire and Leicestershire were approaching the area from Nottingham. The following morning, the Lincolnshire forces withdrew, enticing the royalists after them.[612] This enabled the Midlands parliamentarians to approach the royalists from their left flank and rear. What followed appeared to be induced by panic rather than by defeat on the field. The royalists, perceiving the enemy to their rear, fell into disorder, and if the parliamentarian accounts have any honesty about them, to the amazement of their opponents, fled the field, not by the route to their left rear towards Belvoir, which was still open to them, but through the closes to their right rear. Many found themselves trapped in the enclosed fields and others attempted to swim the mill pond below the castle hill. This resulted in many men and horses being drowned. In the panic, Parliament were able to capture between 600 and 800 men.[613]

It was a devastating defeat, the blame for which fell squarely on Byron's shoulders as he had led the royalist forces at the battle. Within Newark factions developed, one supporting Byron and desiring his retention as governor, and another which sought to replace him with John Digby, the man who as high sheriff in 1642 had done much to turn the town into a royalist stronghold. The argument dragged on for three months following the battle of Denton until Byron was replaced by Richard Willis in 1645. The chief casualty was the North Midlands Army, which was never to fight again as a combined unit, as its fragmentation became increasingly pronounced. With the arrival at Newark, in mid September, of the Northern Horse, Shallcross' regiment temporarily joined other North Midlands Army regiments in the town. Eyre had reformed his regiment after the disaster at Boyleston and it was now at Newark as was Molyneux. Hacker was also in the town. Freshville was still absent, flirting with Parliament's cause though he was soon to reappear in Newark with his horse.[614] Hastings himself, it appeared to Parliament, was under a cloud. 'General Hastings is like to be removed from his government of Ashby-de-la-Zouch and another made Commander of his Counties in his Place whereby it appeareth that the cavaliers begin to suspect their own party', wrote the *Court Messenger*, and *Weekly Account* heard that 'he hath many causes of distaste, then that he hath laid down his commission'.[615] Whether further suppositions that he was at Oxford attempting to gain other employment had any substance or not, the Lieutenant General was not to be removed from his present charge.[616]

November 1644 – April 1645: Isolation and Division

During this winter several strands in the history of the North Midlands Army can be identified. Firstly, the fragmentation of the army which now spent much of its time within its composite garrisons. Secondly and concurrently,

Parliament sought to increase its hold on the counties. Thirdly, as a result of victories in the west, the royalists began a resurgence of activity in March and April.

Parliamentarians at Derby and Leicester spent the early weeks of November, in the wake of the battle of Denton, debating the establishment of a garrison close to Hastings' command centre at Ashby-de-la-Zouch. Between them they agreed to garrison Sir John Beaumont's house at Coleorton, within three miles of Hastings' headquarters. Leicester provided 200 horse and 300 foot, Derby 300 horse and dragoons. This force was in position by 18 November.[617] Such a large proportion of horse assigned to the garrison gives an indication of the nature of intent. The Coleorton forces were to disrupt, as much as possible, Hastings' collection of taxes and provisions from the hundreds appropriated to Ashby. It would be possible, given Coleorton's proximity to Repton and Gresley Hundred in Derbyshire, for the garrison to hinder Tutbury's taxation effort too.

At this time the town and castle at Ashby had, in addition to the county's commissioners of array, a force of 1,000 soldiers. These would be the core regiments of the North Midlands Army, Hastings', Pate's, Nevill's and Parkyns' being amongst them. Hastings himself was reportedly at Oxford, giving rise to the suggestions that he wished to hand over his command.[618]

There was, in addition to the increasing difficulty of maintaining any grip on the counties, the problem of the power vacuum created by Newcastle's departure from the country. It is not known, due to the lack of documentary evidence, who was considered to be Hastings' superior. In the case of Staffordshire it was still Prince Rupert who had assumed command there from Newcastle in or around March 1644. Thus it was to him that Leveson turned to for help when he accused Bagot of disrupting the collection of contribution by force of arms in November 1644.[619] Rupert's command passed under his brother Maurice's generalship in December as did the responsibility for sorting out the Staffordshire quarrels.[620] It is possible that the rest of Hastings' regional command came directly under the authority of the commander of the King's forces, in effect under Rupert, from December. As Maurice was responsible for sorting out the Leveson/Bagot quarrel, it is clear that no attempt was made to reunify Hastings' command by separating Staffordshire from the Marcher counties.

During December the royalists' position crumbled further. In the first half of the month the garrison at Crowland, established by Belvoir in September, surrendered, cut off as it was from its parent garrison.[621] By the 20th, it was reported confidently in London that the Ashby garrison was safely cooped up. Derbyshire markets had now recovered and the sad state of the county economy, witnessed by parliamentarians in the previous winter, had been reversed.[622] By the turn of the year the situation had changed so completely from the halcyon days of the royalist war effort: from being masters of four counties, with the exception of the county towns, they were now holding on to much reduced areas of territory surrounding their garrisons. Even in these areas they were subject to parliamentarian interference. Newark, Tutbury and Ashby were permanently watched by small enemy forces. Those at Newark were under Rossiter's command and derived from Derbyshire,

Nottinghamshire and Lincolnshire. It does not seem that this army was a permanent fixture, though London presses referred to it as a leaguer – a siege force. By the 3rd January, Rossiter moved further away from the town – he had hitherto been at Southwell six miles from Newark. As a result, the garrison was able to collect contribution despite the fears that the hovering menace had earlier produced.[623]

The Bagot/Leveson quarrel, begun anew at the end of 1644, dragged on through the following January. Leveson claimed that the Staffordshire commissioners of array refused to collect contribution to pay his regiments' back pay.[624] For their part, the commissioners were in the process of joining with the gentry of Shropshire, Worcestershire and Herefordshire, in demanding a greater say in the running of the war effort. They wished to raise an armed force themselves and appoint its officer. This was an extension of the idea Leveson had had the previous year when he attempted to use *posse comitatus*. In this case however regular officers, such as Leveson, were deliberately excluded from the proposed county orientated forces. By 15 February the King had agreed to the association of the Marcher counties.[625] In a way, this royal recognition of an accomplished unity was reminiscent of his handling of the unity achieved under Hastings in February 1643. Charles limited the powers of the association's commissioners: Maurice was to choose and appoint the officers for the newly raised forces; but on the other hand, the commissioners had greater control over the use of excise and sequestration income. (It will be remembered that in Chapter 2, it was suggested that this latter may have been a recognition of fact rather than right.) Again, by recognising this position, the King had reinforced the division of the North Midlands counties, thereby ensuring that the breakdown of the unity of the North Midlands royalist war effort was not due solely to the difficulty of holding on to the ever decreasing territorial hold, but also to the internal realignments made by the royalists themselves. Maurice managed to get Leveson and Bagot to reach an agreement without recourse to Rupert's suggestion of recalling them both to Oxford and thus achieved temporary stability in Staffordshire.

With these commanders in agreement, Maurice was able to draw troops from both their garrisons in order to construct the army he needed to reconquer the west. Troops from Ashby and Tutbury were also incorporated in this army.[626] Leveson alone contributed 300 men. It seems that little regard was paid to the safety of the royalist garrisons in the North Midlands; as a result of Leveson's diminution of forces, Patshull House, one of his satellite garrisons, fell to the enemy.[627] Once again there was to be no immediate success derived from the drawing out of men from the North Midlands to fight elsewhere. As Maurice's army entered Chester, enemy forces from Wem attacked and captured Shrewsbury.

However the situation in the North Midlands was confused, for not everything was working against the royalists. On Hastings' eastern flank, the relief force consisting of the Northern Horse sent from Oxford to Pontefract, defeated Rossiter's horse at Melton Mowbray and then drove the rest of his troops from the vicinity of Newark. Whilst in Derbyshire, Colonel Molyneux's horse captured members of the Derbyshire committee at Wingerworth as they attempted to collect assessments.[628]

Nevertheless Hastings was disillusioned as he witnessed his territory being divided up and his Ashby and Staffordshire soldiers being again led off into the west. On his own doorstep, the inhabitants of Leicestershire petitioned him regarding the activities of Gervase Lucas at Belvoir. Their complaints he added to his own about Lucas not attending councils of war and his reappropriation of North Midlands Army weaponry, and sent them on to Prince Rupert.[629] Hastings went to Oxford in March, perhaps to make some personal representation on the matter. His general unhappiness with the situation was obvious. Digby urged Rupert to settle the problems to Hastings' satisfaction as he was still of 'great importance' and to ensure that he 'be not sent home discontented, as here he appears to be highly'.[630] It is not known what solution was made to the Lucas problem though it is likely that Rupert followed Digby's advice as no further complaints seem to have arisen from either side. Presumably the Prince simply reaffirmed Hastings' command over the region and over Lucas.

Staffordshire was the only county where the Marcher Association was pursued conscientiously. The county commissioners, with their few newcomers like the Earl of Ardglass, continued to plan their renewed administration. They had secured Bagot's and Kniveton's agreements to the system but Leveson, as ever, continued in his opposition to civilian government. This time it was Leveson who won. Rupert was dispatched from Oxford to help his re-establishment of royalist control in the Marcher counties and relieve Chester from a siege.[631] Hastings linked his forces with those of the two Princes during April and was a part of their successful rescues of both Beeston and Chester. The achievements of the Princes encouraged the appearance of small royalist garrisons in the Marches but also strengthened the position of the regular officers, the so-called swordsmen, as opposed to the projected civilian armies of the Marcher Association.[632] By the end of April, Rupert ordered the Staffordshire commissioners, in the King's name, to cease their work. The county then seems to have returned to the system established by the original commissioners of array but now effectively run by the garrison commanders.[633]

A resurgence of royalist activity followed the removal of the threat of Rossiter's forces upon Newark and the victories of the Princes and Hastings in the west. Leicestershire's royalists attempted to take possession of the county town in March by means of a complicated plot which failed to mature.[634] Whilst Leveson and Bagot's forces still operated in the Marcher counties, the Staffordshire commissioners were able to meet in Uttoxeter.[635] Nottinghamshire royalists who had roamed around Lincolnshire for a month after Rossiter's departure launched another attack on Nottingham and Major Hacker again became the governor of the Trent Bridge fort. This time he held it for a week until Rossiter's forces returned to throw him out. Parliament was sufficiently worried by the turn of events to dispatch John Hutchinson home from the enquiry into his activities as governor, brought about as a result of conflicts between the civil administration of the town and his own military command. Parliament expressed its continued confidence in him by sending him back to Nottingham to handle affairs in what they saw as a time of crisis.[636]

Thus there was somewhat of a resurgence of activity on the part of the royalists after a period of extreme difficulties. True, they were still largely fragmented and had no real hold on Derbyshire but they proved that the local parliamentarians could not rest on their laurels. This resurgence was to receive added impetus within a few weeks, when the King's Field Army moved out of Oxford to relieve Chester which had fallen under siege again from Sir William Brereton, once the Princes had left the area.

May–June 1645: Renaissance

The intervention of the King's Field Army brought hope to the local royalists. It forced the local parliamentarians to abandon various small garrisons and at the same time provided the royalists with a major new one – a potential nerve centre from which to administer the newly regained territory.

The King left Oxford on 7 May and had, by the 8th, joined the Princes at Stow on the Wold. By the time his army had reached Staffordshire on the 22nd, Brereton had again abandoned his blockade of Chester.[637] The King's Army continued to march north through Staffordshire, prompting Parliament to warn its chief garrisons from Leicester to York to prepare for a possible siege. From Uttoxeter, which he reached on the 24th, the King had a force of 4,000 horse including Bagot's and Leveson's regiments which together contributed 350 men, and 5,000 foot also including units from Lichfield and Dudley. At the same time as the King heard that Brereton had withdrawn from Chester, he also heard that Sir Thomas Fairfax and his army, a composite force made up of the old armies of the Earls of Essex and Manchester and Sir William Waller, topped up with conscripts, was establishing a siege of Oxford.[638]

The King's Army turned east. It had been decided that Fairfax's army, the New Model, had to be drawn away from Oxford. To do this, it was proposed that a Midlands parliamentarian garrison should be stormed. There were, of course, four immediate choices: Derby, Stafford, Nottingham and Leicester. Derby was discounted, perhaps from being too far to the north and because there was a large contingent of parliamentarian horse concentrated there under Gell and Vermuyden at the time. Nottingham's castle had resisted attempts to take it several times and was thus ruled out. Stafford was fairly insignificant and was outclassed by the nearby Lichfield. On the other hand, Leicester, where the committee had continually prevaricated over the building of strong defensive works because it would have meant the destruction of some members' houses, was ideal. The garrison was small, having a regular force of only 240 horse and 480 foot which were expected to man a defensive line over three miles in length. The excessive size of the outer defences was to enable it to encompass the committeemens' houses.[639]

Accordingly, Charles' army moved into Leicestershire. At Ashby, it picked up 100 horse from Hastings' regiment and then moved on Leicester. Between the 27th and the 30th the army established itself around the county town and built gun batteries against the weakest area of the walls, the part known as the Newarke. The garrison had been reinforced by a unit of dragoons under Major Innes, up to 100 horse from the abandoned garrison of Kirby Bellars and armed civilians, giving a total strength of around 2,000. The committee refused Rupert's summons to surrender and the cannon opened fire. Within three hours there was a breach in the walls.[640]

At midnight the town was attacked, and after a brief hard fight, entered. By 2:30 a.m., on the 31st, resistance ended and the royalists were masters of the town. The following day, Hastings became titular governor with Sir Matthew Appleyard as his deputy. Hastings' command of the North Midlands appears to have been reaffirmed and Sir George Lisle was appointed lieutenant general under him, with responsibility for Leicestershire.[641] Whether Hastings was at this time or earlier in the year, raised above his rank of lieutenant general is unknown, but the fact that he now had a person of that rank under him would suggest that he was.

As the King's Army rested south of Leicester, and then marched south to dispatch convoys of food to Oxford via Daventry, Hastings began a two fold task. Immediately he was faced with repairing and strengthening Leicester, the new capital of his command. To do this he undertook what the committee failed to do and began demolishing houses in order to contract the defensive line. Secondly and more importantly he began to raise new recruits. Before the King's forces had even left the town on the 2 June, he had raised 1,000 men. At one stroke the county had become wholly royalist as all the little parliamentarian garrisons melted away.[642] Gell with the forces of Nottinghamshire and Derbyshire were still hovering in the Derby area but did not venture into Leicestershire. The Scots Army, summoned by Parliament to move south to oppose the King and join with Brereton's forces, remained put in Yorkshire.

It was the New Model Army which was to provide the only sufficient opposition to the royalist resurgence. Whilst the King's Army lingered at Daventry for five days, waiting for the return of an escort of horse sent with the convoy of provisions to Oxford, Fairfax, released from his dependence upon the Committee of Both Kingdoms, moved north towards it.

By 12 June, apprised of Fairfax's approach, the King's Army retired towards Market Harborough. This was in order that Goring and the 3,000 horse dispatched to the south-west on 8 May and recalled on the 19th, with orders to go to Market Harborough, would be given time to do so. The royalist army was, without Goring, woefully small, numbering somewhat less than 8,000 men.[643] The following day, Fairfax was joined by his second in command Oliver Cromwell and the New Model reached a strength of around 14,600.

In the King's small army were several elements of the North Midlands Army. Bagot's and Leveson's units have already been referred to. Hastings' Horse appears to have remained at Leicester but elements of Molyneux's, Freshville's and perhaps Eyre's were with the Newark Horse, and Shallcross' were still with the Northern Horse, under Langdale.

On the morning of the 14th, the two armies shifted position westwards after Fairfax and Cromwell decided that the New Model's position was too strong and would deter the royalists from attacking. After mirroring this movement, the royalists stood on Dust Hill, a mile or so north of the village of Naseby, facing south. Across the Broad Moor, a heath land area with three strips of cultivated land running roughly north to south and planted with corn, stood the New Model, almost twice the size of the King's Army, on the reverse slopes of Red Hill. On the royalists' right flank, and to their front the New Model dragoons were ensconced in Sulby Hill Close, an enclosure projecting from the Naseby side of the boundary hedge of Sulby Parish.[644] The North Midland Army units were positioned as follows: Bagot's and Leveson's Horse were in Sir Thomas Howard's Brigade, which was a total of 880 men split into three bodies amongst the foot units of the royalist centre; Molyneux and Freshville, in the Newark Horse, stood in reserve to the rear of the horse on the left flank; Shallcross' Horse was in the front line of the left wing.

The battle lasted less than three hours. Though no convincing account has yet been written of the fight, the action was fairly straightforward. The royalists advanced and as they did so found themselves outflanked to their left as they emerged from the strictures of the parish boundary hedge on that flank. At the same time their left flank would also enter the broken ground, pitted with rabbit warrens. As they negotiated these, they were hit by the first wave of Cromwell's attack.

On the royalist right, the horse advanced towards Commissary General Ireton's horse and as they did so a small number of royalist horse became enmeshed in the hedges of Sulby Close which housed Okey's Dragoons. Most of the royalist regiments avoided this obstacle and charged home. After a stiff fight, they broke Ireton's wing and most of his horse scattered.

In the centre the outnumbered, but far more experienced, royalist foot of the King's Army under Lord Astley, pushed back the opposition. However, Cromwell's horse consisting in the main of his excellent Eastern Association regiments, broke the royalist horse under Langdale and ploughed into Astley's flank. By the time Rupert, who had led the royalist right flank to victory, extricated his men from the parliamentarian baggage train and returned to the field, the battle was lost. An attempt by the King to lead a counter-attack was prevented when the Earl of Carnwath swore at him and pulled him aside by the bridle of his horse. On seeing this the reserve forces joined in the general retreat. The King's Army had been defeated chiefly due to their pitiful lack of numbers which prevented their being able to stem the advance of the numerically superior New Model, once the latter had begun to gain the upper hand.

The royalist foot were, for the most part, captured, but the horse fled by various routes towards Leicester. Here, during the ensuing 24 hours, they deposited their wounded with Hastings, and followed the King, via Ashby, to Lichfield.[645]

The renaissance of the royalists in the North Midlands was over, destroyed by the madcap enthusiasm of the King's Army. Again, outside interference, though initially offering hope, had damaged the North Midlands royalist war effort. Four days after the Battle of Naseby, Hastings was forced to surrender Leicester. He managed, under cover of darkness on the 17th, to sneak 500 horse out of the town, but with the newly repaired walls of the town battered down by the very guns, now under new ownership, which had damaged them before, he was faced with an impossible task.[646] In his letters of explanation he expressed his conviction, after a council of war involving him, Lisle and the rest of the officer corps in the town, that surrender was a better option

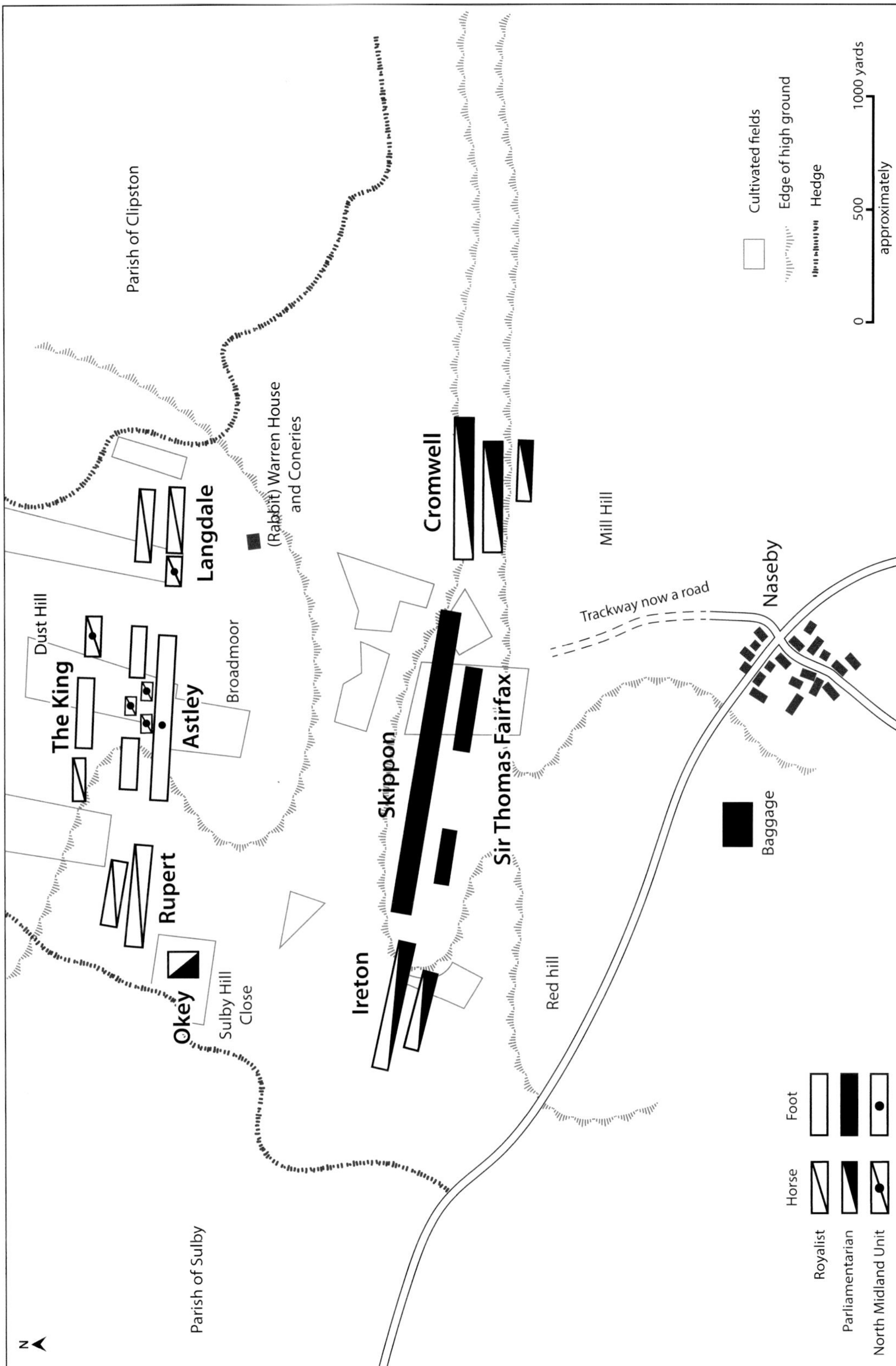

Map 9 The North Midlands Army at Naseby.

than fighting it out. At least this way, he asserted, the garrison was neither slaughtered nor taken prisoner. But he lost all the arms he had in the town and 500 horses as a result of the surrender conditions.[647]

Parts of the New Model along with Gell's forces contemplated the capture of Ashby-de-la-Zouch but nothing was done.[648] The parliamentarian garrisons were reoccupied and the royalists became yet further restricted in their movements and, as a result of Naseby and the surrender of Leicester, much reduced in both weaponry and manpower. Gell was accused of not trying hard enough to prevent the King leaving the area after the battle, for he certainly had the manpower to do so. Hastings too was to suffer the acrimony of his superiors.

A War of Attrition: July 1645–July 1646

During this final stage of the war, the North Midland counties finally succumbed to a reversal of the position at the end of 1643. Small pockets of resistance were now surrounded by a territory largely dominated by parliamentarian forces. However, the indigenous royalists continued a potent guerrilla war against their enemies. It is this image of the North Midlands Army which has survived and presented itself in all hitherto histories. Whereas the army had been a cohesive force until October 1644, it had now become small, isolated but determined groups of warriors.

Despite the disaster of Naseby, the royalist forces were not thoroughly dismayed. On 16 July Freshville's Horse, their colonel recently returned to the royalist fold and with his regiment based at Newark, recaptured Welbeck in Nottinghamshire. Bolsover, across the county border in Derbyshire, also fell to royalist forces. Thus while Gell had been concentrating his efforts on Tutbury, large parts of north Derbyshire were opened up for the collection of royalist contribution.[649]

Richard Bagot had received his death wound at Naseby and Rupert proposed to replace him with his own adjutant, John Scrimshore. Both Hastings and the King objected to the move, on the grounds that Scrimshore had, along with Bagot, argued with Hastings. Thus they asserted, if he were given the governorship, the disputes would continue. That Rupert conceded by the end of July, and allowed Hastings' candidate Harvey Bagot, Richard's brother, to have the post, shows that Hastings was still considered as an important figure by the Prince.[650] The King, it would appear, was not so sure; he had wanted the post to go to Lieutenant General George Lisle. Parliament's newspapers had reported that Hastings had been imprisoned by the King after the surrender of Leicester. But if he did fall into such disfavour, he was in some measure restored, probably by the Prince's intervention, by the end of July. If the Prince had intervened there is no doubt that the letters Hastings had written to him regarding the surrender would have been a factor in this.[651]

The southward march of the Scots Army through the area does not seem to have hampered the activities of some of the local royalists. Newark forces were raiding, on a pragmatic basis, deep into Lincolnshire throughout

August and were threatening to remove the county's harvest produce.[652] In the second week of the month, Charles began a new march into the region having been forced to make concessions to localism in Wales. He took, as usual, soldiers from the garrisons en route. In Staffordshire he was forced to re-establish the Marcher Association. By the time he reached Welbeck on 13 August, he had added 100 foot from Lichfield, and as many as 250 foot from the Nottinghamshire forces to his small army of 4,000.[653] The King's sojourn in the area was, as ever, a mixed blessing. Despite the loss of men to the marching army the royalists could collect contribution from throughout Derbyshire despite parliamentarians from Stafford, Derby and Nottingham, hovering in the area.[654] Leicestershire was still recovering from the effect of the past months. The committee requested the right to compound with royalists who were surrendering in increasing numbers, to supplement their income. The committee also refused to supply Fairfax with 1,500 men, who, they claimed, could not be raised by them.[655]

Throughout this period, from June to November, Ashby Castle was almost inoperative. Plague had broken out in May probably spurred on by the overcrowded conditions in the town and castle caused by the presence of the army. The garrison of the castle had been forced to live in the parklands to the south. By the end of September, it was estimated that there were only 60 men left in the garrison, the rest having moved to other nearby garrisons. Hastings, when not with the King while the latter coursed the North Midlands, seems to have resided at Lichfield.[656]

Charles' departure, after less than three weeks of planning a march to Scotland with his army to join Montrose, returned the North Midland shires to the position held before his arrival. Gell's forces reassumed the task of containing the royalist garrisons within decreasing pockets of territory. Throughout September the situation remained unchanged; the King, having returned to Oxford, then marched out to rescue Hereford from the Scots' siege. At the end of the month, Freshville's garrison of Welbeck, with troops from Newark and Bolsover, recaptured Chatsworth House. Shallcross' Horse, based at Newark since Naseby, became the garrison there. When the regiment had been Milward's Chatsworth had been their base, shared with Eyre's.[657]

By the beginning of October, the King and his roving army returned to the region. He based himself around Newark for a month, and again brought the artificial control of increased areas of the country to the North Midlands war effort.[658] Newark forces were able to exact contribution, albeit on a more pragmatic basis, from parts of Lincolnshire as far away as the Lindsey coast.[659] The Staffordshire commissioners, with Hastings actively involved, had again come into conflict with Leveson over the collection of contribution. Whilst in Leicestershire, as Princes Maurice and Rupert rode to Newark to plead the latter's case for his seeming precipitous surrender of Bristol, Ashby was reoccupied. The re-established forces soon began to conduct raids on nearby parliamentarians. The King ordered Hastings not to allow the two princes to stay at Ashby Castle. Charles' given reasons were that they might use up precious provisions; in reality he probably feared that they would persuade Hastings that they had a just cause and that he would allow them to remain at the castle where they would be a challenge to the King's authority over the North Midlands officers.

Four days before the letter to Hastings, the princes had, with officers loyal to them, attempted to challenge the King's power to decide the governorship of Newark. The King, by replacing Willis, Rupert's friend, had been attempting to placate the commissioners who had grievances against Willis' command. Rupert's action in trying to get the King to retain Willis can be seen in the light of Rupert's attempts to favour army officers, the swordsmen against the civil authorities, as he had done in the case of Leveson.[660]

However, in this instance the King's presence could not prevent the tightening grip of parliamentarian forces on the region for long. By the end of October, the Scots Army which had entered the North Midlands stormed Shelford House, one of Newark's outposts and the garrison was put to the sword.[661] Prompted by this, the King left Newark on 3 November, having effected Willis' replacement with John Belasyse.[662] Following the King's departure, the minor royalist garrisons collapsed. Rowland Hacker surrendered Wiverton House, Welbeck was abandoned by Freshville and Chatsworth and Bolsover followed suit. In Staffordshire Wrottesley House was abandoned by the royalists and parliamentarians took up residence to watch over Dudley Castle. Sydenham Poyntz and the Scots established themselves around Belvoir Castle and before the end of November had captured the stables.[663]

By the beginning of December, the only royalist garrisons remaining were Dudley, Lichfield and Tutbury in Staffordshire, Ashby and the besieged Belvoir in Leicestershire, and Newark in Nottinghamshire. Each of them had a small parliamentarian force stationed nearby to watch over their movements and attempt wherever possible to disrupt their activities. With the possible exception of Lichfield the disruption meant the severe curtailment of contribution collection. Lord Astley's appointment, in December, as Lieutenant General of the Marcher Counties was specifically aimed at maintaining the remaining garrisons and relieving and supporting Chester, which was again under siege from the indomitable Brereton.[664] To do this Astley and Hastings worked together to build an army from the garrisons of the Marches and from remnants of the North Midlands Army. Units of horse from the latter had been already assigned to Sir William Vaughan who was attempting to harass Chester's besiegers. By the end of October Vaughan's forces had been scattered and he spent the ensuing two months trying to weld them together again.

Hastings and Harvey Bagot fell out at the end of December, probably over Hastings' involvement in the renewed Marcher Association. Lichfield was, at this time still able to collect money regularly from the majority of Offlow Hundred and parts of two other hundreds. Given the general condition of the royalist cause, this was quite remarkable especially as it covered about seven eighths of the garrison's expenditure. Hastings' power to examine the accounts of all the region's garrisons would have contravened the local autonomy of the governors, particularly the successful Bagot. It is probable that this led directly to the arguments in Lichfield in late December and to the expulsion of Hastings and other commissioners on the 29th.[665]

Hastings' real authority was now at an end. Astley replaced Bagot with Thomas Tyldesley (though Bagot was retained as deputy governor), and

Kniveton was replaced at Tutbury by the commander of the remains of the Northern Horse, Sir William Blakiston.[666] Thus, by January 1646, Hastings, cut off from Belvoir and Newark by the Scots and denied command of his Staffordshire garrisons, was left with only his forces at Ashby. During January, Ashby troops along with some Newark forces were taken by Astley to create the Chester relief force. An unspecified number joined him early in the month but on the 28th, Colonel Roper and Lieutenant Colonel Stamford led 300 foot and 300 horse out of Ashby.[667] News that Ormonde in Ireland had been unable to reach an agreement with the Catholics, aimed at sending an army to England to help the King, changed the situation. Chester, which had been the designated landing point for the army, was now redundant and under the extreme pressure that it was, the garrison surrendered on February 2nd. A day later Belvoir followed suit. The Ashby forces, sent to Astley, drifted home.[668]

Throughout January, Hastings had conducted highly successful raids on the enemy. He had hindered the progress of the siege of Belvoir by capturing ammunition and weapons. On the 19th January, part of the Ashby garrison marched through Leicestershire into Northamptonshire and captured Castle Ashby, taking the governor home with them.[669] It would appear that this was a flexing of muscles aimed at showing the potential of the garrison forces. Hastings, disgruntled by the harsh treatment of the King and Astley, appears to have been thinking of surrender. Even as the garrison raided the Tamworth area, Hastings' elder brother, the 6th Earl of Huntingdon, was at Leicester negotiating terms. On the last day of February an agreement was made. Hastings obtained excellent terms for himself and his fellow commanders in Ashby – no less than five North Midlands Army colonels were in the garrison at the time. The forces as a whole had three months to leave the castle under arms, as long as they dismantled the new fortifications first. However, not all the garrison wished to surrender and fights broke out between those wishing to lay down their arms and those who wanted, even at this stage, to continue fighting for the King.[670]

Other Colonels also wished to continue the fight. Blakiston at Tutbury held out until April, Leveson and Belasyse until May, and the latter only surrendered Newark on the express orders of the King. Tyldesley and Bagot kept Lichfield in royalist hands until July.[671] The final stages of the First Civil War in the Midlands was reflected in the rest of the country. Parliaments forces proceeded to mop up pockets of royalist resistance which held out in castles and mansions up and down the nation. In the North Midlands the majority of the work was done by local forces particularly those of Sir William Brereton and Gell; the latter was more of a hindrance to the former in the case of the siege of Tutbury where he attempted to maintain his own siege separate from the one established by Brereton! Even though the Scots Army was responsible for the capture of Shelford, Belvoir and Newark, local forces who had been an ever-present menace to Hastings were present at each of the leaguers.

In this chapter the course of the decline of royalist power in the North Midlands has been traced. It has been shown that there were several factors in this decline. Interference in the North Midland Association war effort by outside forces was thoroughly piecemeal and never aimed at an overall strategy. Instead, the resources of the area were used to bail out other royalist regions which had not been established to the same level of success that the North Midlands were. Even when the intervention was potentially of help to the region, such as Rupert's actions in March 1643 and March 1644, it was never fully realised. Though Hastings might have been able to contain the threat of local parliamentarian action he was never able to eradicate it. It was always to be a drain on his resources, limiting his ability to provide a solid springboard from which to launch a royalist offensive. The potential for Rupert and later Charles to help Hastings throw off the parliamentarian albatross was never exploited: in all cases the intervention was curtailed by the outside armies leaving the area too soon or by military disaster. In many cases outside intervention had no useful purpose. The King's personal meddling resulted in several instances of disputes breaking out, or being aggravated, which though they alone would not have wrecked the system, did nothing to strengthen it.

Probably the chief cause of the defeat of the North Midlands was the period in May and June 1644 when the area was stripped of resources and manpower to provide for the attempt to relieve York. The single-minded and shortsighted nature of this policy rendered the North Midlands vulnerable to any parliamentarian action. Indeed, as a result, the area's future was entirely dependent upon the military victory in the north which never came. The resultant deluge of parliamentarian offensives fell upon a territory incapable of a successful defence: had Manchester pressed on into the area instead of turning into Lincolnshire, the collapse may well have come much sooner. However the renaissance of May and June 1645 revealed the ability of the North Midlands activists to re-establish themselves in favourable times: even after the disaster of Naseby the events in the area during the King's August intervention revealed the still present potential for them to do so.

The individual officers and commissioners of the North Midlands showed themselves as competent men. What they lacked was a firm foundation in which to work. The inability of even Hastings himself to be certain that his work was not to be overruled or ignored had severe and debilitating effects upon the overall running of the war effort. The division of his command, under two superior commanders, was surely a contribution to this. It is little surprise that Hastings was disillusioned in late 1644 and early 1645, and it is possible that the surrender of Ashby has to be also seen in this light. Hastings was hamstrung by the fact that his success led to the abuse of the resources of the area and his failures brought castigation and ill treatment.

Chapter 7

Conclusions: The North Midlands and the English Civil War

During the course of this book, five counties have been treated as a combined unit, a region. This collection of counties was perceived as such a unit by the royalist and, with some geographical differences, by the parliamentarian central authorities. There were, within the region, diverse localist attitudes which worked either overtly, or covertly, against regionalism. It is possible that Gell sought to defy the regional commander, Lord Grey, and that the desire to preserve county boundaries brought county committees into dispute with each other. On the other hand, even Gell realised that united efforts were needed to control Ashby-de-la-Zouch's still active garrison late in the war. Similarly, ventures against Newark always involved regional forces. For the royalists' part, their financial system, whilst recognising, as did Parliament's hundredal boundaries, was based on a cross-county border allotment of territory.

Whilst Parliament's committee sought to keep, and succeeded in keeping, other counties' financial demands out of their county, the royalists did not. Staffordshire garrisons drew money from Derbyshire and Warwickshire, Ashby from Derbyshire whilst Belvoir and Newark were partly financed by money from Lincolnshire. Regionalism, as practised by the royalists, was broken down by Parliament's growing military supremacy, not by inherent localism. Dissent by royalist commanders, such as the arguments between Bagot and Leveson, were not innate county-based sentiments coming to the fore; they were disputes over military needs involving assignments of territory in several counties.

From the middle of 1644, after Manchester entered the region following Marston Moor, the indigenous parliamentarians, with the help of outside forces, were able to exercise control over increasingly large parts of the five counties. This inevitably led to the royalists losing the power to co-ordinate actions by their increasingly isolated forces. Even so, Hastings continued his regional policy, attempting the utilisation of regiments unrestricted by a county-based attitude. If in this case, 'country' meant anything less than England as a whole, it certainly meant no less than the region.

The royalist regional policy involved the use of the resources of the communities thus embodied, irrespective of their county but based on their proximity to fortified towns and garrisons. This system was not, for the major period of the war, run on an ad hoc basis and, if the evidence from Lichfield in 1645 is not wholly unique, it was never run that way. The royalist war effort was based on a system of regularly collected taxes taken from the communities in a pseudo-legal fashion given its authority by the presence of war. Traditional organs of government, the warrant, the offices of sheriff and constable, were utilised in order to give the system a validity which was accepted as sufficient to impel compliance by all but the most politically motivated members of the North Midlands communities. Further appearance of legality was given by the right of appeal to the commissioners of the peace, members of which were incorporated into the commissions of array. Moreover, as the study of the membership of the commissions has shown, those involved were part of the communities upon which they imposed their taxation system. These men were not, for the most part, magnates with huge cross-county landholdings; they included representatives of a broad spectrum of gentry society, though most of them were esquires and titled gentry. Between them they were able to muster no small degree of administrative experience, having held county offices such as sheriff and deputy lieutenants. Many could also bring experience of higher education together with legal training to the commissions. All of this would have contributed to the efficiency of wartime administration, which had to be an organised system bringing in enough money to finance an army and pay for defensive works and other materials of war. They also brought to the commissions the vital experience of local knowledge, a sense of knowing what the community could or would bear and what it would not.

Parliament's committees in the region were derived from a similar social group, although from the outset they utilised a greater proportion of people from the lower rungs of the gentry ladder, urban gentry and even yeoman stock. Nevertheless, these men were predominantly land owners who would have the same qualms as their royalist counterparts about the effect of war on the community. The parliamentarian committeemen brought less previous experience to their task than did the royalists. Even so similar ex officers of the counties were present, although in fewer numbers, and their knowledge could be utilised. Yet, Parliament's war effort at the outset was less effective than the royalist alternative, but the inexperience of local administration was not entirely responsible for the dire financial straits that the county committees found themselves in during the autumn of 1643. Though failure to collect money would affect Parliament's military effort, the local royalist military effort was aided substantially by the Marquis of Newcastle's intervention. This gave the royalists the breathing space to form new regiments to control the counties and to put into effect the full rigours of their administration. When the tables were turned, it was parliamentary intervention on the part of Manchester which gave the county committees the ability to extend their system into increasingly larger areas of the North Midlands.

The two systems which operated side by side were, thus, handled by men of some experience who had, for the most part, a vested interest in the community. Their local involvement ensured that the area would never become a waste land like parts of Germany. The instances of actual or attempted cooperation, whereby at least one attempt at bilateral agreement was made, indicate that both sides were aware of what a thorough prosecution of war, regardless of its effects on communities, could entail. The fact that many of the villages, whose constables left accounts, show that the communities could afford to pay both sides (whilst occasionally going into arrears) adds strength to the assertion. The point that, despite the constant presence of garrisons manned by both sides and two rival war efforts, there were no clubman risings in the counties, also indicates that the systems, if not popular, were at least tolerable for the largely rural communities upon which they were imposed.

The study of the county commissioners reveals that the number of activists was quite small. Of the royalist commissioners appointed, a mere 58 percent of them were activists, and of the parliamentarian committeemen, 75.6 percent. The reasons for the higher proportion of parliamentarian activists, chiefly that Parliament made its choices once the war had begun and could therefore choose potentially active supporters, have been dealt with. But this leaves us with no less than 19.5 percent of appointees to either the commissions or the committees who did not take part in the system and for whom there appears no reason such as death, disqualification or service elsewhere. These men were either passive supporters or more likely, men who attempted to maintain a certain distance from the war. These neutrals were the victims of both sides and friends of none, subject to financial exactions by both sides during the war and by Parliament once it was over. If the number of almost 20 percent does not seem particularly high, it must be remembered these were men thought to be dependable supporters of one cause or another by those who nominated them. If these men remained neutral, those who were not specifically chosen were more likely to hold a neutralist attitude or desire merely for self preservation during a war in which neither side could attract their active support.

Yet the figures also show the degree of commitment shown by those who did become activists for both parties. Families were willing to risk their fortunes in the name of a cause. The numbers of heads of families or eldest sons who were active indicate that personal and familial commitment was high. Risking not only personal fortunes but the fortunes of one's posterity was not an example of flippant opportunism. If it were in any way opportunist, then it was a calculated gamble, aimed at increasing territorial or political stakes in the community. It is more likely, however, that there was a degree of political commitment involved and it was this that impelled the activists along their chosen course.

The royalist war effort in the North Midlands met with no small success. By the end of 1643, due both to the efforts of its own army and that of the Marquis of Newcastle, the royalist war machine came to dominate the region. During this period, it not only maintained its own growing forces (regiments of Freshville, Eyre and Milward were added at this time), but also catered for the Marquis' forces until January 1644. Though local disputes and shortages were experienced, the area could finance its own army in the field as it did during the relief of Newark. The royalists in the North Midlands could not raise sufficient troops to undertake such a project on their own but neither could their opponents; the parliamentarian force at Newark was composed, in part, of regiments from outside the region. Hastings never felt confident of his regional army's ability to storm the key towns of Derby, Leicester, Nottingham or Stafford but he practised the cheaper expedient of denying those places of a constant income. It was, then, a limited success, weakened as much by lack of forethought on the part of Hastings' superiors as by anything else.

Hastings' greatest problem from the beginning of 1643, and for the ensuing 18 months was, paradoxically, his own success. His ability to raise an army meant that his regiments were constantly required to bolster up less successful royalists elsewhere. He helped Capel in the west in 1643, Byron in Cheshire and the Lincolnshire royalists at various times. In 1644, he was expected to send troops into the north whilst the Oxford royalists did little to protect his rear. At least one regiment was taken away by the Oxford Field Army. The result was that often his forces were scattered and incapable of suppressing problems within the North Midlands area. The success of the regional financial system led to the absurd situation in May 1644, when the area was used as a feeding ground by both Goring and the Northern Horse and Rupert's army, whilst at the same time providing regiments for both. The result of this dual drain was catastrophic. Hastings appeared confident of mustering a small field force in July 1644, but only a victory in the north could have saved the North Midlands. Economic recovery would have required time and the return of the regiments sent with Rupert and Goring. The defeat on Marston Moor deprived it of both.

Left on its own, the North Midlands royalist war effort had provided for the army, which in this book had been termed the North Midlands Army. This force was, for much of the time, in garrisons performing a task roughly equivalent to that of an armed police force. Parts of it would aid in tax collection, guarding convoys and stopping carriers to ensure that they were not trading with enemy garrison, as well as the purely military tasks of raiding enemy billets and attacking their convoys. Whenever necessary, the army could unite in missions to outside areas or to act in their own territory as they did successfully at Newark or fatally as at Denton.

The army was officered by men drawn from quite a wide social spectrum. Within this officer corps, involvement of the nobility was limited, although Hastings and Fitzherbert were of noble birth and in a way, they were both representing their fathers. The majority of the field officers were esquires but only a small proportion were titled gentry.

The regimental ranks were peopled by men of very low gentry standing or below. There were also the occasional tradesmen, vintners, and shoemakers ranking as high as captain. For the most part the regimental officers had little to lose by their involvement in the war, unlike the majority of their field officers or, more particularly the commissioners of array. Conversely they could expect some gains, estates or even minor county office, which, without the 'locomotive of war' they would ordinarily have been denied. As it was, they fought for the wrong side and defeat in 1646 resulted in some of them being fined. It would appear that the majority had little wealth upon which to base a fine, either as a result of impecunity brought on by wartime expenditure or simply because they were of generally impoverished origins. Even if their financial loss had been slight, defeat denied them the opportunities for any form of reward for their services. The return of the monarchy, 14 years later, did not, for the majority, change this circumstance. Seven thousand officers who fought for Charles I and his son and who were considered indigent in 1663, were presented with a meagre £60,000; this, even if divided equally, would give them a mere £8-10s each – hardly fit reward for staking their pitiful all on the King's cause, and no substitute for lost opportunities, which had been as mirages before their eyes. For them the war was a means of social advancement which had failed to materialise.

The royalist war effort in the North Midlands was in the hands of two distinct groups of men. On the one hand it involved men determined to preserve the counties and their communities from the effects of the war; on the other it embraced an element of men who wished to increase their stake in that society. These men saw the war, and the fighting of it, as a vehicle of social advancement. To gain the advantage from it, the vehicle had to be driven hard; victory in the war was essential, and it must be a military, as opposed to a negotiated, victory. In short, it must be one in which these opportunists were seen to play a crucial role, a part deserving reward. This brought men like Thomas Leveson into conflict with the commissioners and led to the infighting between the two elements of the war effort; thus were the swordsmen of the region at odds with the administration. Leveson, in particular, was reluctant to do the bidding of the commissioners unless ordered to do so by the leading swordsman, Rupert. The command of the North Midlands never passed into the hands of a local man selected purely on his military prowess, as did occur in other regions. Hastings, the representative of the great magnate, the Earl of Huntingdon, had sufficient ability to ensure that this never happened. He himself was never a pure swordsman despite his military tenacity evidenced whilst holding on to Ashby in the dark days of January 1643 and in his ability to lead effective cavalry charges at Hopton Heath and the relief of Newark. Hastings also possessed experience of local government and came from a family with long experience of dominating political affairs in Leicestershire as well as being involved heavily in the affairs of adjacent counties. The result was that Hastings came into conflict with those who had risen in the royalist war effort simply due to their military abilities, notably Leveson and Lucas, but also Richard Bagot, who, though from a family with experience of local government, was a younger son and owed his preferment to his military aptitude. When Richard's elder brother, Harvey, succeeded him to the governorship of Lichfield he did so by dint of military effort and Hastings' preferment. Yet at the end of 1645, he resented Hastings' administrative power over his running of the garrison at Lichfield, and threw the Lieutenant General out of Lichfield. It is likely that Harvey had become very much a swordsman during the war and the expulsion of Hastings was perhaps the final act of the swordsman versus administrator conflict in the Midlands.

Thus we have the picture of the North Midlands at war. A royalist war effort run by local men, several of whom had experience of county government gained before the outbreak of war. They ran a pseudo-legal system of taxation, along what was as near to traditional lines as they found possible. This system was able to support an army more than capable of maintaining control of the region as long as the time all or part of it spent outside was kept to a minimum. The war effort collapsed, not because of internal strife between the commissioners and officers, although these wrangles did nothing to strengthen the system, but because of the gross misuse of the territory's resources by central command.

It is time to turn to the wider aspects of the war and the implications which this work had on our understanding of it. The financial administration of the North Midlands shows that such a system was not only possible but viable in an area subject to parliamentarian incursion as well as a low level parliamentarian presence. Though the constant necessity for a large army within its borders meant that the area could not provide for the royalists in the same manner as the relatively trouble free Eastern Association could provide for Parliament, it does indicate that self sufficiency could be achieved. This had implications for the royalist cause as a whole. It indicates that, despite not possessing the financial might of London, the royalists need not have been at a great financial disadvantage compared with Parliament. The potential for financing the war effort was within royalist grasp. The reasons for their defeat were not entirely financial. Even a flawed collection system such as that in the North Midlands at the end of 1643 and the early months of the following year, could generate enough income not only to function, but also to expand.

County studies have obscured any picture of an overall royalist strategy; this study has indicated that there never was one. Whilst regional royalist administration was not pragmatic, royalist strategy was. Though the original error of draining the North Midlands of royalist activists in the autumn of 1642 was rectified during the ensuing winter, no serious attempt made to help Hastings fully secure his territory was ever pushed to a conclusion. Rupert's intervention in April 1643 was curtailed as soon as Lichfield was recovered. The Queen's army's potential for reducing Derby at the very least, in July 1643, was never realised as she marched it away to join her husband, covetous as he was for not only his wife but for the soldiers and weapons she had with her. Even the Marquis of Newcastle's portentous intervention in late 1643 was left unfinished. Again in March 1644, Rupert's march through the region ended almost immediately after he and Hastings had relieved Newark. In each of these cases the four county towns in parliamentarian possession were left virtually undisturbed. Yet had any of these towns been taken by one of the royalist commanders who entered the region, the royalist cause, as a whole, would have benefited greatly from the enhanced income and stability that increased territorial control would have brought.

The constant drain on the resources of the North Midlands war effort reveals a piecemeal attitude to the prosecution of the war. It made the counties less stable than they could have been, leaving the system open to disruption by the local parliamentarians. Conflicting instructions which meant that Hastings could not always utilise his full potential to tackle any of the military ventures he was ordered to undertake outside his own region limited his chances of success. In the end, the failure of the Oxford politicians to placate the Scots resulted in their entering the war, with devastating consequences. The greatest potential for royalist victory was perhaps the period at the end of 1643, when the Marquis of Newcastle's forces were in the North Midlands. Had it proved possible to use this sizeable army in the south, the history of the Civil War might have been very different. However the entry of the Scots rendered this impossible. Newcastle's departure and the subsequent collapse of the royalist north resulted in the great Northern Army's incapacitation and the necessity for its rescue. Hastings cannot shoulder the blame for Belasyse's defeat at Selby; the commander he instructed to march into Yorkshire sought, and possibly received, Rupert's permission not to do so. Hastings obviously could not move north himself as this would have left his eastern flank under threat and involved him in conflict with a force at least equal to his total field army under a proven daunting adversary, Thomas Fairfax. The additional error of the central command, that of draining the North Midlands of resources to provide for the relief forces of both Rupert and Goring, effectively made the region dependent upon a victory in the north. This was not an act commensurate with the pursuance of a long-term war. Rather it was akin to the mentality of autumn 1642, when the war was envisaged as a short, sharp shock. The lesson of Edgehill and the ensuing few months had not been learned. The royalists had not fully understood that the war was a long-term feature and which should have been conducted accordingly, not by means of a series of pragmatic and damaging measures.

Despite the deluge which followed Marston Moor, the North Midlands royalists maintained a grip sufficient to provide resources for the large garrisons left to them after the summer of 1644. Any chance of a renaissance was the prerogative of an outside field force. When such an intervention occurred in May 1645, the North Midlands royalists showed themselves more than willing and able to resurrect their war effort. Even the lesser interventions of Charles' miniscule army in the following autumn showed such potential. Yet little genuine success was achieved at perceiving the war in long-term aims and objectives and no serious attempt was made to re-establish royalist power bases in either the north or the North Midlands. Just as Peter Newman revealed that the potential to regain the northern counties for the royalist cause existed, this book indicates that this was equally true of the North Midlands.

The collapse of the North Midlands royalist war effort, then, gives us an insight into the defeat of the royalists in the First Civil War.

The decline of Hastings' command, was due largely to the activities of outside influences; royalist malpractice and parliamentarian military supremacy gained as a result of that malpractice and the intervention of the Scots in January 1644. For there to be any truth in Huttons' assertion that the royalists were defeated by a popular antipathy to the war as a whole, then this antipathy must be seen as a final nail in a coffin that had already been made. The mortal blow to the royalists came, this work would indicate, as a result of the absence of a general strategy which brought about a pragmatic military effort which led to military defeat. This defeat had little to do with the way the finances of the royalist war effort were run at the local level. Parliament's victory was won largely on the field of battle, not in the field of economics, where they fared little, if at all, better than their adversaries.

Finally this book, through its study of the royalist activists, has revealed that the royalist cause appealed not simply to the upper ranks of society, who in any case tended to lay fairly low. Active support came equally, if not more so, from the lower reaches of the gentry and below. Men of low social standing were inspired to stake their all on the cause of Charles I. If Joyce Malcolm is right to say that the royalists at Oxford saw themselves as purely a social elite, they were mistaken to do so. The cause did appeal to lower social groups.

Hastings' army may have had too many officers, but they were not alone in their desire to fight for the King. Beneath them were soldiers ready to fight and die for Charles I, on the fields of Hopton Heath, Marston Moor and Naseby. Moreover, the scuffles which broke out at Ashby-de-la-Zouch in 1646, when Hastings chose to surrender, reveal that many of the soldiers wished, even then, to fight on. It was a pity, for them, that the Oxford command was not worthy of their trust and loyalty.

Notes to the Appendices

These are not intended to be comprehensive biographies. They are only guides to the information used in compiling the statistics presented in chapters 2, 3 and 4.

Personal Details Abbreviations

b = born; d = died; m = married; s = son of, i.e. 2s = second son of; bro = brother of

DL = Deputy Lieutenant; HS = High Sheriff; JP = Justice of the Peace; MP = Member of Parliament. In each case, if known, these are followed by the last two digits of the year office commenced.

Ox = Oxford Univ.; Ca = Cambridge Univ. These are followed by year of entry or matriculation whichever is known. Then if appropriate degree and year; fell com = fellow commoner; pleb = plebeian; siz = sizar; sch = scholar; pens = pensioner

RC = Roman Catholic

Source Details

AO; Foster J. (ed.), *Alumni Oxonienses*, 1500–1714, Kraus, 1968

AC; Venn, (eds), *Alumni Cantabrigienses*, 4 vols, Cambridge, 1922–7

BL; British Library

Black *Docquets*; Black W.H., 'Docquets of Letters Patent', unpublished, PRO

Bod Lib; Bodleian Library, Oxford

CCAM; *Calendar of the Committee for Advance of Money*, Kraus, 1968

CCC; *Calendar for the Committee of Compounding*, Kraus, 1968

CSPD; *Calendar of State Papers Domestic Series*, Kraus, 1968

DNB; *Dictionary of National Biography*

Dore; Dore R.N., *The Letter Books of Sir William Brereton*, vol.1, 1984

DV; Dugdale W., *The Visitation of Derbyshire*, 1663, London, 1879

FH 133; Northamptonshire County Record Office, Finch-Hatton Mss 133, Dugdale's Transcripts of Commissioners and Committeemen

Gardiner *Documents*; *The Constitutional Documents of the Puritan Revolution*, 1979

Glover; Glover S., *The History of, Gazetteer and Directory of Derbyshire*, Derby, 1826

Hutchinson; Hutchinson L., *The Life of John Hutchinson*, Oxford, 1973

JHC; *Journal of the House of Commons*

JTB; Brighton J.T., *Royalists and Roundheads in Derbyshire*, Bakewell, 1981

HMC Hastings; *Historical Manuscripts Commission Report on the Papers of Reginald Rawdon Hastings*, HMSO, 1930

HMC Portland; *Historical Manuscripts Commission Thirteenth Report The Manuscripts of the Duke of Portland*, HMSO, 1891

GA; Foster J., Rylands W., *Grantees of Arms*, Harleian Society, 1915

GEC; GEC, *The Complete Baronetage*, Exeter, 1902

VL; Fetherstone FSA, *The Visitation of the County of Leicester*, 1619 Harleian Society, 1870

Metcalfe *Knights*; Metcalfe W.C., *A Book of Knights*, 1426–1600, London

PN; Newman P., *Royalist Officers in England and Wales, 1642–1660*, Garland, 1981

NV; Marshall G., *The Visitations of the County of Nottingham, in the Years 1569 and 1614*, Harleian Society, 1871

Prest; Prest W., *The Inns of Court Under Elizabeth I and the Early Stuarts*, Longman, 1972

RS; Harleian MSS, 984, The Notebook of Richard Symonds

RV; *The Visitation of the County of Rutland*, Harleian Society, 1870

IR; Peacock (ed.), *Index of the Name of the Royalists whose estates were confiscated in the Commonwealth*, Index Society, 1878

Shaw; Shaw S., *The History of the County of Staffordshire*, EP, 1976

Symonds' Diary; Long E.R., *Symonds' Diary of the Marches of the Kings Army*, Harleian Society, 1859

SP; Armytage G., Rylands D., *Staffordshire Pedigrees*, Harleian Soc. 1912

Thoresby; Thoresby, *The Antiquities of the County of Nottinghamshire*, EP, 1972

Wood; Wood A., *Nottinghamshire in the Civil War*, SR, 1971

Wright; Wright J., *The History and Antiquities of the County of Rutland*, EP, 1973

Young Edgehill; Young P., *Edgehill 1642*, Roundwood Press, 1967

Young Naseby; Young P., *Naseby 1645*, Century Press, 1985

Appendix I

The Commissioners of Array

Derbyshire

Active Commissioners

Simon Avery, Bart, Eggington, 1603–1649
1s, John; app. 27/6/42, 21/12/43.
b Northants; JP; MP (Leics.) 40, Ox, Wadham 18; MT 20; Bart 41.
At Oxford part of war, Newcastle's sixth Derbyshire colonel, but served in Oxford Parliament. Receiver of Duchy of Lancaster, 1643 onwards.
Compounded for Eggington Estates. Assessed at £2,000, 1645.
Sources: FH133; AO, 475; CCC, 2448; DV 13; CCAM, 1096; SP 16/405, Fisher F., 'The Every Family and the Civil War' DAJ 74, 1954, JTB, 23.

John Bullock, Esq., Underwood, Darley and Norton
1s John; JP 11 24 26; HS 16.
Signed 1641 petition to King from Derbys.
Compounded 1649; assessed at £800, sequestered for non-payment, 1650.
Sources: FH133; CCC, 1132; CCAM, 1068; PRO, CH 193/12; SP, 16/405; JTB, 16.

Christopher Fullwood, Esq., Middleton by Youlgrave, 1590–1643
1s, Sir George, of Holborn; app. 27/6/42, 21/12/43.
Gray's, 28; JP 28 36.
Described as an opponent of puritan element at Gray's. Enlisted in King's Lifeguard in 42, Wounded Nottingham Feb, 43. Died at Caulton, Staffs. Estate confiscated.
Sources: FH133; SP 16/405; JTB, 27; Glover, 1, app, 76; Prest, 215.

Sir John Fitzherbert, Kt, Norbury, ?–1649
1s, Anthony, 17th Lord Norbury; app. 27/6/42, 21/12/43. JP 26; HS 26; DL 42; (41), col. H+F; Kt 24.
Roman Catholic. In Stafford garrison in early 1643, at Tutbury subsequently, see chapters 5 and 6.
Sources: HMC Hastings, 2, 91, 116, 117; RS, 95; CCC, 1598; CCAM, 864; Metcalfe *Knights*, 183; Gell B, 74; FH133; PRO Sheriffs, 31; C193/12;

Black *Docquets*, 70; PN, no. 519; JTB, 25; BL Harl. MS, 6852, f.1; Gardiner *Documents*, 279.

John Freshville, Esq., Staveley, 1607–1682
1s is Peter; app. 27/6/42, 21/12/43.
Ox Magdalene 21; MT 24; MP shire 28; DL 39–40; (MP, 61, Baron 44) see chapters 4, 5, 6.
Sources: DRO Gresley, 803m, ff.93–97; Derby Gent., 21; HMC Portland, 1, 141; CSPD, 63–64, 226, 64–65, 73, 527; PN, 568; GEC *Peerage*, V, 578–579; Black *Docquets*, 68; RS, f.93; DV, 14; JBT, 26, 72; GA, 94, AO, 532; FH133.

Sir John Harpur, Bart, Swarkestone, 1602–1677
1s Sir Richard; app. 27/6/42, 21/12/43.
Ox Brasenose, 16; JP 36; HS 36; KT 39.
Compounded Nov 45. Fined £4,583, reduced to £4,000. Assessed 47, at 1/20th. Reputed to be richest man in county. Fortified Swarkestone 43, Gov, Burton-on-Trent, July 43–?Jan 44. Gave up arms, Aug 44, back in service by Naseby, gave up again Nov 45. See chapters 4, 5, 6.
Sources: AO, 625; GEC *The Complete Baronetage*, II, 2; FH133; CCC, 1921, 2107; CCAM, 650–651; CJ, II, 662; TO, co1.63; DV, 28; RS, 94; JBT, 32, 70; PN, no. 683.

Henry Hastings, Esq., Oakthorpe, Leics., Ashby-de-la-Zouch, 1609–1667
2s 5th Earl Huntingdon; App, 27/6/42, 21/12/43.
Ca Queens, 27; DL Leics. 38, see chapters 1, 2, 4, 5, 6, 7 (and relevant footnotes).
Sources: RS f.91b; AC 2, 329; HMC Hastings, 2, 83–153; FH133; Dugdale.
Ms 19; Black *Docquets*, 95, 120; Hans Mss, 2043, f.26; GEC *Peerage*, VIII, 166–168; Luke, 192; *Symonds' Diary*, 176, 178, 181, 184; HMC Portland, 1, 280; Warburton, 294, 297, 445, 501, 503, 504, 505; TO col. 187; PN, 691; CSPD, 1663–1664, 289; DNB; Bennett M., *Lord Loughborough, Ashby-de-la-Zouch and the English Civil War*, Ashby Museum, 1984, 'Henry Hastings and the Flying Army of Ashby-de-la-Zouch', *Transactions of the Leicestershire Archaeological Society*, LVI, 1980–1981.

Sir Andrew Kniveton, Bart, Bradley, ?–1669
1s Sir Gilbert; app. 27/6/42, 21/12/43.
Sequestered 46–51; ass 5th and 20th, cut to £150, in 1648. Died ruined, sold all estates.
Col. of H+F. Governor of Tutbury, March 1643–Jan 1646. See chapters 2, 4, 5, 6, 7.
Sources: FH133; *Symonds' Diary*, 175; HMC Hastings, 2, 132; CCC, 1578; CCAM, 865; GEC *The Complete Baronetage*, I, 51; RS, 926; IO co1. 180; PN, no. 842; JBT, 34, 71.

Sir Thomas Milward, Kt, Eaton, 1575–1658
1s William; app. 21/12/43.
Ox Baliol 1591; BA 95; MA 1600; Kt 38; Lord Chief Justice of Chester. Comp, 1646, 49, fined, £360 at 1/3rd, 1651 assessed at £100.
Sources: FH133; DV, 1; CCC, 1464; CCAM, 1375; JBT, 39.

John Milward (Melward), Esq., Snitterton, Eaton, 1599–1670
2s John, of Ash; HS 35, app. 27/6/42.
Col. H+F, based at Chatsworth, fought at Marston Moor, laid down arms after battle. See chapters 2, 4, 5, 6. DL 1660; MP Derbys., 1660s.
Compounded fined £1,000.
Sources: RS, f.95; CCC, 1025; IO, co1.195; HMC Poll Gell Mss, 390; RO, Sheriffs, 31; FH133; PRO, MPs, 521; PN, no. 980; JBT, 38, 72.

Sir Edward Vernon, Kt, Sudbury (Houndshill Staffs.), 1585–1657
1s Walter; app. 27.6.42, 21/12/43.
Ox Baliol 02; BA 06; MA 09; Kt 24; HS 27; JP 36; DL 40–42.
Compounded 45.
Sources: FH133; CCC, 1038; SP 16/405; Petition of the Derbyshire Gentry DAJ, XIX, 22; JTB, 48.

Uncertain Cases

John Agard, Esq., Foston
2s William, heir of brother Henry; app, 27/6/42, 21/12/43. HS 39; (JP 55, Committee of Militia, 59; HS 61).
Only Irish estates sequestered, and those by mistake.
Sources: FH133; DV, 16; CCC, 2982; JTB, 13.

Passive Supporters or Neutrals

Sir John Harpur of Caulke. HS 42; active in the first month, but thereafter avoided all association with cause. The recent acquisition of the Harpur/Crewe papers might reveal more but they are not available at the time of this book being written. See JTB, 33.

Edward Lowe, Esq., Alderwasely; 1592–1653
Fined by Parliament, £221, plundered by royalists. See JTB, 36.

Sir Henry Willoughby, Bart
Though app. 27/6/42, 21/12/43; DL 1640, appears to have played no role at all. FH133.

Elias Woodroffe, Esq., app. 21/12/43. JP, 36? Unidentifiable; FH133.

Leicestershire

Active Commissioners

George Ashby, Esq., Quenby, 1589–1653
1s George; app. 11/6/42.
JP 26.
Sources: FH133; GA, 7; VL, 13; CCC, 110; Nichols, ITT, 229–300; PRO, C193/12.

Sir John Bale, Kt; Saddington and Carlton, 1594–pre-1650
11/6/42, 28/11/44 CoP.
HS 22; DL 40–42; son William a lieutenant colonel.
Sources: FH133; GA, 12; VL, 142; *Nichols*, II, 2, 539; CCC, 2298.

Sapcoat, Viscount Beaumont, Coleorton, 1614–1652
1s Thomas. App. 28/11/44, CoP. Brought into administration in 43.
Estates seized in 1650, assessment in 1651 was £500. Comp 46. Active in later stages of war.
Sources: CCC, 109; VL, 61, 121; CCAM, 1046–1047; Black *Docquets*, 117.

Sir Wolstan Dixie, Kt; Market Bosworth; 1576–?
1s John; app. 11/6/42, 28/11/44, CoP.
HS 13; MP shire 25; fell com Ca, Emanuel 09; came from a family of London Merchants. His son Walter was in the King's Army in the south.
Sources: FH133; AC, 2, 46; VL, 116; CCC, 110; PRO, C193/12; Nichols, IV, 2, 495–507.

Sir Erasmus de la Fontaine, Kt; Kirkby Bellars
App. 11/6/42; HS 28–29.
Arms registered only in 1619; Kt 23; married into Noel family; purchased Kirkby Bellars in 03. Family from Essex.
Seq. 43–45, estate garrisoned by Parliament. Fined £1,000 in 1645. In 1636 he had been fined for depopulating parts of his estate.
Sources: FH133; GA, 73; VL, 4; CCC, 109, 3021; Nichols, II, 2, 231–232.

Sir Richard Halford, Kt, Bart (Edith Weston, Rutland), Wistow, ?–?1675
1s Edward; app. 11/6/44, 28/11/44, CoP.
Ca Christ's pens 13; ?HS Rut. 19 31; HS Leics. 20; DL 40–42; BT 41; kt 42. Imprisoned 1640, for slandering Sir Arthur Hesilrige. Claimed in 1644 that he withdrew from CoA as soon as he heard it was illegal. Not believed, fined £2,000, £3,000 worth of his estate had already been sold by Parliament during the war.
Sources: CCC, 109, 835–837; AC, 2, 285; VL, 144; Nichols, II, 1, 869–870.

Henry Hastings, Esq., see Derbyshire

Henry Hastings, Esq., Humberstone, 1578–1649.

2s Walter (brother of 3rd, 4th Earl of Huntingdon); app. 11/6/42; accused of being a Roman Catholic. Ox, Lincoln Coll 93; Gray's 95; MP shire 01 04–11 24–25 26. In 1643 brought onto Commission of the Peace. In 1643, whilst at Ashby laid about a sentry with his cane.
Compounded 46.
Sources: AO, 671; CCC, 110; CCAM, 1046; Black *Docquets*, 112; VL, 73; HMC *Hastings*, 2, 122, Du Pont to Hastings, 28/2/44.

John Pate, Esq., Sysonby, *c.*1600–1659
2s Edward; app. 11/6/42.
Ox, Brasenose 15; MA 18; HS 41.
Colonel of horse, one of the earliest activists in the county. One of the men Hastings gave a Baronetcy to in 1643 when empowered to award three. In 1644 appointed high sheriff, given responsibility to collect the £100,000 loan in 44. See chapters 2, 4, 5, 6.
Compounded 48, fined £1,120, but Oct 1649 increased to 1/3 at £4,316-13s-6d.
Sources: RS, 94; FH133; CCC, 110, 2032, 2033; GEC *The Complete Baronetage*, II, 214; Black *Docquets*, 95; AO, 1125; PN, no.1098; TO, co1. 103; *Royal Martyrs*, 6; Peacock, 82; BL TT E345/2, *Articles for delivering up of Lichfield-Close.*

Eusebius Pelsant, Esq., Cadeby; 1610–?
?1s of William; app. 28/11/44 CoP.
(Kt Leicester July 1642).
Brought in the administration in 1643.
Sources: CCC, 110; Nichols, IV, 2, 578; Black *Docquets*, 117.

Sir Richard Roberts, Kt, Sutton Cheney, 1564–1644.
3s Thomas; app. 11/6/42, 28/11/44 CoP.
HS 37. Freeholder in Peatling Magna 30.
Sons in the North Midlands Army. Despite age appears to have been active.
Sources: CCC, 110; FH133, VL, 118; Nichols, IV, 2, 547.

Sir Henry Skipworth, Kt, Bart; Cotes; 1589–?
1s William; app. 11/6/42, 28/11/44, CoP.
Ca Queens 06; kt 09; bart 22; HS 36; JP 26; gent of Privy Chamber 41.
At the end of the war moved from one surrendering garrison to another, he was at surrender of Dudley and then Hartlebury.
Compounded 46, fined 1/6th, £1,400; Assessed 51 at £600.
Sources: FH133, AC, 4, 87; CCAM, 1388; CCC, 109, 2016; PRO C193/12; Nichols, III, 2, 368–371.

Richard Turpin Gent., Knaptoft, 1593–?
2s William Kt; app. 28/11/44 CoP.
Ox New Coll 11; Gray's 13.
Three sons died in the King's Army, one of them in Ireland in 1649.
Brought into administration in 1643.

Comp 46 at Oxford and elsewhere, 47 fined 1/6th at £930, 48 reduced to £666-13s-4d, but had to alienate the Knaptoft estates to cover costs. Sources: CCC, 111, 1515–1516; Black Docquets, 117; *Nichols*, IV, 1, 217–225.

Uncertain Cases

Edward Farnham, Esq., Quorn, 1594–1654
1s Adrian; app. 28/11/44 CoP.
Left Ashby in 1645 during the plague, it is not known how long he had been there. Claims was present under duress. Kept prisoner at Leicester.
Compounded 45, fined £480, seq. 49 as only paid half. Assessment 48 1/5th 1/20th £45–12s-0d. Was £950 in debt.
Sources: CCC, 111, 941; CCAM, 785; Nichols, TTT, 1, 97–103.

Henry 5th Earl of Huntingdon, Ashby-de-la-Zouch, probably took no part in the war beyond lending money to the King in 1642. Died Oct 1643.
See correspondence in HMC Hastings Vols 2 and 4.

Ferdinando 6th Earl of Huntingdon, Ashby-de-la-Zouch, was a parliamentarian troop commander at the Battle of Edgehill, then laid down his commission. Went into the Ashby garrison only, he said, for his own protection. Argued he took no part in royalist councils but did sign Oxford Parliament's letter protesting at the intervention of Scots. Acted as mediator for the surrender of the castle, 1646. See CCAM, 640; CCC, 1043.

Passive Supporters or Neutrals

Sir Henry Berkeley possibly not even in the county at the time. See Nichols, II, 1, 400, 413.

Sir Thomas Burton, Bart, Stokeston
Paid parliamentarian assessment throughout the war. CCAM, 165; Nichols, II, 2, 817–820.

Theophilus Cave, Barrow
First appears in the CoP of 1644. Does not seem to have acted on it in any capacity.
Nichols, III, 1, 68.

Sir John Cote, Elston
His whereabouts cannot be traced for the war years. VL, 94; Nichols, III, 2, App. 4, 40.

Sir William Jones, Kt.
App. 11/6/42. Whereabouts unknown. FH133.

Nathaniel Lucy, Hoton.
Whereabouts unknown, only appointed to the CoP in 44. Nichols, III, 2, App. 4, 40.

Sir Thomas Merry, Kt, Gopsall
Whereabouts unknown.
Nichols, III, 2, App.4, 40; IV, 1, 855.

Sir Edmund Reeve, Kt.
Whereabouts unknown.
Nichols, III, 2, App. 4, 40.

Thomas Rowe (Rooe) Gent., Normanton Turville
Son in King's Army, but Thomas's whereabouts unknown. Nichols, IV, 2, 1005; III, 2, App. 4, 40.

Sir John Skeffington, Kt, Bart, Skeffington
Cleared of charges of Royalism by Sir William Brereton.
Estates in Leicestershire sequestered in 1650, possibly by mistake. Nichols, III, 2, App. 4, 40; Dore (ed.), *Letter Books of Sir William Brereton*, 1, p.218.

John Villiers, Viscount Purbeck, Brooksby
Whereabouts unknown though was paying assessments by 1646. CCAM, 675; Nichols, III, 1, 197–198; III, 2, App. 4, 40.

Nottinghamshire

Active Commissioners
John Digby, Esq., Mansfield Woodhouse (also estates in Yorks. and Staffs.) is John; app. 18/6/42, 43, 45 (Disputes Commission); HS 42; kt 42.
Helped Lord Newark raise troops for the King in 1642. Turned Newark into a garrison 1642–3. Candidate for governorship in early 1645. Exempted from pardon in the Uxbridge Treaty. Gave up arms Jan 1646. Was involved in Second Civil War. See chapters 2, 5, 6. Assessed at £2,000 in 48.
Sources: FH133; NV, 168; CCC, 1421; Gardiner *Denouements*, 279; RCHM, Newark, 94, 76; CCAM, 435, 881–885.

Sir Gervase Eyre, Kt (Rampton Derbys), ?–1644
1s Gervase; app. 18/6/42.
Gained Rampton by marriage; wounded at the relief of Newark March 1644. Died in the garrison May 1644. Had regiment of horse.
Sources: FH133; NV, 93; CCC, 2744; Wood, 218; Thoresby, 3, 248.

Richard Byron, Esq., Strelley; 1600–1679
3s John of Newstead; app. 18/6/42.
Kt Shrewsbury, Oct 42; Given MA Ox, Nov 42; Governor of Newark 1644–1645. Gave up arms *c.*Sept 45. See chapters 5, 6. Became the second Lord Byron on death of brother John. Fined at 1/10th £120.
Sources: FH133; NV, 11; CCC, 1308; Thoresby, 285; RCHM, Newark, 58–59.

John, Viscount Chaworth of Armagh, Wiverton, 1600–1644
1s Sir George Kt; app. 9/7/42, 43–44, Comm Lincs. Notts.
Ca Persehouse 27; Baron 39. Appears to have submitted to Parliament Feb 44, but claimed that he died in arms. Had been military active, involved in one of the royalist captures of Gainsborough 22/10/43. M daughter of Lord Camden.
Sources: FH133, AO, 265; AC, 1, 327; NV, 128; CCC, 1357; RCHM, Newark, 93; Wood, 217; CCAM, 181–185; Thoresby, 119.

Sir Roger Cooper, Kt, Thurgarton, ?–1657
1s William Esq., app. 1816/42, 43–44, Comm Lincs., Notts.
Ca Trinity 09; Gray's 11; kt 24. House at Thurgarton garrisoned, Cooper was captured there in 1644, but finished the war at Newark.
Fined at 1/6th, £2,256, didn't pay until 50. Assessment in 47 was £1,200, in 49 £80. By 1650 estate mortgaged to sum of £2,000.
Sources: FH133; AC, 1, 392; CCC, 1325; CCAM, 281–285, 806–807; RCHM, Newark, 94; Hutchinson, 1, 254.

Sir Gervase Clifton, Kt, Bart, Clifton, 1586–1666
1s George; App 18/6/42, 45, Committee for Disputes at Newark.
Ca St Johns fell com 03; MA 12; MP shire 14 20 24 28 61; MP Nottingham 26; MP East Retford 40–43.
Married 7 times! Shared his time between Newark and Oxford as in the Oxford Parliament. Surrendered at Newark. Comp 47 1/3rd £7,625-3s-8d. Assessed in 43 £500, 47 £7,000, 49 sequestered for non-payment. Sources: FH133, AC, 1, 356; GA, 54; NV, 18; CCC, 1318; CCAM, 182, 996; Thoresby, 1, 108; RCHM, Newark, 93; Black *Docquets*, 187; signature on a letter of the Newark commissioner, Brown C., *A History of Newark on Trent*, Newark, 1907, 74.

Thomas Holder, South Wheatley, dead before 1650
App. 1643–44. Sequestered for being a commissioner, wife inherited the estate in 1650 when it was still under sequestration. Was active at Newark in 1643–4.
Sources: CCC, 108, 2579; CCAM, 1360; RCHM, Newark, 93–94; Wood, 122.

Robert Sutton, Esq., Aversham, 1594–1668
1s Sir William; App 18/6/42, 45, Disputes Committee.
Ca fell com Trinity 11; JP 26; DL ?40–42; MP shire 24–25, 40–43. Zealous royalist, created Baron Lexington 1645. Present at surrender of Newark. Assessed at £3,000 in 43.
Sources: FH133, CA, 4, 187; NV, 143; CCAM, 436, 281–285; RCHM, Newark, 94; Brown, *op. cit.*, 74; PRO, C193/12; Black *Docquets*, 280.

Thomas Williamson, Esq., East Markham (Gainsborough Lincs.)
1s of Sir Richard of Gainsborough; app. 18/6/42.

Awarded a Baronetcy for efforts in war. Surrendered at Newark. Assessed at £100 in 46, 48 Lincs. estates assessed at £123, already paying £296 pa for Notts. estates.
Sources: FH133; DV, 98; CCC, 1039; CCAM, 652.

Uncertain Cases
Robert Mellish, Ragnall
Claimed at surrender of Newark that he had never been in arms of council.
Sources: CCC, 108, 1249–1350.

Sir Matther Palmer, Kt, Southwell.
App 18/6/42; IIS 23.
Said to have been a lieutenant colonel but service unknown.
Sources: FH133; Wood, 217; NRO M946.

William Staunton (Stanton), Esq., Staunton, dead before 1660
1s Anthony; app. 45 Committee of Disputes.
Certainly was a colonel in arms but no mention of being a commissioner of array. Given an MA at Oxford in Nov 1642.
Fined £40. Assessed at £800 (1/5th and 1/20th).
Sources: CCC, 1382; CCAM, 817; PN, no.1366; RCHM, Newark, 78, 94.

Passive Supporters or Neutrals
John Gregory, Gent., Nottingham, ?–1654
Whereabouts unknown, possibly never left Nottingham. FH133; *Thoresby*, 2, 41, 93.

Robert Grieves, Gent., Nottingham
Possibly a prisoner in Newark, thrown off the Nottinghamshire town council for suspected royalism. Fined £40 1646.
FH133; CCC, 1278; Records of the Borough of Nottingham, 425–431.

Richard Grieves, Gent., Beely
Probably remained at home, too ill to travel in 1648. FH133; CCAM, 995.

Sir George Lassalls, Kt, Sturton and Gateford, ?–1646. Whereabouts unknown.
FH133; NV, 59; NRO DDA5, 343.

Sir Francis Molyneux, Kt, Bart, Houghton, 1602–1674
Whereabouts unknown, brother Roger was colonel in the North Midlands Army. FH133; Thoresby, 2, 304.

Robert Mellish, Ragnall
Whereabouts and date of appointment unknown. Wood, 220.

John Nevill, Esq., unidentified
FH133.

Nicholas Stringer, Esq., Sutton cum Lound, East Markham. CCC, 108, FH133.

John Wood (?the elder), Esq., unidentified
FH133.

Rutland

Active Commissioners
Bryan Palmes, Esq., Ashwell (also Yorks.), 1590–1654
1s Sir Guy; app. 2/7/42.
Ox Trinity 15; MP Stamford 26; MP Aldborough Yorks. 40 (Short Parliament); Kt (April) 42; Doctor of Civil Law Ox Nov 42.
Compounded 46, fined 47 at 1/6th £681. Assessed 51 at £200.
Sources: FH133; AO, 1111; CCC, 316; CCAM, 1388; DNB.

Sir Guy Palmes, Kt, Ashwell
Father of Bryan, app. 2/7/42.
HS07 17 25; MP shire 21 23 40 (Short Parliament) 40 (Long Parliament, expelled). Fined 47 1/2 at £3,905, reduced 49 to £3,317-13s-4d. Assess 46 £1,500, 49 £800.
Sources: FH133; CCC, 1316; CCAM, 429; Black *Docquets*, 187.

Richard Wingfield, Esq., Tickencote, 1621–1663
1s John; app. 2/7/42.
Ox Magdalene 36; Kt July 42; HS 62.
Claimed that was only a royalist because they had possession of his estate. Fined 46 £746; Dec 46 in debt to £3,000, owed Committee for Comp £112; assessed 45 at £1,000.
Sources: FH133, AO, 1660; CCC, 1056; CCAM, 559–560; Wright, 124.

Baptiste Noel, Esq.; Langham, 1611–1682
1s Edward Lord Camden; app. 2/7/42.
Ca 28; MA ?; MP shire 28 40 (Short Parl.) 40 (Long Parl., expelled); succeeded father March 43; col. of horse, captured 45, released 46; JP 61; lord lieutenant 60–85.
Compounded 46, Fined £19,558, 47 reduced to £11,078.
Sources: FH133, AC, 3, 261; GA, 185; CCC, 946–947; CCAM, 401; PN, no.1051; Black *Docquets*, 59–60.

Richard Bullingham, Esq., Ketton, ?–1657
1s Nicholas; app. 2/7142.
Ca St Johns 12, BA ?
At Belvoir Castle. Fined 47, 1/2 at £375, reduced to £300 with £50 to the church. Claimed could not pay, 48 new fine set at 1/6th £100. Assessed 49 £200.
Sources: FH133; AC, 1, 252; CCC, 1497; CCAM, 1074.

Sir Francis Bodenham, Kt, Ryhall, dead before 1644?
1s Sir William; app. 2/7/42.
Ca Sidney Sussex 01; Gray's 03; HS 14; MP shire 26; JP 26; Kt 16. Estates sequestered for delinquency.
Sources: FH133; AC, 1, 172; CCC, 88–90; Wright, 112; PN, no. 146 passim; PRO C193/12.

Passive Supporters or Neutrals
Thomas Levett, Esq.
Unidentified but may be the T. Levett who was HS 39. FH133.

Staffordshire

Active Commissioners
Sir Simon Avery, Bart. See under Derbyshire

Sir Harvey Bagot, Bart. Blithefield, 1591–1660
1s Walter; app. 26/6/42, 6/8/42.
Ox Trinity 08; JP 26; Bart 27; DL 39; HS 42; MP shire 28–29 40 (Long Parl. expelled).
In the Lichfield garrison where commission generally sat. His 2nd and 3rd sons Harvey and Richard were the governors of the town. Sat at the Oxford Parliament also. At surrender of Lichfield.
Fined 47 2/3rds £1,340, reduced 49 to £1,004–17s.
Assessed 44 at £2,000, 48 at £1,745, had debts of £3,120.
Sources: FH133; AO, 55; CCC, 1476–1477; CCAM, 420; PRO C193/12; Black *Docquets*, 107; *SHC* New Series, XI, 1902.

George Digby, Esq., Sandon, 1601–?
1s Everard; app. 26/6/42, 6/8/42; 45 appointed to Marcher Assoc Com.
Ox Magdalene 20. Accused of being a papist. Didn't comp, fined £1,440.
Sources: FH133; AO, 402; CCC, 2043–2044.

Sir Richard Dyott, Kt, Lichfield, 1590–1659
1s Anthony; app. 26/6/42, 6/8/42.
Ox Corpus Christi BA 07; IT 15 barrister at law; MP shire 21–22 24–25; MP Lichfield 25 26 28–29 40 (Short Parl.); Kt Dublin 35 by Strafford.
High Steward of Lichfield.
Reputed to be a Catholic when in 1640 was in the north with the King. Was fanatically anti-puritan at the TT. At the surrender of Lichfield despite being captured and being held as a prisoner at Shrewsbury in 1645.
Sources: FH133; SP, 76; AO, 483; CCC, 89, 547; Prest, 215.

Thomas Lane, Esq., Bentley, 1572–1660
1s? App. 26/6/42, 6/8/42.

Active until Sept 45. Family not officially armigerous until 1678 and then largely in recognition of John's services. Thomas' son John was a colonel in the North Midlands Army. Compounded 46, fined 1/6th at £225.
Sources: FH133; SP, 152; GA, 149; CCC, 1424; *Staffordshire Historical Collections*, 1910, 174–189.

Sir Richard Leveson, KB, Trentham (Littleshall Salop), 1598–1661
2s Sir John; app. 26/6/42, 6/8/42.
Ox Queens 17; MP Newcastle-under-Lyme 24–25; MP Salop 26; MP Newcastle-under-Lyme (Long Parl. excluded); JP; KB 26.
Shared his time between Oxford Parliament, Staffs. Commission and fighting in Salop. After fall of Shrewsbury was a prisoner for 9 months. Compounded 45, fine £9,846, abated to £3,846, estate at Trentham ruined when used as a parliamentarian garrison, losses thereby claimed to be £24,000. Assessed 44 at £1,500.
Sources: FH133; AO, 904; GA, 154; CCC, 990, 3264; CCAM, 478; SRO D593 Papers of Sir Richard Leveson.

Sir Thomas Littleton, Bart, Kt, Hagley (Frankley Worcs.), 1594–1650
1s John; app. 26/6/42, 6/8/42; Comm of Accounts 44 45.
Ox Balliol 10; IT 13; kt 18; bart 18; HS 41; MP Worcs. 21–22 24–25 25 26 40 (Short Parl.). Colonel of horse and foot, taken prisoner at Bewdley 44, imprisoned in the tower.
Fined £4,000 in 47; assessed 44 and 47 at £1,000.
Sources: FH133, CCC, 863; CCAM, 428, 781; Dugdale 19, 86; Black *Docquets*, 229, 264.

Sir Edward Littleton, Bart, Pillaton Hall, 1599–1657
Ox Brasenose 17; IT 18; bart 27; JP 34–40; MP shire 40 (Short Parl.) 40 (Long Parl.); HS 38.
Shared time between county and Oxford, estate sequestered for much of the war. Assessed at £1,000 and goods belonging to him were sold by Parliament in London. Parliament appointed him to their committees until well into 1643!
Sources: FH133; CCC, 2080–2081; CCAM, 356–357; Black *Docquets*, 108–187.

George Parker, Esq., Park Hall Caveswall, 1591–1675
2s William of Parwich Derbys; app 6/8/42.
Ca Jesus fell com 09; Solicitor at Law and Clerk of Assize in Staffs. Claimed never in arms, fined for commissioner's post £120.
Sources: FH133; SP, 182; AC, 3, 307; CCC, 1028.

Sir Edward Seabright, Kt, Bart (Besford Worcs)
App. 26/6/42, 6/8/42; Comm. for Acc. 45; JP 26; made HS in 44, with responsibility for collection of the £100,000 imposed by the Oxford Parliament. With E. Littleton given power to impress county men into the army in 43. Claimed that he only sat on the commission until just after

Edgehill, bribed witnesses but fined £3,618 in 1650 even though he had served as high sheriff in 1649! His activism is not, now in doubt.
Sources: FH133; CCAM, 671–673; CCC, 2606–2610; PRO C193/12; Black *Docquets*, 108, 176, 264.

Sir John Skeffington, Kt, Bart, Fisherwick, 1582–1651
1s William; app 6/8/42; comm accounts 45.
Ca Jesus 03; MT 04; Kt 24; MP Newcastle-under-Lyme 26; succeeded to baronetcy 35; HS 37. Parliament found actual proof of his guilt as a warrant with his signature came to light – such a find was, and is, rare.
Fined 1/6th 50, £1,132–12s reduced to £961-18s-8d.
Sources: FH133, AC, 4, 84; CCC, 2207; Black *Docquets*, 246.

Ralph Sneyd, Esq., Keele, ?–1650 (Sneyd)
1s Ralph; app. 26/6/42, 6/8/42. HS 21; MP 42; JP 26.
Didn't serve at Oxford Parliament, stayed in Staffs. raising troops in Leek area in 43–44, held rank of colonel. Fined 46 £2,026, abated to £100, finally paid £1,500, assessed at £1,000 in 44, 47 at £2,500.
Sources: FH133; SP, 210; AC, 4, 118 *passim*; CCC, 1033; CCAM, 433; PRO C193/12; HMC Hastings, 2, 117.

Sir Robert Wolseley, Bart, Moreton, ?–1646
2s John; app. 6/8/42, Marcher Comm 45; Clerk of the Peace Staffs. 17–26; Clerk of the Patent Office. Given powers to impress men in Staffs. 43; estate under sequestration until 1647.
Sources: FH133; SP, 251; CCC, 1771; Black *Docquets*, 108; Stephens E., *Clerks of the Counties*, 1360–1960, Newport, 1961, 158.

Walter Wrottesley, Esq., Wrottesley.
App 26/6/42; DL 34; JP; bart 42.
Garrisoned Wrottesley as an outpost of Dudley garrison. Petitioned to compound 54. For years he was assumed to have been inactive, but his commitment to the cause and activism is obvious.
Assessed 44 £500, 45 £1,500, 46 £600.
Sources: FH133; SRO D948/4/6/2–5; CCC, 1056; *Coll for Staffs. Hist*, New Series, VI, 2, 306.

Uncertain Cases

Walter Chetwynd, Esq., Rugeley, Grendon (also Warwicks. estates) 1598–1669
1s Anthony of Grendon; app. 26/6/42, 6/8/42.
Was made HS in 48 but then it was realised that he had furnished Lichfield, Dudley and Ashby with iron from his works. His land value was only £7 pa, but his ironworks were £4,000 pa. Fined 1/10th £464 in 1650. This may therefore be a case of an excellent cover up.
Sources: FH133; SP, 49; AP, 269; CCAM, 1184.

Thomas Crompton, Esq., Bridgnorth, Stone, 1607–?
App. 26/6/42, 6/8/42; MP shire 28 53; DL 34; was at Lichfield during the war but this is the only link with the administration.
Sources: FH133; SP, 64; GA, 66; CCC, 1324 (described as commissioner).

Passive Supporters or Neutrals
Thomas Broughton, Broughton. Whereabouts unknown.
Sources: FH133; SP, 37; CCAM, 783.

Richard Bowyer, Esq., Siddow Lane. Whereabouts unknown.
Sources: FH133

Sir John Pershall, Bart, Pershall, 1620–1680?
Whereabouts unknown though was in the Tower 46. Plotted with Robert Shirley of Staunton Harold Leics. and Ralph Sneyd in 1649, with the aim of supporting Charles II. In Stafford gaol in 1680.
Source: FHI33; SP, 186; CCC, 1207; CCAM, 1371.

Sir William Powell, Kt, Tutbury. Whereabouts unknown.
Source: FH133; CCC, 1985; CCAM, 1388.

William Howard, Viscount Stafford
2s Earl of Arundel. At Oxford? Source: FH133.

Charles Twisden, Dr at Law, whereabouts unknown
Source: FH133; AO, 1526.

Other Categories of Commissioners Not Serving In Their County

Dead or Captured pre-April 1643
Thomas Broome, Notts.; arrested early 1643; FH133; Wood, 217.

Thomas Calthorp, Leics.; died early 1643; Nichols, IV, 1, 49.

Griffin Dybell (Divall), Notts.; arrested Jan 43; FH133; Wood, 217.

Sir John Fitzherbert Kt, Derbys; died in August 1641; FH133; Wright, 78.

Henry Noel, 2s of above; died in prison London after being captured by Lord Grey in Feb 43, d. Jul 43; F1-J133, Wright, 78.

Phillip Earl of Chesterfield; Garrisoned Bretby Derbys. Nov 42, driven out went to Lichfield and in March 43 surrendered it to Gell, he went into semi-voluntary captivity; FH133; JTB, 45. See Chapter 5.

Activists Elsewhere

Sir Thomas Blackwell, Notts.; in the south; PN, no. 126.

Sir John Byron, Notts., Field Marshall in Cheshire, PN, no. 230.

William Cavendish, Earl of Devonshire, Derbys., left the country; CCC, 2831; CCAM, 402, 996.

William Cavendish, Earl of Newcastle, Derbys. Notts. Staffs.; commander of the Northern Army. See chapters 5, 6.

Sir Henry Griffiths, Staffs.; in the north. CCC, 1375; CCAM, 809.

Sir Christopher Hatton, KB, Rut; at Oxford; FH133; CCC, 1581–1582; CCAM, 986, 1207.

Edward Heath, Esq., Rut; at Oxford and in the SW; FH133; Wright, 40.

Sir John Lamb, Kt; Leics.; with the Queen and then at Oxford; FH133; Nichols, IV, 1, 322, III, 1, 748.

Francis Leke, Lord Deincourt, Derbys; at Oxford; FH133; Toynbee M. (ed.), *Strangers in Oxford*, Phillimore, 1973, 57–58.

William Lord Paget, Staffs.; at Oxford; FH133; CCC, 872–873.

Isham Parkyns, Esq., Notts.; governor of Ashby-de-la-Zouch. See chapters 4, 5, 6.

Henry Pierrepoint, Viscount Newark, Notts.; active in 42 then in the Oxford garrison; FH133; CCC, 1482–1484.

Thomas, Viscount Saville, Leics.; in the north; AC, 4, 22.

Sir William Saville, Bart, Notts.; in the north; FH133; CCAM, 436.

Sir Richard Shilton (Shelton), Kt; in Oxford; FH133; SP, 201.

Robert Tredway, Esq., Rut; Served as a CoA for Lincs.; FH133; CCAM, 1073: CCC, 1355.

Parliamentarians

Joseph Bent, Gent. Leics.; CCC, 941–942; Nichols, IV, 1, 161.

Robert Buxton; Served on the Notts. council throughout; FH133; See *Records of the Borough of Nottingham, passim.*

James Chadwick, Esq., Notts.; see Notts. Committee.

Sir John Coke, Kt, Derbys; MP Westminster; FH133; JTB, 21.

William Gregory; Served on Nott Council throughout; *Records of the Borough of Nottingham*, 425–431; FH133.

Sir Thomas Hartopp, Kt; see Leicestershire Committee.

Richard Hurdment; Nott; Served on Notts. Council throughout; FH133; *Records of the Borough of Nottingham*, 425–431.
159.

Sir Edward Leach, Kt, Derbys; in Westminster at HoL; FH133; JTB, 36; CCAM, 343.

Martin Lister, Gent., Leics.; MP Westminster. See Parliamentarians Active Elsewhere.

John Manners, Earl of Rutland, Derbys; in HoL; FH133; JBT, 37.

William Nixe, Notts.; served as Mayor of Nottingham 43–45; FH133; *Records of the Borough of Nottingham*, 425–431.

Gervase Piggott, Esq., Notts.; see Notts. Committee.

Francis Toplady, Notts.; served on Nottingham. Council throughout; FH133; *Records of the Borough of Nottingham*, 425–431.

Sir George Villiers, Bart, Leics.; stayed in Leicester; FH133; Nichols, III, 1, 197–198.

Appendix II

Committeemen

Derbyshire

Active Committeemen
James Abney, Willesley, 1599–1693
1s George; app. 27/3/43, Delinquents Estates.
Ca Emanuel 16; IT 19; HS 55; family possibly drapers. Sources: FH133; GA, 1; JTB, 13, 58.

Ralph Clarke, Brampton ?Ashton; 1599–1661
3s Ralph; app. 1644–?
Ox 11; IT 16; was a merchant in Brampton, and father's heir. Sources: JTB, 19; DV, 25; GA, 53.

Sir John Curzon, Bart, Keldeston; 1598–1686
1s John; app. 12/3/42.
Ox Magdalene 18; IT 20; JP 26; HS 37; DL 40; MP Brackley 28; MP shire 40 (Long Parl.); Bart 41. Receiver of the Duchy of Lancaster.
Sources: FH133; PRO C193/12; JTB, 23.

Sir John Gell, Bart, Hopton; 1593–1671.
1s Thomas; app. 12/3/42, 27/3/43 Delinquents Estates; 8/4/43 Sequestration.
Ox Magdalene 10; captain trained bands 24; HS 35; JP 38; bart 42; DL 42. Governor of Derby after seizing it in 1642. Relentless but not always effective opponent of Hastings. Led one of the factions on the committee; in 46 flouted Committee of Both Kingdoms' instructions and became mistrusted by Parliament. See chapters 5, 6.
Sources: JTB, 27–28, 58, 62; FH133; AO, 556; GA, 98; JHC, 3, 556.

Sir George Gresley, Kt, Bart; Drakelow, 1580–1651
1s Sir Thomas Kt; app. 12/3/42, 8/4/43 Sequestrations
Ox Balliol 94; IT 98; bart 11; kt 12; JP 14 24; MP Newcastle-under-Lyme 28–29; DL 42; HS 45. Refused to pay ship money in the 1630s. Supporter of Gell on the committee. Kept a detailed copy book of committee letters. See chapters 5, 6.

Sources: JTB, 31, 58; DRO 830 M29; JEC, 3, 454.

Christopher Horton, Gent., Carleton, 1582–1659.
1s Walter; app. 12/3/42.
Ox Balliol 98; BA 1600; MT 02; HS 40; JP 47.
Source: FH133; JTB, 33, 58.

Sir Edward Leach, Kt, Shipley, ?1570–1656
1s Robert of Chester; 3/12/42.
Ox Brasenose BA DCL; Gray's, called to the bar; DL 42; HS 54; JP 54. Spent some time at the HoL in the war.
Sources: FH133; JTB, 36, 58.

Francis Mundy, Esq. Markeaton, 1577–1648
1s ? Mundy; app. 3/13/42.
Ca Corpus Christi 93; HS 17; DL 42.
Accused of delinquency by Gell in 46. Cleared.
Sources: FH133; DV, 2; JTB, 40, 58.

Sir Samuel Sleigh, Kt, Pool and Etwall, Ash, 1603–1670
1s Gervase; app. 3/12/42.
Ca Christ's fell com 21; Gray's 23; Kt 41; DL 42; MP Essex 54–56; MP Derbyshire 56–58; Clerk of Peace 44.
Sources: FH133, JHC, 3, 627; DV, 8; GA, 231; JTB, 46, 58.

Edward Charleton, Sandiacre, 1604–1659
1s Thomas; app. 1644–
Opposed Gell in 1645. Captured by royalists in 1645.
Sources: GA, 50; JTB, 19, 58.

Thomas Chalmer
App. 1644– Sequestration.
Almost unidentified but seems to have been active at some time after appointment.
Sources: JHC, 3, 454.

Sir Edward Coke, Bart, Longford, ?–1669.
1s Clement; app. 3/13/42, 44 Sequestration.
Bart 41; DL 42; JP 47; HS 46. Opposed to Gell, managed to outvote Gell's attempt to have him thrown off the committee.
Sources: FH133; JHC, 4, 5; JTB, 22, 58.

Richard Dale, Moneyash, 1591–?
Younger son of Richard of Flagg and Chelmorton. App. 45; receiver for High Peak.
Sources: JTB, 23.

Robert Eyre, Highlow
1s Thomas of Highlow; app. 8/4/44 Sequestration. Captain of foot. Active 1644–
Garrisoned Wingfield 1644 onwards. JP 58; HS 58.
Sources: JHC, 3, 454; JET, 25.

Thomas Gell, Esq., Wirksworth, 1594–1656
2s Thomas; app. 3/12/42, 8/4/44 Sequestration; IT bar 20; lawyer; recorder Derby 40s; MP 45; lieutenant colonel of Gell's Foot. Brother to Sir John.
Sources: JHC, 3, 454; GA, 98; JTB, 28–29, 58.

Robert Mellor, Derby, ?1612–1656.
1s Henry; app. 8/4/44 Sequestration.
Opposed Thomas Gell's election to Parliament in 45. Thereafter opposed to the Gell faction on the committee. A mercer by profession. captain of foot.
Sources: DJ, 31; JHC, 3, 454; JET, 38.

Rowland Morewood, Gent., Alfreton
1s Anthony of Hemsworth; app. 1644.
Captured by Hastings in 1643? Accused of Delinquency in 1646 by Gell but cleared.
Sources: DV, 2; JTB, 40.

John Mundy, Esq., Markeaton, ?1601–1681
1s Francis; App 44–
Captain in Derby garrison until 43? then active on the committee.
Sources: JTB, 40.

George Pole, Gent., High Edge, 1604–1674
1s George; app. 1644–
Committee member for 13 years.
Sources: DV, 4; GA, 202; JTB, 41.

Francis Revel, Esq. Ogston and Carsthwaite
1s Edward; app. 3/12/42, 17/3/43 del est.; DL 42 Nov.
Charged with desertion and helping the royalists, by Gell. However charges did not lead to him being thrown off committee, as he served 10 years.
Sources: FH133; JTB, 42.

Samuel Roper, Gent., Heanor, 1597–1658
1s Thomas of Appleby, 1644–
Ca fell com Emanuel 13–14; Lincolns 16; colonel of horse. Antiquarian, assisted Dugdale.
Sources: AC, 3, 487; JTB, 43.

Thomas Saunders, Gent., Little Ireton, 1610–1695
1s Collingwood; app. 1643? Was absent for part of time until 44–. Educated at Repton and Derby. Bitter enemy of Gell throughout the war.

Sources: JHC, 3, 463; JTB, 43.

Luke Whittington, Derby
App. 3/12/42, 8/4/44 Sequestration.
Alderman of Derby; bailiff 30; mayor 41, 43–44; receiver of plate 42.
Sources: JUG, 3, 454; FH133; JTB, 48.

Henry Wigfall, Renishaw, 1583–1651
3s Henry of Ridgeway; app. 3/12/42, 8/4/44 Sequestration.
Ca Caius 99; DL 42.
Sources: JHC, 3, 454; AC, 4, 401; JTB, 48.

John Wigley, Gent., Wigwell, 1617–?
1s Richard; app. 8/4/44 Sequestration.
Ca Magdalen 34. Married Gell's daughter Bridget.
Sources: JHC, 3, 454; DV, 36; JTB, 49.

Nicholas Wilmot, Gent., Chaddesden, 1612–1682.
3s Robert; App 1645–
Ox Magdalene 26; Gray's 37; barrister at law; kt 79. Opposed Gell. Canvassed for Mellor in 45 election.
Sources: GA, 281; JTB, 49.

Uncertain Cases

Robert Allestree, Alveston ?–1665
?3s William. Town Clerk in the 40s. DV, 15.

Leicestershire

Active Committeemen
Evers Armyn, Esq., Leicester, ?–1680
1s William of Osgodby Lincs.; app. 3/3/43.
Ca Sydney Sussex 14; Gray's 16; barrister 22; MP Grantham 25–26; JP ?
Sources: FH33; CA, 1, 39.

Thomas Babington, Esq., Rothley Temple, 1612 or 1615–?
2s Thomas; app. 15/12/42, 1/4/43, Scandalous Ministers 44; Militia Comm.
Ca Lincoln 28; BA 31. Fought? at the siege of Leicester.
Sources: VL, 206; FH133; AO, 52.

John Bainbridge (Bembrigg), Esq., Lockington, 1616–?
1s Thomas; app. 1/4/43 Sequestration, Scandalous Ministers, 3/8/43 Money for Army.
Sources: FH133; VL, 182.

William Bainbridge (Bembrigg), Esq., Lockington, 1604–1669
1s John; app. 15/12/42, 9/9/43 Sequestration, 10/7/44 Militia.
Ca pens Christ's 21.
Cousin of the above. In charge of the slighting of Ashby-de-la-Zouch in 1648–1649.
Sources: JHC, 3, 326; AC, 1, 69; VL, 182; Nichols, 3, 2, App. 2, 31, 32, 33

Thomas Beaumont, Staunton Grange
3s Thomas; app. 15/12/42, 17/3/45.
Ox Wadham 13.
Sources: VL, 61; FH133; AO, 97.

Richard Brent, Esq., Enderby, Cosby
App. 15/12/42, 3/8/43 Money for Army.
Sources: ?VL, 159; FH133; Nichols, 3, 2, App. 4, 31–32.

John Browne, 1589–?
App. May 45. Militia.
Ox Christ Church 06; BA 10; MA 13.
Sources: BL TT E303/13; AO, 194.

Thomas Cotton, Esq., Laughton, 1595–1653
1s Thomas; app. 15/12/42, 3/8/43 Money for Army, 17/3/45.
Ca Trinity Pens 09.
Sources: JHC, 3, 50; VL, 192; CA, 1, 404; Nichols, 3, 2, App. 4, 38; FH133

Edmund Craddock, Leicester
App. 164 Militia 45.
Alderman, chamberlain 38–39; steward of the fair, 41–42; mayor 45–46.
Sources: Nichols, 3, 2, App. 4, 38; Stocks, 601.

William Danvers, Esq., 1593–?
App. 15/12/42, 1/4/43 Sequestration, 3/8/43 Money for Army, 17/3/45.
Sources: VL, 87; FH133; Nichols, 3, 2, App. 4, 38.

Thomas Goddard, Gent., Peatling Parva, ?Croston, 1617–?
1s William; app. 17/3/45.
Ox Lincoln 34; BA 37.
Sources: VL, 190; Nichols, 3, 2, App. 4, 41.

John Goodman (Goodwyn), Esq.
App. 15/12/42, 1/4/43 Sequestration, 3/8/43 Money for Army, 44 Militia.
Unidentified but active on several committees including that sitting during the siege.
Sources: FH133; BL TT E303/13; Nichols, 3, 2, App. 4, 38.

Valentine Goodman, Gent.
Militia May 45. Unidentified but active in 45.

Sources: BL TT E303/13; Nichols, 3, 2, App. 4, 42.

Theophilus Grey, Esq.
App. 44 Militia.
Captain in Lord Grey's Foot in the garrison at Leicester. Sometime Gov.
Sources: BL TT E303/13; Nichols, 3, 2, App. 4, 35.

Thomas Lord Grey of Groby, Groby, Bradgate Park, 1620–1657
1s Henry Earl of Stamford; app. 15/12/42 and on all subsequent committees Commander of the East Midland Association 1643–1644. Assisted at Pride's Purge, later became a 5th Monarchist. See chapters 2, 3, 4, 5, 6.
Sources: See Nichols, 3, 2, App. 4; Hollings.

Francis Hacker, Esq., East Bridgford Notts., ?–1660
?1s; app. 3/8/43 Money for Army, 44 Militia Comm.
Brother of Major Rowland Hacker of Hastings' Horse. Captured at Melton in 1644. Became colonel of horse, assisted at King's execution. Executed 1660 as a regicide.
Sources: Nichols, 3, 2, App. 4, *passim*; JEC, 3, 50, 434, 444; DNB.

Sir Edward Hartopp, Kt, Buckminster, 1608–1657
1s Sir Edward Bart; app. 15/12/42, 1/4/43, 3/8/43, 17/3/45.
Ca Christ's 24; Lincolns 27; kt 34; succeeded to baronetcy 52.
Commander of the parliamentarian horse at the siege of Newark 1644 and therefore, at the Battle of Cotes. See Chapter 5.
Sources: Nichols, 3, 2, App. 4, 31–33; CA, 2, 321; GA, 117; VL, 197; Bennett M., 'The Civil War Battle of Cotes', *The Leicestershire Historian*, 1984–1985; FH133.

Sir Thomas Hartopp, Kt, Burton Lazars, 1600–?
1s Sir William; App 1/4/43 Sequestration, Scandalous Ministers, 3/8/43 Army Money, 45 Militia.
Ca Queens 16; Gray's 19; kt 24.
Sources: Nichols, 3, 2, App. 4, 38; CA, 2, 321; GA, 117; VL, 9, 197.

Thomas Hesilrige, Esq., Nosely
2s Thomas; app. 15/12/42, 1/4/42 Scandalous Ministers, 3/8/43 Money for Army, 44 Militia. Brother of Sir Arthur. Captured at Melton Mowbray 1644.
Sources: Nichols, 3, 2, App. 4, *passim*; VL, 16; FH133. See Chapter 6.

William Hewitt, Esq., Dunston
1s William; app. 15/12/42, 1644 Militia.
? Ca Christ's fell com 21; Gray's 22.
Sources: Nichols, 3, 2, App. 4, 31; BL TT E303/13, FH133; AC, 2, 362.

Richard Ludlam, Leicester
App. 15/12/42, 3/3/43 Sequestration 3/8/43 Money for Army, 44 Militia.

Steward of fair 37–38; chamberlain 31–32; mayor 42–43. Argued with Lord Grey and sent as prisoner to Burleigh House. Released March 44.
Sources: FH133; JHC, 3, 226; Nichols, 3, 2, App. 4, 38.

William Nowell Esq., Wellesborough
1s William; app. 15/2/45 Scots Army pay.
Sources: Nichols, 3, 2, App. 4, 41; VL, 42.

Archdale Palmer, Esq., Wanlip, 1612–1673
Born in London; app. 45.
Ca Sidney Sussex pens ?30; MT 31.
Had been high sheriff at the time of the issue of the commissions of array. His dithering allowed royalists to send some warrants out in the name of his office. Attempted to arrest Hastings, 23/6/42.
Sources: Nichols, 3, 2, App. 4, 41; AO, 1173; VL, 106.

William Quarles
App. 17/3/45 General Committee. Perhaps only active briefly.
Sources: Nichols, 3, 2, App. 4, 41.

Francis Smalley, Gent.
App. Sept 43, added to General Committee May 45. Active at the time of the siege.
Sources: JHC, 3, 226; BL TT E303/13.

William Sherman, Gent., Newalke Leicester, 1585–?
App. 1/4/43 Scandalous Ministers, 17/3/45 added to the General Committee.
Ca St Johns Pens 04.
Sources: VL, 204.

Henry Smith, Esq., Withicock, 1620–?
App 44, 45.
Ox Magdalene pleb 38; MP county 45–53. Regicide, died in the Tower.
Sources: AO, 1372; GA, 235; VL, 66; BL TT E303/13.

Arthur Staveley, Esq., Leicester, 1591–?
1s Thomas of Bignell Oxon; app. 15/12/43, 1/4/43 sequestered; 3/8/43 Money for Army, 44 Militia; HS 45.
Captured at Melton in 44 with Hacker. See Chapter 5.
Sources: Nichols, 3, 2, App. 4, 38; FH133; JHC, 4, 45; VL, 136.

John Stafford, Esq.
App May 45.
Active at the time of the siege.
Sources: BL TT E303/13.

William Stanley, Leicester.
App. 15/12/42, 3/3/43, 1/4/43 seq., 3/8/43 Money for Army, 44 Militia. Leics. coroner 37–38; steward of the fair? 04–05, 42–43. Alderman.
Sources: BL TT E303/13; Stocks, 602; Nichols, 3, 2, App. 4, 38.

John Swynfen, Gent., Sutton Cheney, 1595–?
1s Richard; May 45 Militia. Active at time of the siege.
Sources: VL, 134; BL TT E303/13.

Peter Temple, Esq., Temple Hall, Leicester
App. 15/12/42, 1/4/43 seq. 3/8/43 Money for Army, May 44, Militia, burgess 41; HS 43; MP 45. Active until recruiter election of May 45.
Regicide. Family were London drapers.
Sources: Nichols, 3, 2, App. 4, 31–33; FH133; JHC, 3, 354.

John Whatton
App May 45.
Active at the time of the siege.
Sources: BL TT E303/13.

Uncertain Cases

John St John, Esq., Cold Overton, 1623–?
App. 15/12/42.
Ox Lincoln 38; Gray's 40; Does not appear to have acted 42–45 though appears to be considered a member in May 45.
Sources: Nichols, 3, 2, App. 4, 31; FH133.

Simon Ridgley (Rudgley)
App. 15/12/42, 1/4/43 Scandalous Ministers
Unidentified, does not appear to have been reappointed after April 43.
Sources: FH133

Sir Roger Smith, Kt
App. 1/4/43, Scandalous Ministers; May 45 Militia.
Possibly active in 45 but uncertain, was not on a major committee between April 43 and May 45 and possibly inactive on the Scandalous Ministers Committee.
Sources: GA, 235; BL TT E303/13.

William Villiers, Leicester
2s Clement; app. 3/8/43.
This was his only appointment.
Sources: VL, 31; Nichols, 3, 2, App. 4, 32.

Passive Supporters or Neutrals

Robert Bilters, Alderman
App. 3/7/43 added to the Sequestration Committee.
Whereabouts unknown.
Nichols, 3, 2, App.4, 32.

Nottinghamshire

Active Committeemen
Edward Ayscough, Esq., Nutall, 1590–?
2s Sir Roger Kt; app. 7/5/44.
Ca Caius 08; Gray's 08 called to the bar 17; opposed to Hutchinson in 44.
Sources: JHL, 4, 543; Wood, 126, 128, 130–131; NV, 77.

James Chadwick, Esq., Nottingham
App. 3/12/42, 27/3/43 Delinquent Estates.
Barrister described as being of low origins but clever; recorder of Nottingham, Stafford and Derby. Opposed Hutchinson in 44.
Sources: Hutchinson, 142; Wood, 223; FH133.

John Hooper
App 17/11/45.
Had been a captain of foot in the garrison previous to this date.
Sources: JHC, 4, 346; Wood, 223.

George Hutchinson, Esq., Owthorpe, 1618–?
2s Sir Thomas Bart; app. 3/12/42 and every subsequent committee.
Brother of John, lieutenant colonel of his brother's regiment. In charge of the garrison on brother's absence.
Sources: Hutchinson, *passim*, Wood, 29, 32, 34, 58–61, 89–91, 124, 127–128, 131, 135; FH133.

John Hutchinson, Esq., Owthorpe, 1615–1664
1s Sir Thomas; app. 3/12/43 and every subsequent committee.
Ca fell com 32; MP shire 46–53 Nottingham 60 excluded.
Governor of the castle and town 1643. Seized Nottingham at end of 42. See chapters 2, 3, 4, 5, 6. Died in prison at Jersey.
Sources: Hutchinson; Wood.

Henry Ireton, Esq., Attenborough, Nottingham, 1610–1651
1s German; app. 22/2/43, 27/3/43 Delinquent Estates.
Ox Trinity 28; BA 29; MT 29.
Married Cromwell's daughter Bridgit. Active in Notts. until 44. Commissary General of New Model at Naseby. Politically active in the army 47–49. Regicide; Lord Deputy of Ireland 50, died at Limerick.

Sources: FH133; AO, 789; JHC, 4, 346; see Chapter 6. Wood, pp.12–13, 15, 27, 32, 34–36, 47, 51, 93, 124, 126, 128, 135, 156, 158, 192; Hutchinson, *passim*; Young, *Naseby*, *passim*.

John James, Nottingham
App. 27/3/42 Delinquent Estates, 17/11/45.
Alderman; Mayor 34–35 41–42; Lucy Hutchinson described him as being the only parliamentarian of 7 aldermen.
Sources: JHC, 4, 246; Wood, 15–16, 35, 124, 128–9, 133; Hutchinson, 1, 69.

Gervaise Lomax (Lomas), Thrumpington, 1607–?
App. 17/11/45.
Ca Christ's pens 24; captain of foot.
Sources: JHC, 4, 346; Wood, 32, 124, 127–128, 130–131.

John Mason, Nottingham
App. 1644. Rebel on the committee in 44. Captain of foot.
Source: Wood, 126–128, 133–134, 164, 166.

Gilbert Millington, Felley Abbey, ?1598–1666
App. 27/3/43 Delinquent Estates; barrister; MP ?; rebel on the committee in 1644.
Sources: Wood, 11, 16, 25, 34, 61, 90, 111, 124, 127, 130–131, 156–157, 175, 180–181, 183, 197; FH133.

William Nixe, Nottingham, 1590–1650
App. 14/10/44.
Alderman; mayor 1636–37 1643–44.
Captain of foot until 1643. Opposed Hutchinson in 1644.
Sources: Wood, 32, 124–126; Hutchinson, 75; FH133.

Richard Pendock, Gent., Tollerton, 1595–?
1s John; app. June 1645.
Active after the county was absorbed into the Northern Association.
Sources: Wood, 34, 126, 128–129, 131; Firth and Rait, 1, 703–714. NV, 107.

Francis Pierrepoint, Esq., Nottingham, ?–1658
3s Robert, Earl of Kingston; app. 3/12/42, 17/3/43 Delinquent Estates.
Only noble representative on the committee; became MP for the town in the recruiter elections of 1645.
Sources: Hutchinson, *passim*; Wood, 16, 29, 32, 34, 38, 50, 54, 95, 124, 127–130, 135, 140, 144, 157, 161, 164, 171, 176; DV, 56; FH133.

Gervase Pigott, Esq., Thrumpington, 1616–1669
1s Gervase; app. 15/12/42.
Ca St Catherine's then Christ's fell com 32; Lincolns 34; JP ?
Sources: Wood, 25, 34, 124, 128, 130–131; Firth and Rait, 49–51; Hutchinson, 73, 74, 136, 141, 145.

Dr Huntingdon Plumtree, Nottingham, 1601–1660
1s Henry; app. 22/2/43, 27/3/43 Delinquent Estates.
Ca St Johns 20; BA Trinity; MA 26; D Med St Johns 31.
Possibly gave up his parliamentarianism in 1643.
Sources: AO, 1173, AC, 3, 374; FH133; Wood, 124, 128–129, 131; Hutchinson, 26, 74, 98, 149.

Henry Sacheverill, Radcliffe or Reresby
?1s Henry of Radcliffe or is of Raffe of Reresby; app. 3/12/42.
Sources: FH133; NV, 165.

Thomas Salisbury, Gent., Nottingham
App. 27/11/43.
Secretary and treasurer to the committee. Opposed Hutchinson in 44.
Sources: JHC, 3, 322; FH133; Hutchinson, 73, 74, 105, 120, 135, 139, 144, 152, 153.

Clement Spelman, Gent., Narborough Norfolk, ?1598–1679
4s Sir Henry of Longham; app. June 45.
Ca Queens pens 11; Gray's 13; barrister 24; bencher 60.
No lands in Notts. until the war. Only on the committee after the county became part of the Northern Association.
Sources: Firth and Rait, 1, 703–714; Wood, 126, 128, 130, 131.

Francis Thornhaugh, Esq., Fenton and Gotham, 1622–1648
1s Sir Francis; app. 3/12/42, 27/3/43.
Ox Magdalene 35; IT 37; HS 43; MP East Retford 46–48.
Killed at Preston in 48. Colonel of horse regiment at Cotes.
Sources: FH133; JHC, 3, 354; AO, 1480; GA, 252; NV, 70; Wood, 34–36, 77–78, 85–88.

Sir Francis Thornhaugh, Kt, Fenton, 1593–1643
1s John; app. 3/12/42, 27/3/43, Delinquent Estates.
Ca fell com Emanuel 06; Lincolns 09; HS 37; DL 27; kt 15.
Father of above. Though died 43 did help put the committee into action.
Sources: FH133; AC, 3, 231; GA, 252; NV, 70; Wood, 11, 32, 34, 38, 124, 126, 135.

Sir Hardolph Watneys, Kt (Wastneys), Hedon
1s Gervase; app. 3/12/42.
May have been passive supporter after initial stages.
Sources: FH133; Wood, 124–125, 171.

Charles White, Esq. Newthorpe
App. 2/12/42, 27/11/43 Sequestration, 27/3/43 Delinquent Estates.
Raised troop of dragoons became captain, later colonel. ? Ca Sidney Sussex pens 24.
Sources: FH133; JHC, 3, 322; CA, 4, 386; Wood, 32, 38, 57–58, 124, 127–128, 130, 132, 148–150, 164–166, 176–177, 181, 202.

Joseph Widmerpool, Esq., Widmerpool
2s George; app. 27/11/43 Sequestration, 2/12/42, 27/3/43 Delinquent Estates.
Sources: FH133; Hutchinson, 73, 74, 104, 136, 150, 184.

Passive Supporters or Neutrals

Nicholas Charlton, Chilwell
App. June 1645. Whereabouts unknown.
Sources: Wood, 34, 126, 130–131; Firth and Rait, 703–714.

John Gregory, Gent., Nottingham
App. 27/3/43. Whereabouts unknown.
Source: FH133; Wood, 128.

Robert Reynes, Esq., Stanford
1s Nicholas; app. 27/3/43 Delinquent Estates. Whereabouts unknown.
Sources: FH133; Wood, 128–129, 171.

Rutland

Active Committeemen

Samuel Barker, Esq., North Luffenham

App. 3/12/42, 20/6/45.
Active between appointments and after 1645.
Sources: FH133; JHC, 4, 181.

Abel Barker Esq., North Luffenham, ?–1661
1s Samuel (above); app. 20/6/45. Called 'gent' in JHC.
Ca pens Emanuel 34–35; BA 37–38; MA 41; later rector of Lyndon?; HS 46.
Sources: JHC, 4, 181; AC, 184; LRO DE730 Barker Mss.

Christopher Brown, Esq., Toulthorpe, Casterton, 1619–1692
1s John; app. 2/12/42, 27/3/43 Delinquent Estates, 8/10/44.
Ca Sydney Sussex fell com 34; Gray's 38; MP shire 46; HS 47.
Sources: FH133; JHC, 3, 655; AC, 2, 232; Wright, 16.

John Cole, Clipsham
App. 29/1/44. Served as treasurer.
Source: JHC, 3, 381.

Sir Edward Harrington, Bart, Ridlington, ?–1653
1s James; app. 3/12/42, 8/10/44.
Ca fell com Christ's 98, Sydney Sussex 1600; kt 09; succeeded baronetcy 14; HS 21 36; DL 42.
Sources: JHC, 3, 655; FH133; Wright, 16; AC, 2, 318.

John Hatcher, Esq.
App. 8/10/45. Active but largely unidentified.
Source: JHC, 3, 655.

Robert Horseman Senior, Esq., Stretton
App. 2/12/42, 8/10/44.
Ca Kings 05; BA 08; MA 11; HS 40 (this may be his son).
Sources: Wright, 16; FH133; JHC, 3, 655; AC, 2, 336.

Robert Horseman Junior, Esq., Stretton Kensington, 1615–?
1s Robert (above); app. 2/12/42, 8/10/44.
Ca Sydney Sussex fell com 32; Gray's 34; HS 40 (this may be the father).
Sources: FH133; JHC, 3, 655; Wright, 16; AC, 2, 336.

Thomas Levett, Esq.
App. 20/6/45.
HS 39; active in the later stages of the war.
Sources: JHC, 4, 181; Wright, 16.

John Osbourne, Esq., Thorpe by Warter
App 2/12/42, 8/10/44.
HS 24 45.
Sources: FH133; JHC, 3, 655, 4, 79; Wright, 16; RV, 18.

Thomas Waite (White)
App. 27/3/43 Delinquent Estates, 8/10/44.
MP 45. A Colonel and in charge of the county's military forces. Captured Burleigh House from the royalists. Sir James Harrington petitioned Parliament about his opposition to the rest of the committee. Waite was summoned to Committee of Both Kingdoms in Dec 45. Later became a regicide. See Chapter 5.
Sources: JHC, 3, 655, 4, 365; CSPD, 1645, 245.

Thomas Lord Grey of Groby
App. 20/6/45. See Leicester Committee.

John Green, Gent.
App. 20/6/45.
Unidentified but active after appointment.
Source: JHC, 4, 181.

William Busby, Gent., Barleythorpe, 1616–?
4s Geoffrey; app. 20/6/45. Active after appointment.
Sources: JEC, 4, 181; RV, 13.

Staffordshire

Active Committeemen

Thomas Backhouse, Stafford
App. 21/2/45.
Burgess, Mayor 34–35 44–45 54–55. Was an Ironmonger.
Source: Pennington/Roots, 349.

Leicester Barbour, Gent., Tamworth, 1610–?
1s George; app. 7/6143. Captain in garrison.
Sources: JHC, 3, 119; SP, 17; Pennington/Roots, 349.

William Bendy, Shutt End Kingswinford, 1620–?
App. 18/10/44.
Ox pleb New Hall 34; BA 38; Lincoln's 39; clerk of peace 45. Chancellor of law 80.
Sources: SP, 22; AO, 105; Pennington/Roots, 349.

Sir William Brereton, Bart, Handforth Cheshire, 1604–1661
App. 27/3143.
Military commander of Cheshire.
Ox Brasenose 21; Gray's 23; BT 27; MP Ches. 28–29 40 (Short Parl.) 40 (Long Parl.), Rumper in 59. See chapters 4, 5, 6.
Sources: FH133; Pennington/Roots, 350; AO, 176; Dore, *The Letter Books of Sir William Brereton*, Record Society of Lancashire and Cheshire, 1984. DNB.

Edward Broughton, Gent., Longdon, 1610–1674
1s Edward; app. 7/6/43. Had legal connections.
Sources. FH133; SP, 38; Pennington/Roots, 350.

Lewis Chadwick, Mavesyn Ridware
App. 4/2/43, 7/6/43 Sequestration.
Governor of Stafford until Dec 44. Supporter of the Denbigh faction. Removed from governorship by Brereton largely because of this. Trumped-up charges of treachery could not stick. Chadwick was present at the Uxbridge Negotiations, presumably with Denbigh. Was a colonel.
Sources: FH133; JHC, 3, 119; Dore, *op. cit.*, 19; Pennington/Roots, 350.

John Chetwood (Chetwode), Hively Cheshire, 1600–1667
App. 2/2/43.
Ox Trinity 19; BA 21; MA All Souls 25; IT 19; MP shire Barebones Parliament. Family had mercantile connections.
Sources: FH133; AO, 268; Pennington/Roots, 351.

Thomas Crompton, Esq., Stone.
1s Thomas; app. 18/10/44.
Lincoln's 21; MP shire 47–53, Stafford 54 56 59.
Sources: GA, 66; Pennington/Roots, 351.

William Foxall, Stafford
App. 4/12/43; Captain in the garrison.
Burgess, removed as a suspected royalist, reappointed 49; mayor 46–47.
Source: Pennington/Roots, 352.

Robert Gregg, Hapsford Cheshire.
?s Edward; app. 25/11/43.
Collector of the excise 46.
Source: Pennington/Roots, 352.

Phillip Jackson, Gent., Wall, Stanhope, ?1593–1675
?s Henry; app. 7/6/43.
Ox University College 10; BA 12; JP 75; captain in the garrison.
Sources: JRC, 3, 119; SP, 138; AO, 795; FHI33; Pennington/Roots, 352.

William Jolley, Gent., Caveswall Castle
1s Thomas; app. 30/5/43, 7/6/43.
Mercer and Grocer. His first wife was Henry Hastings' sister Mary.
Sources: SP, 145; FH133; JHC, 3, 119; Pennington/Roots, 352.

Edward Leigh, Esq., Rushall, 1602–1671
2s Henry of Shawell; app. 22/2/43, 7/6/43.
Ox Magdalene 17; MA 23; MT 24; historian later incorporated at Cambridge; MP shire 45, excluded 48. Colonel.
Sources: FH133; SP, 156; AO, 897; AC, 3, 62; Pennington/Roots, 353.

Michael Lowe, Pipe Ridware
1s John of Lichfield; app. 22/2/43; daughter m Leicester Barbour (above).
Sources: SP, 159; FH133; Pennington/Roots, 353.

Thomas Pudsey, Seisdon, 1611–1676
1s Nicholas; app. 7/12/43.
Sources: SP, 190; Pennington/Roots, 353.

Simon Rugeley, Esq., Hawksyard, Hansley, ?–1665
1s Richard of Shenstone; app. 7/6/43, ditto Sequestration.
Ca Queens 18; HS 43; colonel in the county.
Sources: FH133; SP, 197; JHC, 3, 119, 354; AC, 3, 457; Pennington/Roots, 354.

John Simcox
App. 4/2/43.
Served as treasurer. Ironmonger.

Source: Pennington/Roots, 354.

Henry Stone, Gent., Windmill Walsall
App 30/5/43, 7/6/43 Sequestration.
Plymouth merchant who succeeded to Staffs. estates. Became governor of Stafford after Chadwick displaced.
Sources: JHC, 3, 199; FH133; Pennington/Roots, 355.

John Swinfen (Swinson), Gent., Weeford
App. 7.6.43, ditto Sequestration.
Sources: FH133; DNB; Pennington/Roots, 355; JHC, 3, 119.

Passive Supporters or Neutrals

Ralph Addesley
Whereabouts unknown.
Source: Pennington/Roots, 349.

Michael Biddulph
Whereabouts unknown.
Source: Pennington/Roots, 350.

John Birch
Source: Pennington/Roots, 350.

Thomas Brough, Gent.
Whereabouts unknown.
Source: Pennington/Roots, 350.

Walter Brown
Unidentified.
Source: Pennington/Roots, 350.

Thomas Coke
Unidentified.
Source: Pennington/Roots, 351.

Thomas Daintree
Unidentified.
Source: Pennington/Roots, 351.

Oliver Emery
Whereabouts unknown
Source: Pennington/Roots, 351.

Richard Flyer (Floyer), Esq.
Whereabouts unknown.
Source: Pennington/Roots, 351.

Thomas Fulke, Esq.
Whereabouts unknown.
Source: Pennington/Roots, 352.

Richard Grosvenor (Gravenor)
Whereabouts unknown.
Source: Pennington/Roots, 352.

Edward Mainwaring Junior, Esq.
Whereabouts unknown.
Source: Pennington/Roots, 353.

Mathew Moreton, Esq.
Whereabouts unknown.
Source: Pennington/Roots, 353.

Michael Noble, Gent.
Whereabouts unknown though possibly sitting in Parliament.
Source: Pennington/Roots, 353.

Richard Pyott, Esq.
Whereabouts unknown.
Source: Pennington/Roots, 353.

Anthony Rudyard, Esq.
Whereabouts unknown.
Source: Pennington/Roots, 354.

Ralph Rudyard, Esq.
Brother of above, whereabouts unknown.
Source: Pennington/Roots, 354.

John Smethfield
Unidentified.
Source: Pennington/Roots, 354.

John Smyth
Unidentified.
Source: Pennington/Roots, 355.

Samuel Terrick, Gent.
Possibly in Parliament.
Source: Pennington/Roots, 356.

George Thorley
Acted as a solicitor for Sequestration but not as a committeeman.
Source: Pennington/Roots, 355.

John Turton, Gent.
Whereabouts unknown.
Source: Pennington/Roots, 355.

Henry Vernon
Whereabouts unknown
Source: Pennington/Roots, 355.

Joseph Whitehaulgh
Whereabouts unknown.
Source: Pennington/Roots, 356.

Richard Whitehaulgh, Gent.
Whereabouts unknown.
Source: Pennington/Roots, 356.

Ex Officio Members of the Committee
Basil Fielding Earl of Denbigh
Source: Pennington/Roots, 356.

Thomas Doleman
Source: Pennington/Roots, 356.

Colonel John Bowyer
Source: Pennington/Roots, 356.

Other categories of the Committeemen not serving in their county

Dead, captured or in any wan incapacitated from serving
Sir Thomas Burdett, Derbys
Captured by Hastings in Feb 43 then died.
Source: JTB, 17.

William Drury, Notts., Alderman.
Arrested by Hutchinson for revolt in July, held thereafter at Derby.
Source: Wood, 54.

Activists elsewhere
Colonel Robert Haughton, Staffs.
Serving in Cheshire?
Source: Pennington/Roots, 352.

Sir Arthur Hesilrige, Leics.
At Westminster and in Essex's Army.
Sources: Nichols, 3, 2, App.4, *passim*; VL, 16.

Colonel Richard Grevis, Staffs.
In South Midlands?
Source: Pennington/Roots, 352.

Lt Colonel Daniel Watson, Staffs.
On active service.
Source: Pennington/Roots, 356.

Lt Colonel Sanders, Staffs.
Serving out of county, not fully identified.
Source: Pennington/Roots, 354.

Nathaniel Hallowes, Derbys
In London, MP.
Sources: JTB, 58, GA, 111.

Sir John Coke, Derbys
In London, MP, and at Westminster Assembly 45.
Source: JTB, 21.

Sir Martin Lister, Kt, Leics.
In London, MP.
Sources: GA, 186; Nichols, 3, 2, App. 4, 32.

Henry, Lord Grey of Ruthin
In London, MP, then HoL.
Sources: Nichols, 3, 2, App. 4, 32; Rushworth, 3, 1, 626–627 (he still dabbled with royalism in mid 42).

Sir James Harrington, Rutland
In London, MP.
Sources: RV, 39; FH133; Wright, 16.

Sir Richard Skeffington, Kt, Staffs.
Spent his time on the Coventry Committee, Warwickshire was his home county.
Source: Pennington/Roots, 354.

Royalists

John Millington, Notts.
Source: Wood, 220.

William Roberts, Esq., Leics.
Sources: Nichols, 3, 2, App 4, 31–32; VL, 118.

William Jervis, Leics.
Sources: Nichols, 3, 2, App.4, 31.

Thomas Merry, Leics.
Source: AO, 1004.

Thomas Brudenell, Esq., Leics.
Source: VL, 143.

Sir George Villiers, Leics.
Sources: Nichols, 3, 2, App. 4, 30–31; VL, 171. George Ashby, Esq. See Royalist Commissioners for Leics.

Sir Edward Littleton, Staffs.
See commissioners of array for Staffs.

Sir Wolston Dixie, Leics.
See commissioners of array for Leics.
Walter Wrottesley, Staffs.
See commissioners of array for Staffs.

Appendix III

The Officers of the North Midlands Army

The arrangement of this appendix differs from the two previous ones. Though for many of the field officers and some of the regimental officers there will be an amount of information similar to that given for the commissioners and committeemen; for the vast majority all that is available is the rank, name and the source of the information; in many cases simply IO and/or RS. Officers are listed by regiment. Where possible, men are grouped into their troops or companies.

Lord Loughborough's (Henry Hastings') Regiments

Horse

Colonel Henry Hastings
See Derbyshire commissioners.

Lt Colonel ? Langley
?Present at Edgehill.
Source: BL TT E83/9 only.

Lt Colonel William Bale Esq., Saddington, Carlton, 1620–?
2s Sir John (see Leicestershire commissioners)
Ox Lincoln 35; IT 37.
Served earlier under Marmaduke Langdale as a major. Then transferred to Hastings then to Pate. Placed as a 'spy' in Belvoir where he annoyed Lucas.
Sources: IO, 6, 82, 87, 150; CCC, 110; RS, 92, 94; VL. [Missing Text] 2, 128; AO, 61; Burke, *Dormant Baronetcies*, 33.

Lieutenant Henry Monk, Clement Danes, London
RC?
Sources: IO, 87; SP 16/495/1-/E

Cornet William Misson, Leics.
Source: IO, 6.

Lt Colonel Edward Stamford, Esq., Perry Hall Staffs., 1619–1675
1s William; RC; captain 42; fined 46 £375. 49, in treaty with Venice to fight Turks. Captured at Kidderminster 44; exchanged 45. In Jan 46, commanded 100 horse to relieve Chester. See Chapter 6.
Sources: PN, 1356; AP, 216; *Symonds' Diary*, 278; CCAM, 861; CCC, 1192; JHC, 4, 167; Dore, 1, 120, 402; BL Ms 6852, 1; IO, 87.

Major C. Roper (See under ?own regiment)

Major ? Stanley
Edgehill campaign only; RC?
Sources: BL TT E83/9, E244/2

Major Barnabus Scudamore, Esq., Holme Lacy Hereford, ?–1652
Younger brother to John, Viscount Sligo; kt 45; compounded 51 1/6th at £100, cut to £87–10s. Estate worth £50 pa. Had been involved in Second Civil War. Had been a captain in 1640, in 42 helped Hastings raise trained bands. Was Hastings' Major in Hopton Heath campaign, left before 1644. Later became governor of Hereford.
Sources: RS, 93; BL Add Mss, 36307; PN, 1291, IO 118; PRO SP29/159/45; *Symonds' Diary*, 168, 195; CSPD, 1645–1647, 456; 1648–1649, 139; CCC, 897; CCAM, 1347; Metcalfe *Knight*, 203.

Major Sir Hugh Calverley, Esq., Lea Hall Cheshire, 1613–?
1s Sir Hugh
Ox Brasenose 31; kt 42; comp, £1,855 in 48. Newman did not think that Calverley held field rank.
Sources: RS, 93; PN, 359.

Major Rowland Hacker, Esq., East Bridgford Notts., Colston Bassett, ?–1674
Younger brother of Francis (see Leics. committeemen). Replaced Scudamore. Governed Trent Bridge fort and then Wiverton House. Before being in Hastings' was a captain in Richard Byron's (see Notts. commissioners).
Sources: IO, 87; RS, 93b; HMC Hastings, 2, 120; Wood, 219; DNB; Newcastle, 87; HMC Sutherland, 175; CSPD, 1660–1661, 339, 494.

Lieutenant Robert White, Gent., Notts.
Source: IO, 87.

Major Edmund or Thomas Bale, ?Saddington, Leics.
3 or 4 s Sir John, bro to William above. One of this name killed at Ashby.
Sources: IO, 87; Fosbrooke, 21.

Lieutenant Nathaniel Duncome, Middlesex.
Sources: IO, 87; Fosbrooke, 22.

Cornet Wolstan Roberts, Gent., Sutton Cheney, Leics.
s of Sir William Kt.
Sources: IO, 87; CCC, 110; GA, 215.

Captain Richard Archer, ?Snelson Derbys., 1608–?
1s John; Ca Queens pleb 26; BA 27; MA 29. Based at Newark in 1644 with his troop. May possibly have been a prisoner at Stafford in Jan 44, exchanged for Thomas Leving a prisoner at Ashby.
Sources: IO, 87 / HMC Hastings, 2, 128; WSL Minute book, 55.

Lieutenant Henry Bend, Notts.
Source: IO, 87.

Captain Adam Claypool, Esq., West Deeping Lincs., ?–1673
Ca fell com Queens 38; fined £600 in Dec 45. Three years in the regiment.
Sources: RS, 93; CCC, 1063.

Captain Jonathan Cooke, Warwicks.
Source: IO, 87.

Captain James Dupont (Duport), Gent., Shepshed, Leics.
With Hastings in Nov 42 at Oxford, signed consignment of munitions out of Oxford Stores. Described as a servant of Hastings. Wife's estate seized in 46 as he was not included in the Ashby terms, therefore he had not compounded. Was worth £40 pa at the time. He had gone with Hastings 'beyond the seas'. Was temporary governor of Ashby in 43.
Sources: Roy, 1, 170; IO, 87; CCC, 1746; HMC Hastings, 2, 119, 122.

Captain ? Fisher
At Edgehill.
Source: BL TT E83/9 only.

Captain Ralph Fitzherbert, Hints, Staffs.
1s Robert; d before father.
Source: SP, 87.

Captain Henry Fleetwood, Staffs.
Sources: IO, 87; CCC, 2287.

Captain William Fleetwood, Staffs.
Garrisoned Wooton Lodge and captured ammunition from Moorlanders early 43. Bro to Sir Thomas.
Sources: IO, 87; CCC, 2283.

Captain ? Fryer
At Edgehill.
Source: BL TT E83/9 only.

Captain Gregory
With Bale and Archer was to collect rents of the Earl of Rutland and other delinquents in Leics.
Sources: RS, 93; IO, 87; HMC Hastings, 2, 128.

Lieutenant Thomas Gilbert, Gent., Thrussington, Leics., 1616–?
1s William.
Sources: IO, 87; VL, 189.

Captain ? Griffiths, Junior
Source: RS, 93.

Captain ? Griffiths, Senior
Source: RS, 93.

Captain Sir Robert Harding, Kt, King's Newton, Derbys.

1s Nicholas; Ox Lincoln 36; Gray's 39; barrister 45.
Joined Hastings at Swarkestone in Jan 43. Impoverished estate alienated.
Sources: JTB, 32; DV, 27.

Captain Walter Hastings, Esq., Humberstone, Leics.
2s Henry. Transferred to Wolseley's. Present at surrender of Ashby. ?Later a colonel.
Sources: IO, 87, 93; PN, 693.

Lieutenant John Everard, Leics.
1s John of Pickleton.
Sources: IO, 87; VL, 142.

Captain Hodges
At Edgehill only.
Source: BL TT E83/9 only.

Captain ? Johnson
Edgehill only.
Source: BL TT E83/9 only.

Captain Thomas Mawson, Wigston Magna Leics.
Father Thomas a successful tanner b 1580, bought Wigston in 42. Family granted arms 1692.
Sources: IO, 87; CCC, 108.

Captain John Middleton, Middleton Hall Westmorland
Killed at Hopton Heath.
Sources: RS, 93; York City Library, Battle of Hopton Heath; Y942, Civ 3; Young P., 'The Battle of Hopton Heath', *JSAHR*, 33, part 133.

Captain ? Rooksby
Source: IO, 87.

Lieutenant William Hobman, Yorks.
Source: IO, 87.

Captain William Ruddings, Essex
Source: IO, 87.

Captain Phillip Stanhope
Cited in IO by a quartermaster. Could he be one of the Earl of Chesterfield's sons, later the Colonel Stanhope killed at Shelford House in 1645?
Source: IO, 87.

Captain William Squire, Gaddesby Leics.
Ended up at Oxford, fined 48 at 1/10th £40.
Sources: IO, 87; CCC, 109.

Captain Geoffrey Stanley
Source: IO, 87.

Captain George Thorpe, Dixley Leics.
Gave £80 to garrison and 'rode next to Lord Loughborough with a sword in his hand'.
Source: CCAM, 1158.

Captain William Trimnell, Gent., Stoke Golding, Leics., 1605–?
1s Basil.
Sources: IO, 87; CCC, Ill; VL, 176

Captain Poole Turville, Castle Gresley Derbys.
RC, estate forfeited 53.
Sources: JTB, 47; CCC, 3151; IR, 39.

Captain John Warton, London and Westminster
Sources: IO, 87; Fosbrooke, 22.

Captain Daniel Wright
Source: IO, 87.

Cornet James Harrington, Leics.
Source: IO, 87.

Cornet Henry Waldron, Leics.
Both he and above in Wrights'.
Source: IO, 87.

Captain Yates, Leics.
Possibly bro to Yates in Lucas'. Died in war as Hastings refers to father in his complaint to Rupert about Lucas.
Sources: RS, 93; BL Add Mss 18982, f.47.

Captain Lt John Caesar, Gent., London and Westminster
Source: IO, 87.

Lieutenant John Barnwell, London and Westminster
Source: IO, 87.

Lieutenant Henry Dudley, Swepstone, Leics.
1s Thomas the Vintner. Henry captured at a fight near Melton Mowbray 43. Described as 'that great robber of the country'.
Sources: IO, 87; CCAM, 1033; BL TT E 69 117, *Certaine Informations*, 25 Sept–2 Oct.

Lieutenant Ambrose Grey, Staffs.
Source: IO, 87.

Cornet Roger Gibbs, Notts.
Source: IO, 87.

Cornet ? Lassals, Derbys.
Sources: IO, 87; Fosbrooke, 23.

Cornet Thomas Mosely, Leics.
Source: IO, 87.

Foot

Lieutenant Colonel Sir Arthur Gorges, Kt, Chelsea, 1598–1661
1s Sir Arthur the poet.
Ox Christ's 16; kt 21; fined at 1/2 £806-5s, reduced to 1/6th £512. Debts of £5,000 in 1650.
Was Hastings' agent at Oxford during 43 and 44.
Sources: RS, 93; Roy, 1, 302–303; CCC, 961–962; AO, 588; Metcalf, *Knights*, 179; CCAM, 1337, HMC *Hastings*, 2, 120.

Captain John Adler, Leics.
A Shoemaker.
Source: RS, 93.

Captain Thomas Bailey, Gent., The Mythe Leics.
Left service during the plague at Ashby. Fined 1/6th at £412, reduced to £352-17s-6d.
Sources: IO, 87; CCC, 110, 1373.

Captain Sigismund Beeton
Later a colonel and governor of Bolsover.
Sources: RS, 93; PN, 94. Newman says he was killed in 43.

Captain Samuel Benchkin, London and Westminster
Sources: IO, 87; Fosbrooke, 22; LJRO D30, LIIIB.

Lieutenant George Loosemore, Cambridge
1s Henry; Ca Jesus 40; Music Doctorate 65 Trinity.
Sources: IO, 87; AC, 3, 104.

Ensign Lawrence Fisher, London and Westminster
Sources: IO, 87; LJRO D30, LIIIB.

Captain Henry Bowman, Leics.
Source: RS, 93.

Captain Henry Butler, Bilston, Leics.
Ox 16; BA 21. Fined £128–16s in 46.
Sources: RS, 93; CCC, 1133; AO, 222.

Captain James Hare, Milson Salop, or London and Westminster.
Sources: IO, 87; ?CCC, 1613.

Captain George Hitchcock, Wilts.
Source: IO, 87.

Captain John Holden
Source: IO, 87.

Captain Daniel Robinson
A tailor.
Source: RS, 93.

Lieutenant William Kelton
Of Robinson's company. There were three Robinsons!
Source: IO, 87

Ensign Daniel Robinson, Leics.
Again same problem as above.
Source: IO, 87.

Captain Geoffrey Robinson, Notts.
Either this one or next was governor of King's Mills fort. Bro of below.
Sources: IO, 87; Fosbrooke, 23; RS, 93; HMC Hastings, 2, 112.

Captain Thomas Robinson, Notts.
Source: RS, 93.

Lieutenant John Dixon, London and Westminster
Source: IO, 87.

Ensign John Wakefield, Notts.
Source: IO, 87.

Dragoons
Captain Daniel Roberts
Source: IO, 87.

John Pate's Regiment of Horse

Colonel John Pate
See Commissioner of Array for Leics.

Lt Colonel William Bale
See Hastings' Horse.

Major Elias Whalley
1s in Lichfield garrison in 43, warning Hastings that Lichfield soldiers are being incited against him by their officers. He was possibly captured at Naseby though he is called a captain.
Sources: RS, 94; PN, 1552; HMC Hastings, 2, 111; BL TT E262/19.

Captain William Bent, Gent., Narborough Leics., 1618–?
1s John of Enderby.
Sources: IO, 103; CCC, 110; VL, 159.

Lieutenant Christopher Bent, Enderby or Hoby Leics.
Source: IO, 103.

Cornet Andrew Randall, Leics.
Source: IO, 103.

Captain Henry Bowman
Had transferred from Colonel Dudley's.
Source: RS, 94.

Cornet Robert Wooland, Leics.
Source: IO, 87.

Captain Nathaniel Digby, Gent., Kettleby Leics., 1610–?
3s Edward of Holwell.
Sources: IO, 103; CCC, 110.

Cornet Francis Barnwell, Lincs.
Source: IO, 103.

Captain George Smith, Gent., Queniborough, Leics.
s of George of Withicotes? Estate sequestrated 43–50. Signed the petition of the Indigent Officers under Hastings' name.
Sources: IO, 87; RS, 94; CCC, 2411–2412; VL, 66; Fosbrooke, 23.

Cornet William Brown, Surrey
Source: IO, 103.

William Nevills's Regiments

Horse

Colonel William Nevill, Esq., Holt Leics., Tottenham Middlesex and Cressing Temple Essex, ?–1661
1s Henry of Holt. Possibly a captain in Hastings' Horse in 42, though possibly came to take over father's regiments after the fall of Holt in Jan 43. Assessed 1/5th and 1/20th at £500.
Sources: RS, 92; Fosbrooke, 21; IO, 99; PN, 1041; *Symonds' Diary*, 225; CCC, 111; CCAM, 507, 699, 1376; HMC Portland, 1, 87, 93, 94; BL Add Mss, 19892, 47.

Lt Colonel Thomas Nevill, Holt, 1625–1712
2s Henry bro to above. Discharged from sequestration 48. Comptroller of Petty Customs at Restoration. 1st Bart.
Sources: RS, 94; PN, 1040; GEC *The Complete Baronetage*, 3, 203; CCC, 111; CSPD, 1661–1662, 224.

Major Povey (Purvey, Penery, Powey), Gent. Surrendered at Ashby in 46.
Sources: RS, 94; PN, 1156; Fosbrooke, 23.

Captain Thomas Mason, Northants.
Source: IO, 99.

Lieutenant Daniel Colston, London and Westminster
Source: IO, 99.

Captain Lt Robert Davis, London and Westminster
Source: IO, 99.

Captain Lt William Ellis, Leics.
Source: IO, 99.

Cornet Geoffrey Wellstead
In the same troop as the two previous captain lieutenants. It is possible that one of the above was a successor to the other.
Source: IO, 99.

Lieutenant Henry Hawes, Lincs.
Source: IO, 99.

Foot
Major Thomas Bywaters, London and Westminster
Prisoner at Lichfield in July 1646.
Sources: RS, 94b; PN, 237; IO, 99; BL TT E345/2.

Captain Thomas Bagshaw, Lincs.
Source: IO, 99.

Captain James Claughton, Northants.
Source: IO, 99.

Lieutenant William Claughton, Northants.
Source: IO, 99.

Rowland Eyre's Regiments

Horse
Colonel Rowland Eyre, Esq., Bradway and Hassop, Derbys., 1600–1674
1s Thomas; RC
Ox 17; BA 19; Lincoln's 18; lessee of lead mines from the King. Raised regiments in late 43 and 44. Fought at Marston Moor, later based at Newark, had been based at Chatsworth. Surrendered at Lichfield. Estates forfeited as he was a papist in arms.
Sources: RS, 95b; PN, 494; IO, 45; AO, 477. CCC, 62, 89, 110, 2090, 2319; HMC Hastings, 120; Hutchinson, 442; PRO SP29/159, 45; BL TT E345/2; CCAM, 1436; JTB, 24; DAJ, XIX, 22.

Lt Colonel William Eyre, Esq., ?Hassop, 1603–1653
2s Thomas, bro to Rowland
Ox 17; Lincoln's 21. Prisoner at Oxford 1649. RC.
Sources: JTB, 22; PN, 496; AO, 478; IO, 45; CSPD, 1649–1650, 251, 1650, 263.

Cornet Matther Barker, Derbys.
Source: DO, 45.

Major ? Spratt, Staffs.
Sources: RS, 95; PN, 1352.

Captain Howard Brock, Gent., Brough Derbys.
1s Robert; RC; Signed petition of the Northern Horse. 'A very good commander'.
Sources: IO, 45; JTB, 71, 16; PRO SP29/66, 35 A List of Gentlemen in Derbyshire and how they stand affected.

Captain Rowland Furnis, Derbys.
Source: IO, 45.

Foot
Lt Colonel Tamworth Reresby, Yorks.
Source: JTB, 71.

Major (later Lt Colonel?) ? Jordan, Scots.
Successor to Reresby, Symonds indicates that he was 'once Major to ye Lrd Loughborough', but there is no other verification.
Sources: RS, 95; JTB, 71.

Captain ? Allan, Crosby Derbys.
Possibly sequestered for delinquency.
Sources: IO, 45; JTB, 71; ?CCC, 3068.

Lieutenant John Bold, Notts.
Source: IO, 45.

Captain ? Aston, Derbys.
Sources: RS, 95; JTB, 71.

Lieutenant John Bradbury, Derbys.
Sources: IO, 45; JTB, 71.

Lieutenant Francis Rowland, Derbys.
Sources: IO, 45; JTB, 71.

Dragoons
Captain James Tunstead, Tunstead Derbys.
1s Francis; RC. In 1650 had £50 annuity (as had his father) for taking the King's game in Derbys.
Sources: IO, 45; DV, 33; JTB, 47.

Sir John Fitzherbert's Regiments

Horse
Colonel Sir John Fitzherbert
See Derbyshire Commissioners.

Lt Colonel William Fitzherbert, Gent., Tissington, Derbys.
1s Sir John Fitzherbert of Tissington; RC; garrisoned home in 43 44. Served also at Tutbury and Lichfield. Fined £1,000 in 48, reduced to £817. Assessed at £200 pa in 49, sequestered for non-payment in 50.
Sources: IO, 48; DV, 13; PN, 521; CCC, 1488, 1490; JTB 25–26; 69.

Cornet Thomas Dixwell, Derbys.
Sources: IO, 48; JTB, 69.

Captain Charles Barnesly, Aldmonkton, Derbys.
RC; at Tutbury. Fined at 1/2 £800, reduced to 1/6th £20. Assessed 48 at £500, sequestered for non-payment.
Sources: JTB, 69; CCC, 89; CCAM, 958.

Captain Arthur Bennett, Derbys.
Sources: IO, 48; JTB, 69.

Captain John Bingley, Derbys.
Sources: IO, 48; JTB, 69.

Lieutenant John Statham, Tansley, Derbys.
1s Henry of Morley. Fined 1/6th £29–10s in 49.
Sources: IO, 48; JTB, 69.

Captain John Eyre, Hathersage, Derbys.
1s Thomas. Earlier in Freshville's. ?RC.
Sources: IO, 51; JTB, 69.

Cornet George Eyre, Hathersage, Derbys.
1s John (above). RC.
Sources: IO, 51; JTB, 69.

Captain Reynold Eyre, Yorks.
Sources: IO, 48; JTB, 69.

Captain Edward Fitzrandolph, Surrey
Sources: IO, 48; JTB, 69.

Cornet Richard Wyld, Notts.
Sources: IO, 48; JTB, 69; ?GA, 289.

Captain George Fitzrandolph, Surrey
Either this man or above captured on Bosworth Field Sept 45.
Sources: IO, 48; JTB, 69; BL TT E302/11, *City Scout* 9.

Captain Arthur Lowe, Hazelwood Derbys.
4s Edward. Bro of John below. He, bro and father fined at 1/6th £221. Both at battle of Willoughby field in 48.
Sources: ID, 48; CCC, 2008; JTB, 69; Glover, 2, 7.

Lieutenant Ferdinando Lowe, Alderwasley, Derbys.
?s of Edward, Bro to above.
Sources: IO, 48; JTB, 37, 69.

Captain John Lowe, Gent., Alderwasley, Derbys.
?2s of Edward, bro of 2 above. Heir to Edward as eldest, Anthony d at Gainsborough. Served at Wingfield then Lichfield until Bagot reduced size of garrison.
Sources: IO, 48; JTB 69. CCC

Lieutenant Charles Lowe, Derbys. ?s of John, bro to 3 above.
Source: JTB, 37, 69.

Captain Robert Moore, Surrey
Sources: IO, 48; JTB, 69.

Cornet Thomas Hodgson (Hodgekinson), Staffs.
Sources: IO, 48; JTB, 69.

Foot
Lt Colonel Simon Heveningham, Staffs., London and Westminster
2s Nicholas; RC; bro to Christopher in Leveson's; had served in Leveson's earlier, was major before his brother.
Sources: RS, 95b; IO, 48, 153; SP, 124; PRO SP16/495, 1E; PN, 731; JTB, 69

Captain John Cawsley (Cosley), Lancs.
'An old soldier'.
Sources: RS, 95b; JTB, 69.

Captain ?Anthony Colleridge (Colwich), Stud, Derbys.
s of below.
Sources: RS, 95b; DV, 26.

Captain ?William Colleridge (Colwich), Stud, Derbys.
Sources: RS, 95; DV, 26.
Captain Thomas Royston, Notts. Sources: IO, 48; JTB, 69.

John Freshville (Freschville)'s Regiments

Horse
Colonel John Freshville
See Derbyshire Commissioners.

Lt Colonel Henry Hunlocke, Esq., Wingerworth Derbys., ?–1648
1s Henry, Ca fell comm Corpus Christi 33; Gray's 36; father involved in iron mining and smelting. At Edgehill with Freschville, kt on field for bravery. Possibly had garrison at Wingerworth while Freschville at Staveley. Baronet 43. Lost use of right hand in fight at Newstead Abbey 44. Surrendered Nov 45. Gell used his mines for 3 years. Fined £1,458. d June 48 after discovery of fraudulent estate valuation.

Sources: JTB, 72; Young P., *Cavalier Army*, ?142; Black *Docquets*, 12; CCC, 1089; AC, 2, 432.

Major John Beversham, London and Westminster, ?–1670
Served first in Sir William Saville's; fought against English at Battle of the Dunes 58. Styled Colonel when buried at Westminster Abbey 1670. Seized 50, on (correct) suspicion of not having compounded.
Sources: IO, 51, 116; PN, 115; JTB, 72; CSPD, 1650, 438, 1660, 195; *Nicholas Papers*, Camden Soc, XXXI, 58.

Captain Richard Allsop, Derbys.
Sources: IO, 51; JTB, 72.

Captain John Eyre
See Fitzherbert's.

Lieutenant Thomas Eyre
Bro of above?
Sources: IO, 51; JTB, 72.

Cornet George Eyre
See Fitzherbert's.

Captain John Lowe, Oldgreave, Hasland Derbys., 1616–1677
2s Anthony? Troop scattered at Marston Moor then joined Newark. Gave up arms Dec 45. Fined £133-6s-8d. Assessed at £200 in 49. Claimed that Earl of Newcastle sequestered him for aiding Gell!
Sources: JTB, 37, 73; DV, 30; CCC, 960; Glover, 2, 7; IO, 51.

Lieutenant William Fletcher, Derbys.
Sources: IO, 51; JTB, 72.

Captain Edward Nichols, Beds.
Sources: IO, 51; JTB, 72.

Cornet Clifton Rhodes, Sturton Derbys.
Sources: IO, 51; JTB, 72.

Captain George Pole (Poole), Gent., Spinkhill, Wakebridge Derbys. ?–1644
1s Francis; RC; d fighting against parliamentarians.
Sources: IO, 51; DV, 5; Glover, 2, 324; JTB, 41, 72.

Lieutenant Ignatius Pole (Poole), Derbys.
Relative of above?
Source: IO, 51.

Foot
Lt Colonel ? Betteridges
Sources: RS, 95; JTB, 72.

Major John Jammott, Brussels.
Professional soldier. Recaptured Welbeck in July 45. See Chapter 6. Lucy Hutchinson thought he was killed at Cotes in 44.
Sources: *Symonds' Diary*, 224; JTB, 72; CSPD, 1650, 257; *Nicholas Papers*, 2, 205; PN, 804.

Captain William Bates, Notts.
Sources: IO, 51; JTB, 72.

Sir John Harpur's Regiments

Horse
Sir John Harpur, Bart.
See Derbyshire Commissioners.

Lt Colonel William Bullock, Esq., Darley and Norton Derbys., 1617–1686
3s John; Ca pens St John's 35; BA 39; MA 42. Fined at 1/6th £40. House pulled down during the war.
Sources: RS, 94; ID, 63; AC, 1, 253; DV, 22; JTB, 17, 70; CCC, 491, 1133; PRO SP29/66, 35.

Lieutenant Andrew Scriven, Derbys.
Sources: IO, 63; JTB, 70.

Lieutenant William Smith, Derbys.
Either he or above succeeded the other.
Sources: IO, 63; JTB, 70.

Cornet Richard Whinyates, Derbys.
Sources: IO, 63; JTB, 70.

Major Thomas Bates, Derbys.
Sources, RS, 94; JTB, 70.

Captain Durand Alison, Chesterfield, ?–1671.
1s Robert; Ca pens Trinity 27; IT 25.
Sources: IO, 63; JTB, 14, 70; AC, 1, 24; CCAM, 1233.

Lieutenant William Ogle, London and Westminster
Sources: IO, 63; JTB, 70.

Cornet Thomas Alison, Chesterfield, London and Westminster
Bro of Durand.
Sources: IO, 63; JTB, 70.

Captain Thomas Baker, Leics.
Fled to Parl. in 45 but a Major Baker was taken at Ashby in 46. Ca Emanuel 31; BA 35; MA 38; Fellow 35.
Sources: RS, 95; PN, 60; AC, 1, 72.

Captain John Bullock, Esq., Darley and Norton, Derbys.
1s John; comp 46. Unable to pay assessment of £800, sequestered for non-payment 50
Sources: JTB, 16, 70; RS, 94; CCC, 1132; CCAM, 1068.

Captain John Lowe, Denby Derhys, 1616–1660
1s Vincent; compounded 47, at 1/6th £480.
Sources: IO, 63; JTB, 70; DV, 30; CCC, 2034.

Cornet Richard Mason, Derbys.
Sources: IO, 63; JTB, 70.

Captain Anthony Mozine, Notts.
Sources: IO, 63; JTB, 70.

Lieutenant John Jellico, Worcs.
Sources: IO, 63; JTB, 70.

Cornet Francis Mozine, Notts.
Sources: IO, 63; JTB, 70.

Captain Robert Sykes, Markfield Leics.
At siege of Leicester.
Sources: IO, 63; CCAM, 1245; JTB, 70.

Cornet William Willcocks, Gent., Ashwell Rutland, 1601–?
1s William.
Sources: RV, 10; IO, 63; JTB, 70.

Captain Lt John Whinyates, Notts.
Belonged to Captain Kniveton's troop. This indicates that he served before the creation of Kniveton's own regiment, possibly under Peter or Gilbert Kniveton.
Sources: IO, 63; JTB, 70.

Foot
Major Mallory
Sources: RS, 94; PN, 930; JTB, 70.

Captain Arthur Grant, Derbys.
Sources: RS, 94; JTB, 70.

Captain ? Tythal (Tyndal)
Source: RS, 94.

Dragoons
Captain Richard Corbet, Gent., Salop
Sources: RS, 94; JTB, 70.

Lieutenant Andrew Cook, Salop
Sources: IO, 63; JTB, 70.

Cornet Andrew Pitchford, Salop
Sources, IO, 63; JTB, 70.

John Milward's/John Shallcross' Regiments

M = indicates served only in Milward's; S = only in Shallcross'

Colonel John Milward, Esq.
See Derbyshire Commissioners.

Lt Colonel, later Colonel John Shallcross, Esq., Shallcross, Derbys., 1603–1673
1s Richard; JP 36; HS 38; (HS 45). Governor of Chatsworth Aug 45. See Chapter 4. Fined 1/10th at £400, cut to £100 if paid £200 of a debt of £600. Gaoled for debt 51. Active royalist 1659.
Sources: IO, 119; PRO SP29/159, 45; PRO List of Sheriffs, 31; Warburton, 3, 71; CCC, 750, 1031–1032; CCAM, 791; HMC Portland, 1, 578; CSPD, 1651, 209; HMC Hastings, 2, 120; PN, 1301; DAJ, 28, 1906.

Captain William Clement, S, Yorks.
Sources: IO, 119; JTB, 72.

Captain Edward Vernon (Venner), Gent., S, Sudbury Staffs., 1624–?
2s Sir Edward; Ox Trinity 40; possibly in Hastings' at Edgehill, was so afterwards. Possibly the young Vernon who told Sir Edward Littleton Lord Keeper about Hastings plundering those who would not pay voluntarily thus starting the attacks on Hastings in the Oxford Parliament. Colonel at Pontefract in Second Civil War. JP 61; DCL 77.
Sources: PN, 1497; BL TT E83/9; Fosbrooke, 23; HMC Hastings, 2, 121.

Captain Lt William Penketh, Lancs, S
Sources: IO, 119; JTB, 72.

Cornet Thomas Herrod, S, Peak Forest Derbys.
RC; lead miner. Goods seized 50.
Sources: IO, 119; JTB, 33, 72; CCAM, 1207.

Captain Lt John Rudyard, Gent., Staffs., 1616–?
1s Thomas; Ox Trinity BA 37. Family had faked arms 1579.
Sources: JTB, 72; IO, 119; GA, 219; AO, 1288.

Foot
Lt Colonel Robert Bonny, M.
Earlier in Hastings' as major; virginal player; lieutenant 40.
Sources: JTB, 70; PN, 154; RS, 93b.

Captain Francis Bruce, M, Beds.
Sources: IO, 95; JTB, 72.

Lieutenant Thomas Polt, M, Derbys.
Sources: IO, 95; JTB, 72.

Ensign Francis Cotterel, M, Derbys.
Sources: IO, 95; JTB, 72.

Captain David Ellis, M, Derbys.
Sources: IO, 95; JTB, 72.

Captain John Todd, M, Lincs.
'Governor of Wingfield under ye rebels', wrote Symonds'.
Source: RS, 95.

Sir Andrew Kniveton's Regiments

Horse
Colonel Andrew Kniveton
See Derbyshire Commissioners.

Lt Colonel Peter Kniveton, Esq., Bradley Derbys.
2s Sir Gilbert. Was a major in Fitzherbert's.
Remained at Tutbury after brother's replacement in 46.
Sources: IO, 80; RS, 92b; PN, 843; JTB, 34, 71.

Cornet Richard Allestry, Gent., Alveston Derbys., 1622–1681.
1s Richard of Uppingham Salop; Ox Christ Church Comm. 36; BA 40; MA 43; Doctor of Divinity 60.
At Restoration was chaplain to Charles II and Regius Prof Divinity Ox.
Sources: IO, 80; JTB, 13, 72.

Major John Bunnington (Bannington), Barcote Derbys., ?–1645
Ca Emanuel 07; Gray's 09; later became major of Prince Rupert's Firelocks.
Killed at siege of Leicester.
Sources: RS, 92b; JTB, 72; PN, 208; *Royal Martyrs*, 7; *Symonds' Diary*, 181.

Major Gilbert Kniveton, Esq., Derbys.
3s Sir Gilbert. Prisoner at Derby in Oct 45. Bro of Andrew and Peter. Ex-captain in Fitzherbert's.
Sources: RS, 92b; JTB, 34, 72; JHC, 4, 318.

Captain Thomas Brough, Staffs.
Sources: IO, 80; JTB, 72.

Cornet Thomas Kniveton, Gent., Bradley Derbys.
Youngest bro of Sir Arthur.
Sources: IO, 80; JTB, 35, 72.

Captain ? Menhill
Killed 44.
Sources: RS, 92b; HMC Hastings, 2, 132.

Captain Henry Merry, Barton Park Derbys.
?1s John; RC; may also have had lands at Kegworth, Leics. Claimed never in arms! Fined at 1/6th £1,943 in 46; reduced in 49 to £1,600.
Sources: DV, 31; CCC, 1380; JTB, 38.

Captain Alexander Walsall (Walthall), Eggington Derbys., ?–1657
Cryer at Derby assizes. Fined £164. Surrendered at Tutbury.
Sources: RS, 92b; CCC, 1315; HMC Hastings, 2, 133; JTB, 48, 71.

Captain Lt Henry Dudley, London and Westminster
Sources: IO, 80; JTB, 71.

Cornet Roger Fletcher, Derbys.
Source: IO, 80.

Cornet William Doddington
Sources: IO, 80; JTB, 71.

Foot
The only two surviving names for the foot are those of Lt Col Peter Kniveton and Major Bunnington.

Roger Molyneux's Regiments

Horse
Colonel Roger Molyneux, Esq., Teversal Notts.
?s of Sir John Bart. Governor of Wingfield 43–44. See Chapter 6.
Then moved on to Newark. Fined June 46 £200. Assessed at 1/5th and 1/20th £120 in 47. In arms 48, fined at 1/6th, £250.

Sources: RS, 96; HMC Hastings, 2, 114, 116, 117; PN, 989; IO, 95, 96; RCHM, Newark, 77; CCC, 1335; CCAM, 788; Burke's *Dormant Baronetcies*, 361; Young P. *Naseby*, 68.

Lt Colonel William Whichcot (Whichcote), Dunston Lincs., 1618–?
?2s Sir Haman; Ca Emanuel pens 34; Gray's 37; captured at the Battle of Denton 44. Compounded 50 at 1/6th £5.
Sources: CCC, 2301; Burney's Newspapers, 26, *Perfect Occurrences* no. 30; RCHM, Newark, 77; Young, *Naseby*, 69; CA, 4, 382.

Major Thomas Eyre, Esq., Dronfield Derbys., ?–1645
1s Edward; attorney; was a major to Sigismund Beeton (see Hastings' Horse) when he was a colonel. Was a major at Wingfield. Wounded at Naseby and taken by Gell to Derby where he died.
Sources: RS, 96; IO, 9, 154; PN, 495; *Symonds' Diary*, 196; JTB, 24–25, 73 suggests he was a lieutenant colonel.

Major Norris Fiennes (Fines), Esq., Christhead and Whitehall Lincs.
?s of Sir Henry. A hostage at surrender of Wingfield, laid down arms at this point. Fined 46 £50.
Sources: IO, 75, 95, 96; CCC, 1213; PN, 516.

Captain Anthony Wilkinson, London and Westminster
At Wingfield. Promoted from captain lieutenant.
Sources: RS, 96; IO, 95.

Lieutenant Richard Evans, Derbys.
Sources: IO, 95; JTB, 73.

Cornet John Wilkinson, Lincs.
Source: IO, 95.

Cornet John Belson, Derbys.
Source: IO, 95.

Cornet ? Kermet
At Wingfield 44.
Source: DRO 803 m/211.

Foot
Captain ? Basford
At Wingfield.
Source: DRO 803 m/211.

Captain ? Boles
At Wingfield.
Source: DRO 803 m/211.

Captain ? Chippendale
At Wingfield.
Source: DRO 803 m/211.
Captain Henry Statham, Notts.
Sources: IO, 95; RS, 96.

Ferdinand Stanhope's /John Barnard's Regiments

S = Stanhope's only; B = Barnard's only

Horse
Colonel Ferdinando Stanhope, Esq., Bretby, 1615–1644.
4s Earl of Chesterfield.
Ca fell com Sydney Sussex 36; BA 36; DCL Ox Dec 42 MP Tamworth Long Parl. Raised troop in 42 at Edgehill. Returned to Derbyshire. in Dec 42. Captured at Hopton Heath. Killed Nov 44.
Sources: RS, 92; PRO SP28/69, 45; AC, 4, 146; AO, 1408; *Royal Martyrs*, 4; PN, 1361.

Major, later Colonel John Barnard, Northants.
?CoA Northants. Took regiment south in 44 either all, after death of Stanhope, or part as a new regiment before Stanhope's death. Gov of Abbey Cwm Hir surrendered 13/1/45 and later governor of Cannon Frome. He and garrison massacred by Scots.
Sources: RS, 92, 92b; BL TT E252/6; IO, 6–7; *Symonds' Diary*, 211; ?FH133; CSPD, 1644–1645, 181; PN, 72.

Captain Lt Thomas Leving, Gent., S, Parwich Derbys., 1619–?
1s Timothy; Ox Balliol 36; IT barrister 41; clerk of peace Derby 29–45. Wounded at Hopton Heath.
Sources: RS, 92; GA, 155; BL TT E262/9; JTB, 36.

Captain William Milward, Gent., S, Chilcote Derbys.
1s Sir Thomas of Eaton. Lincoln's?; at Tutbury under Kniveton at some time. Surrendered to Gell in July 45. No order for fine.
Sources: RS, 92; CCC, 1605; DV, 7; JTB, 39.

Lieutenant John Mather, Staffs.
Source: IO, 87.

Cornet Thomas Milward, Staffs.
Source: IO, 87.

Captain ? Mynn, Gent., S
s of Sir Richard.
Source: RS, 92.

Captain Lt John Pickering, Gent., B, London and Westminster, ?Giles Cripplegate.
?RC.
Sources: IO, 6; PRO SP16/495, 1E.

Captain Arthur Warren, Gent., S, Wissendine Rutland
Fined in 47, £450 owed £900, had to sell estates in Bucks. Assessed at 1/20th £500.
Sources: RS, 92; JTB, 71; GA, 268; RV, 35.

Foot

Lt Colonel Richard Dudley, Gent., B, Swepstone, Leics.
Ex-captain of Hastings' Horse. POW in 44 at Upton Warren Worcs. Exchanged. Fined at 1/10th £106 in 49.
Sources: IO, 87; CCC, 108, 190, 1879; RS, 92b; PN, 455; Fosbrooke, 23.

Major Thomas Jennings, B, Warwicks.
Cow gelder and farmer, according to Symonds.
Sources: RS. 92b; IO, 7; PN, 810.

Captain John Brisco, B, London and Westminster
Source: IO, 6.

Isham Parkyns' (Perkins') Regiments 1601–1671

Horse

Colonel Isham Parkyns, Esq., Bunny Notts.
1s Sir George. Estate of £1,000 pa; JP 42; CoA Notts.
Governor of Ashby-de-la-Zouch.
Sources: RS, 96; CCC, 111–112; CCAM, 1432; PN, 1119; Fosbrooke, 21.

Captain Geoffery Trees (Treace), Notts.
Source: IO, 103.

Foot

Captain ? Greene
Butler and Falconer to Lord Loughborough.
Source: RS, 96.

Captain George Stanley
Source: RS, 96.

Richard and Harvey Bagots' Regiments

R = only in Richard's regiment; H = only in Harvey's

Horse
Colonel Richard Bagot, Esq., Pipe Hayes Staffs., 1619–1645
4s of Sir Harvey (see Staffs. CoA); earlier in Paget's Foot; arrived in Staffs. early 43, or late 42. Governor of Lichfield 43–45; wounded at Hopton Heath, see chapters 2, 4, 5, 6.
Sources: RS, 93; *Symonds' Diary*, 172; HMC Hastings, 2, 115–116; PN, 55; Roy, 1, 159; Young, *Edgehill*, 222; LCL MS Lich 24.

Lt Colonel, later Colonel Harvey Bagot, Esq., Pipe Hayes Staffs., 1618–1674
2s to Sir Harvey; elder bro to above. Ox Trinity 35; MT 37; captain of trained bands in 42. Second to younger bro as Richard was a professional soldier. Succeeded to colonelcy and at Hastings' instigation, the governor of Lichfield on bro's death. Threw out Hastings in Dec 45. Made assistant governor to Tyldesley in Jan 46. See Chapter 6.
Sources: RS, 93; PN, 54; *Symonds' Diary*, 227; LJRO D30, LIIIB; CCC, 1203, 1814; AO, 55.

Major Cecil Cooper, R
Captured at Willoughby 48.
Sources: RS, 93; PN, 342; RCHM, Newark, 79.

Major William Warner, Northants.
A clerk. In June 45 accused of plundering £1,000 from tenants on his uncle's estates at Thorpe Lubenham, Warwicks. Surrendered at Ashby 46.
Sources: IO, 5; CCC, 37; PN, 1524; Fosbrooke, 22.

Captain Thomas Bennett, R
Yeoman's Son of Staffs.
Source: RS, 93.

Captain William Bodley (Baggeley), Staffs.
Sources: IO, 5; RS, 93; SP, 13; LJRO D30, LIIIB.

Captain William Dibdale, R
?Preacher and chaplain to Richard.
Sources: RS, 93; BL TT E258/14.

Captain ? Dinwick, R
Possibly in regiment April 43.
Source: LCL MS Lich 24.

Captain William Gibbons, Gent., R, Coventry, ?–1646
1s William; father an attorney; Ca 35; MT 35.
Sources: RS, 93; IO, 5; AC, 2, 209.

Cornet Vincent Scudamore, R, London and Westminster
Source: IO, 5.

Captain H. Rugely, Gent.
Source: IO, 5.

Lieutenant Thomas Underhill, R, London and Westminster
Source: IO, 5.

Captain ? Trevor, R
With Bagot in April 43?
Source: LCL MS Lich 24.

Lieutenant Walter Beardmore, R, Staffs.
Source: IO, 5.

Lieutenant Lewis Milton, R, London and Westminster
Source: IO, 5.,

Lieutenant John Roade, R, Derbys.
Source: IO, 5.

Cornet Edward Chiles, R, Warwicks.
Source: IO, 5.

Foot

Major Roger Harsnett (called Robert), Packington Staffs., ?–1663
Servant to Prince Charles. In 1660, said to be 'the oldest serving officer in England'.
Sources: RS, 93; PN, 686; LJRO D30, LIIIB; CSPD, 1660–1661, 77, 1661–1662, 508, 1663–1664, 404; HMC Hastings, 2, 134.

Captain Francis Collier, H, Darlaston, Staffs.
1s Henry; was only a lieutenant in 45; by end of year had 15 in his company. Lands confiscated in 52.
Sources: IO, 6; IR, 47; Young, *Naseby*, 88; LJRO D30 LIIIB.

Ensign Ralph Wuckridge, H, Salop
Source: IO, 6.

Captain Anthony Dyott, Freeford Staffs., 1617–1662
1s Sir Richard of Lichfield
Ox 34; IT 52; barrister, and recorder of Tamworth. ?Captured at Naseby.
Sources: RS, 93; AO, 438; SP, 77; LJRO D30, LIIIB; IO, 5; BL TT E262/9.

Lieutenant Robert Blenhorne, Staffs.
Only an ensign when captured at Naseby; lieutenant by Oct.
Sources: IO, 5; LJRO D30, LIIIB; Young, *Naseby*, 87.

Captain Jeffery Glazier, Lichfield
A chorister; was the garrison treasurer; captured at Naseby but released/exchanged. Surrendered at Lichfield.
Sources: RS, 93; CCC, 3, 1664; BL TT E262/9; LJRO D30, LIIIB; LCL Ms Lich

Captain Hugh Henne
Killed at Faringdon?
Sources: IO, 5; *Royal Martyrs*, 8.

Lieutenant Michael East, Staffs., 1580–1680
Composer and choirmaster from 1618, at Lichfield.
Sources: IO, 5; LJRO D30 LIIIB; Young, *Naseby*, 88.

Captain Zacharia Turnpenny, Lichfield
In the choir at Cathedral; led the citizens' company.
Sources: IO, 5; LJRO D30, LIIIB; Young, *Naseby*, 89.

Ensign Zacharia Bakewell, Staffs.
Source: IO, 5.

Captain Lt Ralph Swift, York?
Captain in Harvey's?
Source: RS, 93.

Captain Lt Timothy Startin, Uttoxeter
Prisoner at Nantwich Oct 45. Estate confiscated 52. Compounded 49 1/6th at £171–10s. Asked for review 51.
Sources: IO, 5; CCC, 2010; LJRO D30 LIIIB; RI, 47c; Young, *Naseby*, 88.

Lieutenant ? Baggeley, H, Corbyn Hall, Worcs.
Sources: LJRO D30, LIIIB; Young, *Naseby*, 89.

Captain ? Benskin, H
Source: LJRO D30, LIIIB.

Lieutenant ? Burden
At surrender of Ashby?
Sources: LJRO D30, LIIIB; Fosbrooke, 23.

Lieutenant ? Cowper, R
A reformado captured at Naseby.
Source: Young, *Naseby*, 87.

Lieutenant ? Robinson, H
Sources: LJRO D30, LIIIB; Young, *Naseby*, 88.

Lieutenant John Stowe, H
Sources: LJRO D30, LIIIB; Young, *Naseby*, 8.

Lieutenant Thomas Waldron, H, London and Westminster
Source: IO, 5.

Lieutenant Alexander Ward, R. Captured at Naseby.
Source: Young, *Naseby*, 87.

Lieutenant Richard Warnesley, Staffs.
Possibly only a lieutenant in Oct 45.
Sources: LJRO D30, LIIIB; IO, 5.

Ensign John Bud, H, Garton Yorks.
Ca Magdalene 18–35.
Sources: IO, 5; AC, 1, 115.

Ensign ? Butler, H
Sources: LJRO D30, LIIIB; Young, *Naseby*, 88.

Ensign Francis Fisher, H, Warwicks.
Bro to Sir Clement.
Sources: LJRO D30 LIIIB; Young, *Naseby*, 89.

Ensign Walter Petty, R, Staffs.
Source: IO, 5.

Ensign ? Pyott, H
In prison at Nantwich Oct 45.
Source: LJRO D30, LIIIB.

Ensign ? Sharpe
Source: LJRO D30, LIIIB.

Ensign ? Stanford
New in Oct 45.
Sources: LJRO D30, LIIIB; Young, *Naseby*, 88.

Ensign ? Thomas, R
Captured Naseby, still in prison in Oct 45.
Sources: LJRO D30, LIIIB; Young, *Naseby*, 87.

Dragoons
Cornet Timothy Eamon, Bucks.
Sources: IO, 5; LJRO D30, LIIIB.

John Lane's Regiment of Horse

Colonel John Lane, Esq., King's Bromley, Bentley Wolverhampton Staffs.

1s Thomas (see CoA Staffs.); earlier in Lord Digby's. Gov of Stafford then Rushall 43; surrendered Rushall May 44; wounded at Asherton Fair 44, rescued by Hastings. Fined £250. Became MP for Lichfield at Restoration. Bro to Jane who helped the young Charles II escape after Worcester 52.
Sources: IO, 16, 18; HMC Hastings, 2, 98; CCC, 89, 112; CCAM, 1252; BL Harl. MS 2043, 28; PN, 850; Fosbrooke, 21; PRO Return of MPs 1, 528; *Staffordshire Historical Collections*, New Series XIX, 1910.

Captain Fulke Grosvenor, Wednesbury Staffs.
In charge of the church at the siege of Rushall May 44.
Source: CCC, 1486.

Captain John Lassalls, Derbys.
Sources: JTB, 73; Fosbrooke, 23; IO, 81.

Lieutenant Richard Fairley
Source: IO, 81.

Thomas Leveson's Regiments

Horse

Colonel Thomas Leveson, Esq., Wolverhampton, ?–1652
2s Sir Walter; DL 40; RC.
Leveson returned from France at the beginning of the war. He was a part of the King's initiative in the North Midlands in late 42. First he garrisoned Wolverhampton, then Dudley. He held the latter until the end of the war gaining a reputation as being ruthless; an extension, no doubt, of his ability to make himself thoroughly unpopular with his fellow gentry, exhibited before the war. Argued at length with Richard and Harvey Bagot, Hastings and the various commissioners. See chapters 2, 5, 6, 7. Like Hastings he was labelled 'Rob-Carrier' by the hostile press.
Sources: IO, 84; *Symonds' Diary*, 168, 182; HMC Hastings, 2, 104, 106, 114, 121, 127; PRO SP29/159, 45; HMC Portland, 1, 570; JHC, 6, 700; CCC, 89, 2483–2486; Black *Docquets*, 35, 108; WSL SMS, 550; RS, 95b; PN, 881; CCAM, 427; CSPD, 1649–1650, 41.

Lieutenant Colonel Walter Giffard, Esq., Hyon Staffs.; 1611–1680.
1s Peter of Chillington; RC; Estates confiscated 53.
Sources IO, 84; CCC, 89; SP, 104; IR, 47c; PN, 604, *Staffordshire Historical Collections*, New Series IV, 1895.

Lieutenant Richard Collier, Staffs.
Source: IO, 84.

Lt Colonel George Parker, Sutton Coney Staffs.
RC.
Sources: CCAM, 90, 1429; Roy, 321; PN, 1094; SP, 182.

Lt Colonel Francis Beaumont, Barrow on Trent, Derbys., 1599–1661
1s William; In charge at Dudley in Leveson's absence during the Marston Moor campaign.
Sources: RS, 95b; IO, 84; Shaw, 1, 62; PN, 88.

Major Christopher Heveningham, Gent., Pipehill, Staffs., 1616–?
3s Nicholas bro to Simon (see Fitzherbert).
Captain in 43; promoted following transfer of bro to Fitzherbert's.
Ox Trinity 32; BA 32; MA 35; Compounded 48. RC.
Sources: RS, 95; CCC, 1804; CCAM, 1415, 1433; SP, 124; IO, 84; AO, 699.

Lieutenant Francis Fortesque, Warwicks.
Source: IO, 84.

Major Simon Heveningham
Preceded Christopher Heveningham (see Fitzherbert's).

Major ? Mole
'An officer in Ireland'.
Source: RS, 95.

Captain Richard Astley, Esq., Patshull Staffs., 1625–1688
1s Walter; kt during war; bart 62. Garrisoned father's house until it was captured Feb 46, then he went into Dudley. Perhaps had been in Hastings' before Leveson's. Pious RC.
Sources: CCAM, 1415; PN, 40 (as a lieutenant colonel); Young P., Roffe M. *The English Civil War Armies*, Osprey, 1979, 21, 33, plate C.

Captain William Carlos (Carless, Carlosse), Gent., Bromhall, Staffs., ?–1689
RC; commanded Tong garrison. Became a colonel after First Civil War. At the battle of Worcester 51; hid with Charles II in tree.
Sources: GA, 46; PN, 246; WSL, Chetwynd Papers, AL 565.

Captain John Potts, Staffs.
RC.
Sources: IO, 84; CCAM, 141.

Lieutenant Richard Caney, Staffs.
Source: IO, 84.

Captain Lieutenant John Birch, Gorstock Staffs.
RC. Possibly the garrison treasurer. May have been captured in Jan 45.
Sources: IO, 84; CCC, 89; BL TT E258/14; Shaw, 1, 60.

Cornet John Dunn(e)
Possibly trumpeter only. Deserted and went to Stafford where he became trumpeter? to Colonel Rugeley.
Sources: Pennington/Roots, 106; Guttery D.R., *The Great Civil War in the Midland Parishes*, Birmingham, 1950, 56.

Foot

Captain Lt ? Parker
Leveson's company.
Source: Young, *Naseby*, 90.

Ensign Phillip Draycott, London and Westminster
Lt Col Beaumont's company.
Sources: IO, 84; CCAM, 1202.

Ensign Robert Harris, Salop
Lt Col Beaumont's company
Source: IO, 84.

Ensign William Copplewood, Staffs.
Of Simon Heveningham's company as he too held dual command in the foot and horse.
Source: IO, 84.

Ensign William Hickman, Staffs.
Heveningham's company.
Source: IO, 84.

Captain Thomas Gifford, Esq. Chillington Staffs.
?s of Peter. RC.
Sources: IO, 84; SP, 104; GA, 100.

Ensign Walter Stanford, Staffs.
Source: IO, 84.

Captain Lt Charles Colles, London and Westminster
Source: IO, 84.

Lieutenant Francis Colles, Gent., London and Westminster, ?Silver Street
?RC.
Sources: IO, 84; PRO SP16/495, 1E.

Ensign John Rumney, London and Westminster, ?St Martins in the Fields ?RC.
Sources: IO, 84; PRO SP16/495, 1E.

Lieutenant ? Johnson
Prisoner at Stafford 44.
Sources: WSL Minute Book of the Committee at Stafford, 58; Young, *Naseby*, 90.

Devereaux Wolseley's Regiments

Horse
Colonel Devereaux Wolselev, Esq., Orme Staffs., ?–1663
Governor at Bagworth May 43. See chapters 4, 5. Surrendered at Ashby.
Sources: RS, 91; HMC Hastings, 2, 103; Fosbrooke, 21; PN, 1600; IO, 144.

Captain Walter Hastings
See Hastings' Horse

Cornet Edward Aston, Staffs.
Source: IO, 144.

Foot
Lt Colonel Knapper
'Clerk to Lord Chief Justice Banks when he was an Attorney'.
Sources: RS, 91; IO, 144; PN, 838.

Lieutenant Hopkin Matthews, Glamorgan
Source: IO, 144.

Major Thomas Roberts, Gent., Sutton Leics. (and Cheltenham and Hereford)
5s Sir William; bro to Wolstan (see Hastings' Horse – cornet).
Peter Newman suggests he is John Roberts. RS says Tho.
Sources: RS, 91; CCC, 110; VL, 118; PN, 1211.

Captain ? Masters
Source: RS, 91.

Captain William Orme, Gent., Longdon Staffs., 1615–1665
ls William.
Ox Corpus Christ's pens 31; IT 32; 46 fined at 1/10th £1,395; 49 reduced to £558 to be only £372 if tithes of £18 pa settled on local minister. June 51 discharged from sequestration and tithes and assessment of £500.
Sources: CCC, 1684; SP, 178; GA, 186.

Gervase Lucas' Regiments

Horse

Colonel Gervase Lucas, Gent., Fenton Lincs., 1611–1668
ls Anthony. Governor of Belvoir 43–46. Bart 44, one of Hastings' creations? Argued with Hastings. See chapters 2, 4, 5, 6, 7. Commissioner for surrender of Lichfield where he had gone after surrender of Belvoir. Governor of Bombay after Restoration.
Sources: IO, 87–89; RS, 92b; HMC Hastings, 2, 110, 114, 135; *Symonds' Diary*, 228, 278; BL TT E345/2; GEC *The Complete Baronetage*, 2, 226; Warburton, 2, 98; Black *Docquets*, 230; CSPD, 1601–1661, 72, 1667–1668, 278; PN, 916.

Major George Plunkney (Plunkett), Ibstone Staffs., ?–1643
?RC; had been a captain in regiment. Described as (a) an ex-Irish rebel now fighting for the Protestants, (b) when he was killed at Sproxton Heath in Dec 43, as the 'vilest villain of all the cormorants at Belvoir Castle or Newark either'. Several Plunketts had been MPs in Ireland.
Sources: RS, 92b; *Royal Martyrs*, 6; HMC Portland, 1, 165; CCC, 110; BL TT E81/8; Nichols, 2, 1, 52; PN, 1143; Kearney H.F., *Strafford in Ireland*, MUP, 1961, 260–261.

Major James Hardy, Grimsby Lincs.
Possibly major following Plunkney's death. Had been a captain in the regiment. Compounded 46, fined £120.
Sources: RS, 92b; PN, 681; CCC, 1449; BL TT E345/2.

Captain ? Archer, London.
'Used to sell gloves at the Cheapside Cross'.
Source: RS, 92b.

Captain ? Barton
Source: IO, 89.

Cornet Edward Bates, Northants.
Source: IO, 89.

Captain William Corby, Rutland
Source: IO, 89.

Lieutenant Anthony Wright, Yorks.
Source: IO, 89.

Captain ? Deane
'Came from the Parliament'.
Sources: RS, 92b; Guilford E., 'The Accounts of the Constables of Stathern', AJ, 69, 1912, 148.

Captain ? Harding
Source: IO, 89.

Captain Timothy Lucas, Gent., Fenton Lincs., ?–1652
?s of Anthony. When Gervase was at Bolsover in the winter of 43–44, Timothy was in charge of the castle and argued with William Bale.
Ca fell com Peterhouse 26. Comp on Newark Articles. Fined at 1/6th £750 in 47. In 49 begged leave to pay £300 and rest after Michaelmas, granted. June 50 discharged.
Sources: Line Pedigree, 615; HMC Hastings, 2, 110; CCC, 1330; AC, 3, 114.

Captain Thomas Mason, Ashwell Rutland
Parson. The 'commander of the Fen Robbers' (Oct 45). Imprisoned many times for reading the common prayer. His quartermaster regularly collected contribution from Waltham on the Wolds and from Branston. See section on contribution in Chapter 2.
Sources: RS, 92b; Nichols, 2, 52; LRO Waltham CA, 68–70, Branston CA, 60–62.

Captain Peter Needham, Staffs.
Source: IO, 89.

Cornet William Rawson, Lincs.
Source: IO, 89.

Captain ? Yates, Leics.
Killed at Melton. Son of the Mr Yates Lucas was collecting money from despite having lost two sons in the cause. Bro to Yates in Hastings.
Sources: RS, 92b; *Royal Martyrs*, 10; BL Add Mss, 18981, 47.
Cornet Gervase Jackson Source: CCAM, 1361–1362.

Foot
Captain George Brellisford, Harleston Lincs., London and Westminster
Estates confiscated in the 3rd Confiscation Act.
Sources: IO, 89; IR, 45a.

Captain Andrew Broome, Grantham Lincs.
Apothecary.
Sources: IO, 89; CCC, 881, 2766.

Lieutenant Joseph Locker, Essex
Source: IO, 89.

Captain John Stevens, Lincs.
Source: IO, 89.

Lieutenant Henry Page, Leics.
Source: IO, 89.

Francis Wortley's Dragoons (Perphaps later Dud Dudley's)

Colonel Francis Wortley, Esq., Wortley Yorks., 1620–1665
1s Sir Francis the first person to raise horse for the King. Under Hastings at the beginning of 43. See Chapter 5. Fined at 1/6th £671-13s-4d reduced to £408-6s-8d if he would compound for another royalist who owed £1,850 to his wife. Active in 50s.
Sources: PN, 1609; CCAM, 779.

Major Dudley Dudley of Dudley, 1599 1684 (also of Tipton Staffs.)
2s illegitimate of Edward Lord Dudley. Ironmaster, supplied iron to Staffs. garrisons and Oxford. Was active in North Staffs. in late 43, suggesting that he and Wortley returned to the area with the Northern Army, having gone north after Hopton Heath, not, as Edward Nicholas suggested to Hastings, before. At Colchester in Second Civil War. Sentenced to be shot but escaped twice. Estates confiscated in 52. Were worth £200 pa in late 40s.
Sources: IO, 146; IR, 47d; PRO SP29/159, 45; SP, 45; PN, 435; CCC, 89, 261, DNB; CSPD, 1660–1661, 45, 73–74, 220.

Cornet Jeffery Dudley, Rushall Staffs. Married to Dud's sister.
Source: IO, 46.

Cornet Robert Heaton, Worcs.
Source: IO, 146

John Corbet's Regiments

Horse

Colonel Sir John Corbet, Esq., Stoke Adderley Salop, 1620–?
1s Sir John
Ox 34. Had been captain in Hastings' Horse, was colonel by 1644, operated in the Marcher counties after this. Fined in 50, £1,000, imprisoned but released on £2,000 bail with sureties for good behaviour. Baronet 62.
Sources: RS, 93b; CCC, 735, 205; PN, 345; GEC *The Complete Baronetage*, 2, 33; *Symonds' Diary*, 252; CSPD, 1650, 519; IO, 31.

Foot

Captain ? Hawlet, Leics.
Source, IO, 10.

? Colonel Christopher Roper's Foot

This regiment may be either a part of Hastings' regiment given to Roper in 1645, or a creation of the Second Civil War.

Christopher Roper, Aston-on-Trent Derbys. and Leics.
In Lord Moore's Regiment in Ireland 41; Possibly MP for Dingle, Munster in Irish Parliament 40. In Nov 43 he came over to England to be the major in Hastings' Foot. There were (possibly) abortive attempts to bring his company over as well. He had a foot unit in early 46 which he led towards Chester but the town's surrender resulted in him leading it back to Ashby where he surrendered in Feb. This may have only been part of Hastings' regiment.
Sources: IO, 110; CCC, 112; *Symonds' Diary*, 278; WSL SMS, 550, Hastings to Rupert, 29/11/43; Bod Lib, Carte Calendar, 12, 580; HMC Ormonde, 1, 140; PN, 1226; Kearney, *op. cit.*, 261; Fosbrooke, 21.

Captain Lt Charles Smith, Salop
Source: IO, 110.

Other Officers who appear to have served at some time in the North Midlands Army, but whose Regiment is unknown.

Major Thomas Brudenell, Stanton Wyvill, Leics., 1613–?
1s Thomas. Cornet in 41.
Sources: PN, 198; CCC, 109; Fosbrooke, 21.

Major John Trevor, Llys Trefor, Denbighshire, ?–1658
At Holt Castle in 43; surrendered at Ashby; died in Wrexham Gaol.
Sources: Fosbrooke, 21; IO, 100; PN, 1453.

Captain Robert Poudrell, West Hallam Derbys., 1623–1662
Was an officer at Dudley and a Papist.
Source: CCAM, 1433.

Captain Edward Beck, Frasby Staffs.
Was a captain as early as Edgehill. In the garrisons of Ashby, Tutbury and Lichfield. Involved in an attack on Bagworth when it was in parliamentarian hands.
Source: CCAM, 1909.

Endnotes

1 Alan Everitt, *The Community of Kent and the Great Rebellion,* Leicester University Press, 1973; J.T. Cliffe, *Yorkshire Gentry from the Reformation to the Civil War*, University of London, 1969; Anne Hughes, *Politics, Society and Civil War in Warwickshire, 1626–1660*, Cambridge University Press, 1987; Clive Holmes, *Seventeenth Century Lincolnshire*, Society of the History of Lincolnshire, Lincoln, 1980.

2 Alan Everitt, *The Local Community and the Great Rebellion*, Historical Association, London 1969; Ronald Hutton, *The Royalist War Effort*, Longman, London 1980.

3 Martyn Bennett, 'Leicestershire Royalist Officers and Their War Effort in the County', *Transactions of the Leicestershire Archaeological and Historical Society,* LIX, 1984–85, 1985; 'The Civil War Battle of Cotes', *Leicestershire Historian* Vol 3, part 3, 1984; 'The Sinews of War: Royalist Finances in the North Midlands, 1642-1646', *The Historian*, 22, 1989; 'Contribution and Assessments; Financial Exactions During the Civil War', *War and Society*, XXX; 'Between Scylla and Charybdis: The Establishment of Rival Administrations in the English Civil War', *Local Historian*, 22, 4, 1992; 'The King's Gambit: Charles I and Nottingham in the Summer of 1642', *Transactions of the Thoroton Society of Nottingham*, XCVI, 1992; 'Damnified Villagers: Taxation in Wales during the First Civil War', *Welsh History Review*, Vol. 19, 1, June 1998.

4 4 'My Plundered Townes, My Houses Devastation: The Civil War North Midlands Life, 1642–46', *Midland History*, XXII, 1997 and *A Nottinghamshire Village in War and Peace: The Accounts of the Constables of Upton, 1640–1666*, Thoroton Society Records Series, Nottingham 1995. 'Roman Catholic Officers in the North Midlands: 1642–1646', *Journal of Military and Strategic Studies*, 6, Winter 2003–Spring 2004.

5 Martyn Bennett, *The Civil Wars in Britain and Ireland 1639-1651*, Blackwell, Oxford, 1997 and *The Civil Wars Experienced, Britain and Ireland, 1638–1661*, Routledge, London, 2000.

6 Martyn Bennett, *Oliver Cromwell*, Routledge, London, 2006 and *Cromwell at War: the Lord General and His Military Revolution,* I.B. Tauris, London, 2017.

7 Jeffrey Richards, *Aristocrat and Regicide: The Life and Times of Thomas, Lord Grey of Groby,* New Millennium, 2000; and *The Siege and Storming of Leicester*, New Millennium, 2001.

8 Ian Atherton, 'Royalist Finances During the English Civil War: the Case of Lichfield Garrison, 1643–5' *Midland History,* Vol 33, No 1, 2008.

9 Brian Stone, *Derbyshire in the Civil War*, Cromford, 1992; Andrew Polkey, *The Civil War in the Trent Valley*, Bristol, 1992.

10 Peter Edwards, *Dealing in Death: The Arms Trade and the English Civil War*, Sutton Publishing, Sutton, 2000; Gavin Robinson, *Horses, People and Parliament in the English Civil War*, Ashgate, Farnham, 2012.

11 By doubly defeated I mean that they were defeated in the war against Parliament and that they were defeated in their attempts elevate their social standing by siding with a victorious king, for whom they had ventured their lives and estates.

12 David Fleming, 'Faction and Civil War in Leicestershire', *Transactions of the Leicestershire Archaeological and Historical Society*, Vol. LVII, (1981–2). He had developed this from his MA thesis at Leicester University, in 1976. I had unknowingly developed the same idea in my undergraduate dissertation at Loughborough some five years later and published a reference to it and Fleming's pioneering work in 'Leicestershire Royalists and their War effort in the County, 1642–1646', *Transactions of the Leicestershire Archaeological and historical Society*, Vol LIX, (1984–85).

13 Roberts, Michael. 'The Military Revolution, 1560–1660' (1956), reprinted in Clifford J. Rogers (ed.), *The Military Revolution Debate: Readings on the Military Transformation of Early Modern Europe*, Avalon Publishing, 1995; Geoffrey Parker, *The Military Revolution*, Cambridge, 1996 second edition; Jeremy Black, *A Military Revolution? Military Change and European Society 1550–1800*, Basingstoke, Macmillan, 1991. Jeremy Black, 'Was there a Military Revolution in Early Modern Europe?', *History Today*, 58/7 (2008).

14 This subject is explored in great detail by Paul Scannell in his book, *Conflict and Soldiers' literature in Early Modern Europe The Reality of War*, London, Bloomsbury, 2015. Very good examples are John Cruso *Instructions for the Cavallrie*, Cambridge, University of Cambridge, 1632, and William Barriffe's *Military Discipline or the Young Artillery Man*, London, 1635. There were also discussions of and histories of the current war on the Continent such as the *Swedish Intelligencer*, published in London during the 1630s, which reported on battles and tactics.

15 Sherwood R.E., *Civil Strife in the Midlands*, Phillimore, 1974

16 Holmes C., *The Eastern Association in the English Civil War*, Cambridge University Press (CUP), 1974; Hutton R., *The Royalist War Effort*, Longmans, 1982

17 Newman P., unpublished D. Phil Thesis 'The Royalist Army in Northern England 1642–1645', York, 1978

18 Blackwood B.G., *The Lancashire Gentry and the Great Rebellion*, Chetham Society, 1978; Newman P., *The Royalist Officers of England and Wales 1642–1660*, Garland Press, 1981, and 'The Royalist Officer Corps 1642–1660. Army Command as a reflection of the Social Structure', *The Historical Journal*, 26, 4, 1983

19 Malcolm J., *Caesar's Due: Loyalty and King Charles 1642–1646,* Royal Historical Society, 1983

20 Wanklyn M., Young P., 'A King in Search of Soldiers: Charles I in 1642: A Rejoinder', *The Historical Journal,* 24, 1, 1981, p.149

21 Ensberg J., 'Royalist Finance during the English Civil War 1642–1646', *Scandinavian Economic History Review*, 14, 2, 1966

22 Dietz F.C., 'The Receipts and Issues of the Exchequer during the Reigns of James I and Charles I', *Smith College Studies in History,* 3, 4, 1928

23 Roy I., unpublished PhD thesis, 'The Royalist Army in the First Civil War', Oxford, 1963

24 Morton-Thorpe A.M., unpublished MA thesis, 'The Gentry of Derbyshire 1640–1660', Leicester, 1971; Beats L., unpublished PhD thesis, 'Politics and Government in Derbyshire 1640–1660', Sheffield, 1978

25 Lloyd P., unpublished M.Phil thesis, 'Politics and the Personnel of Politics in Nottingham 1642–1688', Nottingham, 1978

26 Pickles J.T., unpublished MA thesis, 'Studies in Royalism in the English Civil War 1642–1646, with Special Reference to Staffordshire', Manchester, 1968

27 Newman (1978), *op. cit.*

28 Hughes A., 'Warwickshire on the Eve of the Civil War: A County Community?' *Midlands History,* 7, 1982

29 Hutton R. (1982), *op. cit.*

30 Young P., *Edgehill 1642: The Campaign and the Battle,* Roundwood, 1967

31 Young P., *Marston Moor 1644: The Campaign and the Battle,* Roundwood, 1970; *Naseby 1645: The Campaign and the Battle,* Century, 1985

32 Blackwood (1978), *op. cit.*

33 Brighton J.T., *Royalists and Roundheads in Derbyshire,* Bakewell and District Historical Society, 1981

34 Newman (1978), *op. cit.*, p.34

35 Newman (1981), *op. cit.*

36 Newman (1983), *op. cit.*, p.951

37 The Royal Commission on Historical Monuments, *Newark upon Trent: The Civil War Siegeworks,* HMSO, 1964

38 LRO 66/34 The Petition of the Inhabitants of the County of Leicester

39 Kenyon J.P., *Stuart England*, Pelican, 1985, p.164

40 Wedgewood C.V., *The King's War 1642–1647*, Penguin, 1983, p.446

41 Nichols J., *The History and Antiquities of the County of Leicester*, 1804

42 Shaw S., *The History and Antiquities of the County of Staffordshire*, E.P. Publishing, 1976; Glover S., *The History, Gazetteer and Directory of the County of Derbyshire*, 1829

43 Thoroton R., Throsby J., *The Antiquities of Nottinghamshire*, E.P. Publishing, 1972, orig. 1677; Wright J., Harrod W., *The History and Antiquities of the County of Rutland*, E.P. Publishing, 1973, orig. 1684–1712

44 Dickenson Rastell W., *A History of the Antiquities of the Town and Church of Southwell in the County of Nottingham*, 1787
45 Hollings J.F., *The History of Leicestershire During the Great Civil War*, 1840
46 Hensman E.W., *Loughborough During the Civil War,* Echo Press, 1921; 'Henry Hastings, Lord Loughborough and the Great Civil War', in Dryden A. (ed.), *Memorials of Old Leicestershire,* Ballantyne and Hanson, 1911
47 Wood A., *Nottinghamshire in the Civil War*, S.R. Publishing, 1971 edn
48 Everitt A., *The County of Kent and the Great Rebellion*, Leicester University Press, 1973; Cliffe J.T., *The Yorkshire Gentry from the Reformation to the English Civil War*, Athlone Press, 1969; Blackwood, *op. cit.*
49 Everitt A., *The Local Community and the Great Rebellion,* Historical Association, 1969, p.6
50 Holmes C., *Seventeenth Century Lincolnshire,* History of Lincolnshire Committee, 1980; Hughes, *op. cit.*
51 Everitt (1969), *op. cit.*
52 Fleming D., unpublished MA thesis, 'Some Aspects of the Gentry in Jacobean and Carolian Leicestershire', Leicester, 1976; 'Faction and Civil War in Leicestershire', *Transactions of the Leicestershire Archaeological and Historical Society* (*TLAHS*), 57, 1980–82
53 Gruenfelder J.K., 'The Electoral Influence of the Earls of Huntingdon 1603–1640', *TLAHS*, 50, 1974–75
54 Lloyd (thesis)
55 Pennington D., Roots I., *The Committee at Stafford 1643–1645,* Staffordshire Historical Collections, 1957; Pickles (1968), *op. cit.*
56 Morton-Thorpe (1971), *op. cit.*
57 Beats (1978), *op. cit.*
58 Brighton (1981), *op. cit.* and 'The Gell Family in the Sixteenth and Seventeenth Centuries: A Case of Rising Gentry', *Journal of the Bakewell and District Historical Society*, 1980; 'Sir John Gell and the Civil War in Derbyshire', *JBDHS*, 1981
59 North. RO, Finch-Hatton MSS 133; Bod Lib, Dugdale Ms 19; Black W.H., 'Docquets of Letters Patent and other Instruments of Government', unpublished and kept in the PRO
60 Everett-Green A.M. (ed.), *The Calendars of the Committees for Compounding,* Kraus, 1967; *The Calendars of the Committee for the Advance of Money,* Kraus, 1967
61 BL Add MSS 29548, ff.7–9, 34217, f.70; Han l MSS 6851, f.130; Edgerton MSS, 2986, f.212
62 Pennington, Roots, *op. cit.*; WSL Salt MSS, 48/49; NRO, Hall Books 1642–1647 and printed version, *Records of the Borough of Nottingham*, vol. 5, 1625–1702, Nottingham, 1900; LRO BR/18/22–24 and printed version, Stocks H.E. (ed.), *Records of the Borough of Leicester 1603–89*, CUP, 1923
63 BL E83/9, *A Catalogue ...*, printed as, Peacock E., *The Army Lists of the Roundheads and Cavaliers containing the names of the Officers in the Royal and Parliamentary Armies of 1642,* 1863
64 PRO SP 29/68, 19
65 BL Harl. MS 986
66 Foster J.A. (ed.), *Alumni Oxonienses 1500–1714,* 1–2, Kraus, 1968; Venn J., Venn J.A. (eds), *Alumni Cantabrigienses* Part 1, 1–4, Cambridge, 1922–7; Foster J.A. (ed.), *The Register of Admissions to Gray's Inn 1521–1889,* London, 1889
67 Morrill J., 'The Northern Gentry and the Great Rebellion', *Northern History*, 15, pp.66–87
68 HMC, *Report on the Manuscripts of the Late Reginald Rawdon Hastings*, HMSO, 1930; *The Manuscripts of His Grace the Duke of Portland*, HMSO, 1891; *The Manuscripts of His Grace the Duke of Rutland*, HMSO
69 WSL Salt MSS 479–564; Warburton E., *Memoirs of Prince Rupert and the Cavaliers*, 1849
70 DRO Gresley MSS D803 m29
71 Hutchinson L., *The Life of Colonel John Hutchinson,* Longman, Orme, Rees and Brown, 1822
72 Margaret, Duchess of Newcastle, *The Life of William Cavendish, Duke of Newcastle*, 1886; Parsons D. (ed.), *The Diary of Sir Henry Slingsby of Scriven Bt.*, 1836; Hamper W. (ed.), *The Life, Diary and Correspondence of Sir William Dugdale Kt.*, Harding and Lepard, 1857
73 Philips I.G. (ed.), 'Journal of Sir Samuel Luke', *Oxfordshire Record Society*, 29, 31, 33, 1950–1953; Webb J. Webb T.W. (eds), *Military Memoirs of Colonel John Birch*, Camden Soc., 1873
74 Clarendon, Earl of, *History of the Great Rebellion*, OUP, 1969
75 *Firth and Rait,* pp.1–6
76 North. RO, Finch-Hatton MSS 133
77 CSPD 1627 p.193; HMC *Hastings*, 4, p.209

78 HMC, *op. cit.*, 4, p.67; Gruenfelder J.N., 'The Electoral Influence of the Earls of Huntingdon', *Transactions of the Leicestershire Archaeological and Historical Society*, L 1974–5
79 Hutchinson L., 'Memoirs of the Life of Colonel John Hutchinson', OUP, 1973 edn (Hutchinson *Life*), pp.56, 64
80 SRO D948/4/6/2–6 Letter from George Thorley to Walter Wrottesley; G. Wrottesley, 'History of the Wrottesley Family', *Collections for a History of Staffordshire*, New Series VI part 2, pp.312–319
81 Gardiner S.R., *Documents of the Puritan Revolution*, OUP, 1979 edn, p.259
82 *Rushworth*, 3, 2, p.676
83 *Rushworth*, 3, 2, p.669; Nichols J., *The History and Antiquities of the County of Leicestershire*, III, 2, Appendix 4, pp.19–22
84 Nichols, *op. cit.*, III, 2, App. 4, p.19
85 Gardiner, *op. cit.*, pp.245–7
86 BL Add MSS 34217, f.70, Instructions to the Northamptonshire Commissioners
87 Nichols, *op. cit.*, III, 2, App. 4, pp.20–21
88 *Rushworth*, 3, 1, p.618
89 LRO Borough Records, BR 18/22/155; *Rushworth*, 3, 1, p.669; Nichols, *op. cit.*, III, 2, App. 4, pp.22–4
90 HMC *Hastings*, 2, p.84; *Rushworth*, 3, 1, p.670; Nichols, *op. cit.*, 2, App. 4, p.24
91 North. RO, Finch-Hatton MSS 133
92 JHC, II, p.645
93 HMC *Hastings*, 2, p.85, Charles I to the Earl of Devonshire 27/6/1642
94 Hutchinson, *Life...*, p.54
95 Nichols, *op. cit.*, III, 2, App. 4, pp.28–9
96 Clarendon Earl of, *History of the Great Rebellion*, OUP, 1969 edn, p.242
97 Brighton J.T., 'Sir John Gell and the Civil War in Derbyshire', *Journal of the Bakewell and District Historical Society*, VIII, 1981, p.8; Dias J., 'Lead, Society and Politics in Derbyshire before the Civil War', *Midlands History*, VI, 1981, p.53
98 Malcolm J., *Caesar's Due: Loyalty and King Charles I*, RHS, 1983, p.43
99 Hutton R., *The Royalist War Effort*, Longman, 1982, p.24; Morrill J., *The Revolt of the Provinces*, Longman, 1980, p.37
100 HMC Hastings, 2, pp.85–6
101 Hutton (1982), *op. cit.*, p.22
102 Bod Lib, Dugdale Ms 19, f.6, Black, 'Docquets of Letters Patent and Other Instruments of Government', unpublished volume in the PRO, p.9; HMC Hastings, 2, pp.94–5
103 Individual commissioners of array's personal details may be studied in Appendix I
104 For a discussion of the seventeenth century family structure see, Slater M. *Family Life in the Seventeenth Century*, Routledge and Kegan Paul, 1984; Slater M., 'The Weightiest Business: Marriage in an Upper Gentry Family', *Past and Present*, 72, 1976; Mendelson S.H., 'Debate: The Weightiest Business...', *Past and Present*, 85, 1979; Larminie V., 'Marriage and the Family: The Example of the Seventeenth Century Newdigates', *Midlands History*, IX, 1984
105 Prest W., *The Inns of Court under Elizabeth I and the Early Stuarts 1590–1640*, Longman, 1972, p.37
106 *Ibid*., p.215
107 See for instance, CSPD *Charles I 1626*, p.370, and various letters in HMC *Hastings*, IV, pp.204–212
108 Hutton (1982), *op. cit.*, p.36
109 Bod Lib, Dugdale Ms 19, Black, *op. cit.*; North. RO, Finch-Hatton MSS 133
110 WSL, SMS 479–564
111 LCL Ms 24; LJRO, D30 LIIIB
112 Porter S., 'The Fire Raid in the English Civil War', *War and Society*, 2, 2, 1984
113 Everett E., *The Community of Kent and the Great Rebellion*, Leicester University Press, 1973, p.130
114 BL TT E69/12, *Certaine Informations*, no. 37, 26 Sept–2 Oct 1643
115 BL Add MSS 5752, ff.398–9 Royal Commission on Historical Monuments, *Newark upon Trent: the Civil War Siegeworks*, HMSO, 1964, pp.93–4
116 Glover S., *The History, Gazetteer and Directory of the County of Derbyshire*, 1829, 1, App. , p.66, 'A True Relation of What Service has been done by Colonel John Gell...'; BL TT E105/27, *Certaine Informations* 21, 5–11 June, 1643

117 SRO D3712/4/1 Mavesyn Ridware Parish Book (Mavesyn PB); LJRO D30 LIIIB, Lichfield Accounts
118 See Royal Commission on Historical Monuments, *op. cit.*
119 The Ottley Papers, *Shropshire Archaeological Transactions* (SAT) 8, p.245
120 Bod Lib, Dugdale Ms 19 f.86
121 Wheeler J., unpublished Ph.D. Thesis, 'English Army Finance and Logistics', Berkeley, 1980, Chapter 4
122 Hutton (1982), *op. cit.*, p.93
123 Bod Lib, Dugdale Ms 19 ff.83, 105. Black, *op. cit.*, pp.210, 262
124 BL TT E308/1 *An Order Concerning the Excise*
125 Beats L., unpublished Ph.D. Thesis, 'Politics and Government in Derbyshire 1640–1660', Sheffield, 1978
126 An easily accessible account can be found in Nichols, *op. cit.*, III, 2, App. 4, p.30
127 BL TT E94/24, *A Declaration and Ordinance for the Seizing and Sequestering Estates*
128 BL TT E97/3, *Certaine Informations*, 17 April 1643; DRO D803 M29, Copybook of Sir George Gresley f.109; LRO DE730, Barker Correspondence, IV, p.15
129 Bod Lib, Dugdale Ms 19 ff.30, 115
130 LJRO D30 LIIIB
131 Dietz F.C., 'The Receipts and Issues of the Exchequer...', *Smith College Studies*, 3, 4, pp.152–3
132 Wheeler (1980), *op. cit.*, p.65
133 Hutton (1982), *op. cit.*, p.36
134 HMC *Hastings*, 2, p.116; DRO Gell MSS Box 30/5/n
135 DRO Gell MSS Box 60/16; BL Harl. MSS 6802, f.224
136 BL Add MSS 18982, f.42
137 NRO D35/5 Toton Rentals p.95; PRMW 13/2 Accounts of William Dand of Mansfield; PR 1710 Upton Constables' Accounts (Upton CA); PR 5767 Constables' Accounts of Thorpe (Thorpe CA); PR 1531 Coddington Constables' Accounts (Coddington CA)
138 BL TT E303/16, *Mercurius Veridicus*, 20–27 Sept 1645
139 BL Add MSS 5752, ff.398–9
140 LCL, MS Lich 24; LJRO, D30 LIIIB
141 Shaw S., *The History and Antiquities of the County of Staffordshire*, EP Publishing, 1976 edn, p.48
142 SRO D3451/2/2 Pattingham Parish Book (Pattingham PB) p.108; Shaw, *op. cit.*, I, pp.60–2; HMC *Hastings*, 2, pp.105, 126–7
143 BL TT E78/33, *Mercurius Aulicus*, 47th Week, 1643
144 SRO 1039, Extract of Uttoxeter Churchwardens' Accounts; Shaw, *op. cit.*, I, p.48
145 See analysis above and Appendix I
146 SRO D1454/2 Rugeley Constables' Accounts (Rugeley CA), np
147 NRO PR2130, Edwinstowe Constables Accounts (Edwinstowe CA), p.16
148 Mavesyn PB, np
149 Morrill (1980), *op. cit.*, p.37
150 Upton CA, p.15; Mavesyn PB, np
151 Pickles J.T., unpublished MA thesis, 'Studies in Royalism in the English Civil War, 1642–1646, with Special Reference to Staffordshire', Manchester 1968, p.94
152 BL TT E59/1 *Certaine Informations*, 26 June–3 July, 1643
153 BL Harl. MSS 6851, f.130, Instructions to the Commissioners of Worcestershire, f.133–4, Orders of a Council of War, March 14, 1643
154 WSL, SMS, 48–9, p.8
155 See Upton CA for the best example of this practice
156 Warrants, like receipts, were paid for: at Coddington they were 2d but at Upton they were 4d, and at Mavesyn they were 6d
157 Mavesyn PB, np
158 *Ibid.* and LRO, DE 720/30 Branston Constables' Accounts (Branston CA), pp.60–2
159 LRO D 1605/56, Stathern Constables' Accounts (Stathern CA), p.72
160 *Ibid.*; Coddington CA *passim*
161 LRO DE 625/60 Waltham on the Wolds Constables' Accounts 1608–1706 (Waltham CA), p.68
162 Branston CA, p.55; Nichols, *op. cit.*, II, 1, p.55
163 Waltham CA, pp.68–70; Branston CA, pp.60–62
164 Mavesyn PB, np; LCL, MS Lich 24, LJRO, D30 LIIB
165 Shaw, *op. cit.*, I, p.60

166 Guilford E. (ed.), 'The Accounts of the Constables of the Village of Stathern, Leicestershire', *Archaeological Journal,* 69, p.149; Branston CA, pp.58–62
167 Mavesyn PB, *passim*
168 Upton CA, *passim* for examples
169 Mavesyn PB, various pages
170 Branston CA, p.62; Waltham CA, pp.68, 70
171 Thorpe CA, np; Upton CA, pp.35–45
172 Welbeck was 'straitened' from October 22 to November 22, 1645, HMC *Portland,* I, p.290; NRO D71/1 Agreement for disgarrisoning Welbeck; DRO Gell MSS Box 30/5/n
173 LCL, MS Lich 24; LJRO, D30 LIIIB
174 LRO DE 1965/41, Belton Constables, Churchwardens and Overseers Accounts 1602–1739 (Belton CA), np
175 SRO D3539/21, Biddulph Parish Book 1630 onwards (Biddulph PB), np
176 Edwinstowe CA, p.12
177 Rugeley CA, np
178 BL Add MSS 18982, f.111
179 Long C.E. (ed.), Symonds R., *Diary of the Marches of the Royal Army,* Camden Society 1859, p.168
180 Based on the Lichfield Accounts, Staffordshire's royalists could expect around £20,000 per annum and the Scarsdale sum would if consistent throughout the county only render £6,754 per annum: thus £30,000 does not seem an underestimate
181 Mavesyn CA, np
182 Porter S., unpublished Ph.D. Thesis, 'The Destruction of Urban Property in the English Civil War 1642–1651', London 1983, pp.148–157; Porter (1984), *op. cit.,* p.37
183 LAO, Addlethorpe and Ingolmells Constables' Accounts, 12, 1637–1684, *passim*; Biddulph PB, *passim*; Branston CA, passim
184 HMC *Portland,* I, p.158, Staveley and Hacker to William Lenthall, 24/11/43
185 BL TT E77/6, *Certaine Informations,* no. 49, 20–27 November 1644; WRO, D30 LIIIB; Beats L. (Thesis), p.140
186 Waltham CA, p.70; Upton CA, pp.39, 41; Mavesyn PB, np
187 Upton CA, p.36; Guilford *op. cit.*, p.141; Mavesyn PB, np
188 Guildford *op. cit.*, p.149; Mavesyn PB, np; Upton CA, pp.16, 23
189 This does not take into account the officers' wages, nor does it include the numbers of men still in the garrisons during the field campaign; the figure will thus be an underestimate. NRO DD 49 55/49, billeting costs in Devon on Lady Button's estates show the cost of one night's billet for horse and man as being 4d each
190 LCL, MS Lich 24; HMC Hastings, 2, pp.115–6; WRO, D39 LIIIB
191 HMC Hastings, 2, p.132
192 *Ibid.*, 2, p.119
193 BL Add MSS, 5752, f.402
194 CCAM, p.1184
195 LCL, MS Lich 24
196 Rushworth; Firth and Rait
197 Everitt A., *The Community of Kent and the Great Rebellion*, Leicester University Press, 1973; Holmes C., *The Eastern Association in the English Civil War*, CUP, 1974; Wheeler J., PhD Thesis, Berkeley, 1980, 'English Army Finance and Logistics 1642–1660'
198 Firth and Rait I, p.49; North. RO, Finch Hatton MSS 133; Nichols J., *The History and Antiquities of the County of Leicestershire,* London, 1804, 3, 2, App 4, p.31
199 For full coverage see Chapter 5
200 DRO Gresley MSS D803 M29, Copybook of Sir George Gresley (Gresley Copybook) and Glover S., *The History and Gazetteer and Directory of the County of Derby,* Derby, 1829, 1, App. 'A true account of the raising and imploying of one foote regiment under John Gen' (Gell B page number following the abbreviation refers to the page in Glover)
201 Nichols *op. cit.*, 3, 2, App 4, p.31
202 *Firth and Rait,* I, pp.49–51
203 *Ibid.*, pp.85–100
204 *Ibid.*, pp.106–117; North. RO, Finch Hatton MSS
205 Details regarding each individual will be found in Appendix II
206 DRO, Gresley Copybook, pp.68–70

207 Nichols *op. cit.,* 3, 2, App 4, pp.39–40; BL TT E8/16, *Court Mercury* 9, E16/19, *Thomas Beaumont's Speech at the handing over of the Leicestershire Petition*
208 Pennington D.H., I. Roots (eds), *The Committee at Stafford, 1643–1645*, Staffordshire Historical Collections, 1957
209 Stone L., *The Crisis of the Aristocracy 1558–1641*, Clarendon Press, 1965, p.668; Stone L., 'The Educational Revolution in England', *Past and Present*, 28, 1964, p.67
210 Prest W.R., *The Inns of Court under Elizabeth I and the Early Stuarts 1590–1640*, Longman, 1972, p.37
211 BL TT E78/16, *Mercurius Aulicus*, 48th Week, 1644; Newcastle, Duchess of, *The Life of William Cavendish, Duke of Newcastle* (Newcastle *Life*), London, 1886, p.344; *Mercurius Belgicus, or a brief relation of the Battles, Sieges, Conflicts and other most Remarkable Passages…*, London, 1685 edn (*Mercurius Belgicus*), np.
212 *Firth and Rait,* 1, pp.202–214
213 Wheeler (1980), *op. cit.,* p.145
214 DRO Gresley Copybook, pp.47-48; BL TT E9/7, *Mercurius Civicus*, no. 69, 12–19 Sept, 1644, these give just two examples of such raids
215 WSL SMS 48/49 The Minute Book of the County Committee at Stafford, f.1
216 BL IT E258/4 *Perfect Occurrences*, no. 19, 13–19 December, 1644
217 Wheeler (1980), *op. cit.,* p.149
218 DRO Cell MSS 34/10, pp.3–4
219 *Journal of the House of Lords,* 1644–5, p.570, cited by Beats L., Sheffield PhD thesis, 1978, 'Politics and Government in Derbyshire 1640–1660', p.242
220 *Firth and Rait,* I, pp.106–117
221 *Ibid.*, pp.106–7; BL Harl. MSS 6851, f.158
222 *Firth and Rait,* I, pp.437–441
223 Wheeler (1980), *op. cit.,* p.140
224 SRO D260 m/f/4/18, The Composition Book of the County of Stafford
225 CCC, pp.107–112; WSL Transcription of the Papers of the Committee for Compounding with Delinquents, 6 vols
226 DRO, 258/m/58/28 Order for the Sequestration of Francis Revell's Estates
227 NRO DA18/11, Receipts of the Sequestered Estates of Robert Waring
228 Pennington and Roots, *op. cit.,* p.xxxvii
229 WSL 48/48 Minute book *passim; ibid.*, pp.163–4
230 *Ibid.*, pp.169, 178
231 See previous chapter
232 *Firth and Rait,* I, pp.85–100, 614–626; Wheeler (1980), *op. cit.,* p.174
233 *Firth and Rait,* I, pp.86–7
234 PRO SP16/348/5/1; DRO Gell MSS 31/33g, 31/10 a, b
235 WSL, SMS, 48/49 Minute book, ff.11, 17, 18
236 Pennington and Roots, *op. cit.,* pp.121–122, 209
237 *Ibid.*, p.194
238 *Ibid.*, pp.242–244
239 LRO D720130 Branston Constables' Accounts (Branston CA) pp.60–63; D625/60, Waltham on the Wolds Constables' Accounts (Waltham CA) p.67
240 NRO PR1710 Upton Constables' Accounts (Upton CA) pp.26–48
241 Malcolm J., *Caesar's Due: Loyalty and King Charles I 1642–1646,* Royal Historical Society 1983, p.185
242 Shaw S., *The History and Antiquities of Staffordshire,* EP Publishing, 1976 edn, p.48; SRO 139, Extract of Uttoxeter Churchwardens Accounts 1644–1646
243 Pennington and Roots, *op. cit.*, pp.315–330
244 Wheeler (1980), *op. cit.*, pp.102–103; Firth and Rait, I, p.615
245 *Ibid.*, pp.49–51, 53–58; Rushworth, III, 2, pp.66–67
246 Hutton R., *The Royalist War Effort 1642–1646,* Longman, 1982, pp.145–147
247 CSPD, 1644, pp.34, 52
248 Pennington and Roots, *op. cit.*, pp.lxxiv–lxxxi; Dore R.N., *The Letter Books of Sir William Brereton*, The Record Society of Lancashire and Cheshire, 1984, I, pp.18–19
249 Gell B, p.71, and the same work, Glover, *op. cit.,* I, app, 'A True Relation of what Service hath beene done by Collonell Sir John Gell' (Gell A), p.63. See also Chapter 5
250 DRO Gresley Copybook, p.106; BL TT E53/11, *Weekly Account*, no. 44, 26 June–3 July 1644; Gell A, p.67

251 See both Gell A, p.62 and Gell B, p.71; Hutchinson L., *The Life of Colonel John Hutchinson*, OUP, Oxford, 1973, p.97 (Hutchinson *Life*)
252 *Ibid.*, p.68, Lucy Hutchinson accused the Derbyshire committee of doing as much damage to Nottinghamshire as the royalists; DRO Gresley Copybook, pp.80–81, 96
253 Branston CA, p.63
254 NRO DD294/1 Replies to the Petition of the Vale of Belvoir Dwellers
255 DRO Gell MSS, Box 30/5n
256 Roy I., 'England turned Germany? The Aftermath of the Civil War in its European Context' *Transactions of the Royal Historical Society,* 5th Series, 28, 1978
257 Roy I., unpublished PhD thesis, 'The Royalist Army in the First Civil War', London, 1963; Wanklyn M., unpublished MA thesis, 'The King's Armies in the West of England, 1642–1646', Manchester, 1966; Newman P., PhD Thesis, 'The Royalist Army in Northern England, 1642–1645', York, 1978
258 Young P., *Edgehill 1642: the Campaign and the Battle,* Roundwood Press, 1967; *Marston Moor 1644: the Campaign and the Battle,* Roundwood Press, 1970; *Naseby 1645: The Campaign and the Battle,* Century Press, 1985; Newman P., *The Battle of Marston Moor,* Anthony Bird Publications, 1981
259 Smith G.R., Toynbee M., Young P., *Leaders of the Civil Wars, 1642–1648*, Roundwood Press, 1977; Newman P., *Royalist Officers in England and Wales, 1642–1660*, Garland Press, 1981
260 Newman P., 'The Royalist Officer Corps, 1642–1660: Army Command as a Reflection of the Social Structure', *The Historical Journal*, 26, 4, 1983; Blackwood D.C., *The Lancashire Gentry and the Great Rebellion, 1642–1660*, Chetham Society, 1978
261 Newman P., *Royalist Officers in England and Wales…*
262 Roy I. (ed.), *The Royalist Ordnance Papers 1642–1646*, Oxfordshire Record Society, 1964; see also Peter Young's contribution to Royal Commission on Historical Monuments, *Newark Upon Trent, the Civil War Siegeworks*, HMSO, 1964, pp.18–19
263 Newman (1978), *op. cit.*, p.11
264 Brighton J.T., *Royalists and Roundheads in Derbyshire,* Bakewell and District Historical Society, 1981
265 HMC Hastings 2, p.85, Charles I to Hastings, 1/8/42
266 BL TT E83/9, *A Catalogue…, of the King's Marching Army*
267 HMC Hastings 2, p.87, Charles I to Hastings, 22/11/42
268 Phillips W., 'The Ottley Papers Relating to the Civil War', *Shropshire Archaeological Transactions, 1894–6*, (Ottley Papers) 6, p.49, Hastings to Ottley, 12/12/42; Glover S., *The History, Gazetteer and Directory of the County of Derby*, Derby, 1929, 1, Appendix, 'A True Relation of what service hath been done by Collonell Sir John Gell', (Gell A), p.62
269 Warburton E., *Memoirs of Prince Rupert and the Cavaliers,* London, 1849, 2, p.96, Hastings to Prince Rupert, 17/1/43; 'Ottley Papers', 6, p.74, Eyton to Ottley, 18/2/43
270 BL Add MSS 36913, f.125
271 Long C.E. (ed.), Symonds R., *The Diary of the Marches of the King's Army*, Camden Society, 1858, p.181 (*Symonds' Diary*)
272 Fosbrooke T.H., Ashby-de-la-Zouch Castle, Leicestershire, Leicestershire Museums and Art Gallery, nd, pp.21–23; *ibid.*, p.281
273 Roy 1964, pp.169–170
274 Gell A, p.62
275 BL TT E67/7, *Mercurius Aulicus*, 35th Week, 1643
276 *Rushworth,* III, 2, p.772
277 HMC Portland, I, p.82
278 BL TT E85/45, *Certaine Informations*, no. 1, 16–23 Jan, 1643
279 BL Harl. MSS 986, *Notebook of Richard Symonds* (*Symonds' Notebook*); Fosbrooke, *op. cit.*, pp.21–23; HMC Hastings 2, p.129
280 PRO SP 29/68, 19, A List of Officers Claiming to the £60,000 etc Granted by his Sacred Majesty for the Relief of His Truly Loyal and Indigent Party (List), col. 103
281 Fosbrooke, *op. cit.*, pp.21–23
282 *Symonds' Notebook*, f.95
283 CSPD, 1644, p.191
284 *Symonds' Notebook*, f.95
285 HMC Hastings 2, p.90
286 Brighton, *op. cit.*, pp.26, 41; Newman, *Royalist Officers…*, nos 568, 115

287 *Symonds' Diary*, p.224; *Mercurius Belgicus, or a brief chronology of the Battels, Sieges, Conflicts and Other Most Remarkable Passages from the beginning of this Rebellion to the 25th of March, 1646* (*Mercurius Belgicus*), ?London, 1685, no pagination; RCHM, *op. cit.*, p.77; Gell A, p.68
288 HMC Hastings 2, p.123; CSPD, 1644, p.191
289 Hutchinson L., *The Life of Colonel John Hutchinson*, OUP, 1973 (Hutchinson *Life*), p.122
290 BL TT E29/9, *Mercurius Aulicus*, 1st Week, 1644; Gell A, p.64, and same work, 'A True Account of the raising an imploying of one Foote Regiment under John Gell' (Gell B), p.74
291 *Symonds' Notebook*, f.94
292 See Appendix III
293 Young P., *Marston Moor*, (facing) p.145, De Gomme's Map
294 Brighton, *op. cit.*, p.44; Young, *Naseby*, p.74
295 *Symonds' Notebook*, f.92; list, col. 80
296 HMC Hastings 2, p.132
297 *Ibid.*, p.114; DRO 803/M/211
298 BL TT E8/20, *Mercurius Aulicus*, 33rd Week, 1644
299 DRO Gell MSS, Box 66/2/i; *Mercurius Belgicus*, np
300 *Symonds' Notebook*, f.95; list, col. 144
301 BL TT E325/22, *Perfect Passages*, no. 28, 1646; CSPD, 1645–6, p.352
302 Gell B, p.70
303 Glover, *op. cit.*, 1, app. , p.81, William Brereton's Account of the Battle of Hopton Heath
304 HMC Hastings 2, p.111
305 BL Add MSS 11043, f.15; Webb J., Webb T.W., ads, *Military Memoir of Colonel John Birch*, Camden Society, 1873, p.113
306 Young, *Edgehill*, p.221
307 BL TT E99/18, *The Battle of Hopton Heath*
308 LCL, MS Lich 24, The Accounts of Collonel Bagot
309 HMC Hastings 2, pp.116, 121, 127; *Symonds' Notebook*, f.93
310 *Symonds' Diary*, p.172
311 LJRO D30 LIIIB, Contributions to the Garrison in the Close
312 LCL MS Lich 24
313 *Symonds' Notebook*, f.93
314 LJRO D30 LIIIB
315 Young, *Edgehill*, p.211
316 HMC Hastings 2, p.98
317 WSL SMS 480, Bagot to Hastings, 22/4/44; CSPD, 1643–4, p.178
318 Fosbrooke, *op. cit.*, pp.21–23
319 Black W.H., 'Docquets of Letters Patent and other Instruments of Government', unpublished, PRO Chancery Lane (Black *Docquets*), p.35
320 *Symonds Diary*, p.169
321 *Mercurius Belgicus*, np, referring to June 1644; Shaw S., *The History and Antiquities of the County of Staffordshire*, E.P. Publishing, 1976, pp.60–63
322 See Appendix III
323 HMC Hastings 2, p.127; WSL SMS, 550, several letters; BL Add MSS 18981, f.89
324 *Symonds' Notebook*, f.95; HMC Hastings 2, pp.105–6, Nicholas to Hastings, 14/10/43
325 *Ibid.*, p.102; BL TT E71/22, *Certaine Informations*, no. 40, 16–23 Oct 1643
326 *Symonds' Notebook*, f.92; list, cols 87, 144
327 Fosbrooke, *op. cit.*, pp.21–23
328 Warburton, *op. cit.*, 2, p.98
329 BL Add MSS 18982, f.42
330 *Symonds' Notebook*, f.93
331 HMC Hastings 2, p.110, Lucas to Hastings, 10/11/43
332 List, col. 110; *Symonds' Diary*, p.116; *Symonds' Notebook*, f.93
333 HMC Hastings 2, p.117
334 Dugdale MS 19, ff.42b, 85b; Black, *Docquets*, p.163
335 *Symonds' Notebook*, f.95
336 Parliamentarians certainly thought this was so, see CSPD, 1644, p.191
337 LRO OS 126, Hastings to Rupert, ?summer 1643
338 *Symonds' Diary*, p.173
339 There is little evidence to suggest how drastic this was, the burial details of St Helen's Ashby were not kept for the duration of the plague. *Mercurius Veridicus* of September 27th, 1645 reported

that the garrison was down to 60 men, cited Nichols J., *The History and Antiquities of the County of Leicester* (Nichols Leicestershire) III, 2, App. 4, p.65

340 Malcolm J., *Caesar's Due: Loyalty and King Charles, 1642–1646*, Royal Historical Society, 1983, pp.190–193.

341 This is if regimental strengths are accepted as 1,300 for foot and *c*.500 for horse, see above

342 List, full title above no. 24

343 See no. 23

344 Bod Lib, Dugdale Ms 19; Black, *Docquets*

345 BL TT E83/9

346 Blackwood (1978), *op. cit.*, p.166

347 Morrill, J.S., 'The Northern Gentry and the Great Rebellion', *Northern History*, 15, 1979, is one good example

348 See Appendix III, for details of individuals

349 See Chapter 2, no. 30 for the details of this discussion

350 Kearney H.F., *Strafford in Ireland: A Study in Absolutism,* Manchester University Press, 1961 edn, p.261

351 See CCC and CCAM; Peacock M.G.W., *Index of the Royalists whose Estates were Confiscated during the Commonwealth,* Index Society 1878; also, the WSL Transcripts of Staffordshire Composition Papers; SRO D260, M/F/4/18, The Composition books of the Committee of Stafford; BL Harl. MSS 2043, f.11, List of Leicestershire Gentry who Compounded

352 CCC, p.1022

353 *Ibid.*, pp.946–7

354 CSPD, 1646, p.325

355 CCC, p.1089

356 CCC, pp.961–2

357 Newman, *Royalist Officers...*, no. 359 (Sir Hugh Calverley)

358 BL TT E81/19, *Mercurius Aulicus*, 52nd Week, 1643; *Mercurius Belgicus*, np; Dore, R.N. (ed.), *The Letter Books of Sir William Brereton,* Record Society of Lancashire and Cheshire, 1984, 1, pp.300–1

359 Newman, *Royalist Officers...*, no. 453

360 Newman (1978), *op. cit.*, pp.34, 43–9

361 Blackwood (1978), *op. cit.*, p.166

362 Newman, 'The Royalist Officer Corps...', HJ, 26, 4, p.949

363 *Symonds' Notebook*, f.93

364 CCC, p.1380 (Captain Merry)

365 Malcolm, *op. cit.,* pp.149–158; BL TT E273/13, *Mercurius Aulicus*, 8th Week, 23 Feb–2 Mar 1645, report of an enemy trumpeter's assertion that the royalist officers were younger sons of gentry, no tradesmen. If Malcolm is correct about the royalists' elitist self-perception, then this may be a piece of royalist fiction.

366 CCC, p.1684 (Captain Orme)

367 *Ibid.*, p.2010; Peacock, *op. cit.*, p.47

368 *Ibid.,* p.1207; Brighton, *op. cit.,* p.33

369 CCC, p.1202

370 Foster J. (ed.), *Alumni Oxonienses, 1500–1714*, Kraus, 1968; Venn J. and J.A. (eds), *Alumni Cantabrigienses*, Part One, Cambridge, 1922–7

371 Stone L., 'The Educational Revolution in England, 1560–1640', *Past and Present*, 28, p.76

372 *Ibid.*, p.67

373 Prest W., *The Inns of Court under Elizabeth I and the Early Stuarts, 1590–1640*, Longman, 1972, pp.27–9

374 Newman P., 'Catholic Royalists in the North of England, 1642–1645', *Northern History*, 1979, p.94

375 See Appendix III

376 Bossy J., *The English Catholic Community 1570–1850,* Darton, Longman, Todd, 1975, p.100

377 Newman, 'The Royalist Officer Corps...', pp.945–958

378 HMC Hastings 2, p.153

379 Fletcher A., *The Outbreak of the English Civil War,* Arnold, 1981, p.365; Hutton R., *The Royalist War Effort,* Longman, 1982, pp.19–21; HMC *Hastings* 2, p.86

380 Nichols J., *The History and Antiquities of the County of Leicester*, Leicester, 1804, III, 2, App. 4, p.30

381 *Ibid.*, p.31; Stocks H.E. (ed.), *Records of the Borough of Leicester 1603–1689*, Cambridge University Press (CUP), 1923, pp.317–319
382 See Hutton, *op. cit.*, p.24, for a discussion of this.
383 Firth C., 'The Journal of Prince Rupert's Marches', *English Historical Review*, XIII, (JPR), p.730
384 *Ibid.*, p.730; Hutton (1980), *op. cit.*, p.25
385 JPR, p.730
386 Freshville served with Wilmot's Horse, and so did his later major John Jammot, giving rise to the suggestion that the eventual regiment that Freshville had in the North Midlands Army was created from his troop in Wilmot's.
387 JPR, p.730
388 DRO D830 M29, Copybook of Sir George Gresley; Glover S., The *History, Directory and Gazetteer of the County of Derby*, Derby, 1829, I, Appendix, 'A True Relation of What Service Hath been Done by Collonell Sir John Gell' (Gell A), p.62
389 Gell A, p.62
390 Pickles J.T., unpublished MA thesis, 'Studies in Royalism in the English Civil War, 1642–1646, With Special Reference to Staffordshire', Manchester, 1968, p.61
391 SRO, Quarter Sessions Records, 15/11/42, f.1
392 Pickles (1968), *op. cit.*, p.63
393 HMC Hastings 2, p.87, Charles to Hastings, 22/11/42; Roy I. (ed.), *The Royalist Ordnance Papers*, Oxfordshire Record Society, 1964, 1, p.70
394 Gell A, p.62
395 *Ibid.*, p.62
396 Phillips W., 'The Ottley Papers Relating to the Civil War', *Shropshire Archaeological Transactions, 1894–1896* (Ottley Papers), 6, p.94
397 HMC Portland 1, p.82, Henry Nevill to the inhabitants of Liddington, Stoke and Bisbrooke, 28/12/42
398 Nichols, *op. cit.*, III, 2, App. 4, p.31
399 *Ibid.*, III, 2, App. 4, p.31
400 Rushworth, II, 1, pp.66–67
401 Hutchinson L., *The Life of Colonel John Hutchinson*, OUP, 1973 (Hutchinson *Life*), p.74
402 Glover, *op. cit.*, appendix, 'A True Account of the Raising and Employing of one Regiment of Foote under Sir John Gell' (Gell B), p.70
403 Rushworth, III, 1, pp.66–67
404 Gell A, p.62; Gell B, p.70
405 DRO, Gresley Copybook, f.49
406 *Ibid.*, ff.47–48
407 *Ibid.*, f.50
408 BL TT E86/22, *Mercurius Aulicus*, 2nd Week, 1643; Gell A, p.62; Gell B, p.71
409 Warburton E., *Memoirs of Prince Rupert and the Cavaliers*, London, 1849, 2, p.96, Hastings to Rupert, 17/1/43; BL TT E86/1, *Special Passages*, no.24, 17–24 Jan, 1643; Gell A, p.63;; Gell B, p.71; HMC Hastings 2, p.88, Rupert to Hastings, 22/1/43
410 BL TT E85/45, *Certaine Informations*, no. 1, Jan 16–25, 1643
411 Gell A, p.63; Gell B, p.71
412 HMC Hastings 2, p.88
413 JPR, p.732
414 *Ottley Papers*, 6, p.65, Bridgeman to Ottley, 25/1/43; BL Add MSS 3691, ff.124–126; Hutton, *op. cit.*, pp.44–45
415 Warburton, *op. cit.*, 2, p.98
416 HMC Hastings 2, p.88
417 *Ibid.*, p.89
418 *Ibid.*, pp.89–90
419 *Ibid.*, p.91, Littleton to Hastings, 9/2/43
420 Ottley Papers, 6, p.74
421 *Ibid.*, 6, pp.75–76
422 HMC Hastings 2, p.93, Nicholas to Hastings, 21/2/43; Ottley Papers, 6, pp.75–76, James to Ottley, 25/2/43
423 Roy, *op. cit.*, 2, p.202; BL Add MSS, 36913, Aston Papers, 3, f.125
424 Hutchinson *Life*, pp.74–76; BL TT E92/3, *Certaine Informations*, 20 Feb–6 Mar; E86/41, *Mercurius Aulicus*, 9th Week
425 BL TT E91/23, *Special Passages*, 34, 23 Feb–2 Mar

426 Philip I.G. (ed.), *Journal of Sir Samuel Luke*, Oxfordshire Record Society, 1950–1953 (Luke), 1, p.20; Ottley Papers, 6, pp.75–6, 78
427 WSL, Burney's Newspapers, p.6; *Perfect Diurnal*, 28 Feb–6 Mar; BL TT E92/8, *Special Passages*, 28 Feb–7 Mar
428 Gell A, p.63
429 Shaw S., *The History and Antiquities of Staffordshire*, E.P. Publishing, 1976 edn, 1, p.52
430 Ottley Papers, 7, p.276, James to Ottley, 10/3/43
431 Shaw, *op. cit.*, p.52
432 SRO D868/2/69, Account of the Battle of Hopton Heath
433 Brighton J.T., 'Sir John Gell and the Civil War in Derbyshire', *Journal of the Bakewell and District Historical Society*, 8, pp.55–56
434 SRO D868/2/69 and *Mercurius Aulicus*, 12th Week, 1643 as cited by Brighton *op. cit.*
435 HMC *Hastings* 2, pp.94–95, Nicholas to Hastings, 25/2/43; BL TT E92/20, *Certaine Informations*, 20 Mar–3 April
436 Brereton's account can be found in Glover, op. cit, 1, app, pp.55–56; LCL MS Lich 24; Young P., 'The Battle of Hopton Heath', *Journal of the Society for Army Historical Research* (*JSAHR*), 33, part 133, p.35
437 HMC Hastings 2, pp.94–95, Nicholas to Hastings, 25/2/43
438 *Ibid.*, 2, p.96, Bromley to Hastings, 22/3/43; WSL SMS, 487, Falkland to Capel, 26/3/43; *Historical Collections for a History of Staffordshire* (HCS), 1941, p.139, Hastings to Rupert, 27/3/43
439 JPR, p.733; HMC Hastings 2, p.97, Nicholas to Hastings (2), 5/4/43; HMC Portland 1, p.106; BL TT E94/29, *Certaine Informations*, no. 11, 27 Mar–3 Apr; *Mercurius Belgicus or a Brief Chronology of the Battles, Sieges, Conflicts and Other Most Remarkable Passages from the beginning of this Rebellion to the 25th of March 1646*, ?London 1685 edn, np (*Mercurius Belgicus*)
440 WSL SMS 550, Hastings to Rupert, 13/4/43
441 Luke, 1, p.63
442 Warburton, *op. cit.*, 2, p.171, Charles to Rupert, 16/4/43
443 JPR, p.733
444 *Ibid.*, p.733; *Mercurius Belgicus*, np
445 LCL MS Lich 24
446 BL Harl. MSS 6851, ff.140, 155
447 JPR, p.733
448 HMC Hastings 2, p.981 Nicholas to Hastings, 19/4/43
449 *Ibid.*, same letter; Luke, 1, p.56; BL TT E100/10, *Certaine Informations*, 24 Apr–1 May; Verney, F. Parthenope, *Memoirs of the Verney Family during the Civil War* (Verney), Tabard Press, 1970, pp.154–156
450 BL Add MSS 18980, f.36, Hastings to Rupert, 4/4/43; WSL SMS 550, Hastings to Rupert, 7/5/43
451 HMC Hastings 2, pp.98–99, Nicholas to Hastings, 315143; Warburton *op. cit.*, 2, p.1891 Nicholas to Rupert, 11/5/43
452 HMC Hastings 2, p.1011 Nicholas to Hastings, 14/5/43
453 BL TT E101/2, *Certaine Informations*, 1–8 May, 1643; Gell A, p.64
454 HMC Hastings 2, p.98, Lane to Hastings, 20/4/43
455 *Ibid.*, 2, p.102, Wolseley to Hastings, ?/25/43
456 *Hutchinson Life*, p.81
457 BL TT E101/19, *Kingdomes Weekly Intelligencer*, 9–15 June, 1643
458 HMC *Hastings* 2, pp.102–103, Henrietta Maria to Hastings, 1/6/43
459 HMC *Portland* 1, p.120, Skeffington to Lenthall, 24/6/43
460 Gell A, p.64; BL TT E60/8, *The Parliament Scout*, 6–13 July, 1643
461 York Central Library (YCL), 942 CW3, Collections of Civil War Pamphlets, 'Two Intercepted Letters'; BL TT E60/8 as above
462 BL TT E61/11, *Mercurius Civicus*, no. 8, 1643
463 JPR, pp.733–734
464 Hutchinson *Life*, p.87
465 BL TT E105/27, *Certaine Informations*, 5–11 June, 1643; E244/16, *Perfect Diurnall*, 5–11 June, 1643; E59/1, *Certaine Informations*, 26 June–3 July
466 BL TT E64/11, *Mercurius Aulicus*, 30th Week, 1643; WSL SMS, 562, Nicholas to Rupert, 27/7/43
467 BL TT E61/26, *Speciall and Remarkable Passages*, 20–27 July, 1643; E61/25, *Certaine Informations*, 20–27 July; Hutchinson *Life*, p.82

468 BL TT E62/8, *Special and Remarkable Passages*, 21–28 July; E65/13, *Mercurius Aulicus*, 31st Week, 1643; Newcastle M., *The Life of William Cavendish, Duke of Newcastle* (Newcastle *Life*), London, 1886, pp.54–56; Luke, 2, p.127
469 BL TT E64/7, *Certaine Informations*, 29 July–5 Aug, 1643
470 Luke, 2, p.137; BL TT E65/33, *Special and Remarkable Passages*, 10–18 Aug, 1643
471 BL TT E67/3, *Certaine Informations*, 4–11 Sept, 1643; E67/7, *Mercurius Aulicus*, 35th Week, 1643; E250/11, *Weekly Account*, 6–13 Sept; E250/8, *Perfect Diurnal*, 4–11 Sept, 1643; HMC Hastings 2, pp.105–106, Nicholas to Hastings, 14/10/43
472 BL TT E59/1, *Certaine Informations*, 26 June–3 July, 1643; HCS, 1941, p.139
473 BL TT E250/11, *Weekly Account*, 6–11 Sept, 1643
474 BL TT E69/17, *Certaine Informations*, 25 Sep–2 Oct, 1643; E71/8, *Mercurius Aulicus*, 40th Week, 1643
475 LRO DE 2161, Newcastle to Hastings, 18/9/43
476 *Hutchinson Life*, pp.96–100; Brown C., *The Annals of Newark upon Trent*, London, 1907, pp.101–121; Brown C., *The History of Newark upon Trent*, London, 1879, p.63
477 *Newcastle Life*, p.60; HMC *Hastings* 2, pp.105–106, Henderson to Hastings, 11/10/43, Widdrington to Hastings, 12/10/43
478 *Ibid.*, 2, p.102, Nicholas to Hastings, 5/10/43, p.106, Hastings to Capel, 16/10/43
479 BL TT E71/22, *Certaine Informations*, 16–23 Oct, 1643; Brown (1907), *op. cit.*, pp.120–121
480 HMC *Hastings* 2, p.107, Newcastle to Hastings, 17/10/43; BL TT E252/3, *Perfect Diurnal*, 16–23 Oct, 1643
481 Trease G., *Portrait of a Cavalier*, Macmillan, 1979, p.122
482 Bod Lib, Dugdale Ms19, f.37b; Black W.H., 'Docquets of Letters Patent and other Instruments of Government' (Black *Docquets*), unpublished copy in PRO, p.95
483 BL TT E75/30, *Certaine Informations*, 6–13 Nov, 1643; E75/9, *Shropshire's Misery*, E252/18, *Perfect Diurnal*, 23–30 Oct, 1643
484 BL TT E7618, *The Parliament Scout*, 10–17 Nov, 1643
485 BL TT E77/6, *Certaine Informations*, 20–27 Nov, 1643
486 BL TT E78/16, *Mercurius Aulicus*, 48th Week, 1643; Newcastle *Life*, p.344
487 Nichols, *op. cit.*, III, 2, App. 4, p.32, Grey to Parliament, 7/12/43
488 WSL SMS 550, Hastings to Rupert, 29/11/43; BL TT E77/31, *Weekly Account*, 30 Nov–6 Dec, 1643; E78/10, *Remarkable Passages*, no.5, 1643
489 Gell B, p.73
490 Newcastle *Life*, p.346; HMC Portland 1, p.162; Luke, 3, p.202
491 HMC Hastings 2, p.110, Lucas to Hastings, 10/12/43
492 Newcastle *Life*, pp.62, 342; BL TT E80/8, *Mercurius Aulicus*, 51st Week, 1643; Gell A, p.64; Gell B, pp.73–74; Luke, 3, pp.224–225
493 Brighton J.T., *Royalists and Roundheads in Derbyshire*, Bakewell and District Historical Society, 1981, pp.26–27
494 HMC Hastings 2, pp.114, 116, 120
495 *Ibid.*, p.116
496 Gell B, p.74
497 HMC *Hastings* 2, p.117
498 BL TT E77/6, *Certaine Informations*, 20–27 Nov, 1643
499 BL TT E78/33, *Mercurius Aulicus*, 48th week, 1643
500 See above for references to Leicestershire; Gell B, p.73; *Newcastle Life*, pp.63, 65; BL TT E78/10, *Remarkable Passages*, no.5, 1643, *Mercurius Belgicus*, np; Hutton, *op. cit.*, p.125
501 Newcastle *Life*, p.63; BL Harl. MSS 986, Notebook of Richard Symonds (*Symonds' Notebook*), f.92
502 Newcastle *Life*, p.65
503 HMC Portland 1, p.165; BL TT E81/8, *Certaine Informations*, 1–8 Jan, 1644
504 See Bennett M., 'Contribution and Assessment; Financial Exactions in the English Civil War', *War and Society*, 4, 1
505 Hutchinson *Life*, p.113
506 Brown (1879), *op. cit.*, pp.64–65, Petition of Newark to King Charles
507 Warburton, *op. cit.*, 2, pp.372–373, Hastings to Rupert, 6/2/44
508 Gell A, p.64
509 HMC *Hastings* 2, p.120, Hastings to ?, 14/2/44
510 *Ibid.*, 2, p.119, Leveson to Hastings, 7/2/44, p.121, Nicholas to Hastings, 16/2/44; WSL SMS, 550, Leveson to Rupert, 8/2/44; LCL MS Lich 24

511 Hamper W. (ed.), *The Life Diary and Correspondence of Sir William Dugdale* (Dugdale *Diary*), London, 1857, p.51; HMC *Hastings* 2, pp.122–123, Freshville to Hastings, 29/2/44
512 Letter as above and HMC *Hastings* 2, p.123, Archer to Hastings, 29/2/44
513 Gell A, p.64
514 Rushworth, III, 2, p.304
515 Wood A., *Nottinghamshire in the Civil War*, S.R. Publishers, 1971 edn (original 1937); Young P., 'The Royalist Army at the Relief of Newark', *JSAHR*, 30, no.124, 1952; Royal Commission on Historical Monuments, *Newark on Trent: The Civil War Siegeworks*, HMSO, 1964
516 HMC *Hastings* 2, p.120, Byron to Hastings, 12/2/44
517 *Ibid.*, 2, p.124, Thorold to Sutton, ?7/3/44
518 Wood A.C. (ed.), *Memorials of the Holles Family* (*Holles Family*), Camden Society, 1937, pp.188–189
519 Warburton, *op. cit.*, 2, p.3711 Lucas to Rupert, 2/3/44; and the Thorold letter cited in no.139
520 HMC *Hastings* 2, p.123, Freshville to Hastings, 3/3/44; Wood, *op. cit.*, p.74, citing *Fairfax Correspondence*; 'The Civil War', pp. 82–84
521 HMC Hastings 2, p.1231 Hastings to ?, 6/3/44
522 *Ibid.*, p.124
523 *Ibid.*, 2, p.125, Rupert to Hastings, 9/3/44
524 Nottingham County Library, Civil War Pamphlets, *Prince Rupert's Raising of the Siege of Newark upon Trent*
525 JPR, p.735
526 Rushworth, III, 2, p.305
527 BL Add MS 18981, f.89, Hastings to Rupert, 16/3/44
528 NRO, 1710, Upton Constables' Accounts, p.16; *Hutchinson Life,* p.122
529 BL Add MS 18981, f.89, letter as above no.149
530 Hensman E.W., 'Mountsorrel', Dryden A. (ed.), *Memorials of Old Leicestershire*, Ballantyne, 1911, pp.126–127, citing 'The Examination of Captain George Palmer'
531 BL Add MSS, 18981, f.90, Hastings to Rupert, 17/3/44
532 Hensman, *op. cit.*, pp.126–127; *Hutchinson Life,* p.122
533 JPR, p.735
534 NRO, DD2B/3/36, Brief of the case between Arnold and Dahill, refers to enclosures destroyed in March 1644; JPR, p.735
535 Nottingham County Library, Civil War Pamphlets, 'His Highness…'
536 Wood, *op. cit.,* and Young, 'Royalist Army at the Relief of Newark', for example
537 JPR, pp.735–736
538 CSPD, 1644, p.77
539 Hutton R., *The Royalist War Effort,* Longman, 1982, p.100
540 HMC Hastings 2, pp.106, 114
541 BL Harl. MSS, 986, 'Notebook of Richard Symonds' (*Symonds' Notebook*), f.93; Newman P., *Royalist Officers in England and Wales 1642–1660,* Garland Press, 1981, no. 94
542 Glover S., *The History, Directory and Gazetteer of the County of Derby*, Derby, 1829, 1, Appendix, 'A True Account of the Raising and Employing of one Regiment of Foot under Sir John Gell' (Gell B), p.74, here Bolsover is referred to as Newcastle's own garrison
543 Hutton (1980), *op. cit.*, p.100
544 HMC Hastings 2, p.106
545 *Ibid.*, 2, p.116, Bagot to Hastings, 16/1/44
546 *Ibid.*, 2, p.106, Nichols to Hastings, 17/10/43
547 *Ibid.*, 2, p.108, Nichols to Hastings, 28/11/43
548 *Ibid.*, 2, pp.109-110, postscript to Nichols to Hastings, 10/12/43
549 *Ibid.*, 2, p.116, as note 7, p.121, Gorges to Hastings, 16/2/44; Lichfield Cathedral Library (LCL), MS Lich 24
550 HMC *Hastings* 2, p.119, Leveson to Hastings, 7/2/44; WSL SMS 550, Leveson to Rupert, 8/2/44
551 HMC Hastings 2, p.12I, as note 11, pp.121-122, Gorges to Hastings, 22/2/44; Hutton, *op. cit.*, p.101
552 HMC Hastings 2, p.116, Freshville to Hastings, 18/1/44
553 *Ibid.*, 2, pp.116-117, Molyneux to Hastings, 19/1/44; DRO 803m/211, Orders regarding well usage at Wingfield
554 HMC Hastings 2, p.114, Nicholas to Hastings, 14/1/44
555 BL Add MSS 18982, f.47

556 Wood A.C., *Nottinghamshire in the Civil War,* S.R. Publishers, 1971 edn (original 1937), and Royal Commission on Historical Monuments, *Newark on Trent the Civil War Siegeworks,* HMSO, 1964
557 HMC *Hastings* 2, p.114, as note 16; BL Add MSS, 18982, f.47
558 Newman P., 'The Defeat of John Belasyse: Civil War in Yorkshire, January–April, 1644', *Yorkshire Archaeological Journal,* 52, 1980, pp. 128–129
559 *Ibid.*, p.131
560 Warburton E., *The Memoirs of Prince Rupert and the Cavaliers,* London, 1849, 2, p.523, Porter to Rupert, 30/3/44
561 WSL SMS 550, Hastings to Rupert, 6/4/44
562 *Ibid.*, Hastings to Rupert, 8/4/44
563 Warburton, *op. cit.,* 2, pp.453–454, Newcastle to Charles, 18/4/44
564 HMC *Hastings* 2, p.126, Charles to Hastings, 17/4/44
565 WSL SMS 550, as note 24
566 HMC *Hastings* 2, pp.126-127, Bagot to Hastings, 21/4/44
567 As note 24
568 WSL SMS 550, Hastings to Rupert, 13/4/44
569 HMC *Hastings* 2, p.126, Charles to Hastings, 17/4/44
570 *Ibid.,* 2, as note 28; WSL SMS 550, Bagot to Hastings, 22/4/44
571 HMC *Hastings* 2, as note 28; WSL SMS 550, Hastings to Rupert, 2, 13 and 16/4/44
572 CSPD, 1644, p.191
573 HMC *Hastings* 2, p.127, Goring to Hastings, 26/4/44, p.126-127, Nichols to Hastings, 30/4/44
574 *Ibid.,* p.128, Freshville to Hastings, 5/5/44
575 *Rushworth,* III, 2, p.621; Firth C., 'The Journal of Prince Rupert's Marches' (JPR), *English Historical Review,* XIII, p.736
576 BL TT E49/21, *News from Prince Rupert*
577 BL TT E49/29, *Letters…*, letter of 29/5/44
578 BL TT E49/21, *News from Prince Rupert*; JPR, p.736
579 *CSPD,* 1644, p.178; BL Stowe MSS, 155, f.179
580 JPR, p.736
581 BL TT E53/11, *Weekly Account*, 26 June–3 July, 1644
582 Long C.E. (ed.), Symonds R., *The Diary of the Marches of the Kings Army* (*Symonds' Diary*), Camden Society, 1858, p.13; *Rushworth,* II, 2, p.676; 'Mercurius Belgicus or a Brief Chronology of the Battles, Sieges Conflicts and other Most Remarkable Passages from the beginning of this Rebellion to the 26th March 1646' (*Mercurius Belgicus*), ?London, 1685 edn, np; Hutton, *op. cit.,* p.146
583 Hutton, *op. cit.*, pp.146–147; WSL Burney's Newspapers, p.21, *Perfect Occurrences*, 15–22 June
584 This account is the result of study of, Young P., *Marston Moor 1644: The Campaign and the Battle,* Roundwood Press, 1970, in particular the primary sources contained within, and Newman P., *The Battle of Marston Moor,* Anthony Bird Publications, 1891
585 CSPD, 1644, p.191
586 See previous chapter
587 Newman, *Marston Moor,* p.119, the chapter in which the quotation is contained takes its title from it
588 HMC Hastings 2, p.120, Hastings to his cousin, 14/2/44
589 *Ibid.*, 2, pp.129–130, Byron to Hastings and Byron to Rupert, 6/7/44
590 *Ibid.*, 2, p.131, Byron to Hastings, 8/7/44
591 Glover, *op. cit.,* 1, App. , 'A True Relation of what has been done by Colonel John Gell' (Gell A), p.65; HMC *Hastings* 2, pp.131–132, Byron to Hastings, 19/7/44
592 Gell A, p.67
593 WSL, 'Burney's Newspapers', pp.22–23, *Perfect Occurrences*, 19–26 July, 1644
594 DRO D830 M29, 'Copybook of Sir George Gresley' (Gresley Copybook), p.88, Hastings to Bagot, 30/7/44; JPR, p.736
595 Gell A, p.66
596 WSL, 'Burney's Newspapers', p.23, *Perfect Occurrences*, 2–9 Aug, 1644; BL TT E8/20, *Mercurius Aulicus*, 33rd Week, 1644; Gell A, p.66
597 Gresley Copybook, p.87, Molyneux to Hastings, 30/7/44
598 WSL SMS 550, Hastings to Rupert, 27/?4/44

599 Newcastle M., *The Life of William Cavendish, Duke of Newcastle* (Newcastle *Life*), London, 1886, p.164; *Rushworth*, III, 2, p.644; Turberville A.S., *A History of Welbeck Abbey and its Owners, 1, 1539–1755*, Faber and Faber, 1937, p.112
600 Gresley Copybook, p.91, Fairfax to the Derby Committee, 7/8/44; *Rushworth*, III, 2, p.644; Wood A.C. (ed.), *Memorials of the Holles Family* (*Holles Family*), Camden Society, 1937, p.161
601 Newcastle *Life*, p.164; Rushworth, III, 2, p.664
602 Gell A., p.69; DRO Gell MSS, 56/28e; WSL, 'Burney's Newspapers', p.25, *Diary or Exact Journal*, 21–28 Aug
603 WSL, 'Burney's Newspapers', p.25 *ibid.*
604 Holmes C., *Seventeenth Century Lincolnshire*, History of Lincolnshire Committee, 1980, p.174
605 BL TT E10/19, *Mercurius Aulicus*, 35th Week, 1644; E8/19, *True Intelligencer*, 17–24 Aug, 1644
606 BL TT E8/20, *Mercurius Aulicus*, 33rd Week, 1644; Beats L., unpublished PhD Thesis, 'Politics and Government in Derbyshire, 1640–1660', Sheffield, 1978, p.159; 'The East Midland Association, 1642–1644', *Midlands History*, IV, 1978, pp.170–171
607 Gresley Copybook, p.102, Leicestershire Committee to the Derbyshire Committee, 16/9/44
608 BL Add MSS, 18982, £47
609 BL TT E10/7, *Kingdomes Weekly Intelligencer*, 17–24 Sept, 1644
610 HMC *Hastings* 2, p.132, Kniveton to Hastings, 11/9/44; Gresley Copybook, p.109
611 BL TT E8/16, *Court Mercury*, 31 Aug–8 Sept, 1644; E16/19, Thomas *Beaumont's Speech at the handing in of the Leicestershire Petition*; Nichols J., *The History and Antiquities of the County of Leicester*, III, 2, App. 4, pp.39–40
612 Holmes (1980), *op. cit.*, p.175
613 Gell A, p.64; BL TT E13/11, *Perfect Passages*, 30 Oct–6 Nov, 1644; E13/14, *Mercurius Civicus*, 31 Oct–7 Nov, 1644; E13/15, *The Parliament Scout*, 31 Oct–7 Nov, 1644
614 Holles Family, p.161
615 BL TT E12/4, *Country Messenger*, 4–11 Oct, 1644; E13/10, *Weekly Account*, 16–23 Oct, 1644
616 BL TT E256/30, *Perfect Occurrences*, 22–29 Nov
617 Gresley Copybook, pp.106-107; Gell A, p.63; BL TT E256/30, *Perfect Occurrences*, 22–29 Nov
618 Gresley Copybook, p.107, BL TT E256/30 as above
619 WSL SMS 481, Bagot to Rupert, 21/11/44, SMS 547, Leveson to Rupert, 1/12/44
620 Hutton, *op. cit.*, p.153
621 BL TT E258/1, *Perfect Occurrences*, 6–13 Dec, 1644
622 BL TT E258/4, *Perfect Occurrences*, 13–20 Dec, 1644
623 Warburton (1849), *op. cit.*, 3, pp.49–50, Rhodes to Rupert, 10/1/45; Gell A, p.68; BL TT E258/9, *Perfect Occurrences*, 27 Dec 1644–3 Jan 1645
624 WSL SMS 547, Leveson to Rupert, 10/1/45
625 Hutton (1982), *op. cit.*, pp.156–159
626 BL TT E258/24, *Perfect Occurrences*, 7-14 Feb, 1645
627 WSL SMS 547, as in note 86; BL TT E258/28, *Perfect Diurnal*, 21–28 Feb, 1645
628 *Mercurius Belgicus*, np; Warburton, *op. cit.*, 3, pp.67–68, Langdale to Rupert, 6/3/45
629 BL Add MSS, 18982, ff.42–3
630 Warburton (1849), *op. cit.*, 3, pp.65–67
631 *Ibid.*, 3, p.69, Rupert to Legge, 11/3/45
632 *Mercurius Belgicus*, np; BL TT E260/3, *Perfect Passages*, 19–25 Mar, 1645; Dore R.N. (ed.), *The Letter Books of Sir William Brereton*, Record Society of Lancashire and Cheshire, 1984, 1, p.77, Brereton to Lord Fairfax, 14/3/45
633 WSL SMS 502, Digby, Wolseley and others to Charles, 5/5/45
634 BL TT E277/44, *Exact Journal*, 3–10 Apr, 1645
635 Dore, *op. cit.*, 1, p.241, Committee of Shropshire to Brereton, 17/4/45; WSL, 'Burney's Newspapers', p.41, *Perfect Occurrences*, 11–18 Apr, 1645
636 Dore, *op. cit.*, pp.300–301, Lloyd to Lord Byron, 26/4/45, p.285, King to Brereton 23/4/45, *Mercurius Belgicus*, np; Gell A, p.68; BL TT E278/29, *Exact Journal*, 17–24 Apr, 1645; E284/1, *Mercurius Aulicus*, 20–27 Apr; E279/12, *Weekly Account*, 23–29 Apr
637 JPR, pp.738–739; Dore, *op. cit.*, 1, p.391, Intelligence report of the Committee of Northamptonshire, p.415, Committee of Coventry to Brereton, 13/5/45
638 *Symonds' Diary*, p.169; JPR, p.739
639 For a descriptive account, see Hollings J., *The History of Leicestershire During the Great Civil War*, Leicester, 1840, pp.45–63
640 *Symonds' Diary*, p.171; JPR, p.739; Dore, *op. cit.*, p.494, Colonel Duckenfield to Brereton, 26/5/45, p.498, Barton to Brereton, 27/5/45; *Mercurius Belgicus*, np; Hamper W. (ed.), *The Life,*

Diary and Correspondence of Sir William Dugdale (Dugdale *Diary*), London, 1857, p.80; BL TT E286/20, *Kingdomes Weekly Intelligencer*, 27 May–3 June, 1645; Parsons D., *The Diary of Sir Henry Slingsby of Scriven Bart* (Slingsby), London, 1836, p.147

641 *Symonds' Diary*, p.184

642 *Slingsby*, p.148; Nichols, *op. cit.*, III, 2, App. 4, pp.45–54; JPR, p.738; *Dugdale Diary*, p.80

643 JPR, p.739; HMC *Portland* 1, p.224, Digby to Goring, 19/5/45, pp.224–225, Rupert to Goring, 19/5/45

644 This interpretation is based on the study of the 1630 Estate Map, held at the Suffolk County Record Office, Acc no. 2803, as well as on Slingsby's account and Okey's both conveniently printed in Young P., *Naseby 1645: The campaign and the Battle*, Century Press, 1985, pp.301–377, along with other accounts which have been consulted. In the view of the present author no good secondary account has been written on the battle and none appears to use the estate map satisfactorily, although Woolrych A., *Battles of the English Civil War*, Pan, 1961, pp.112–138, does mention its existence. The field itself has, of course, been visited by the present author.

645 *Slingsby*, p.153

646 *Mercurius Belgicus*, np; BL TT E289/17, *Moderate Intelligencer*, 19–26 Jun; E290/15, *Parliaments Post*, 24 Jun–1 Jul, 1645; *Rushworth*, IV, 1, p.50; *Dugdale Diary*, p.80

647 WSL SMS 550, Hastings to Rupert, nd, ?July, 1645, and Hastings to Rupert, 30/7/45

648 BL TT E290/5, *Scottish Dove*, 20–27 Jun, 1645

649 BL TT E292/19, *Exact Journal*, 3–10 Jul, 1645; E293/21, *Kingdomes Weekly Intelligencer*, 15–23 Jul, 1645; E293/29, *Scottish Dove*, 18–25 Jul; *Mercurius Belgicus*, np; Gell A, p.68; *Symonds' Diary*, p.224

650 WSL SMS 497, Charles to Rupert, 13/7/45, SMS 550, Hastings to Rupert, 21/7/45

651 Wedgwood C.V., *The King's War 1641–1647*, Penguin, 1983, p.475; WSL, 'Burney's Newspapers', p.57, *Perfect Occurrences*, Aug 13–21, p.58; *Perfect Diurnal*, 18–25 Aug, 1645

652 *Mercurius Belgicus*, np; HMC *Portland* 1, pp.237–238, Lister to Lenthall, 4/8/45

653 HMC *Portland* 1, p.241, Tuthill to Stone, 8/8/45, p.251, Gell to Lenthall, 15/8/45; *Symonds' Diary*, pp.223, 275

654 HMC *Portland* 1, p.254, Gresley to Lenthall, 18/8/45

655 *Ibid.*, 1, p.253, Temple to Lenthall 16/8/45

656 LRO DE 1013, St Helens, Ashby-de-la-Zouch, Parish Register, 1561–1881, pp.155–157; BL TT E303/16, *Mercurius Veridicus*, 20–27 Sept, 1645

657 Gell A, p.64

658 *Symonds' Diary*, p.224; HMC *Portland* 1, p.282, Gell to Lenthall, 7/10/45

659 BL TT E304/25, *City Scout*, 7–14 Oct, 1645

660 BL TT E307/6, *True Informer*, 18–25 Oct, 1645; E327/2, *Perfect Occurrences*, 27 Feb-6 Mar, 1645; Nichols, *op. cit.*, III, 2, App. 4, p.66

661 *Mercurius Belgicus*, np; Hutchinson L., *The Life of Colonel John Hutchinson* (Hutchinson *Life*), OUP, 1973, 2, p.88; *Newcastle Life*, p.164; BL TT E308/21, *Scottish Dove*, 31 Oct–7 Nov, 1645

662 *Dugdale Diary*, p.82

663 *Newcastle Life*, p.163; BL TT E309/7, *Four Great Victories Obtained*; E308/25, *True Informer*, 2–8 Nov, 1645; NRO D7I/1, Welbeck Disgarrisoning; DRO Gell MSS, 30, no.50; HMC *Portland* 1, p.306, Leigh to Lenthall, 10/11/45; BL TT E309/25, *Weekly Account*, 12–19 Nov, 1645; *Mercurius Belgicus*, np

664 Bod Lib Dugdale MSS, 19, f.113; Black W.H., 'Docquets of Letters Patent and Other Instruments of Government' (Black *Docquets*), unpublished, PRO, p.278

665 LJRO D30, LIIIB Dugdale, 19, f.113, Black *Docquets*, p.279; BL TT E314/25, *Kingdomes Weekly Intelligencer*, 30 Dec 1645–6 Jan 1646; *Symonds' Diary*, p.277

666 HMC *Portland* 1, p.339, Gell to Lenthall, 17/1/46

667 BL TT E314/29, *Scottish Dove*, 1–7 Jan, 1646; *Symonds' Diary*, p.278

668 BL TT E320/7, Chester Articles, E320/15, *Weekly Account*, 28 Jan–4 Feb, 1646; *Symonds' Diary*, p.278

669 *Symonds' Diary*, pp.227, 279; *Mercurius Belgicus*, np

670 BL TT E322/21, *Special and Remarkable Passages*, 6–11 Feb, 1646; E327/21, *Scottish Dove*, 4–11 Mar; E323/19, *Perfect Occurrences*, 13–20 Feb, 1646; *CSPD*, 1645–1646, p.352, Needham to Committee of Both Kingdoms, 24/2/46

671 BL TT E344/11, *Kingdomes Weekly Intelligencer*, 21–28 Apr, 1646; E345/2, Lichfield Articles; Rushworth, IV, 1, p.269; WSL, 'Burney's Newspapers', p.77, *Perfect Occurrences*, 1–8 May, 1646, p.78; *Perfect Diurnal*, 11–18 May, 1646

Bibliography

Primary Sources

Manuscripts

Bodleian Library Oxford
Carte Manuscripts
Dugdale Manuscripts 19, List and Descriptions of Commissions sent to the Counties

The British Library
Additional Manuscripts
5752 Various Papers
6688)
6689) Derbyshire Collections
11043 *Scudamore Papers Volume III, Correspondence, 1600–1700*
11331)
11332) *Letterbooks of Sir William Brereton* Vols 1, 2, 3
11333)
15856 Copies of Official Documents during the Reigns of Charles I and II
18981)
18982) Various Letters during the Civil War
18983)
29548 Hatton Papers
34217 State Papers of James I and Charles I
34253 Civil War Papers
35297 Syms J., *Journal of the Civil War, 1642–1649*
36452 Aston Papers, vol.9
36913 Aston Papers, vol.13
46553 Lexington Papers

Edgerton Manuscripts
2986 Heath and Verney Papers concerned with County Rutland vol. 9

Harleian Manuscripts
986 Notebook of Richard Symonds
2043 Historical and Heraldic Visitations
6802 Miscellaneous Letters
6084 Miscellaneous Letters
6851 Miscellaneous Letters

Stowe Manuscripts
155 Miscellaneous Letters

The Derbyshire County Record Office

D258/m/c Committee of Derbyshire Sequestration of Francis Revell
D258/mb 31/33h An order to seize recusant arms
D258/m28/13q Trained Soldier Levy on Hopton, Carrsington and Thorpe Mapleton
D258/m/56/28a Order from Robert Mellor to the Constable of Kedleston
D803/M29 The Copybook of Sir George Gresley
D803/M211 Instructions for using the well at Wingfield

The Leicestershire County Record Office

Borough Records, BR 11/18/22–24
DE 6/126 Deed between Francis Saunders, Thomas Waite and Edward Heath
DE 214/1 Mortgage between Sir William Hartopp and Sir Erasmus de la Fontaine
DE 348/36 Wigston Magna Churchwardens' Accounts
DE 625/60 Waltham on the Wolds Constables' Accounts, 1608–1706
DE 667/62 Loughborough Churchwardens' Accounts
DE 670/14 Edmondthorpe Constables' Accounts, 1635–1677
DE 720/30 Branston Constables' Accounts, 1611–1676
DE 730 Barker Manuscripts Vols 1, 2, 3
DE 734/6 Shawell Churchwardens' and other Accounts, 1609–1775
DE 1013 St Helen's, Ashby-de-la-Zouch, Parish Records 1651–1881, No.1
DE 1605/56 Stathern Constables' Accounts
DE 1784/17 Uppingham Churchwardens' Accounts
DE 1965 Belton Constables' Churchwardens' and Overseers' Accounts, 1602–1739
DE 2161 Letter of the Earl of Newcastle to Henry Hastings, 18/9/1643
DE 2461/55 Preston Churchwardens' and Overseers' Accounts, 1596–1792
DE 2461/135 Preston Civil War Receipts
DE 7/1/70 Survey of Burleigh by Parliamentary Commissioners, 1651
DG 40 (Gretton)/81 Charles I's licence to Henry Skipwith to alienate lands at Prestwold, Burton on the Wolds and Wymeswold
DG 40 (Gretton)/527Instructions to Henry Skipwith as High Sheriff
DG 40 (Gretton)/576Subsidy payments to High Sheriff Roberts
Hartopp Mss 1864 Award of the confiscated Bishop of Ely's Burton Lazars Estates to Sir Thomas Hartopp
OS 126 Letter of Hastings to Prince Rupert, 1643
19/D 33/4 Peckleton Churchwardens' Accounts

Lichfield Cathedral Library

MS Lich 24 A True and Perfect Account of the Expenses of Collonell Richard Bagot

Lichfield Joint Record Office

D30 LIIIB Contributions to the Garrison in the Close, Oct 2nd to Dec 29th, 1645

Lincolnshire Archives Office

Addlethorpe and Ingolmells No 12; Constables' Accounts, 1637–1684
ANC XII/A/5 Commission to Lord Willoughby for raising a regiment issued by Charles I, Aug 5, 1642
ANC XII/6 His Majesties Commission to Lord Willoughby to be a colonel of horse, Aug 5, 1642
ANC XII/14 Commission of Array for the county, 4th July 1642 South Kyne no.12; Constables' Accounts, 1639–1685

Northamptonshire County Records Office

Finch/Hatton Mss 133 Dugdale's Transcripts of Commissioners for several counties

Nottinghamshire County Records Office

D71/1 Order for disgarrisoning Welbeck, Nov 1645
DA 18/11 Receipt for Sequestered Land by Robert Waring
DD 2B/2/17–51 Papers Concerned with Roger Cooper's Sequestration

DD 2B/3/36 Brief of the Case Between John Arnold and Richard Dabill
DD 4P 55/49 Billeting Charges in Devon
DD 39/5 Toton Rentals
DD 294/1 Petition of the Vale of Belvoir
DD 816/12 Forced Loan Exacted of Huntingdon Plumtree, by Charles I
DD 816/13 Linen Exactions of the Newark Garrison
DG M 9796 Order for Disgarrisoning Welbeck, August 1644
DD ME (2) 8 Anthony Eyre Entails Estates to his Son, Gervase
DDSR 211/128 Papers regarding the Ironworks at Kimberworth
M22 Hutchinson's Orders to the Garrison
PR 1529)
PR 1530) Coddington Constables' Records, 1625–1769
PR 1531)
PR 1710 Upton Constables' Accounts
PR 2130 Edwinstowe Constables' Accounts
PR 5767 Thorpe Constables' Accounts
PRMW 13/2 Accounts of William Dand
Borough of Nottingham Hall Books, 1642–1647

The Public Record Office, Chancery Lane, London

C193/12, No.2 Justices of the Peace, 1626

State Papers:
SP 16/16, 495/I–E Recusants in England
SP 29/60, f.130–159 Lords Lieutenants and Deputy Lieutenants in England, 1661
SP 29/66, 25 A List of Gentlemen in Derbyshire and How they stand affected
SP 29/68, 19 A List of Officers Claiming to the Sixty Thousand Pounds Etc, Granted by His Sacred Majesty for the Relief of his Truly Loyal and Indigent Party, Alphabetical List of JPs, Rolles Room 20/93

Staffordshire County Records Office

Orders of Sessions, Epiphany, 1659 – Translation 1667, vol. 7
D260 m/f/1/6/5 Assessment for one months pay to His Majesty's Garrisons, 24th August 1645
Walsall Garrison Levy, Nov 7th, 1645
D260 m/f/1/6/6 Assessment for the Garrison at the Close for Two weeks pay
D260 m/f/4/18 The Composition Book of the Committee of Stafford
D593 Papers of Sir Richard Leveson
D593 p/8/1/1 Commission of Array for Shropshire
D868 Papers of the Leveson Family
D868/2/69Royalist Account of Hopton Heath
D984/4/6/2–5Letters of Walter Wrottesley
D948/4/6/6 Letter of Sir John Skeffington
D996/4a Summons of Charles I to Richard Weston to attend him at Oxford
D1054/7/1 Cannock, St Luke's Parish Book
D1454/2 Rugeley Constables' Accounts
D3451/2/2 Pattingham Parish Book, 1582–1646
D3539/2/1Biddulph Parish Book
D3712/4/1 Mavesyn Ridware Parish Book
1039 Extract of Uttoxeter, Churchwardens' Accounts, 1642–1646

Suffolk County Records Office

Purcell-Fitzgerald Collection, Acc No. 2803. Estate Map of Naseby, 1630

William Salt Library, Stafford

Salt Mss 48/49 Minute Book of the County Committee in Staffordshire
Salt Mss 370/V111/I Burney's Newspapers
Salt Mss 479–564 Civil War Letters
Transcripts of the Papers of the Committee of Compounding, concerning Staffordshire

Other Sources

University of Hull. DD HO/1/26, Letter from Hotham to the Earl of Newcastle concerning Hastings

A Catalogue of the Lords, Knights, and Gentlemen (of the Catholic Religion) that were slain in the Late Warre, in Defence of their King and Country

The Royal Martyrs, London 1663, Printed by H.L.

(Both the above lent by Dr Peter Newman)

Pamphlets

The titles of individual tracts are not, in most cases given. The information below gives the necessary accession numbers of documents consulted. The tracts used extensively are referred to in the endnotes and the information given there may be used in conjunction with that given here.

Leicester University Library

Mercurius Belgicus, or a Brief Chronology of the Battels, Sieges, Conflicts and other most remarkable passages from the beginning of this Rebellion to the 25th March 1646, London 1685

Mercurius Rusticus or the County's Complaint of the Barbarous Outrages Begun in the Year, 1642, by the Sectaries of this Late Flourishing Kingdom. Cambridge, 4th edn, 1723.

The Catholic Apology, with a reply to the Answer.

Roger Palmer, Earl of Castlemaine. 3rd edn, 1674. Lent by Dr Peter Newman.

Nottingham County Library

Local History Department. Collection of Civil War Tracts and Ordinances Concerned Chiefly with Nottinghamshire.

The British Library

The Thomason Tracts. In each case the E/Volume number and the tracts from that volume are given.

These pamphlets can now be consulted online by their title, using the Early English Books Online website.

E7: 8, 12
E8: 20
E10: 7, 9
E42: 20, 26
E51: 1
E54: 5
E56: 11
E59: 1
E61: 9
E62: 8
E64: 8, 11
E67: 3, 7, 25
E69: 17
E71: 8, 9, 10, 11, 24, 32
E73: 2, 6
E74: 10
E77: 6, 31, 33
E78: 10, 15, 16
E79: 5, 7, 17, 19
E80: 8, 9
E81: 7, 8, 13, 15, 19, 26
E84: 3, 4
E85: 45
E86: 15, 22, 39, 41
E88: 17

E314: 25, 29
E316: 2, 25, 27
E317: 4
E318: 4
E319: 8, 17, 23, 24
E320: 1, 2, 6, 15, 22
E322: 9, 13, 14, 18, 21, 24, 27, 39
E323: 9
E325: 10, 22
E327: 21
E330: 14
E332: 3
E333: 10, 11, 15, 24
E334: 11, 12
E345: 2

York Central Library

Civil War Tracts, Local Studies Room, York 942, Civ 1–3

Printed Primary Sources

Armytage G.J. & W.H. Rylands (eds), *Staffordshire Pedigree* (London: Harleian Society, 1912)
Armytage G.J. (ed.), *The Visitation of the County of Rutland, 1618–1619*, by William Camden, (London: Harleian Society, 1870)
Baker W.T. (ed.), *Records of the Borough of Nottingham*, vol. 5 (Nottingham Corporation, 1900)
Black W.H. (ed.), 'Docquets of Letters Patent and other Instruments of Government', unpublished, 1837 (in the Round Room PRO)
Bruce J. (ed.), *Calendar of State Papers, Domestic Series, Charles I* (Lichtenstein: Kraus reprint, 1967)
Clarendon, Earl of, *A History of the Great Rebellion* (Oxford: OUP, 1969)
Cox J.C. (ed.), 'Documents Relating to the Sequestration of the Derbyshire Estates of Philip, First Earl of Chesterfield', *Derbyshire Archaeological Journal* (*DAJ*), IX, 1889
Cox J.C. (ed.), 'Proceedings of the Derbyshire Committee for Compounding and Other Commonwealth Committees' *DAJ*, II, 1891 (new series)
Dore R.N. (ed.), *The Letter Books of Sir William Brereton*, vol. I, The Record Society of Lancashire and Cheshire, vol. CXXIII (Gloucester, 1984)
Dugdale W., *The Visitation of Derbyshire, Taken in 1662 and reviewed in 1663* (London: Golding and Lawrence, 1879)
Erickson E.J. (ed.), *Journal of the House of Commons, 1547–1900* (New York: Readex Microprint, 1964)
Everett-Green M.A. (ed.), *Calendar of the Committee for Compounding*, (Liechtenstein: Kraus Reprint, 1967)
Everett-Green M. (ed.), *Calendar of the Committee for the Advance of Money, 1642–1656* (Liechtenstein: Kraus Reprint), 1967
Farnham G.F. (ed.), *Quorndon Records, County Leicester* (London: Mitchell, Hughes and Clarke, 1912)
Fetherstone FSA, *The Visitation of the County of Leicester 1619* (London: Harleian Society, 1870)
Fisher F. 'Civil War Papers of the Constable of Hope', *DAJ*, 70, 1950
Firth C.H. and R.S. Rait (eds), *Acts and Ordinances of the Interregnum 1642–1660* (London: HMSO, 1911)
Firth C.H. (ed.), 'Journal of Prince Rupert's Marches', *English Historical Review* (*EHR*), XIII, 1899
Foster J. (ed.), *Alumni Oxonienses 1500–1714* (Liechtenstein: Kraus Reprint, 1968)
Foster J. & W.H. Rylands (eds), *Grantees of Arms Named in Docquets and Patents to the end of the Seventeenth Century* (London: Harleian Society, 1915)
Foster J. (ed.), *The Register of Admissions to Gray's Inn, 1521–1889* (London: privately printed by the Hansard Pub. Union, 1889)
Gardiner S.R. (ed.), *The Constitutional Documents of the Puritan Revolution* (Oxford: OUP, 1979 edn)

Godfrey J.T. (ed.), *Manuscripts Relating to the County of Nottingham* (London: Sotheran, 1900)
Guilford E.L. (ed.), 'The Accounts of the Constable of Stathern 1631–1646', *Archaeological Journal*, 69, 1912
Hamper W. (ed.), *The Life, Diary and Correspondence of Sir William Dugdale, Kt* (London: Harding, Lepard and Co., 1857)
Historical Manuscripts Commission Second Report, *Lyttleton, Wrottesley and Owen Papers*, (London: HMSO, 1874)
Historical Manuscripts Commission Thirteenth Report, Appendix I and Two, *The Manuscripts of His Grace the Duke of Portland* (London: HMSO, 1891)
Historical Manuscripts Commission, *The Manuscripts of His Grace the Duke of Rutland, KG* (London: HMSO)
Historical Manuscripts Commission, *Report on the Manuscripts of the Late Reginald Rawdon Hastings, of Ashby-de-la-Zouch* (London: HMSO, 1930)
Hutchinson L., *Memoirs of the Life of Colonel John Hutchinson* (London: Longman, Orme and Rees and Brown, 1822)
Hutchinson L., *Memoirs of the Life of Colonel John Hutchinson* (Oxford: OUP, 1973)
Johnson D.A. & D.G. Vaisey (eds), *Staffordshire and the Great Rebellion* (Stafford: Staffordshire County Council Records Committee, 1964)
Long C.E. (ed.), *Diary of the Marches of the Royal Army, During the Great Civil War, kept by Richard Symonds* (Westminster: Camden Society, 1859)
Marshall G.W. (ed.), *The Visitations of the County of Nottingham, in the Years 1569 and 1614, with many descendants of the Same County* (London: Harleian Society, 1871)
Newcastle M., Duchess of, *The Life of William Cavendish, Duke of Newcastle* (London: unknown, 1886)
Ogle O. (ed.), *Calendar of Clarendon State Papers preserved in the Bodleian Library*, (Oxford: Clarendon Press, 1872)
Parsons D. (ed.), *The Diary of Sir Henry Slingsby of Scriven Bt* (London: Longman, Rees, Orme, Brown, Green, and Longman, 1836)
Peacock M.G.W. (ed.), *Index of the names of Royalists Whose Estates were Confiscated During the Commonwealth* (London: Index Society, 1878)
Peacock M.G.W. (ed.), *The Army Lists of the Roundheads and the Cavaliers, Containing the Names of the Officers in the Royal and Parliamentary Armies of 1642* (London: Index Society, 1863)
Pennington D.H. & I.A. Roots (eds), *The Committee at Stafford, 1643–1645* (Manchester: Manchester University Press, 1957)
Philip I.G. (ed.), *Journal of Sir Samuel Luke*, 3 vols (Oxford: Oxfordshire Record Society, 1950–1953)
Phillips W. (ed.), 'The Ottley Papers Relating to the Civil War', *Shropshire Archaeological Transactions*, vols 6, 7, 8, 1894, 1895, 1896
Roy I. (ed.), *The Royalist Ordnance Papers, 1642–1646*, 2 vols (Oxford: Oxfordshire Record Society, 1964)
Rushworth J. (ed.), *Historical Collections*, Vols 4, 5, 6, 7 (London, 1721–1722)
Sotheby's, *Civil War Papers of Charles I, Prince Rupert of the Rhine and Sir Thomas Fairfax* (London: Sotheby's Catalogue, 1980)
Staffordshire Records Society, 'The Account of the Gentry in Staffordshire at the time of the Interregnum; List of Active Parliamentarians; List of Recusants, 1657', *Collections for a History of Staffordshire* Series 4, vol. II (Stafford, 1958)
Stocks H.E. (ed.), *Records of the Borough of Leicester, 1603–1689* (Cambridge: CUP, 1923)
Venn J. & J.A. Venn (eds), *Alumni Cantabrigienses*, Part One, 4 vols (Cambridge: CUP, 1922–1927)
Verney, F. Parthenope (ed.), *Memoirs of the Verney Family During the Civil War* (London: Tabard Press, 1970)
Warburton E. (ed.), *Memoirs of Prince Rupert and the Cavaliers, Including their Private Correspondence* (London: Bentley, 1849)
Webb J. & T.W. Webb (eds), *Military Memoirs of Colonel John Birch* (London: Camden Society, 1872)
Wood A.C. (ed.), *Memorials of the Holles Family by Gervase Holles* (London: Camden Society, 1937)

Secondary Sources

Books and Pamphlets

Ashton R., *The English Civil War: Conservatism and Revolution* (London: Weidenfeld and Nicolson, 1978)

Bailey T., *Annals of the County of Nottingham* (London: Sempkin, Marshall, c.1853)

Bence-Jones M., *The Cavaliers* (London: Constable, 1976)

Bennett M., *Lord Loughborough, Ashby-de-la-Zouch and the English Civil War* (Ashby: Ashby Museum, 1984)

Blackwood B.G., *The Lancashire Gentry and the Great Rebellion* (Manchester: Chetham Society, 1978)

Bossy J., *The English Catholic Community, 1570–1850* (London: Darton, Longman and Todd, 1975)

Brighton J.T., *Royalists and Roundheads in Derbyshire* (Bakewell: Bakewell and District Historical Society, 1981)

Brown C., *A History of Newark on Trent* (Newark: Brown, 1907)

Brown C., *Lives of Nottinghamshire Worthies and of Celebrated and Remarkable Men of the County* (London: Sotheran, 1882)

Brown C., *The Annals of Newark on Trent* (London: Brown, 1879)

Burke J., *The Extinct and Dormant Baronetcies of England* (London: Burke, 1838)

Burke J. & J.B. Burke, *The Dormant and Extinct Peerages of England* (London: Burke, 1969 edn)

Cliffe J.T., *The Yorkshire Gentry from the Reformation to the English Civil War* (Athlone Press, distrib. Oxford University Press, 1969)

Cliffe J.T., *The Puritan Gentry: The Great Puritan Families of Early Stuart England*, (London: Routledge and Kegan Paul, 1984)

Cox J.T., *Three Centuries of Derbyshire Annals* (London: Bemrose, 1890)

Cross C., *Church and People, 1450–1660* (Glasgow: Fontana, 1979)

Cross C., *The Puritan Earl* (London: Macmillan, 1966)

Davies R.G. & J.H. Denton (eds) *The English Parliament in the Middle Ages* (Manchester: MUP, 1981)

Dickenson Rastell W., *A History of the Antiquities of the Town and Church of Southwell in the County of Nottingham* (London, 1787)

Dryden A. (ed.) *Memorials of Old Leicestershire* (Leicester: Ballantyne and Hanson, 1911)

Eller I., *The History of Belvoir Castle* (London: Tyas, 1841)

Everett A.M., *The Community of Kent and the Great Rebellion* (London: Historical Association, 1969)

Everett A.M., *The Local Community and the Great Rebellion* (London: Historical Association, 1969)

Firth C.H., *Cromwell's Army* (London, Methuen, 1967 edn)

Firth C.H., *The House of Lords During the Civil War* (London: Longman, 1910)

Fletcher A., *The Outbreak of the English Civil War* (London: Arnold, 1981)

Fosbrooke T.H., *Ashby-de-la-Zouch Castle Leicestershire* (Leicester Museums and Art Gallery, nd)

Francis H.J., *The History of Hinckley* (Hinkley: Pickering and Sons, 1930)

Gardiner S.R., *History of the Great Rebellion* (New York: AMS Press, 1965 edn)

Garner A.A., *Boston and the Great Civil War* (Boston: Richard Kay, 1972)

G.E. Cokayne, *The Complete Baronetage*, II, 1625–1649 (Exeter: W. Pollard & Co., 1902)

Gladwin I., *The Sheriff, The Man and His Office* (London: Gollancz, 1974)

Glover S., *The History, Gazetteer and Directory of the County of Derby* (Derby, 1829)

Gower Lord Ronald, *Rupert of the Rhine* (London: Kegan Paul, 1890)

Greenall R.L. (ed.) *Naseby: A Parish History* (Leicester: Department of Adult Education, Leicester University, 1974)

Guttery D.R., *The Great Civil War in the Midland Parishes: The People Pay* (Birmingham: Cornish Bros., 1950)

Hardacre P., *The Royalists During the Puritan Revolution* (The Hague: M. Nijhoff, 1956)

Harding A., *A Social History of English Law* (Harmondsworth: Pelican, 1966)

Havran M.J., *Caroline Courtier: The Life of Lord Cottington* (London: Macmillan, 1973)

Hensman E.W., *Loughborough During the Civil War* (Loughborough: Echo Press, 1921)

Hill C., *The English Revolution* (London: Lawrence and Wishart, 1979 edn)

Hill C., *God's Englishman: Oliver Cromwell and the English Revolution* (London: Penguin, 1972)

Royal Commission on Historical Monuments, *Newark upon Trent, The Civil War Siegeworks* (London: HMSO, 1972)

Hollings J.F., *The History of Leicestershire During the Great Civil War*, Leicester, 1840
Holmes C., *Seventeenth Century Lincolnshire* (Lincoln: History of Lincolnshire Committee, 1980)
Holmes C., *The Eastern Association in the English Civil War* (Cambridge: CUP, 1974)
Hutton R., *The Restoration: A Political and Religious History of England and Wales, 1658–1667* (Oxford: Clarendon Press, 1985)
Hutton R., *The Royalist War Effort* (Harlow: Longman, 1982)
Ives W., *The English Revolution, 1600–1660* (London: Arnold, 1978)
Kearney H.F., *Strafford in Ireland: A Study in Absolutism* (Manchester, MUP, 1961 edn)
Kenyon J.P., *Stuart England* (Harmondsworth: Pelican, 1985 edn)
Malcolm J., *Caesar's Due: Loyalty and King Charles 1642–1646* (London: Royal Historical Society, 1983)
Mander G.P. & N.W. Tildesley, *A History of Wolverhampton* (Wolverhampton: Wolverhampton Corporation, 1960)
Manning B., *The English People and the English Revolution 1640–1649* (London: Heinemann, 1976)
Metcalfe W.C., *A Book of Knights 1426–1600* (London: Mitchell and Hughes, 1885)
Money W., *The First and Second Battles of Newbury and the Siege of Donnington Castle during the Civil War AD 1643–1646* (London: Simpkin, Marshall, 1884)
Morrill J. (ed.), *Reactions to the English Civil War, 1642–1649* (London: Macmillan, 1982)
Morrill J., *The Revolt of the Provinces* (London: Longman, 1980)
Nugent Bell H., *The Huntingdon Peerage* (London: Baldwin Craddock and Joy, 1820)
Newman P.R., *Atlas of the English Civil War* (London: Croom Helm, 1985)
Newman P.R., *The Battle of Marston Moor* (Chichester: Anthony Bird, 1981)
Newman P.R., *Royalist Officers in England and Wales, 1642–1660* (New York: Garland Press, 1981)
Nichols J., *The History and Antiquities of the County of Leicestershire*, 4 vols (London: Nichols, 1804)
Pitt W., *A Topographical History of Staffordshire* (Newcastle-under-Lyme: Smith, 1917)
Prest W., *The Inns of Court under Elizabeth I and the Early Stuarts, 1590–1640* (London: Longman, 1972)
Ridley J., *The Roundheads* (London: Constable, 1976)
Ridsdill-Smith G, M. Toynbee & P. Young (eds) *Leaders of the Civil Wars* (Kineton, Roundwood Press, 1977)
Russell C. (ed.) *The Crisis of Parliament* (Oxford: OUP, 1981)
Russell C. (ed.) *The Origins of the English Civil War* (London, Methuen, 1984 edn)
Sandford J.L., *Studies and Illustrations of the Great Rebellion* (London: J.W. Parker & Son, 1858)
Scott W., *The Story of Ashby-de-la-Zouch* (Ashby: Brown, 1907)
Shaw S., *The History and Antiquities of Staffordshire* (Wakefield: EP Publishing, 1976 ed. (1798–1801))
Shaw W.A., *The Knights of England*, 2 vols (London: Sherratt & Hughes, 1906)
Sherwood R.E., *Civil Strife in the Midlands* (Chichester: Phillimore, 1974)
Simmons J., *A City and a County* (Leicester: Leicestershire Archaeological and Historical Society, 1981)
Slater M., *Family Life in the Seventeenth Century: The Verneys of Claydon House* (London: Routledge and Kegan Paul, 1984)
Stephens E. (ed.), *The Clerks of the Counties, 1360–1960* (Newport: Society of the Clerks of the Peace of the Counties and of Clerks of the County Councils, 1961)
Stone L., *The Causes of the English Revolution, 1529–1642* (London: Routledge Kegan Paul, 1977 edn)
Stone L., *The Crisis of the Aristocracy 1558–1641* (Oxford: Clarendon Press, 1965)
Stone L. (ed.), *The University in Society*, vol. 1 (Princeton, NJ: Princetown University Press, 1975)
Tanner J.R., *The English Constitutional Conflicts of the Seventeenth Century 1603–1639* (Cambridge: CUP, 1962 edn)
Thoroton R. & J. Thoresby, *The Antiquities of Nottinghamshire* (Wakefield: EP Publishing, 1972 edn (orig. 1677))
Townsend P. (ed.) *Burke's Peerage, Baronetage and Knightage* (London: Burke, 1970)
Toynbee M., P. Young, *Strangers in Oxford, A Sidelight on the English Civil War* (Chichester: Phillimore, 1973)
Trease G., *Portrait of a Cavalier, William Cavendish, First Duke of Newcastle* (London: Macmillan, 1979)
Turbeville A.S., *A History of Welbeck and its Owners*, vol. 1, 1539–1755 (London: Faber and Faber, 1937)

Underdown, D., *Revel Riot and Rebellion: Popular Politics and Culture in England 1603–1660* (Oxford, Clarendon Press, 1985)
Victoria County History, *A History of the County of Derby*, vol. 2 (Oxford: OUP, 1967)
Victoria County History, *A History of the County of Leicester*, vol. 2 (Oxford: OUP, 1954)
Victoria County History, *A History of the County of Nottingham*, vol. 2 (Oxford: OUP, 1954)
Victoria County History, *A History of the County of Rutland*, vol. 2 (London: St Catherine's Press, 1935)
Victoria County History, *A History of the County of Stafford*, vols 5–8 (London: OUP, 1958–1979)
Ward W.R., *The English Land Tax in the Eighteenth Century* (London: OUP, 1953)
Wedgwood C.V., *The King's War, 1641–1647* (Harmondsworth: Penguin, 1983 edn)
Wenham P., *The Great and Close Siege of York 1644* (Kineton: Roundwood Press, 1970)
Wilshire J. & S. Green, *The Siege of Leicester 1645* (Leicester: Leicester Research Services, 1972)
Wood A.C., *Nottinghamshire in the Civil War* (Wakefield: reprint, S.R. Publishers, 1971)
Woolrych A., *Battles of the English Civil War* (London: Pan, 1966)
Wright J. & W. Harrod, *The History and Antiquities of the County of Rutland* (East Ardley: reprint, EP Publishing for Rutland County Council, 1973 (orig. 1684, 1712))
Young P., *Edgehill 1642: the Campaign and the Battle*, Roundwood, Kineton, 1967
Young P., *Marston Moor: 1644, The Campaign and the Battle* (Kineton: Roundwood Press, 1970)
Young P., *Naseby 1645: The Campaign and the Battle* (London: Century, 1985)

Journal Articles

Beats L., 'The East Midland Association 1642–1644', *Midland History* (MH), IV, 1978
Bennett M., 'Contribution and Assessment: Financial Exactions in the English Civil War, 1642–1646', *War and Society*, V, 1, 1986
Bennett M., 'Henry Hastings and the Flying Army of Ashby-de-la-Zouch', *Transactions of the Leicestershire Archaeological and Historical Society* (*TLAHS*), LVI, 1980–1981
Bennett M., 'Henry Hastings and the Royalist Cause in the East Midlands', Palmer M. (ed.), *The Aristocratic Estate: The Hastings Family in Leicestershire and South Derbyshire* (Loughborough: East Midlands Studies Unit, 1981)
Bennett M., 'Leicestershire's Royalist Officers and their War Effort in the County', *TLAHS*, LIX, 1984–1985
Bennett M., 'The Civil War Battle of Cotes', *Leicestershire Historian*, III, 3, 1984–1985
Daly J., 'The Implications of Royalist Politics 1642–1646', *Historical Journal* (*HJ*), 27, 3, 1984
Diaz J., 'Lead, Society and Politics in Derbyshire before the Civil War', *Midland History* (*MH*), VI, 1981
Dietz F.C., 'The Receipts and Issues of the Exchequer During the Reigns of James I and Charles I', *Smith College Studies in History*, 3, 4, 1928 (Northampton Mass)
Ensberg J. 'Royalist Finance during the English Civil War 1642–1646', *Scandinavian Economic History Review*, 14, 2, 1966
Fisher F.N., 'The Every Family and the Civil War: A Tale of Loyalty', *Derbyshire Archaeological Journal* (*DAJ*), 74, 1954
Fleming D., 'Faction and Civil War in Leicestershire', *TLAHS*, LVII, 1981–1982
Fletcher A.J., 'Petitioning and the Outbreak of the Civil War in Derbyshire', *DAJ*, 93, 1973
Gruenfelder J.K., 'The Electoral Influence of the Earls of Huntingdon 1603–1640', *TLAHS*, L, 1974–1975
Hughes A., 'The King, The Parliament and the Localities during the English Civil War', *Journal of British Studies*, 24, 1985
Hughes A., 'Warwickshire on the Eve of Civil War: A County Community?', *MH*, VII, 1982
Hutton R., 'The Failure of the Lancashire Cavaliers', *Transactions of the Lancashire and Cheshire Historical Society*, 129, 1980
Hutton R., 'The Structure of the Royalist Party 1642–1646', *HJ*, 24, 3, 1981
Hutton R., 'The Worcestershire Clubmen in the English Civil War', *MH*, V, 1980
Lacey A.C., 'Sir Robert Shirley and the English Revolution', *TLAHS*, LVIII, 1982–1983
Larminie V., 'Marriage and the Family: The Example of the Seventeenth Century Newdigates', *MH*, IX, 1984
Maddon F., 'The Gresleys of Drakelow', *Staffordshire Historical Collections*, New Series, I, 1898
Malcolm J., 'A King in Search of Soldiers, Charles I in 1642', *HJ*, 21, 2, 1978

Mendelson S.H., '(Debate) The Weightiest Business, Marriage in an Upper Gentry Family in Seventeenth Century England', *Past and Present* (*PP*), 85, 1979
Meredith R., 'A Derbyshire Family in the Seventeenth Century: The Eyres of Hassop and their Forfeited Estates', *Recusant History* (*RH*), 8, 1, 1965
Morrill J., 'The Northern Gentry and the Great Rebellion', *Northern History* (*NH*), XV, 1979
Newman P., 'Catholic Royalist Activists in the North 1642–1646', *RH*, 14, 1, 1977
Newman P., 'Catholic Royalists of Northern England 1642–1646', *NH*, XV, 1979
Newman P., 'The Defeat of John Belasyse: Civil War in Yorkshire, January–April, 1644', *Yorkshire Archaeological Journal*, CII, 1980
Newman P., 'The Royalist Officer Corps 1642–1660: Army Command as a Reflection of the Social Structure', *HJ*, 26, 4
Newton S.C., 'The Gentry of Derbyshire in the Seventeenth Century', *DAJ*, 86, 1966
Porter S., 'The Fire Raid in the English Civil War', *War and Society*, 2, 2, 1984
Roy I., 'England Turned Germany? The Aftermath of the Civil War in its European Context', *Transactions of the Royal Historical Society* (*TRHS*), 5th Series, 28, 1978
Russell C., 'Why did Charles I Fight the Civil War?', *History Today*, June 1984
Sitwell G., 'The Derbyshire Petition of 1641', *DAJ*, XIX, 1897
Slater M., 'The Weightiest Business: Marriage in an Upper Gentry Family in Seventeenth Century England', *PP*, 72, 1976
Slater M., 'The Weightiest Business... a Rejoinder', *PP*, 85, 1979
Smith T.S., 'The Persecution of Staffordshire Roman Catholic Recusants 1625–1660', *Journal of Ecclesiastical History*, 30, 1979
Stevenson W. 'A Vale of Belvoir Cavalier Family', *Transactions of the Thoroton Society*, VI, 1902
Stone L., 'The Educational Revolution in England, 1560–1640', *PP*, 28, 1964
Shawcross W.H., 'The Owners of Shawcross', *DAJ*, XXVIII, 1906
Wanklyn M. & P. Young, 'A King in Search of Soldiers: Charles I in 1642, A Rejoinder', *HJ*, 24, 1, 1981
Wedgewood J., 'Staffordshire Members of Parliament', *Staffordshire Historical Collections* (*SHC*), New Series, 29, 1920
Wrottesley G., 'A History of the Bagot Family', *SHC*, New Series, XI, 1902
Wrottesley G., 'A History of the Lane Family', *SHC*, New Series, XIX, 1910
Wrottesley G., 'A History of the Wrottesley Family', *SHC*, New Series, V, 1896
Wrottesley G., 'The Giffards of Chillington', *SHC*, New Series, IV, 1895
Yateman P., 'The Recusants of Derbyshire', *DAJ*, X, 1888
Young P., 'The Battle of Hopton Heath, 19th March 1643', *The Journal for the Society of Army Historical Research* (*JSAHR*) XXXIII, part 133, 1955
Young P., 'The Royalist Army at the Relief of Newark', *JSAHR*, XXX, no 124, 1952

Unpublished Theses

Beats L., 'Politics and Government in Derbyshire 1640–1660', PhD, Sheffield, 1978
Fleming D., 'Some Aspects of the Gentry in Jacobean and Caroline Leicestershire', MA Course Dissertation, Leicester, 1976
Lloyd P., 'Politics and the Personnel of Politics in Nottingham 1642–1688', MPhil, Nottingham, 1983
Morton-Thorpe A.M., 'The Gentry of Derbyshire 1640–1660', MA, Leicester, 1971
Newman P., 'The Royalist Army in Northern England 1642–1645', PhD, York, 1978
Pickles J.T., 'Studies in Royalism in the English Civil War 1642–1646, With Special Reference to Staffordshire', MA, Manchester, 1968
Porter S., 'The Destruction of Urban Property in the English Civil Wars 1642–1651', PhD, London, 1983
Roy I., 'The Royalist Army in the First Civil War', PhD, Oxford, 1963
Wheeler J.S., 'English Army Finance and Logistics 1642–1660', PhD, Berkeley, California, 1980